Cold War Crucible

Cold War Crucible

THE KOREAN CONFLICT AND THE POSTWAR WORLD

Masuda Hajimu

 Harvard University Press

CAMBRIDGE, MASSACHUSETTS & LONDON, ENGLAND

2015

Library of Congress Cataloging-in-Publication Data

Masuda, Hajimu.
    Cold War crucible : the Korean Conflict and the postwar world /
Masuda Hajimu.
        pages cm
    Includes bibliographical references and index.
    ISBN 978-0-674-59847-8
    1. Cold War. 2. Korean War, 1950–1953—Influence. 3. World politics—1945–1989. I. Title.
    D843.M265 2014
    909.82'5—dc23   2014013034

Contents

Cold War Crucible

Introduction

What Was the Cold War?

"IF ANY ONE THING more than another could advance the cause to which the western nations are bending their efforts, it would be to stop describing it as the 'cold war.'" So argued the cover article in the British newsweekly the *Economist* on May 27, 1950, maintaining that, whatever the term had meant when first coined, it had the effect in the public mind of making the Western powers appear to be aggressors. The article continued: "It is time the western peoples dropped the term entirely from their political vocabulary and used instead a phrase . . . that genuinely expresses their firm but pacific purposes."[1] Following the outbreak of the Korean War on June 25, 1950, however, critiques of this kind disappeared within a few years, if not months. The manner of spelling out the phenomenon changed as well; the situation that had been described as "a cold war" or "the so-called cold war" in lower case in the late 1940s came to be commonly known as "the Cold War" in capital letters by the mid-1950s. This transition from lower to upper case implies that the bipolar confrontation no longer represented one of a number of disputable perspectives, but one that was now widely accepted as a substantial, irrefutable actuality.

Such a gradual revelation of the Cold War, however, also suggests the constructed nature of a conflict that *became* "reality," as opposed to something that existed as an objective situation immediately following World War II. What made the Cold War different from other wars, such as the two world wars or the Korean War, was that it did not exist at a particular time and place. Rather, it existed not because it was there but because people *thought* that it existed. It was, in this way, an imagined reality that came to be shared and solidified in the postwar era, particularly during the Korean War, which many feared was the beginning of World War III. During the decades that followed, the Cold War appeared to be the "reality" of the world, and, thus, questions tended to focus on how it came about and who created it—a manner of research characterized by looking back on the "origins" of the conflict from a viewpoint accepting its actuality. Today, the Cold War seems to be an event of a past long gone, and the nature of inquiry cannot be the same. We now ask: How did millions of people worldwide come to believe in such an imagined reality, and why? How did such a "reality" become solidified in the early postwar era, particularly during the Korean War? And, after all, what truly was the Cold War?

This book is an attempt to rewrite the formation of the Cold War through synthesizing social and diplomatic history and local and global history.[2] It examines the crucial moment of the Korean conflict, around 1950, and investigates the ways in which actors around the world—from elite policymakers to ordinary people—interpreted the meaning of the Korean War through the lenses of their own local contexts and participated in a multilayered politics of knowledge production in their hometowns, eventually paving the way toward maintaining a particular Cold War world.[3] My principal concern is not when the Cold War began or who initiated it but how the "reality" of the Cold War was produced and consolidated, and why numerous people joined in. Therefore, I look into not only policy-making processes during this period but the integral roles of popular imagination and participation that framed and conventionalized this "reality." My hope is to delineate how such an imagined reality, fueled by fear, antagonism, memories of war, and concerns about disorder at home, eventually *became* the irrefutable actuality of the postwar era. In brief, this is not a Cold War history that presupposes the existence of the Cold War. To be more precise, it is a history of a *fantasy* of the Cold War, focusing on its imagined and constructed nature as well as the social need for such an imagined reality.

In examining the post–World War II period, however, there is one ob-
stacle: our ingrained habit of looking at this historical moment as a prelude
to the Cold War and explaining all conceivable events and phenomena in
terms of the Cold War reality. Here, in looking at the postwar years, we need
to make a distinction between the Cold War as discourse, on the one hand,
and as a "reality" of the world, on the other. The former was engaged in by
policymakers and intellectuals in terms of expressing a set of opinions, often seen as provocative and perceptive. One could easily think of, for instance, Walter Lippmann's series of newspaper articles published in 1947,
George F. Kennan's "Long Telegram" in 1946, or, perhaps, George Orwell's
1945 general description of the nuclear age as a "cold war." Actually, one could
trace such Cold War discourse back to Herbert Hoover's warnings during
World War II or even Woodrow Wilson's concerns following the 1917 Russian Revolution.[4] It is not difficult, indeed, to further trace a prototype of
such discourse to the nineteenth-century writings of Alexis de Tocqueville,
in which he forecast a future Russian-American rivalry (on the grounds
that both had observed rapid population growth in their vast territories).[5]
In short, a discourse of this kind, predicting an eventual and inevitable
competition between the Soviet Union (Russia) and the United States had
existed all along. Yet not all of the time since the age of Tocqueville and
Wilson has normally been considered an epoch of East-West confrontation.
After all, their opinions were simply their opinions.

A "reality" is somewhat different from such discourse. In order for something to be considered an irrefutable reality and a distinctive historical epoch,
there should be one more ingredient: social acceptance and participation.
The distinction between discourse and reality lies not in terms of its essence
but the number of its adherents. To put it plainly, a majority of the population had to believe in and propagate the discourse of the Cold War as a reality
of the world, rather than simply viewing it as someone's opinion. As we will
see below, such a situation evolved along with the outbreak and development of the Korean War in 1950, which was feared in many (but not all)
places in the world as the start of World War III. In the late 1940s, however,
the Cold War did not really exist in this way as a reality of the world, even
though it surely existed as one of many discourses about world situations. In
fact, commentators still described it diffidently as "a cold war" or "the so-called
cold war," written in lower case, rather than taking for granted that they
were living in the age of the Cold War, in capital letters.

Nonetheless, because we tend to mix up these two processes, a couple of historiographical problems arise. First, because we have viewed policy-makers' and intellectuals' Cold War discourse as explanations for the reality of the Cold War, we have not paid much attention to why numerous people came to accept and participate in the reality of the Cold War and what dynamics existed behind such social acceptance. To be sure, while there has been an upsurge in literature that explores the impacts of the conflict on ordinary people's daily lives, much of it has described the Cold War as a given phenomenon—like the weather—rather than a constructed reality, and has not set out to examine the roles of ordinary people in shaping such a reality.[6] In other words, while recent studies have gone far beyond investigating the "origins" of the Cold War in terms of the conduct of Harry S. Truman or Joseph Stalin, the stories of the numerous "adherents" at the grassroots level who ultimately made up the Cold War world have not yet been properly told. What were the choices of ordinary people? How did they participate in or, in some cases, even take advantage of, the Cold War world? What we are exploring here, as the historian John Lewis Gaddis and political scientist Stuart Kaufman have advocated, has less to do with people's "objective" interests than the attitudes, beliefs, and myths that influenced these interests.[7] Therefore, this book does not treat popular myths, rumors, and emotions among everyday people merely as *effects* of the Cold War; rather, it casts light on them as *factors creating* the "reality" of the conflict. As such, we will see that ordinary people were hardly passive in terms of the practice of Cold War politics and that the "reality" of the Cold War during this period was, in fact, maintained and propagated at the people's initiative, parallel to the intentions of high-ranking policymakers.

Another focal point involves more clearly delineating the social and historical background of that particular moment: legacies of World War II and colonialism as well as people's experiences and memories of them. While we might assume that the years of the late 1940s and early 1950s were the prelude to the Cold War era, for many, they were above all the days following years of cruel wars—a postwar era. Yet, because we know what happened later, we have tended retroactively to apply the Cold War paradigm to the preceding era, when the Cold War was not yet a reality of the world. As a result, a wide range of events and phenomena has been viewed as parts, or even origins, of the Cold War, even though these might have had far more diverse local and historical roots. As we shall see in the cases of American, Chinese, Japanese, and other societies, many were, indeed, living with memories of World War II and observed contemporary events, like the Korean War, through that particular lens, contributing to intensifying fear of World War III, which, in turn, solidified a fantasy Cold War world. This point will become much clearer when we look at the fact that the Cold War was not a universal phenomenon at that time. As we will see below, the Cold War "reality" attained its highest level of verisimilitude in this early postwar period in Europe, East Asia, and the United States—that is, areas that were most fiercely involved in the world war—but did not achieve such a degree of plausibility, at least at this point, in other places, such as Africa and Latin America, which were not principal battlefields of the world war.[8] This was because many people in these (post)colonial societies were living with memories of colonialism and observing postwar situations differently. By examining a dividing line in terms of whether to believe in the "reality" of the Cold War, this book reveals the imagined and constructed nature of the Cold War world.

Keeping these points in mind, what we will attempt here is to strip away Cold War imaginings, shedding light on locally specific realities and, in doing so, destabilize our understanding of the Cold War as a single, global conflict that divided the world in two, between the Eastern and Western camps. In this way, my effort to explicate social and historical contexts underlying the Cold War world is in line with a number of other ongoing endeavors, notably the historian Matthew Connelly's advocacy of "Taking Off the Cold War Lens," and the anthropologist Heonik Kwon's encouragement for "Decomposition of the Cold War."[9] It is also in line with the social historian Lizabeth Cohen's observation that much of importance in America's postwar history happened outside the Cold War framework and that applying that framework exclusively can obscure other crucial developments.[10] This observation, in turn, has resonance with the historian Immanuel Wallerstein's recent warning about the danger of looking at the second half of the twentieth century using the Cold War narrative, which he views as "largely a fantasy."[11]

This kind of scholarship, which raises fundamental questions about the Cold War framework, has, indeed, been increasing in recent years, in particular, among scholars outside the circles of Cold War specialists. Kuan-Hsing Chen, a prominent Taiwanese scholar of postcolonial and cultural studies, for instance, has argued for the need to "De–Cold War" in order to analyze and promote the ongoing task of decolonization and deimperialization in Asia.[12] Jodi Kim, a scholar of Asian-American literature, similarly, has conducted critical analysis of what she calls "Cold War compositions" in order to problematize the imperial and gendered racial logic of the Cold War.[13] Also, in an anthology titled *De-Centering Cold War History*, Jadwiga Pieper Mooney and Fabio Lanza, Latin America and China specialists, respectively, have shed light on local, street-level experiences and initiatives that, they argue, were crucial to shaping the Cold War world.[14]

The book takes these viewpoints seriously, and its ultimate goal, certainly, is to think about what the Cold War really was. However, we will not approach this question directly, assuming that the Cold War was a single, global confrontation, shaped through the conduct of elite policymakers and experienced in the same way across the world. Rather, *Cold War Crucible* makes a deliberate detour and approaches it by breaking down and delving deeply into local events usually conceived of as "Cold War" experiences, and, through analysis of local and micro-level events, we will inspect the imagined and constructed nature of the Cold War world as well as the social needs of such a reality on the ground. Below, we look into a number of post–World War II societies, in particular those of China and the United States, and examine the ways in which many events indeed developed outside the Cold War framework, though they came to be seen as part of the Cold War world. Following this detour, we return to our core question concerning the nature of the Cold War.

Readers might ask: if we want to prove these points, don't we need more extensive research on all societies around the world? Ideally speaking, yes, but one book can only do so much. I sincerely hope that this book will spark new interest and research in the areas that I cannot cover here, including the Soviet Union and Germany. I do not provide extensive and detailed narratives on Korea, even though some discussion is provided where necessary. Korea is always at the center of our story, but this is not a book about the Korean War itself. Rather, it explores how the war, which was often interpreted as the beginning of World War III, functioned as a catalyst in the crucible of the postwar world and contributed to the materialization of the Cold War world.

The book has three parts, divided roughly chronologically and thematically. Part I examines the years between 1945 and 1950. Focusing on American, Chinese, and Japanese societies, we will see that domestic societies in this period turned into "battlefields," that the Cold War remained a discourse over which there was considerable dispute, and that various phenomena we usually view as reflecting the Cold War confrontation actually had their own diverse, locally specific realities and social conflicts. Furthermore, through investigating reactions to the Korean War in East Asia, Southeast Asia, South Asia, the Middle East, Europe, and North America, we will see how such a Cold War discourse came to acquire an aura of the "reality" of the world at the time of the Korean conflict, and how memories of World War II created a foundation for this world.

Part II concentrates on the months following the outbreak of the Korean War, exploring the interplay between state and society in the making of American and Chinese foreign and domestic policies, both of which consolidated the imagined reality of the Cold War. It shows that, even though they consequently cemented the Cold War world, Washington's and Beijing's policies had less to do with military strategy or Cold War thinking than with the politics of impression in attempts to dominate the currents of popular attitudes and that policy-making processes were not isolated from social politics and the daily lives of ordinary people. Furthermore, through examining the rise of a particular version of "truth" in these societies, we will analyze how propaganda programs spread, how ordinary people participated in them, and how historical memories conditioned the ways in which "truth" was formed in their societies. What was really achieved in these truth-making campaigns was not necessarily the forging of consensus but merely clarification of dividing lines among populations between "us" and "them."

Part III explores the ways in which such local disagreements were fiercely "resolved" through analyzing the global phenomenon of domestic purges during the Korean War: suppression of counterrevolutionaries in China, the White Terror in Taiwan, the crackdown on "un-Filipino" activities in the Philippines, the Red Purge in Japan, and anti-communist movements in Western societies, such as anti-strike and anti-labor drives in Britain and McCarthyism in the United States. As we will see below, local actors in these domestic suppressions utilized the logic of East-West confrontation in their own social conflicts and culture wars, stifling dissent and "purifying" their societies, and often choosing particular kinds of "order" and "reality" that lasted for decades. Viewed in this way, these local conflicts were not so much results of the Cold War, as is usually assumed; rather, each was itself part of the engine, a core component, of the Cold War, contributing to the realization of a gigantic social construction, with the participation of ordinary people in their own domestic "wars" fought for the sake of order in each society.

In sum, *Cold War Crucible* revisits the immediate postwar period and reappraises what was really going on within the seemingly coherent Cold War paradigm by delving deeper into local histories in a number of postwar and postcolonial societies and listening to ordinary people's whispers and rumors. In this sense, this is a book about the social history of the global postwar world, with an emphasis on American and Chinese societies. In addition, by incorporating such social and local histories with an analysis of Washington's and Beijing's policy-making processes concerning the Korean conflict, this book provides a new mode of diplomatic history for these countries, which explicates interactive relationships between foreign and domestic politics, between state and society, and among policymakers and everyday people.

Exploring the crossroads of such social and diplomatic history, the book also includes a political history of grassroots conservative movements, defined broadly. It chronicles the inceptive moments of social conservative backlash, which functioned primarily to restore and maintain domestic tranquility, regardless of political regime and ideology, in many parts of the world in the chaotic postwar period. To put it differently, this is a story about how grassroots conservatives fought and suppressed various kinds of postwar change under the name of the global Cold War confrontation, and how power operated in such contexts, not just from the top down, but from the bottom up.

By integrating such social, diplomatic, and political histories with local and global history approaches, *Cold War Crucible,* above all, aims to destabilize and challenge the standard narrative of the Cold War, commonly believed to have been a global, geopolitical, and ideological confrontation between the Soviet Union and the United States, orchestrated primarily by the elite policymakers of these states. Instead, by tracing the social construction of a fantasy of the Cold War world, it reveals that the actual divides of the Cold War existed not necessarily between Eastern and Western camps but within each society, with each, in turn, requiring the perpetuation of the imagined reality of the Cold War to restore and maintain order and harmony at home.[15] It was such an acceleration of domestic needs and beliefs in the imagined reality of global confrontation that made the hetero-geneity of local realities invisible and functioned internally to maintain and perpetuate the "real" Cold War for decades. Re-examining the Cold War in this way, *Cold War Crucible* hopes to open up discussion as to why such an imagined reality materialized during the Korean War period, why millions of people throughout the world participated in its formulation, and, finally, what the Cold War truly was.

I

The Repercussions

CHAPTER ONE

Naming the Unnamable

OUR STORY BEGINS in Hawaii, on the morning of Labor Day, September 2, 1946. A sugar plantation worker, "Shirley" Shiroma, got on a train for the first time in his life, heading for Honolulu. For Shirley—so nicknamed because his curly hair resembled that of the late child actress Shirley Temple—getting away from the sugar plantation and going to the city was quite unusual.[1] Like many other plantation workers, he had a life that was tightly controlled by whistle and whip, regularly waking up before 5 a.m., beginning work in the field at 6 a.m., having breakfast at 7:45 a.m. and lunch at 11 a.m. in the field, quitting work at 3:30 p.m., and going to bed at 8:30 p.m.[2] For such a plantation worker, being absent and leaving the plantation without permission were not allowed and visiting friends or traveling to Honolulu would require approval as well.[3]

That day, however, was different. The train bound for Honolulu left Kahuku, at the northern edge of Oahu Island, traveling south by way of Waialua, Waianae, and Ewa, at each stop picking up hundreds of sugar plantation workers who lived nearby. Although the train's passenger coach was nothing special or fancy, with simple, hard, wooden chairs, and although the trip took several hours because the train was extremely slow, Shirley had a lot of fun talking to other plantation workers he had never met before. In Honolulu, they joined in a parade of approximately 3,000 people.[4] At the same time, thousands joined in similar parades on all the major Hawaiian islands, marching with banners and placards that read "Labor Demands Humane Living Wages," "Demand Equality and Justice," "We Helped Smash Nazism," and so on.[5]

It was the second day of the territory-wide strike, involving more than 25,000 workers from 33 sugar plantations, continuing for more than two months and, eventually, challenging and changing the century-old master-servant relationships at the sugar plantations, which workers often compared to slavery and even one executive acknowledged was benevolent despotism.[6] On the surface, the strike took the form of a labor movement, but, as one of its slogans maintained, "Wages Are Not the Issue"; many workers and their families joined the strike not only to improve wages and working conditions. Deep down, the crux of the dispute involved changing the conventional social order and human relations.[7] Although the labor strike had many precedents in Hawaii, prewar strikes were mostly divided by ethnic origin, between, for instance, Japanese and Filipino plantation workers. It was largely World War II experiences that forced them to reconsider and cross ethnic lines, and the 1946 Sugar Strike was the first in which different ethnic groups went on strike under one union.[8] Seldom had the path to great change to terminate a de facto colonial situation seemed so clear.

In the same year, change seemed possible for many African Americans. Regardless of whether they lived in small cotton-mill towns or big cities, North or South, blacks had been in inferior and subordinate positions for a long time. This was particularly the case in the Deep South; blacks could not patronize the same restaurants and theaters as whites and could not ride buses in seats reserved for whites.[9] Even Coca-Cola vending machines had two separate pick-up pockets for white and "Colored."[10] There were no black police officers, no black firefighters, no black office workers, and no black civil service employees. Job opportunities for blacks, regardless of education level, were limited to those marked "Negro jobs," such as janitors, mill hands, and other jobs requiring physical labor, which were a "bit hotter and dirtier" than those desired by white men.[11]

This system of segregation covered many, if not all, details of everyday life and conditioned the conscious and unconscious behavior of ordinary people, whether black or white, adults or children. Many white people tended to assume, for example, that when they passed each other on the street, blacks would step off the sidewalk. One black community leader in Macon, Georgia, remembers how black parents normally told their children: "If you are on the sidewalk, and the white people want the sidewalk, you get off. Let them have it."[12] That was the tradition, and the only way to maintain peace and harmony on an interpersonal and community level. "Colored people are crucified not once a day," pointed out the civil rights activist Aubrey Williams, "but several times a day on trains, buses, in stores, or wherever they live or seek to work."[13]

During World War II, African Americans' expectations for racial equality heightened, and, in 1946, great change seemed possible, or at least promising. In February and March, black World War II veterans spearheaded campaigns to promote black voter registration and organized a demonstration in Atlanta to urge the appointment of black police officers in the city.[14] In July, thousands of African Americans patiently joined long lines to cast votes in the Democratic primary for the first time in their lives, despite being threatened and despite being forced to stand outside for hours due to the poor capacity of polling places.[15] Despite a massive conservative backlash, in September, African-American leaders and white reformers in the North began a nationwide anti-lynching campaign in the hope of protecting African Americans' civil rights.[16] While unpredictable, the wind of change was perceptible and seemed like a tailwind at this point.

At the same time, another significant battle was becoming more clearly visible in postwar America than ever before: workingwomen's struggle for gender equality. In October 1946, for instance, approximately 400 clerks, mostly women, at the most popular department and clothing stores—Kahn's and Hasting's—in Oakland, California, launched a strike to protest the dismissal of a female worker. "Do Not Patronize" and "The Store [Is] Unfair" were slogans carried by female participants in street demonstrations.[17] Described by their male colleagues as the "most militant group of people you ever wanted to see," these female department stores clerks continued their strike for more than two months. In December 1946, it eventually triggered perhaps the most comprehensive general strike in U.S. history, which 100,000 workers joined and during which almost everything in Oakland—from shipyards, factories, and industrial plants to construction sites and transportation services—was shut down for three days.[18]

Women picketing in front of Kahn's, November 1946. (Photograph by Moses L. Cohen. Oakland Museum of California, Oakland Tribune Collection, H96.1.27.)

Historically speaking, women, too, had designated places and roles in society and at home. Women were institutionalized in a way that was similar to the treatment of African Americans and plantation workers, with certain expectations about "men's jobs" and "women's jobs." Opportunities for workingwomen, in general, were limited to those as domestic workers, waitresses, telephone operators, and secretaries as well as salesclerks—and at lower salaries than men.[19] During the war, with the men gone off to fight, the situation was different. To be sure, long before the 1940s, many women had held paid work outside home, but in wartime they were taking what had previously been considered "men's jobs"—as riveters, welders, and crane operators. They worked at shipyards, automobile plants, and manufacturing factories, and many more than before attained positions as doctors, lawyers, journalists, and college professors.[20] During the war, the number of employed women almost doubled, from 11 million to nearly 20 million.[21] Whether working in industries or professions, many workingwomen, for the first time, gained a different kind of work experience, with high wages, respect, and a sense of independence. "[The women of the neighborhood] changed as much as the men who went to war," recalled a Mexican-American war worker, Carmen Chaves: "We had a taste of independence we hadn't known before the war. We developed a feeling of self-confidence and a sense of worth."[22]

As the war came to an end, the large majority of women in factories disappeared almost overnight as the men came home from fighting and received preference in hiring. Between 1944 and November 1945, at the Ford plant in Highland Park, Michigan, for instance, the number of female employees decreased from 5,800 to 300, or from 43 percent to 2 percent of the workforce.[23] Granted, many women willingly returned home, but the seeds of social tension were planted, because many workingwomen wanted to retain their jobs or at least continue to work outside the home. At the Ford plant, for example, the remaining female workers organized a public demonstration in the fall of 1945, carrying placards that read "How Come No Work for Women?," "Stop Discrimination Because of Sex," and so on.[24] Although many workingwomen had to leave the factories nonetheless, others who were fired remained in the workforce at traditional "women's jobs," such as department store clerks and telephone operators. Among them were those who worked at Kahn's and Hasting's, and those who in 1947 actively participated in a nationwide strike of telephone workers—the largest walkout of women in U.S. history—in which 350,000 employees, 230,000 of them women, were involved.[25] For them, women's reality had already transformed radically. For many, a change in the existing gender hierarchy seemed possible and necessary.

Plantation workers, African Americans, and workingwomen: these were merely the tip of the iceberg, only a few examples of profound and extensive social changes following the Great Depression and World War II. Normally these changes are treated separately as Hawaiian history, African-American history, and women's history and certainly are rarely discussed in connection with the global history of the Cold War. Nonetheless, the whispers, mutterings, and outcries associated with these changes aroused strong reactions on the ground, destabilizing old social norms and existing hierarchies and thus sparking a variety of social tensions in postwar America, inflaming the American version of "anti-communism" and eventually swaying domestic politics, which, in turn, affected the conduct of external policies.

Intriguingly, what was happening in American society had unintended and far-reaching repercussions in other parts of the world, often intensifying internal tensions there, and, taken together, the stories of such local tensions were not irrelevant to the evolution of the global Cold War. The primary aim of this book is precisely to show how such micro-level stories within societies connect to stories on a global scale. To begin with, what kind of reactions occurred in American society, how did these relate to the evolution of the American version of "anti-communism," and how did such a development initiate a chain of actions and reactions beyond the U.S. borders?

MASSIVE RESISTANCE

Radical changes that became visible during World War II gave hope to the many people who had been underrepresented previously and who found new opportunities in the turbulent years of the war and postwar periods. Nevertheless, what was hope for these people was, in the eyes of the majority of the population, a challenge to existing social norms and hierarchies, whether in terms of economics, race, or gender. Looking back, in the aftermath of the war what the majority of the people seemed to aspire to was not a radically new society, with revolutionary changes and serious reforms, but a recovery of American society and its dreams as they existed (or at least as they were believed to have existed) before the Great Depression and World War II.

In this sense, the November 1946 issue of *Life* magazine's featured article, "Dreams of 1946," captured well the emotions of the vast majority of the population. According to the article, what many people envisioned was the materialization of a new life, equipped with an electric iron ($10), toaster ($19), portable radio ($60), General Electric television ($190), dual-temperature refrigerator ($199), automatic washing machine ($241), electric stove ($266), dishwasher ($299), and, above all, an automobile, like the Mercury Convertible ($2,209).[26] All of this should be available in a new house, and that house should be home to a new family, including, of course, babies. After all, who could blame the people who had suffered through more than a decade of hardship during the depression and war for dreaming of ordinary happiness? For them, postwar life was expected to be rosier and brighter, in the words of *Life*, "full of air-conditioned peace and electronically controlled plenty."[27]

Nevertheless, real life in postwar America was not so plentiful nor was it peaceful. The average salary for full-time employees was still $2,473 per year, with a railroad worker's total yearly income at $3,055, a public school teacher's at $2,025, and a farm laborer's at $1,394.[28] This meant that, for an ordinary public school teacher, a portable radio cost more than a third of a month's income.[29] Worse still, inflation was rampant, and the cost of living skyrocketed; the price of consumer goods, for instance, rose 15 percent in the second half of 1946, and food prices during the same period rose 28 percent.[30] One magazine noted that the price of shoes for children had reached $6 to $7 a pair, which would pinch large families, as would children's clothes at double, or more than double, their prewar prices.[31] The economic situation in 1946 was still anything but stable and plentiful.

Furthermore, American society was far from peaceful. Most notable, perhaps, was the explosive increase in labor strife. Although wildcat strikes were actually quite frequent during wartime despite a "no-strike" pledge, a genuine, massive wave of strikes hit the United States in the immediate postwar period. By the end of 1946, there had been 4,985 strikes, involving 4.6 million workers—a record high in terms of scale and number of strikes in all of U.S. history.[32] In many cases, these disputes did not represent simply "labor" strife, as they often contained diverse social demands, such as anger over racial and gender inequality and frustration with outdated social norms. These strikes, thus, raised fundamental questions about the existing order, and that is why, on the one hand, they attracted enthusiastic support, while, on the other, they provoked irritation and even animosity. Consequently, massive waves of backlash developed.

Although, in view of ongoing criticism of labor after the war, it is not surprising to see a storm of denunciations of the strike waves in 1946, the intensity of attacks may have been well beyond participants' imaginations. Observing the Oakland general strike, for instance, a Chicago man wrote an angry letter to *Life:* "It made me sick to my stomach to see the stupidity and brutality shown in these strikers. They should be given a compulsory course in American history so that they would have a better appreciation of the principles and ideals behind the system they are endangering by their unthinking acts."[33] Likewise, the mayor of Oakland flatly denied the validity of the strike because it was an attempt to push aside the government created by all the people and to substitute the physical force of mobs for that government.[34] Along similar lines, one business writer even described the situation in 1946 as "nothing less than catastrophic civil war."[35]

The backlash against labor activism in the South was much more severe. From the beginning, any efforts to organize unions among Southern workers—most of them black—in cotton mills or on tobacco plantations were thoroughly and effectively blocked by community-wide resistance and obstruction, including surveillance and threats, as well as physical violence toward union activists and sympathizers.[36] In addition, African-American workers had little support from white workers. At a manufacturing plant in Memphis, Tennessee, for example, white welders warned the manager that they would go on strike after they learned that the company was about to employ a black welder.[37] Indeed, white labor unionists in the Deep South tended to give blacks the cold shoulder; one white union member at a factory in Columbus, Georgia, for instance, told a Northern labor activist: "[I have] nothing against the nigger. He has to buy his groceries in the same store as me and at the prices I pay. But I just don't want to mix and mingle with him."[38]

In terms of fissures within the labor movement, workingwomen, like black workers, were beset with immense difficulties. From the beginning, in contrast to the rise of a new consciousness of rights among working people and blacks in the 1930s and 1940s, not much attention had been paid to the issue of gender inequality.[39] Nonetheless, the backlash came from many directions as soon as workingwomen began to challenge the existing gender hierarchy. Like black workers, women did not always have full support from unions. In some cases, the local union leadership refused to submit grievance reports to management for female members. Even when such grievances were written up, they were, in one case, stored in a male member's locker and later "mysteriously disappeared from the locker."[40] A female labor activist in the San Francisco Bay Area, Betty de Losada, recalls: "Men were very conscious that they were the breadwinner of the family, with children to support, and wives and women's work was ancillary to the man's income." She continued, "And men were not prepared to have women earn the same wages, in the sense that the wife would bring home the same paycheck, because that really affected the male-female relationships in the household."[41] Thus, the backlash toward workingwomen came not just from management but from male union members as well as their husbands. Such reactions increased as workingwomen began attempting to challenge the gender hierarchy.

The conservative backlash to the blacks' struggle for civil rights was even more ruthless and merciless. If civil rights activists appealed for a "Double V" campaign—victory over fascism abroad and racial discrimination at home—Southern segregationists, as the historian Jason M. Ward aptly points out, developed their own version of "Double V": defense of democracy abroad and defense of Southern tradition—Jim Crow practices—at home.[42] It is not surprising that African Americans' voter registration drives inspired massive resistance from white conservatives. Democratic State Representative John D. Long of South Carolina, for instance, spoke bluntly: "We'll fight him at the precinct meeting, we'll fight him at the county convention, we'll fight him at the enrollment books, and, by God, we'll fight him at the polls if I have to bite the dust as did my ancestors!"[43]

Democratic Senator Theodore G. Bilbo of Mississippi was even more brazen. In a radio broadcast on June 23, 1946, he urged listeners to use "any means to keep the nigger away from the polls," because if one handful went to the polls that year, there would be two handfuls the following year, and numbers would continue to grow after that. "Do not let a single nigger vote," said Bilbo; "You and I know what's the best way to keep the nigger from voting. You do it the night before the election. I don't have to tell you any more than that. Red-blooded men know what I mean."[44] It is not clear whether any listeners did "do *it*" the night before the election that particular year, but many incidents of voter prevention did occur in the Deep South in the late 1940s; in Wrightsville, Georgia, for example, three hundred hooded men—members of the Ku Klux Klan, of which Bilbo was a member—gathered and burned a cross on the courthouse lawn on the eve of an election, effectively scaring off blacks from voting.[45]

Conservative white resistance was not limited to the South. Recent studies have shed new light on the civil rights movement in the North, revealing in detail the massive white backlash in Northern cities. In Detroit, more than one-third of the respondents to a survey expressed explicit antagonism toward the influx of black migrants during the war.[46] Such strong attitudes among white residents were pervasive not only among adults but children and teenagers; in East St. Louis, Illinois, for example, more than a hundred high school and junior high students walked out of their classrooms in protest when thirteen black students sought admission to the schools, leaving them to sit in empty classrooms. White students reportedly scribbled, "Down with the Negros" and "The Negroes. If They Stay We Go."[47] Mounting antipathy of this kind came from the whites' irritation that long-held customs and order were increasingly being trampled upon. In order to continue enjoying peace and harmony among whites and blacks and within communities, segregation of the races, it was claimed, had to be maintained.[48]

These waves of backlash toward labor, workingwomen, and African Americans had a common logic: "Our lives and harmony were threatened by outsiders." The identity of "outsiders" differed depending on the situation; sometimes they were migrant blacks in the North, sometimes Northern labor activists in the South, sometimes women in the workplace, and so forth. In Hawaii, the same logic prevailed; a business writer, for example, disapproved of the plantation workers' strike on the grounds that it was led by "mainlanders" and not "local men," while a pastor criticized the coming of unionization to the islands as it posed a challenge to the "aloha spirit" that local people cherished.[49] "Our homes, our schools, our churches, our hospitals, our government, our very lives as residents of Hawaii are at stake," maintained the *Honolulu Advertiser*'s front-page editorial at the height of the 1946 Sugar Strike.[50] This statement, however, is not as clear as it might appear at first glance. After all, whose lives were "our lives" in postwar America, and whose were outsiders'?

WHAT WAS AMERICAN (AND UN-AMERICAN)?

Intriguingly, the moment when diverse social conflicts became visible and a massive backlash developed was also when the term the "American Way," often in capital letters, came into vogue among a large portion of the population. Indeed, the years around 1946–1947 marked the historical period when a patriotic atmosphere appeared to pervade the United States.[51] Nonetheless, the craze for Americanness in this period did not really indicate the beginning of an era of consensus and harmony. In fact, the opposite was true. As the historian Wendy L. Wall astutely observes, the popularity of such terms reveals a deep sense of anxiety that had accumulated through the 1930s and 1940s.[52] The collapse of domestic tranquility required a redefinition of what should (and should not) be deemed "American." It is no coincidence that discussions concerning the definition of "America" emerged following the Great Depression and spread during and, especially, after World War II. In this short period, the reality of America became more diverse, with the result that the promise of prosperity suddenly was in question, social, racial, and gender hierarchies were in flux, and old social norms were challenged, as we have just seen.[53]

In such chaotic circumstances, with visible divisions and conflicts, it is not difficult to imagine the emergence of new phenomena and emotions. When an upheaval is so dramatic and so unusual, sometimes new situations arise that do not easily fit into existing categories of knowledge, so assigning specific and suitable names to them is challenging. If an entirely new vocabulary is introduced, it will not be universally understood. Because one cannot avoid using existing language and value systems, one has to use old language to describe new situations or to express new emotions by rearranging or substituting for the meanings of existing words.

The wartime and postwar periods presented precisely such a challenge. On the one hand, those who were in a position to question existing social, economic, and political orders, such as African Americans and women who aspired to improve their status, tended to find useful vocabularies for critiquing the status quo in leftist thought, even when this stream of thinking did not necessarily fit perfectly with how they felt. On the other hand, those who were alarmed by the decay of the existing version of order and harmony needed names for themselves and their antagonists as well. Words like "conservatism" or "the conservative movement" did not exist as signifiers for grassroots popular sentiments or social activism. The term "Americanism" was useful to some extent but, at the same time, awkward and even troublesome. After all, opponents could claim that their positions and demands were more "American"; sugar plantation workers, for instance, claimed an "American standard for all," while African Americans and women asserted their equal rights based on the core principle in the Declaration of Independence, "all men are created equal." Therefore, those who positioned themselves to defend or attempt to recover a conventional version of order and harmony also needed new terms that would describe their own position as well as their antagonists. As such a demand arose, an old vocabulary returned to circulate increasingly in society, with a new usage and a broader scope: communist and anti-communist.

These terms were inclusive from the outset. The word "communist" was used to describe anything deemed "un-American"—that is, atypical from the majority's viewpoint—which came to the surface as aftereffects of radical social, cultural, political, and economic transformations in the 1930s and, particularly, during the war. By the same token, "anti-communist" was adopted to describe a truly diverse group of people who defined themselves by negating others who were not like them. This version of anti-communism developed in response to various problems and antagonists at home, and, as Colleen Doody's study of the micro-level experiences of the Cold War in Detroit shows, it was more concerned with tensions within American society than those at the international level.[54] From a social point of view, it is thus reasonable to say that the development of anti-communist zeal in the United States was not simply an end result of international situations but had its own domestic dynamics. At its core, the "anti-communist" campaign in postwar America can be seen as a sort of social movement for cracking down on "un-American" activities and individuals—in a sense, a grassroots conservative backlash containing elements of "disturbance" in order to recover an orderly and harmonious society.

In fact, such "anti-communist" campaigns at their zenith in the early 1950s often overlapped with attacks on African Americans, civil rights activists, feminists, immigrants, gays and lesbians, and advocates of New Deal policies, who epitomized radical social change in wartime and postwar America. Such attention to local roots explains why, in the United States, anti-communist rage more rapidly grew in places where social change was particularly conspicuous and why it developed hand in hand with currents in local politics and elections, with a variety of different local forms.[55] The more visible the change, the more intense and furious the backlash: The more labor unions became politicized and the more civil rights, feminist, and New Deal activists became visible, the more this version of anti-communist logic grew in local politics.

The 1946 midterm elections were fought under such circumstances. Candidates were well aware of an angry climate due to domestic issues, such as shortages, high prices, and, in particular, labor strikes, and their voting reflected the irritation, resentment, uneasiness, and disappointment so aptly expressed in a bitingly effective GOP (Grand Old Party) slogan: "Had enough? Vote Republican."[56] Throughout the election campaigns, domestic issues were the central subject, and several magazines, such as *The Nation* and *U.S. News and World Report,* even declared in 1946 that practically no candidates had bothered to discuss foreign policy or the U.S.-USSR rivalry.[57] The issue of "anti-communism," to be sure, was a heated topic in several places, such as California, Wisconsin, Ohio, Michigan, and Idaho; however, these were places where New Dealers and labor activists had been active in local politics. In fact, actual discussions of the "anti-communist" line centered on the question of what to do with labor activism at home following the explosive surge in strikes in 1946.[58] In other words, the topic grew hot because Republican candidates used this version of anti-communist logic as a political tactic to castigate labor activism and New Deal type policies in their districts. Indeed, it worked.

The results of the midterm elections were astonishing. The Republican Party picked up fifty-five seats in the House and thirteen in the Senate and now counted twenty-five governorships out of forty-eight, including Ohio, Pennsylvania, California, and New York. Although the takeover of the House had been widely predicted, Republicans also succeeded in capturing the Senate, which meant they controlled both houses of Congress for the first time since 1932.[59] It was a sweeping Republican victory across the country, and the version of anti-communist tactics that local candidates used in local election campaigns now began extending to national politics. It is no surprise, therefore, that this version of "communist" attacks first heated up among newly elected politicians in the House of Representatives, rather than incumbent politicians in the Senate or the White House.[60] When the new Congress met in January 1947, in fact, Republican representatives, including Fred Busbey of Illinois and Paul Shafer and Bartel Jonkman of Michigan, jumped on anti-communist issues, earnestly urging investigations of the State Department, the Justice Department, and chambers of commerce, all of which had expanded during the New Deal and wartime periods, and all of which had been rumored to have large numbers of communists as members.[61] Their stance was understandable, particularly in view of the popularity of "anti-communist" remarks in Michigan and Illinois, where labor strife had been particularly fierce.[62]

At this point, however, consensus over the reality of the Cold War written and conceived in capital letters as an obvious historical epoch did not exist, and variety of futures seemed possible. Thus, the public was divided over President Harry S. Truman's "anti-communist" initiative in March 1947, namely, the Truman Doctrine, which called for immediate economic and military aid to Greece and Turkey. According to opinion polls, while the majority approved of economic aid to Greece, more than half actually disagreed with sending military advisers to train the Greek army, and, in fact, many openly criticized the president's announcement.[63] The world of the Cold War remained one of a variety of opinions, not yet an irrefutable "reality," simply because it was not yet known and shared widely. In sum, in 1946 the development of the "anti-communist" trend was observed along with a rise in social tensions concerning what was "American" and what was not, and such intense debates and fluid political situations in American society had unintended, far-reaching repercussions beyond the United States, in places such as in Japan.

ANTI-COMMUNISM LEAPING TO JAPAN

The U.S. occupation of Japan formally began in October 1945. In the first six months, there was little significant controversy concerning the conduct of the General Headquarters (GHQ) in Tokyo under the control of the Supreme Commander of Allied Powers (SCAP)—that is, General Douglas MacArthur.[64] The situation, however, changed as a surge in the popularity of Marxist agendas and labor activism became apparent in postwar Japan; labor union membership quickly surpassed its prewar peak of 400,000 by the end of 1945 and reached nearly 5 million by December 1946.[65] Such increasing and overwhelming support for leftist thought in Japan was noticeable even from the United States, and, as soon as criticism toward the New Deal and alleged communist activities grew following the 1946 midterm elections, many American observers began to problematize the "left turn" in Japan under the U.S. occupation. For them, the rapid spread of leftist influence and the sudden development of labor unionism could not be explained without reference to the expansion of Moscow's influence in East Asia.[66]

However, there was a much more fundamental element in the popularity of leftist thought in postwar Japan: the experiences of war and defeat among the Japanese themselves. If victory in the war brought the United States confirmation of wartime values and morale and also heightened trust in the government and patriotism, defeat brought Japan a negation and distrust of all of them. For many in Japan, the immediate reaction was to devalue wartime ethics and reevaluate things that were forbidden during the war. As such, one group was suddenly in the spotlight: the Japanese Communist Party (JCP). After all, the JCP was the only group that maintained opposition to the war while it was going on, and this simple reality gave it the ethical high ground after Japan's defeat. The fact that hundreds of Japanese communists maintained antiwar beliefs, despite harsh suppression, imprisonment, and, in many cases, torture throughout the war made them appear to be martyrs or saints in the postwar period.[67] This was particularly the case for intellectuals, who surrendered their opinions and cooperated in support of the war but felt a deep sense of remorse afterward. For many, the communists' uncompromising attitude toward the war seemed symbolic of true independent thinking—in the buzzwords of the time, a proof of "subjectivity." This term captured people's hearts precisely because many keenly felt that they did not have it.[68]

Like the United States, Japan experienced profound upheavals after the war, with an outpouring of new emotions and phenomena that defied easy labeling. After all, not many vocabularies or systems of knowledge were available to squarely criticize war, militarism, and the emperor in a society that had been at war in one way or another for more than a decade, even, arguably, almost half a century. When such emotions emerged in the postwar era, it was Marxism and the long tradition of labor activism in Japan that gave many people an avenue through which to express their feelings of regret, irritation, and anger about the war and to compensate for their unfulfilled desire for subjectivity during the war. In other words, many contemporary Japanese creatively (or mistakenly) developed leftist thinking as a result of their own experiences of war and defeat. Indeed, as the historian Oguma Eiji suggests, almost all phenomena in postwar Japan grew out of wartime experiences, remorse, and shame.[69] Seen in this way, it is clear that broad support for a Marxist agenda did not represent the spread of the Cold War in East Asia nor did it represent Moscow's influence.

On the other side of the Pacific, such local voices, feelings, and specific demands often faded away. In covering Japan's nationwide May Day demonstrations in 1946, American newspapers and radio shows focused on the "expanding roles of Communism in Japan."[70] Several commentators even asked whether "in the nurturing of the Japanese labor movements" the U.S. occupation had "bred something in the nature of a Frankensteinian monster."[71] Meanwhile, rumors spread, maintaining that a large number of communists and leftists were active inside the GHQ.[72] Groundless rumors of this kind, however, were not simply powerless illusions when they were repeated and grew. They became a sort of "common sense" and, in turn, drove the people involved to look for proof, supplying the tailwind for a red-baiting climate at the SCAP.

"The newspapers are full of the anti-communist investigation and purges now going on in the States, especially in Congress. This is as good a time (*sic*), psychologically, to revive our own situation," wrote Charles Willoughby, chief of the Military Intelligent Section—known as G2—in the GHQ in Tokyo in February 1947.[73] Born in Heidelberg, Germany, Willoughby immigrated to the United States when he was sixteen and later became a military officer and described himself as a zealot for American values. He liked to say that he had "absolute trust" in the justice and truth of the United States and considered progressives, liberals, and communist sympathizers who criticized the country his enemies. "On this point I do not yield an inch," he stressed.[74] Not surprisingly, the SCAP's initial reform-oriented policies looked to him like the result of communist manipulation, and, thus, in early 1947, when the "anti-communist" mood was growing in the United States, he found an opportunity to revive a critique of alleged leftist influence in the GHQ.

Willoughby energetically capitalized on this opportunity precisely because his earlier effort had not been so successful. His section's first intelligence report, "Leftist Classification of Civilian Employees," produced in September 1946, did not capture much attention at first, but, after the retreat of the New Deal in the 1946 midterm elections, it gained notice. The revised version raised its profile with a slightly catchier title, "Leftist Influence in Headquarters," and, by February 1947, a third revision had appeared with a far more eye-catching title, "Leftist Infiltration into SCAP." The report swelled from the original 28-page study to a 110-page survey.[75] Willoughby's correspondence during this period shows his unusual zeal, bordering on paranoia. In drawing up a revised version of older studies that listed nine suspects, he did not hesitate to order that some "facts" be made up. He even wrote to his subordinates, "I am disappointed in the small number of cases. I thought there were 21. We might as well list the other 'suspects' as being under investigation."[76]

Furthermore, MacArthur's political ambitions and opportunistic attitude helped to foster the red-baiting mood. In the early months of the occupation, he accepted the growing popularity of leftist thought and, in fact, stated that the rise of labor unions in Japan was a favorable sign of a "liberal trend," but, within a year, his attitude changed.[77] A key to explaining his capricious outlook is his sensitivity concerning his own public image in the United States. As MacArthur's political advisors observed, the general was highly concerned with how he was viewed and extremely sensitive to any kind of criticism.[78] In line with this, it made sense for him to support New Deal–type policies in the early months of the occupation, as he firmly believed that such policies were still popular in the United States. Thus, after seeing the defeat of the New Deal and the loss of popularity of labor activism in the 1946 midterm elections, he had no reason to stick with such reform-oriented policies.

Such was particularly the case between November 1946 and February 1947. The landslide victory of the Republican Party in the midterm elections confirmed for many people that the next president would be a Republican and that MacArthur would be a formidable candidate. In November 1946, he began receiving letters and telegrams from supporters, ranging from ordinary people to former president Herbert Hoover, many of whom had backed his unsuccessful candidacy in the 1944 presidential election.[79] These supporters now advised MacArthur to return to the United States and give a few talks to bolster the morale of the country. One Chicago man wrote to the general, informing him that he had already begun a "Draft MacArthur Movement." Likewise, a woman in Oregon confessed that, when she was praying, God gave her a vision of Christ, standing by MacArthur's side, saying, "He is my man. . . . I will stand beside him all the way."[80]

No less confident than this woman, MacArthur strongly believed that he could be the next president. Thus, he wanted to know which way the wind was blowing in the United States, and the 1946 midterm election returns showed him, making his judgments on the course of U.S. occupation policy even more capricious.[81] It was no surprise that MacArthur ordered the cancellation of a planned general strike in Japan in January 1947 after having observed the election results and the backlash against the Oakland general strike, which had occurred just a month earlier. It was blindingly obvious that he would be harshly attacked in his homeland if he did not stop it. On this point, he did not need to ask about Washington's direction nor did he need to think about the U.S.-USSR rivalry.

As various headwinds combined—from the defeat of the New Deal in the midterm elections and the rapid increase of negative reports on the SCAP in the American media to the escalation of red-hunting within the GHQ, as well as MacArthur's opportunistic attitude—it was not surprising that the SCAP's young officials who had been promoting radical reform programs in Japan, and began to be criticized as "New Dealers," gradually lost confidence. Theodore Cohen, chief of the labor division at the SCAP between 1946 and 1950, recalled the meaning of the 1946 elections: "Labor was rejected. Business was in the saddle." A graduate of Columbia University, where he specialized in Japanese labor history, and an enthusiastic supporter of New Deal policies, Cohen wrote: "Reforms and reformers lost prestige and even respectability, while many of the Headquarters brass cozied up to GHQ civilians with big business connections."[82] Meanwhile, word spread among SCAP officials in Tokyo that it was becoming increasingly difficult to find a job upon returning to Washington, because they were labeled "too New Dealish" or even "communistic."[83] One ex-SCAP member, who was looking for a job in Washington in the spring of 1948, for instance, found that his work experience at GHQ aroused "much hostility."[84]

The case of Andrew Grajdanzev was even worse. Born in Siberia, and having spent almost his entire life in Harbin and Tianjin, China, before immigrating to the United States in the late 1930s, Grajdanzev was Willoughby's number one target and had been placed under strict surveillance in 1946. He was tailed, his room was secretly searched, and his letters were read, though there was no substantial evidence that he had done anything wrong. A three-week counterintelligence investigation found that he tended to eat by himself, stay at home, and visit the same places frequently. This last behavior did attract an investigator's interest, but it turned out that he was regularly learning Japanese while teaching English.[85] Nevertheless, when he returned to the United States, he could not find a job in government at all, due to rumors and attacks, despite his work experience in the SCAP, a Ph.D. in economics, and fluency in Russian, Japanese, Chinese, and English. Eventually he studied library science, starting over completely, and got a job at a small local library.[86]

Hearing of such experiences, many reformers simply became too discouraged to continue with their programs.[87] A considerable number of staff members decided to leave the SCAP in 1947. One staff member, asked decades later whether that atmosphere had any influence on him, said: "I think I became less enthusiastic about going on in the field. . . . [The climate] dampened my interest. I realized that you could not say just anything you wanted to. If you wanted to continue your career, you could not."[88] Still in their thirties, talented and ambitious, many young SCAP officials wanted to return to and continue their careers in the United States.[89] However, their choices were limited: to leave the SCAP as soon as possible (which many did) or to compromise by toning down liberal reforms, adapting themselves to the newly emerging political culture. SCAP officials' memoirs suggest that changes in day-to-day office policies were the result of their own fears and adaptations between the spring of 1946 and 1947, a trend that accelerated following the 1946 midterm elections. These adaptations were not the result of Washington's Cold War strategy but came from their own conscious and unconscious daily practices. This point sheds new light on the shift in U.S. occupation policy for Japan—commonly known as the "Reverse Course," assumed to have taken place in the late 1940s.

LOCAL POLITICS OF THE REVERSE COURSE

Conventionally, the so-called Reverse Course—from the policy of reforming Japanese society to that of restoring the Japanese economy—has been explained as resulting from the escalation of the Cold War.[90] This explanation maintains that, because the Cold War developed in Europe, the United States decided to take a tougher stance all over the world, including East Asia, thus, abolishing various reform-oriented policies and focusing more on the maintenance of stability and rehabilitation of the Japanese economy to use Japan as a fortress against the threat of Soviet expansion in East Asia. Those in control, according to this narrative, were grand strategists in the State Department, such as George F. Kennan and Walton W. Butterworth, who took new positions in the summer of 1947 as director of the Policy Planning Staff and head of the Far East Division, respectively, and began talking about developing Japan as a buffer state in East Asia.[91]

Kennan, in fact, wrote memorandum NSC-13 in October 1948, officially recommending a change in U.S. occupation policy in Japan, a document that is often seen as the origin of the Reverse Course in Japan. The diplomat later recalled this proposal as his "most constructive contribution," continuing in a self-congratulatory tone, "On no other occasion (except the Marshall Plan), did I ever make recommendations of such scope and import; and on no other occasion did my recommendations meet with such wide, indeed almost complete, acceptance."[92] Emphasizing the unity and consistency of state power and high-ranking policymakers and displaying a seemingly clear and coherent image of the world situation, the story of the Reverse Course originating in Washington as Cold War strategy has since become the dominant narrative in Japan and the United States.[93]

Nevertheless, when the phenomenon is examined more closely such a conventional model is inadequate for explaining the situation. Theodore Cohen recalled that there was nothing like a situation in which the GHQ changed its occupation policy due to the escalation of the Cold War—that was merely historians' suspicious and simplistic scenario, he noted.[94] This recollection is valuable. To begin with, the gradual shift in tone of occupation policy began well before Washington explicated its policy in the fall of 1948. Changes in policy had already occurred in the fall of 1946 in a more fragmented and bottom-up way, as many SCAP officials personally began adapting themselves to the new political climate in the United States, which became visible through the 1946 midterm election. In addition, far more fundamental than State Department officials' considerations were the practical desires of politicians for "trimming the budget" and "protecting American taxpayers."[95] This emphasis on taxpayers, of course, came to the surface in line with popular anti–New Deal sentiments at that time, and, most importantly, with the 1948 presidential election. In short, domestic political considerations were particularly important in terms of supporting the notion of changing the emphasis in U.S. occupation policy.

While State Department officials indeed worked to modify the direction of occupation policy, this was only one of many diverse factors that, in many different ways, contributed to the phenomenon called the Reverse Course. These factors include currents of domestic politics and results of elections, as well as SCAP officials' personal politics, political ambitions, and self-protective attitudes—all of which became less visible under the clear-cut explanation based on the Cold War paradigm. Simply looking at the American side, the shift in U.S. policy seems more personal, fragmented, and domestically political than strategic, systematic, and Cold War oriented. However, there were far more fundamental factors in the change of course—Japanese elements.

When we look at Japanese agency in the dynamics of the Reverse Course, the story of that phenomenon seems far more complicated. At its core, the shift can be seen part of a process of local struggles between two radically different versions of reality, which were captured in two photos. One "reality" was that of a significant number of Japanese people, particularly the young and urban, enthusiastically embracing postwar reforms following the end of World War II. As the historian John Dower points out, many Japanese raised doubts about established orders and values, welcoming radical changes and reforms—the defiant climate that appears in a photo of a May Day demonstration in 1952.[96] Nonetheless, for many others, particularly the elderly and rural, who made up the majority, early postwar reforms looked abnormal, and the trend labeled the Reverse Course appeared more like a return to traditional, accustomed "normalcy"—the mood that can be seen in a photo that captured a cheering crowd of people welcoming the Emperor Hirohito in 1946.

Both versions of "reality" had enormous support in postwar Japan and, thus, were in conflict, with each taking advantage of foreign influence in its own way. From this perspective, the Reverse Course was not simply policy directed from Washington but primarily a process of local struggles among Japanese who wanted a different future for their society. In other words, the phenomenon of the Reverse Course can be seen as a reflection of an emerging conservative backlash at both elite and grassroots levels in the chaotic postwar period, rather than of the global Cold War. Although we cannot go into detail here, we can briefly explore this aspect by taking a look at how initial reform-oriented policies were altered or discontinued.

One of the clearest examples of the Reverse Course as a return to "normalcy" was the radical change in tone of labor policy, from encouraging labor activism to limiting and restricting it. On this point, Japanese conservative politicians played important roles in restraining labor's power. In one case, for instance, MacArthur's "directive" in July 1948 banning strikes among government workers is well known; yet, as the historian Koseki Shoichi reveals, this policy actually emerged in response to Prime Minister Ashida Hitoshi's desire to "stabilize" society.[97] By the same token, Japanese conservatives also utilized the GHQ's authority to restrict communist activities for the purpose of creating domestic tranquility. Such conservative attacks on communists were nothing new in Japan; a quarter-century's memories of communists as illegal at best and, more commonly, as gangsters, fanatics, or even carriers of epidemic diseases did not suddenly disappear from the minds of many people. Although the policy of releasing Japanese communists from prison was enacted in 1945, it was reversed due to mounting objections from both American and Japanese conservatives.

May Day demonstration in Tokyo, May 1952. (MacArthur Memorial Archives, Photographic Collection of Georges Dimitria Boria, No. PHB0167.)

While leftist agendas and labor activism were on the defensive, old bosses came back. The policy of purging former-regime bosses and military officials—often called the "White Purge," in contrast to the "Red Purge" years later—was executed in 1946. However, it was gradually lifted through the tireless efforts of Japanese and American conservatives. Their efforts began bearing fruit in 1948 and afterward with the release of A-class war criminal suspects, such as Kishi Nobusuke, who became prime minister of Japan in the late 1950s.[98] At the local level, more importantly, the White Purge had not been particularly effective because many purged persons could take "pride" in being expelled. One Japanese translator recalled that, when one was purged, people considered him to have been recognized by the GHQ as a "first-rank citizen of Japan." If one was not dismissed, people whispered, "He was such small people [*sic*], so that he was not even purged."[99] This sort of social recognition helped to maintain the old bosses' prestige in their communities, and it is not difficult to imagine the high

Hirohito addresses crowd, November 1946. (Photograph by John Florea. Getty Images,
LIFE Picture Collection, 466287031.)

respect they received when the Reverse Course resulted in their returning
to their hometowns.

Even high-profile policies followed a similar fate. The policy of dissolving
the *zaibatsu* (business conglomerates), for instance, suffered setbacks from
beginning to end. The first problem was bureaucratic and jurisdictional disputes within the SCAP, which occurred between the Government Section,
whose staff was more New Deal oriented, and the Anti-Trust Division, whose
staff derived mainly from American business circles and thus tended to dislike any state control of private companies.[100] The second problem was the
lack of support from Japanese and American business communities. Therefore, it is not surprising that, with mounting criticism in Tokyo and Washington to the effect that they were too "New Dealish," Government Section
staff gradually lost control within a year.[101] As a result, only a handful of giant
companies were dissolved, and most others were able to maintain their wartime forms, as Japanese conservatives had hoped. Finally, even major companies that had dissolved, like Mitsui, Sumitomo, and Mitsubishi, soon set up a
different form of enterprise group, later called *keiretsu* (corporate groupings),
and basically returned to their prewar shape, anyway.

Also reversed were American initiatives to reform the police system, which more or less reflected a peculiarly American idea concerning the importance of local self-government. Based on a typically Jeffersonian idea, the SCAP ordered that each city, town, and village fund and control its own police department. But, since the mid-nineteenth century, Japan had been pursuing the centralization of power; local taxpayers were not enthusiastic about paying for their police because they considered that to be simply inefficient. Local politicians also feared that such local police would be ineffective in monitoring nationwide left-wing networks. Thus, like the *zaibatsu* dissolution, the decentralization of the police system did not last long, mainly because it lacked support from Japanese politicians, bureaucrats, and local people.

By the same token, the U.S. policy of harsh and punitive war reparations, particularly to Asian countries, which was planned and approved in the early period of the occupation, was eventually abolished. Many Japanese remembered (or, more precisely, wanted to remember) World War II as the war against the United States and thus viewed themselves merely as "victims" of the war, rather than as aggressors in Asia. This framework attenuated the angle of war reparations as a central issue of Japan's war responsibility. In fact, except for a few intellectuals, many scholars in Japan tended to discuss the reparation issue within the framework of economic rehabilitation, rather than as an issue of moral or responsibility, and, thus, viewed war reparations only as an economic burden for the recovery. So, the topic appeared to be economic, rather than ethical, and, thus, the cancellation of war reparations went along perfectly with the efforts of many Japanese, particularly conservatives and businessmen.[102]

Finally, what was unmistakable as a sign of the return to "normalcy" was the revival of conservative Japanese politicians and bureaucrats, who had believed that initial occupation programs had swung too far to the left. As they became accustomed to the U.S. occupation, these Japanese actors learned how to take advantage of factional disputes within the SCAP. Prime Minister Yoshida Shigeru, for example, continually stressed the size of the threat of communist influence in Japan. In his dozens of letters to MacArthur, he repeatedly brought up the political and economic instability of his government. Once he learned that this strategy was effective in slowing down, or even canceling, early reform policies, Yoshida and other conservatives repeatedly used similar anti-communist language to achieve domestic and personal goals.[103]

In studies of the Reverse Course, scholars have tended to focus on political and economic aspects. Yet, when the expression *gyaku kousu* (Reverse Course) was first widely circulated among the Japanese population, circa 1951, through the publication of a series of articles in *Yomiuri Shinbun*, the term signified much broader and more diverse phenomena. In fact, *Yomiuri's* series of twenty-five articles included topics that went beyond typical examples of the Reverse Course, such as the failure of land reform and the return of *zaibatsu,* to the renewed popularity of war songs, toy guns, and Shintoism, as well as the revival of moral education and arrogant attitudes among the police, and so forth.[104] Considering that the term originally had such a broad scope, the contemporary focus on politics and economy seems to be the result of a substitution of meanings by later generations of historians. Viewed in this way, while often hidden under the mantle of a seemingly clear and coherent narrative of American Cold War strategy, the Reverse Course was a more local, fragmented, and social and cultural phenomenon. In essence, it was less a result of Washington's Cold War policy than part of a conservative backlash in Japan aimed at the recovery of normalcy and familiar order.

Nonetheless, it is also simplistic to view the subsequent conservative revival as an inevitable, linear development. While the backlash was recognizable in various areas, it also re-energized opposition, particularly among labor, youth, urbanites, and intellectuals, who had been seriously engaged in postwar reforms and transformations. Many workers still continued to fight back. Students began lining up at demonstrations to resist. Many intellectuals actively participated in public debates, publicizing their own agendas for the future of their country. If nothing unusual had happened in the summer of 1950, such substantial struggles and weighty debates in postwar Japan might have continued for much longer, possibly restricting the government's policy of a separate peace treaty and military alliance with the United States, and Japan's rearmament might have followed a different path.

Still, the shift in postwar Japan was noticeable even from abroad; several countries in East Asia and the Pacific, such as Australia, New Zealand, and the Philippines, were alarmed by this emerging trend. And, of course, it disturbed tens of thousands in China.

CHINESE REACTIONS TO THE "REVERSE COURSE"

"It is an iron fact that the American imperialists are helping Japan. It is a 100 percent fact that we do not need even to discuss. The fact of America's restoring of Japan creates a grave threat for China. All Chinese must raise an objection to it. It is very strange that the government remains hostile to such patriotic movements."[105] So said one speaker in one of many forums in Shanghai in the spring of 1948. Whatever the real factors were, the shift appearing in occupied Japan was readily observable across the sea between 1946 and 1948 and sparked popular outcry, which was widely known as *fan MeifuRi* (Oppose U.S. support of Japan). As in Japan, many Chinese viewed the Reverse Course as a deliberate reversal of America's Asian strategy, which indicated a coherent intention to rehabilitate the Japanese economy, revive conservative elements, and use Japan as a fortress from which to invade

Student protest in "Oppose U.S. support of Japan" demonstration in Shanghai, June 1948. (Photograph by Jack Birns. Getty Images, LIFE Picture Collection, 452743767.)

China. In Shanghai, where the movements first became popular, approximately 15,000 college and high-school students joined a demonstration on May 4, 1948, to oppose U.S. policy in Japan. Such demonstrations attracted sympathetic responses nationwide, in Beiping (Beijing), Tianjin, Kunming, Guangzhou, Xiamen, and Changchun, bringing various existing anti-government sentiments together under the banner of *fan MeifuRi*, which generated a long-lasting anti-American movement.[106]

Because of the extremely rapid and vigorous development of these movements, many contemporaries, particularly Nationalist Party members and

Student protest in Shanghai, June 1948. (Photograph by Jack Birns. Getty Images, LIFE Picture Collection, 465279249.)

sympathizers, as well as American observers, believed that communist propaganda and manipulation created them. After observing the spread of student movements nationwide, Generalissimo Chiang Kai-shek (Jiang Jieshi), for instance, angrily wrote in his diary that communist-supported "professional students" had instigated other students.[107] Based on this viewpoint, urban police departments were ordered to investigate and make lists of such "professional students" stirring the movements.[108] The U.S. ambassador to China, J. Leighton Stuart, agreed with the Generalissimo, attributing the students' and intellectuals' opposition to the U.S. government to communist manipulation.[109]

However, it is simplistic to view the development of *fan MeifuRi* and anti-American sentiments merely as products of communist manipulation. Certainly, the Chinese Communist Party (CCP) took full advantage of the situation and greatly benefited from the political climate that the movement fostered, but, at the outset, in the summer of 1946, criticism of the shift of U.S. occupation policy actually began in the nonpartisan and Nationalist Party–leaning newspapers in Shanghai.[110] "Under the moderate U.S. occupation policy, the old forces of Japan wore the mantle of democracy," *Da Gong Bao*, a major nonpartisan newspaper, argued as early as July 1946; "Surely, some of the militarists and *zaibatsu* were cleaned up. But the democratic forces in Japan are still weak, and all of the reforms remain incomplete under the influence of the emperor and senior statesmen."[111] In the midst of the *fan MeifuRi* movement in May 1948, *Da Gong Bao* increased its criticism, asserting, "The threat is extremely grave for China. If Japan rearmed, then naturally China would be the target of an attack. We need to firmly oppose [America's restoration of Japan]."[112] Another popular independent newspaper, Shanghai's *Fei Bao*, was in the same vein: "MacArthur is too generous. The Japanese are maneuvering him deviously and trying to restore themselves," adding that the emperor should bear responsibility for the war and that Japan should pay reparations to China.[113] No wonder both papers vehemently opposed Ambassador Stuart's statement attributing the cause of the movements to a communist plot.[114]

In fact, Nationalist sympathizers similarly disagreed with Stuart's view. Although Chiang's tolerant and moderate policy toward Japan—the "return good for evil" policy—had been praised since Japan's surrender, disagreements from within came to the surface as news spread of "America's policy of rebuilding Japan." Even the Nationalist Party's official newspaper, *Zhongyang Ribao*, expressed dissatisfaction in April 1948.[115] Chiang, nevertheless, publicly reconfirmed his support for U.S. policy the following month, further exacerbating dissatisfaction among party members and their sympathizers. Meanwhile, many Chinese businessmen, who were not typically communist sympathizers, lined up to take part in the *fan MeifuRi* movement. One businessman stated in another forum, "We need to oppose the U.S. policy of helping Japan because the policy is wrong and because it would pose a threat to the lives of the Chinese people." He asserted, "Opposing the [U.S. policy of] restoring Japan is patriotic; not opposing it is a betrayal of our country!"[116]

The CCP, to be sure, had been encouraging anti-government and anti-American demonstrations, actively intervening and promoting student movements. It had decided to take an anti-American stance by July 1946 and pronounced its opposition to the U.S. policy of rebuilding Japan in July 1947, according to a confidential report by the Shanghai Police Department.[117] However, this kind of opposition was not unique to the CCP. A number of independent newspapers, like *Da Gong Bao* and *Fei Bao,* had already expressed a similar view, and it was quite well received at that time.[118] In a sense, it is more reasonable to say that the CCP quickly and aptly adapted itself to the popular mentality of the period.

If CCP control did not explain the scale of the *fan MeifuRi* movement and anti-American sentiments, what did? The key was anticolonial sentiments on the part of millions of Chinese—more specifically, experiences and memories of World War II. This explains why similar sentiments were observed in several countries in the Asia-Pacific region and why such feelings were strongest in China.[119] For many Chinese, World War II meant the War against Japan—the war in which millions of Chinese perished, evoking countless images of brutal Japanese imperialism and widespread slaughter of Chinese. In short, the *fan MeifuRi* movement developed so quickly and broadly because the change in U.S. occupation policy in Japan was observed through the perspective of memories of Japanese imperialism. To spread such sentiments nationwide, the CCP did not need any propaganda or manipulation; after all, it was the Japanese military that invaded the country, including thousands of small towns and villages, conducting operations that the Chinese called "kill all, plunder all, and burn all."[120]

Memories of the war were everywhere. Writers and journalists in newspapers and magazines, as well as panelists, moderators, and students in many forums and demonstrations, almost all referred to their experiences and memories of war when they expressed harsh criticism of U.S. policy in Japan.

One *fan MeifuRi* forum, held June 3, 1948, began with a minute of silence for the war dead. Then, a moderator addressed the audience of 3,500, including prominent guests, such as the mayor of Shanghai, Wu Guozhen, as well as scholars, businessmen, and other Nationalist Party members:

> During the eight years of the War Against Japan, we, each of us, deeply experienced the cruelty of Japanese fascism. Through our own eyes, we saw our fathers and brothers die beneath the sword of Japanese fascism, and saw our sisters violated by Japanese fascism, and our houses were demolished. But in the end we won a victory. This victory was won at the cost of thousands and millions of Chinese people's lives. Today, even before the bloodstain gets dry, Japanese fascism has been reviving with the help of American imperialism.[121]

Eight speakers, including this moderator, gave speeches at the forum; not one failed to refer to experiences and memories of the war recently con-

Anti-American poster at Jiaotong University, Shanghai, June 1948. (Photograph by Jack Birns. Getty Images, LIFE Picture Collection, 452743765.)

cluded. At another forum, on May 26, 1948, seventeen panelists—including the widow of the renowned novelist Lu Xun, as well as an economist, a chemist, a historian, a businessman, a journalist, and various lawyers, editors, professors, and others—spoke, and again everyone alluded to their war experiences as grounds for opposition to U.S. policy in Japan.[122]

Throughout this period, "anti-American" calls were usually anti–American *policy* and anti–American *government* supportive to Japan but not yet really anti-America or anti-Americans, in general. What these appeals shared in common was, rather, skepticism and distrust toward Japan due to bitter memories of the war. Some speakers at these forums even spared time to state that their "anti-American" views represented opposition to the U.S. government, particularly concerning its policy in Japan, but not to the "American people" in general.[123] By the same token, although many local newspapers continued to criticize the Nationalist government's weak diplomatic efforts and

Memories of the War against Japan in "Oppose U.S. support of Japan" rally at Jiaotong University, Shanghai, June 1948. (Photograph by Jack Birns. Getty Images, LIFE Picture Collection, 465279247.)

U.S. policy of restoring Japan, at the core of these critiques lay deep skepticism of Japan, rather than the United States. In other words, the United States was criticized because it appeared to be "supporting Japanese imperialism and conservative elements," and the Nationalist government was condemned for following U.S. policy without expressing any independent opinions.[124] As in many other countries in the postwar period, experiences and memories of World War II created overall contexts in China, through which contemporary foreign and domestic affairs were observed. This effect was particularly strong in political and social arenas, and this point provides a key to understanding the spread of anti-government and anti-American sentiments during the Chinese Civil War.

ANTI-NATIONALIST AND ANTI-AMERICAN SENTIMENTS

The Chinese Civil War between the Nationalist Party (Guomindang, GMD) and the CCP, which resumed in the summer of 1946, was, to be sure, fought on battlefields. Seen purely in terms of military capability, the GMD forces surpassed those of the CCP by roughly four to one.[125] Therefore, at the beginning, the war evolved in a way that was advantageous to Nationalist forces; in fact, they captured the CCP's base camp at Yan'an in 1947, and, at the beginning of 1948, Chiang could still say bombastically that they would be able to sweep out all communists within a year.[126] Nonetheless, GMD forces suffered decisive defeats later in the year, eventually causing them to retreat to Taiwan in 1949.[127] How did this happen? Why did the tide of war turn to the advantage of CCP forces in the end?[128] While we cannot answer these questions in great detail, the key factor involves the nature of this war. It was fought not only on battlefields but within society over a sense of legitimacy and authority, and such "battles" were no less important than physical combat. After all, many cities surrendered to the CCP's People's Liberation Army (PLA) without fierce battles.[129] What mattered in the war was the politics of trust among a large portion of the population. In such a struggle, *minxin* (people's hearts) was crucial.

In these battles over people's hearts, thus, the point of contention was not really ideology nor was it a global confrontation between the East and the West. Many people's problems with the Nationalist government were more local and specific, and what was happening was more about a meltdown of trust—the liquidation of legitimacy.[130] Take Shanghai, for example. A minor problem might have involved only local public policy, as some "reactionary" wall-scribbling read: "Government officials, you don't need to ride trains and go to dance halls; please come to the streets, and look at the piles of trash."[131] Yet even such complaints were severely cracked down on. Two high-school students in Shanghai, for instance, were given a two-year jail sentence with a three-year suspension for putting up seven "reactionary" wall posters.[132] A playwright was placed under police surveillance because his scenarios stressed the violence of American soldiers stationed in China and depicted scenes of the Nationalist Party government fawning over Americans.[133]

In an effort to maintain order, the Shanghai city government banned hundreds of newspapers, magazines, maps, and books, with titles such as *Ideal Marriage, American Public Opinions,* and *Several Problems in the History of Chinese Society.*[134] Likewise, one school administrator ordered tighter controls concerning popular songs on campus that would "instigate disorder, and intend to destroy society and state."[135] None of these controls, however, seemed effective; in many cases, they simply backfired. After all, it is impossible to crack down on popular sentiments. Posters expressing complaints

GMD's crackdown on "communist agents" in Shanghai, 16 May 1949. (Anonymous photographer, Bettmann/Corbis/AP Images, 49051602516.)

and discontent about the government were rampant.[136] Arrests of "reactionary" college and high school students only aroused much larger protest
movements among students, while causing morality and justice among local offices to deteriorate.[137] The surveillance of the aforementioned drama-
tist found only that he frequently had parties at night and that many of his
guests were GMD naval officers, not CCP sympathizers.[138] And the banning of books provoked slogans like "We Have the Freedom to Read!"[139]

Even some intellectuals, who had been skeptical or reluctant to support
the CCP, eventually abandoned the GMD when faced with a situation in
which one could be arrested simply for openly opposing the government.
"If we cannot openly oppose the government, let me ask this; what do we
hope for the government hereafter?" wrote Peking University professor Lou
Bangyan, who ominously prophesied, "An antonym of the open opposition is an underground plot. If the government does not permit open opposition, people's plot for rebellion will eventually develop into an all-out
revolution."[140]

The GMD's harsh crackdown was particularly shocking because it occurred during one of the most liberal-democratic moments in modern Chinese history. In Shanghai alone, during the period following the defeat of
Japan, hundreds of new magazines and newspapers were published, which
provided forums for free and open exchanges of diverse viewpoints.[141] These
new voices boldly expressed their hopes for democracy, freedom, and equality and, thus, often openly took confrontational positions against the GMD
government.[142] One of the most active and prominent was a weekly magazine, Guancha (Observation), which was founded by a journalist, Chu Anping, in September 1946. From the start, the magazine demanded the establishment of a liberal and democratic government and, thus, opposed the
GMD government's repressive attitude and continued to express its support
for the fan MeifuRi student movement.[143]

It is important to note, however, that Chu and his fellow intellectuals
were not necessarily sympathetic to, let alone supportive of, communist ideology. On the contrary, Chu himself did not believe that the people would
achieve fundamental freedom under communist rule or that the CCP would
bring democracy to China.[144] If he had such deep apprehensions about the
CCP, why did Chu take a firm stand against the GMD and accept communist rule? This was the dilemma many intellectuals faced at that time.
The simple answer is that their distrust of the GMD was far more profound

than their uneasiness about the CCP. As Chu wrote in the article, however critical and distrustful he was toward the CCP, he knew that the Nationalist Party would not be able to conduct any social reforms, and that the CCP, by contrast, appeared relatively promising in executing imperative social reforms in the particular circumstances of China in the late 1940s.

Here, again, we see an example of a situation in which a name given to something does not necessarily fit with its substance. As we can see in Chu's case, acceptance of the CCP did not mean support for communist ideology, let alone sympathy for Moscow's policies. Rather, it simply meant objections to the GMD government and the U.S. government, both of which appeared to be supporting the rearmament of Japan. In other words, behind approval of the CCP lay memories of Japanese colonialism. Such a subtle disparity between name and substance was not surprising in view of the chaotic situation in postcolonial China, in which new emotions and phenomena that did not have suitable names erupted all of a sudden. As in postwar Japan, "communist" ideology was translated and adopted based more on local and historical contexts, rather than as the expansion of the Cold War.

In fact, the Cold War paradigm had not yet been consolidated. Like Chu, many liberals, who were distrustful toward communist ideology, actually, kept in step with the CCP, harshly criticizing GMD rule, while staunch anti-communist newspapers openly supported students' protest movements that were anti-Nationalist in nature. For instance, *Laobaixing Ribao,* a small local newspaper in Jilin, generally maintained an anti-communist and Nationalist-leaning stance but, at the same time, published articles sympathetic to student movements, praising them as "patriotic movements," and continued to demand further and dramatic government reforms.[145] Likewise, *Fei Bao,* generally a Nationalist-leaning paper, often criticized the slow pace of government reforms, as in one political cartoon showing a police officer unable to regulate traffic due to too many signs of "privileges" and "exceptions."[146]

The battle line was not the one made through Cold War confrontations; rather, it emerged more through struggles over legitimacy and over *minxin* primarily between these two political parties. While *Fei Bao*'s pro-Nationalist tone did not change, its editorials argued that people were losing trust in the GMD government due to the continuation of the Civil War, the collapse of the economy, and the prevalence of many forms of corruption, concluding that the prestige of the Nationalist Party was declining.[147] "Those who win the hearts of the people gain ascendancy, while those who lose them die out!" the paper's editorial announced in 1948, adding, "The hearts of the people are most difficult to control and to force. The earlier to win them, the more advantageous the position will be."[148]

The GMD leadership, however, almost ignored such voices, even when they came from pro-Nationalist newspapers, while the CCP leadership might have been more sensitive to them. When Zhou Enlai, one of the CCP's top leaders, repeatedly wrote memorandums on how to win people's hearts, Chiang Kai-shek simply lamented in his diary about the "stupidity and ignorance of this population of 400 million."[149] For Nationalist Party leaders, popular sentiments could not be seen as anything but reflections of communist propaganda and manipulation, although frustrations and complaints about the government were, in fact, more fragmented and local, rather than ideological. As the GMD leadership continued to treat popular attitudes accordingly and to crack down on any dissenters as such, it was no surprise that the government quickly lost popular support. Much worse for the GMD government, its oppressive policies reminded many of similar conduct by the Japanese police and military during World War II. The more the GMD resembled Japanese militarists, the more quickly the authority of its government decayed.

Anti-American sentiments developed in this period in a similar manner. Previously favorable images of the United States began to deteriorate in the postwar period for various reasons. The first was, as we have seen, that the U.S. government was seen as supporting and rearming Japan. The second was Washington's continuous support for the increasingly unpopular and repressive GMD government, which culminated in the China Aid Act, passed by Congress in April 1948. Still, another arguably more important factor had to do with thousands of local conflicts arising between local Chinese residents and American soldiers stationed in China in the postwar period. One of these, the Shen Chong incident, for instance, involved the alleged rape of a Chinese college student by a U.S. Marine in December 1946, which triggered widespread protest movements in cities all over China.[150] As the historian Hong Zhang makes clear, however, while anti-American rallies nationwide were surely mounted on the pretext of protesting this alleged rape of a Chinese student, they were not really about that particular incident. In fact, slogans at these rallies read: "China Is Not a

Colony; Why Does America Stay in China?" and "Defend China's Independence and Freedom."[151]

Each incident was emphasized not because it was unique but because it was considered symbolic of a larger phenomenon—namely, colonialism. In this process, again, experiences and memories of the War against Japan played key roles. After all, conflicts between American soldiers and Chinese residents evoked many people's sympathy because they were reminiscent of similar and ubiquitous conflicts between Japanese soldiers and the Chinese. The Shen Chong incident, for example, reminded many of the Japanese atrocities against females during the war.[152] Furthermore, the fact of the U.S. occupation of Japan and the southern part of Korea, combined with allegations concerning U.S. policies for restoring and rearming Japan, caused many people to fear another foreign invasion. In a sense, anti-American sentiments in China developed as American actions were gradually seen as overlapping with images of Japanese imperialism during the war.[153] In sum, the development of anti-GMD and anti-American sentiments in postwar China had more to do with local wariness and historical contexts based on experiences and memories of World War II than with CCP propaganda or international plots emanating from Moscow; they were not part of the Cold War.

In this way, the Japan issue served as a catalyst, evoking bitter war memories and anti-imperial feelings, while generating the basis for long-lasting antigovernment and anti-American feelings. In the midst of the Civil War, how to respond to the shift in U.S. occupation policy in Japan became a litmus test between the two opposing parties over their legitimacy and authority. Because of deep memories of the war, the Japan issue caused cracks to appear in the Nationalist Party, undermining trust in the GMD government from within, while the CCP greatly benefited from the political emotions that evolved during the *fan MeifuRi* movement.

That said, it is simplistic to view the dominance of communist rule in the 1950s as an inevitable outcome. In fact, at the moment of its founding in 1949, the People's Republic of China was not yet a fully socialist or communist state.[154] Nor did Beijing secure social, political, and economic control over the entire country from the outset. Although the CCP took crucial and central roles, it also paid significant attention to bringing together diverse political forces beyond the party line. Practically speaking, the CCP, which had grown out of and ruled primarily rural areas, lacked experience in administrating cities and would not be able to govern the entire country without cooperating with various non-Communist forces, as well as ex-GMD officials and their sympathizers.[155] In short, to administer the country, the CCP had to soften its political agenda and, thus, the leadership recognized that it would take "quite a long time"—perhaps fifteen years by their initial calculations—before it would be able to move on to a fully communist state through the nationalization of private industries and socialization of agriculture.[156] In 1949, the radical shift in Beijing's policies that took place circa 1951–1953 was not yet on the horizon, nor was it preordained at the moment of the establishment of the new regime.

If nothing unusual had happened in the summer of 1950, the CCP's moderate policies in both rural and urban areas would have lasted a little longer, as originally scheduled, and the Beijing leadership might not have chosen radical agendas, as it eventually did alongside the development of the Korean War.[157] In short, however brief it was, there was a period between the civil war and early months of 1950 before something fundamentally changed. Reality was still in flux, and various futures seemed possible.

PERCEPTION OF CHINA IN THE UNITED STATES

On the other side of the world, in the United States, however, the complicated aspects of the *fan MeifuRi* movement and the Chinese Civil War—domestic politics, social contexts, and memories of the War against Japan—were largely omitted, and usually only a simplified version was reported: the expansion of communist influence in East Asia. To be sure, quite a few reports attempted to call attention to the social and historical background to the Chinese Revolution and its aftermath.[158] Yet the large majority of magazines and newspapers ascribed the decay of the GMD regime simply to propaganda and manipulations of the CCP, or even the Kremlin, similar to the way in which they attributed the popularity of leftist thought in Japan solely to communist expansion and "socialistic" SCAP occupation policies.[159]

In the period between late 1947 and mid-1948, the China issue evolved into a nonpartisan topic, as members of both parties and their sympathizers used similar language. Henry Luce's pro-Republican *Life* and *Time* magazines, for example, maintained some of the most hawkish attitudes in the major media.[160] Born in Shandong Province, China, to a Presbyterian missionary family, Luce maintained a strong desire to "save" China, remaining an ardent anti-communist throughout his life, and believed in the role of American foreign policy, a theme he delineated in his famous article in 1941, "The American Century."[161] Luce's influential magazines continually criticized the Truman administration for being too slow and too willing to compromise, asserting, "While the U.S. talks about reform, the communists are winning the war."[162] Of course, this did not mean that Democrats and their sympathizers supported the government's China policy; the pro-Democratic *Newsweek,* for instance, maintained that the United States would not permit all of China to go communist.[163]

Decisive communist victories in China in the fall of 1948 incited many writers to amplify their critiques. Irritated by the progress of the war, a Catholic and far more nationalistic magazine, *America,* urged Washington to support the GMD government to save China from becoming a "Far Eastern puppet of the Kremlin," stating: "There is only one policy for America to adopt toward China: immediate and effective aid, whatever it costs to halt Communism."[164] By early 1949, fifty-one members of Congress had formed a supra-partisan group, arguing that a communist victory would pose a "grave threat" to U.S. national security.[165] One of them, John McCormack, the Democratic representative from Massachusetts, took a firm stand in the House: "We cannot let China become subject to Communist government."[166] Such a rigid claim grew even firmer after the defeat of GMD forces. With mounting critical remarks such as "Who Lost China?" and accusations of being "soft on communism," the "loss" of China was traumatic for Democrats for decades to come.[167]

During this period, sensational and journalistic accounts about China were abundant, and they indicate a number of dominant attitudes regarding China.[168] To begin with, a sense of omnipotence is quite conspicuous. While the "loss" of China was frequently discussed, the question itself was delusional and arrogant; after all, how could Americans "lose" a country they had never governed or possessed?[169] While many magazines insisted firmly that Americans could not "permit all of China to go Communist," from the beginning, none asked why the Chinese needed America's "permission." Yet such claims did not sound strange in the aftermath of World War II. After all, the United States won the war and saved the world (at least, many considered this to be the case). Then, why not save China? Even Walter Lippmann, one of the most prominent intellectuals of the day, did not hesitate to ask, "Why at the zenith of American power was American influence in China paralyzed?"[170] Beneath irritation of this kind was a strong sense of self-righteousness, which had been promoted and consolidated in the wartime and postwar periods.

The other side of such illusions of omnipotence was the incapacitating of "others," particularly Asians. As the journalist Harold Isaacs observed, a large majority of Americans viewed China merely as "a country we have always helped" and the Chinese as "a people to be helped."[171] If the Chinese did not act as Americans wished, they were simply considered "puppets of the Kremlin."[172] Finally, the basic worldview in which this sense of omnipotence was grounded was the popular ideology of global geopolitics, which tended to make sweeping generalizations about the "world," with an assumption that what happened in one place should happen in the same way in other parts, thus, making local complications and historical contexts appear negligible.[173] For a country that fought and won the world war in Europe and Asia-Pacific, this "global" view appeared natural, although such a perspective was no more than local imaginings of the world.[174]

This explains why student movements in China were almost completely ignored in the United States. To begin with, the ideology of geopolitics naturally presupposed conflicts between states and made it difficult to see the development of internal decay and domestic discord. Thus, because internal opposition was simply viewed as the conduct of enemy agents, Chinese student movements were seen by Americans merely as a result of communist propaganda. In addition, this widespread sense of self-righteousness made it difficult to listen to criticism from outside. Questions or protests shouted in the streets in China were viewed in the United States not as proper opinions to be considered but conduct instigated by the enemy. Finally, as the reverse side of the sense of omnipotence, "others" were assumed to be incapable, not proactive and subjective actors who had their own voices and thoughts.

REALITY STILL IN FLUX

However, differing viewpoints did exist. Many observers—including politicians, scholars, journalists, and even everyday people—openly argued against such a popular worldview. A major liberal magazine, *The Nation,* for instance,

was still able to plead in December 1948 that the United States not be mis-
led by pleas of "aiding" and "saving" China, arguing against the idea of
providing military assistance to the GMD government, which "the Chinese people came to despise."[175] Likewise, a renowned Harvard historian,
John King Fairbank, was able to urge readers to look at the actual situation
in China: "The United States must make a distinction between the Chinese
communist movement and the Chinese social revolution. This means that
American policy must be to align ourselves more positively and actively with
social change in China of the type we really believe in, even though we find
ourselves running parallel to Chinese Communism."[176] Along the same lines,
one commentator explicitly argued for the need to think more about how to
get along with the communist world.[177]

This kind of attitude, urging cooperation with Communist China was,
in fact, not limited to liberals and progressives. Even a pro-Republican and
pro-business magazine, *U.S. News and World Report,* observed in February
1949 that U.S. recognition of Communist China was "ultimately to be expected."[178] Similarly, Secretary of State Dean Acheson, often deemed one of
the most hawkish "Cold Warriors," was, in early 1949, actually considering
recommending that the United States eventually recognize Mao Zedong's
regime.[179] Contrary to the later image of Dean Acheson as a primary archi-
tect of the global Cold War, the Acheson of early 1950 actually urged Americans not to regard Asia in the same light as Europe—a suggestion that would
be almost unimaginable for the Acheson of later years, implying the existence
of heterogeneity and flexibility in the politics of the early postwar period.[180]

One example of such heterogeneity involves Henry A. Wallace, who served
as vice president under Franklin D. Roosevelt and was the leader of the Progressive Party and a candidate for president in 1948. Having grown up in a
farming town in Iowa, Wallace was an active protagonist of populist movements, proclaiming himself a true believer in the "people." Whereas Henry
Luce envisaged the "American Century," Wallace imagined "The Century
of the Common Man," as the title of his book indicated.[181] Thus, he pas-
sionately argued, "The Chinese fiasco illustrates the complete bankruptcy
of U.S. foreign policy. Unless Chiang's regime is replaced by a people's government . . . the great bulk of the Chinese people will hate the very words
'America' and 'United States' for generations to come."[182]

Openly defying the notion of the Cold War and insisting on cooperation with the people of China and the Soviet Union, the presence of Henry

Wallace in national politics itself suggests the heterogeneity of American politics in the late 1940s.[183] Although almost no one expected him to win in the 1948 presidential election, Wallace was not a minor candidate; major newspapers and radio programs paid attention to and reported on him, which would have been scarcely imaginable in the 1952 election.[184] Even given his bitter defeat, Wallace supporters did not suddenly disappear. On the contrary, progressives in 1949 actually attempted to set a new tone in calling for a remobilization of the Progressive Party in preparation for the 1950 midterm elections.[185]

Therefore, it would be a mistake to view the period between 1945 and 1950 simply as a prelude, a transitional period, leading to the era of the Cold War and McCarthyism. Because we know what happened in the years that followed, we tend to draw a straight line between "similar" events over time. Yet the consolidation of the Cold War did not develop in such a linear and accumulative manner. Since we are familiar with the heyday of the Cold War in the 1950s, we have tended to view 1949 as a moment of rising tension between the two superpowers, a half-landing on the stairs leading up to the Cold War. But quite a few contemporaries did not see their era this way. In fact, a White House staff member, Eben Ayers, regarded 1949 as a year of "rest," rather than that of rising tension in the Cold War. The strike wave was over (1946), the presidential election was won (1948), and, finally, the Berlin crisis—the Soviet blockade of the city, which developed into a major international conflict—was over, as well (1948–1949). With a feeling of assurance, Ayers could take a three-week vacation from late September to early October, without much concern about the founding of the People's Republic of China. In retrospect, 1949 might appear to be a moment of rising tensions leading to the Cold War, but it did not necessarily appear that way at the time.

By the same token, the explosion of anti-communist sentiments after 1950 was not predestined nor was it inevitable; the anti-communist climate, indeed, did not develop in a straight line. In Michigan, one of the places where the politics of anti-communism first developed in earnest, the use of Cold War rhetoric actually backfired, at first; according to the historian Colleen Doody, Governor Kim Sigler exaggerated the communist threat so much in his re-election campaign of 1948 that he undermined his credibility and lost the election.[186] A similar situation could be seen in Hawaii, another location where red scare politics first developed in the United States after the

1946 Sugar Strike. "I don't care if they call my leader a communist. . . . So what," said a sugar plantation worker.[187] Indeed, unlike at the height of Mc-Carthyism in the following years, expressing disagreement and discontent were still quite common in the late 1940s. Bearing in mind the extremes at the peak of McCarthyism in the early 1950s, anti-communist politics in the late 1940s appears rather nonchalant and even casual.

In national politics as well, the tactics of red-baiting were not as success-ful in the late 1940s as they were in the early 1950s. The first big wave of "anti-communist" campaigns in postwar America came with the defeat of the New Deal in the 1946 midterms—a wave stirred up by newly elected Republican representatives, such as Fred Busbey of Illinois, as well as Paul Shafer and Bartel Jonkman of Michigan. Nevertheless, their claims did not really mark an era that would inspire terms like "Busbeyism," "Shaferism," or "Jonkmanism," despite the fact that their anti-communist and anti–State Department claims were almost identical to those of a Wisconsin senator years later. Instead of marking an epoch, they were criticized for their ground-less allegations. The *Washington Star,* for instance, denounced Representa-tive Shafer for making "reckless" claims, and declared that he "offered not a shred of substantiating evidence for his insinuations."[188]

Actually, this was the kind of criticism that Senator Joseph McCarthy, Republican from Wisconsin, faced in the spring of 1950. Although McCarthy gave his (in)famous speech in February, declaring that 205 communists had infiltrated the State Department, the senator was initially more criticized than believed.[189] Even *Life* magazine castigated McCarthy, as did *Time.* After ignoring his charges for two months, an editorial in *Life* insisted that there was a right way and a wrong way to fight communism and that Mc-Carthy's was the wrong one. "What you can best do for America and for American principles is not to join in the McCarthy lynching bee," pro-claimed the magazine.[190] Likewise, the Tydings Committee, a senatorial committee organized in March to investigate McCarthy's charges, publicly concluded in early June that not one of the persons accused was either a "disloyal employee or a Communist."[191] One White House staff member concluded in April 1950 that McCarthy was losing credibility, as he could not offer any evidence to support his accusations.[192]

If nothing unusual had happened in the summer of 1950, the dark days of McCarthyism might not have come or, at least, could have been post-poned for some time. The name of McCarthy might have been forgotten, like those of many of his colleagues, such as Paul Shafer. Children might not have needed to practice air raid drills in elementary schools, with the comical (in retrospect) song, "Duck and Cover."[193] Nor would children in New York State have had to wear identification tags in case of death from an atomic attack.[194] Perhaps, Mike Hammer, the main character in best-selling hard-boiled crime novels, would not have needed to change his targets from street gangs to "commies."[195] Likewise, Hollywood might not have felt the need to mass-produce tales of the red scare, which it did, releasing about 200 such films between 1951 and 1953. Furthermore, the memorandum NSC-68, which recommended a far more militaristic and aggressive stance on the side of the United States and which the historian Walter LaFeber called the "American blueprint for waging the Cold War," might have been shelved and not seen the light of day, as it was so in the spring of 1950. As such, commentators might have continued describing U.S.-USSR relations as "a cold war" or "the so-called cold war," in lower case, if the summer of 1950 had gone by uneventfully. With the cooling down of the Berlin blockade in 1949, the situation we now call the Cold War in the second half of the twentieth century might have developed into a situation called a "Cold Peace."[196] Without overwhelming support by the large majority of populations all over the world, the particular discourse of the Cold War would not have become an irrefutable "reality" of the world, had nothing unusual happened in the summer of 1950.

But something did happen, thousands of miles from the United States. The event might not have been as significant as many people thought at that time. It *became* important because millions of people imagined it to be, because it brought back memories of World War II, because it made them fear a possible World War III with atomic attacks, and, finally, because it provided a logic of global war that local people could use to end various social struggles and culture wars in many places of the world under the imagined reality of the Cold War. That event, which eventually triggered the social and political consolidation of the "reality" of the Cold War at home and abroad, was, of course, the full-scale outbreak of the Korean War on June 25, 1950.

CHAPTER TWO

Local Translation

AROUND NOON on Sunday, June 25, 1950, Kim Song-chil (Kim Seong-chil) was working in the fields at a village on the outskirts of Seoul. A 37-year-old historian at Seoul University, Kim did not need to go to school that day and thus was doing what he usually did on weekends. This ordinary day, however, was shattered with the news that a neighborhood storeowner brought. The shopkeeper, who had just returned from the city, told Kim that, after an invasion of forces from the north on that morning, fierce battles had been going on along the 38th parallel, that military personnel in the city had been urgently called up, and that the city was filled with tension. "I'm not sure whether this is just one of the frequent clashes that repeatedly occur along the dangerous 38th parallel or an invasion on a massive scale, as he told me," he wrote in his diary on that day. "But, judging from his look of panic after seeing the situation in the city, the matter seems quite urgent."[1]

The next day, he waited for a bus for quite a long time early in the morning, but it never came, so he ended up going to the university on foot. Perhaps all the buses were requisitioned, he thought. At school, as always, two of his students were studying in his office (Kim had left his door open for students who were working on a project for him). As had been recommended, Kim attended what was to be a regular Monday morning gathering for the first time, although he was disappointed with the university president's mediocre speech. It did not have any scholarly depth or patriotic enthusiasm, he thought, despite the critical situation facing them. On the way home, Kim felt as if the town was becoming more tumultuous than the school. "The war will expand," he thought, feeling dizzy while looking at military vehicles passing at full speed: "The killing among our kind, which has frightened us for five years, has finally come."[2]

The following day, Kim went to a nearby shop. On the street, passersby were gathering here, there, and everywhere, murmuring and whispering. Some began leaving the village, and others began taking refuge in the mountains behind the village. At the store, Kim bought eggs, noodles, tobacco, an alcoholic beverage, and some sweets, preparing to stay at home. "Even if we seek refuge, in a land as tiny as a palm, where can we find a safe place south of the 38th parallel?" he thought.[3] Eventually, however, he took his family and went to his brother-in-law's house, which was located on the northern outskirts of Seoul. By that night, the sound of artillery came closer, and it did not stop throughout the night. At dawn, the fighting became much fiercer, with gunfire getting closer and closer.[4]

After the cannons' roar died down as the sun rose on the morning of June 28, he peeped outside, looking over the city. People were already walking in the streets. Furthermore, a troop of soldiers wearing unfamiliar uniforms was marching down the street. Although the people looked relieved as the gunfire stopped, the world had been turned upside-down overnight. Around noon, Kim and his three children left his brother-in-law's house, heading back home on foot. Already, people in town were shouting, "Manse! Manse! [Hooray! Hooray!]," with red flags waving in their hands. The national flag of the Democratic People's Republic of Korea (North Korea), which he had only heard about, was fluttering over a school. He saw tanks, automobiles, horse-drawn carriages, and a crowd of foot soldiers gathering and talking together.[5] He wrote in his diary that day:

> They have a hard northwestern accent, but they are our kind, sharing the same language, customs, and blood. At a glance, somehow, they don't look like the enemy. They look more like brothers, who left home and lived some-

where far away, just making a visit after a long absence. Nobody feels animosity when seeing them speaking calmly with smiles.[6]

As he returned home, Bill—his dog—happily rushed up to Kim. Other than that, nothing was unusual. Just like Kim and his family, neighbors who had evacuated during the battle returned to their homes one after another, almost all at once. Everyone seemed glad to see one another, though no one dared to speak about topics relating to war and politics. By that evening, young people coming and going were already wearing communist red armbands; among them, Kim noticed, was a young man who, until only yesterday, had worn a different armband, that of an official right-wing organization in the Republic of Korea (South Korea).[7]

This was the beginning of Kim's wartime days, which, unfortunately, ended abruptly in October 1951, when Kim was killed while traveling to his hometown, Yongchon (Yeongcheon). He could not write a history of the events that he had scrupulously recorded (he was a specialist in Korean history), but his diary sheds light on several interesting points. First, he saw the invasion on June 25 as part of an ongoing domestic conflict that had been in progress for five years. In addition, he did not necessarily view soldiers from the north as the enemy—the hateful other. What is most interesting is that quite a few people, including Kim and his family, as well as many of his neighbors, chose to stay in Seoul, however resignedly, instead of fleeing to the south in a panic.

Kim's somewhat calm attitude and everyday experiences of warfare and occupation were, perhaps, not particularly unusual. In fact, a baseball game continued at Seoul Stadium while news of the invasion was announced and the radio broadcast a command for military personnel to return to barracks.[8] Many peasants in southern areas, too, simply continued their work in the fields, even though they knew that North Korean forces were moving southward; they reportedly thought that the soldiers would not harm them, anyway: "they are our kind, after all."[9] However lacking in tension they were in spite of warfare, local residents' reactions of this kind were quite common.

Nevertheless, such experiences on the ground have been shoved to the byways of history in many ways. First, the meanings and experiences of the Korean War were "understood" quite differently overseas, depending on from where and how the war was observed. In some areas, the war was dominantly perceived as the beginning of World War III. In others, it was more often considered as overlapping with anticolonial (or even anti-Western) struggles. Still, there were areas where the Korean conflict stirred relatively little excitement, making it appear a somewhat distant, local war. As we will see below, such a difference was rooted mostly in the diversity of historical backgrounds, particularly, of World War II experiences.

Second, intriguingly, such a process of local translation was not limited to foreign countries. Even within South Korean society, stories of everyday experiences have been superseded by the Cold War–based national history, which has commonly described the war as the "6.25 [June 25] War," emphasizing the abruptness of the war and de-emphasizing the historical roots of the war.[10] In a sense, the mechanism of "translation" operated even within local society. Why did this happen? How did people around the world—in East Asia, Southeast Asia, South Asia, the Middle East, Europe, and the Americas, as well as within Korea—observe and understand the war, respectively, and why did they do so in quite different ways?

FEAR OF WORLD WAR III

The moment of this attack was shared on the other side of the world almost immediately. Viewed from the United States, the situation looked far grimmer and more urgent, because North Korea's attack was assumed to be a direct challenge from Moscow, against which Americans should stand firmly. Although many Americans might not have known much about the Korean Peninsula, details of geography or culture did not really matter.[11] The significant point was that the "enemy" had come to attack. Based on this view, many Americans took to their pens, sending messages to the president. In just four days following the North Korean attack, the White House received approximately 900 telegrams and 276 letters; such correspondence, like a flood, continued to arrive every day for the next several months, with the majority asking the president to take a tougher stance, some proudly and others more in a panic.[12] One man in Indianapolis wrote a letter to the president on July 25:

> Communism is a bad thing and must be met with strong measures, since
> that is the only thing they understand or respect. . . . I'm convinced that we

are never going to have any peace until that "hell hole" in Russia is cleared out. Let's take the *offensive*. We have been sitting back waiting and spending ourselves into bankruptcy, the Russians definitely have the upper hand in this sort of game. The longer we wait the stronger they will get and by the same token we will grow weaker.[13]

Similarly, an Oklahoma man urged: "Dear Mr. Truman. I don't know much about the war but I want to know what you think of this. Why don't you load up a few B-29s with Atomic Bombs, fly over to Russia and let them drop. It's an awful thing to do. But if we don't do it first Russia will."[14] Likewise, a mother in Plainfield, New Jersey, resolutely informed the president: "My husband served overseas in the second [world] war. My son is 1A Plus for the third if the blunders of Manchuria, Ethiopia, and Czechoslovakia are repeated."[15]

Glancing over hundreds of these letters, one might easily note that the majority never even mention "Korea." Most, instead, focus on the "Kremlin" and "Stalin," implying that many Americans assumed that the Korean War began with an invasion of Soviet forces on June 25, 1950, and that North Koreans were merely tools of Moscow, with North Korea's attack instigated by Joseph Stalin.[16] Although significant numbers of people disagreed with this viewpoint, as we shall see, many viewed the Korean War as part of a carefully laid scheme by the Kremlin, which, to many Americans, meant the opening phase of a war between the USSR and the United States.[17] As such, *Chicago Daily News* reporter Keyes Beech's observation from Seoul on July 1, 1950, did not appear strange or absurd to American society: "I have a feeling that I have just witnessed the beginning of World War III."[18]

In fact, nearly two-thirds of respondents to a Gallup Poll believed that the United States was already engaged in World War III and that the Russians would drop the atomic bomb on American cities.[19] Several popular magazines reflected such feelings by presenting estimations of the potential damage of a nuclear attack on American cities—New York City, in particular. A notable example was Chesley Bonestell's illustration depicting an ominous mushroom cloud over Manhattan Island, an image that he prepared for the popular magazine *Collier's* piece of fiction "Hiroshima, U.S.A.," published on August 5, 1950, which aroused considerable reaction among both governmental officials and the general public.[20]

"Hiroshima U.S.A." (Illustration by Chesley Bonestell. Reprinted with permission.
New-York Historical Society, No. 1956.7.)

Memories of World War II were still fresh, and many housewives, who
worried about the possible outbreak of a full-scale war and subsequent scarcity of goods, began hoarding commodities.[21] A New York housewife plac-
ing two large orders for sugar reportedly said, "I'm just trying to get some
before hoarders buy it all."[22] Another housewife in Bethesda, Maryland,
with four new refrigerators in her kitchen reportedly complained when a

dealer would not sell her two more.[23] These cases of extreme hoarding were based on the illusion of shortages. In spite of rapidly rising prices of commodities following the outbreak of the Korean War, nationwide scarcity did not occur.[24] But hysteria did. For instance, Joseph Bildner, president of Kings supermarket in New Jersey, put 2,400 five-pound bags on display in his Plainfield store to prove that there was plenty of sugar. Within four hours, however, all 6 tons had been sold.[25] This phenomenon of hoarding in the summer of 1950 exemplified how widely anxiety and fear of war had spread throughout the country.

The initial U.S. strategy concerning the outbreak of the Korean War was formulated in this environment.[26] Enjoying a vacation in his hometown, Independence, Missouri, on the night of June 24, President Harry S. Truman did not see the situation, at its outset, as a burning crisis. Rather, he remarked to an aide that he would not cut short his visit to Independence unless something developed, because that would alarm people.[27] What changed his attitude by the next morning, however, were close communications with officials and politicians in Washington, including a telephone conversation with Secretary of State Dean Acheson and a memo forwarded from John Foster Dulles, a Republican and a special adviser to Secretary of State, who happened to be visiting Seoul and Tokyo at that time and frankly recommended that Washington use military force in Korea.[28] Truman quickly modified his stance, asserting, "If we are tough enough now . . . they won't take any next steps. But if we just stand by, they'll move into" other parts of the world in the future.[29] Interpreting North Korea's attack as a clear sign of communist aggression controlled by Moscow, the Truman administration decided to dispatch U.S. forces to Korea and the Taiwan Strait.[30]

In the People's Republic of China (PRC), the outbreak of the war was not big news. America's intervention in Korea and the Taiwan Strait, however, created far more serious and complex repercussions. Immediately, rumors in Northeast China maintained that "Chiang Kai-shek has already landed nine divisions in South Korea. Now both American and Japanese forces have entered the war, and World War III will be inescapable. Shenyang cannot avert air raids."[31] In Tianjin, a rumor at the end of June predicted that a world war would begin the following September. In Kunming, in Southwest China, local rumors had it that Ho Chi Minh, a Vietnamese communist leader, had already evacuated from Vietnam to Yunnan Province, that U.S. forces would attack China from Vietnam, and that Chiang had been flown to Tibet to command counterrevolutionary forces.[32] In Chongqing, one landlord suddenly stopped renting his property in mid-July; it turned out that he foresaw a rise in housing rents because many people living along the lower Yangtze River would have to evacuate to Chongqing following the outbreak of a general war.[33] In the Hualing district of Shanghai, local people gossiped that the CCP would have no way to survive if a world war were to break out, whispering that the its anti-American signature-collecting campaigns would be of no use at all.[34]

Because of such fear of World War III, commodity prices rose quickly in most cities throughout China, while stock prices in Beijing, Shanghai, and Tianjin fell rapidly.[35] In Tianjin, for instance, stock prices plummeted by nearly half, while the price of gold escalated by 133 percent in the first week following the U.S. intervention.[36] Observing the situation, a communist official in Rehe, in Northeast China, lamented, in a report written on July 22, 1950:

> The people's minds appear to be in a state of sheer terror. Ordinary people do not trust the value of our paper money any more, rushing to buy gold and silver, leading to a surge in gold prices. People do not believe our news reports of the victory of North Korean forces. . . . There have been fear of [a U.S.] atomic attack, which have caused some to forecast the end, resulting in parties of heavy drinking and eating in some areas. Some say, "Let's drink today all liquor we have today."[37]

As we shall examine later, reactions were even more diverse than we see here. However, the fear of World War III was unmistakable in Chinese society, and this was why many were even thrilled about the news of war. For those who had been skeptical, or even antagonistic, toward the communist regime, America's intervention in Korea and the Taiwan Strait seemed a rare opportunity to fight back.

If anyone saw an opportunity in this way, perhaps, no one exceeded the degree of zeal of members and sympathizers of the Nationalist Party, which had evacuated the mainland to Taiwan only about half a year earlier. Chiang wrote in his diary on July 1: "The United States has already started World War III. For the purpose of our counteroffensive to the mainland, we need to study ways in which we can support South Korea."[38] Two days later, Chiang made a speech in the new Nationalist capital city of Taipei, declaring that the Korean War would be an opportunity not only to create a framework of cooperation between Taiwan and the United States but also to form an alliance in East Asia against the threat of communism.[39]

In this line of thinking, the Korean War, as defined by the Nationalist Party, appeared to be part of a larger battle between Russians and Asians. The official GMD newspaper, *Zhongyang Ribao,* for example, editorialized that the outbreak of the war signified "another" invasion of Russian imperialism in Asia, arguing that the war in Korea should be seen as a struggle between the Asian people and Russian imperialism and that the GMD's effort to launch a counterattack should be seen as part of such a struggle, not just that between Taiwan and mainland China.[40] Viewed in this way, the outbreak of the Korean War marked a golden opportunity for Taiwan, with the United States on its side. On the same day that he made the speech mentioned earlier, Chiang actually informed General Douglas MacArthur, with great enthusiasm, that Taiwan could dispatch land troops to South Korea within five days.[41]

One poet expressed these fervent hopes in a poem, "A Signal of July," immediately following the U.S. intervention in Korea and the Taiwan Strait:

> In the season of dense cloud
> A thunderbolt with anger
> > sounds across the low sky of July
> A storm has come
> It is a signal
> > not a prophecy
> Vibrant days
> Spirited hearts
> Every depressed life
> > all become amazed and exuberant
> The song we passionately sing
> > thunders out in July
> We will find fruits
> > that the storm shall make them fall.[42]

Of course, this was not the only reaction in Taiwan in 1950; such feelings of delight were, more or less, limited to newly arriving Chinese settlers and evacuees from the mainland, called *waishengren,* whose numbers dramatically increased with the arrival of GMD armies, refugees, and their families after the defeat of the Nationalist Party on the mainland in 1949. Many of them believed that the Korean War should not be just a local conflict in Korea but a continuation of their own battles, as part of a "global war" against communism. Therefore, the war represented an unmistakable "signal" of fighting back, not an untrustworthy "prophecy," as the poet above described.

Because it appeared to be such a rare opportunity for a counterattack, some even felt irritated with the pace of the United States. His offer to send troops to Korea rejected by Washington, Chiang became increasingly impatient and distrustful, expressing his anger in his diary on July 27: "For these three years the United States has abandoned China, and taken a policy of supporting Japan. That policy in China and East Asia continues now. That is America's crude and shortsighted strategy in East Asia. How can such a country lead the world?"[43]

Hope and disappointment of this kind appear to have been shared on the other side of the world in Eastern Europe. In Sofia, Bulgaria, for example, a British diplomat discerned a "good deal of excitement" among local residents immediately following the U.S. intervention in Korea. Bulgarians, who were bitterly opposed to the communist regime but saw no chance of upsetting it without general upheaval, according to his observations, were talking in elated and vengeful terms of such an upheaval having just begun.[44] As in Taiwan, much disappointment was observed among such Bulgarians, however, because the U.S. government–sponsored radio network Voice of America retained a moderate tone, instead of making bold and sensational comments.[45] Still, rumors in Romania in mid-July maintained that regular transports of guns westward had been observed in Galati, on the Danube River; that the Soviet Union had already demanded that Romania invade Yugoslavia; and that there was "evidence" of road and rail movements of Romanian and Soviet troops near Bucharest.[46] In a fearful and suspicious frame of mind, the Norwegian ambassador to London inquired of a British minister: "[A]ny information to suggest that Russians were making preparations . . . elsewhere?"[47]

In other parts of Europe, too, in this climate of impending world war, even trivial daily occurrences appeared extremely serious. This was because there was a certain "common sense" view of the situation—that North Korea's attack occurred under Stalin's orders, that the Soviet Union chose Korea merely as a test, and that there could, or must, be a similar and larger attack in Europe.[48] In short, many in Western Europe feared that the Korean War was merely a feint operation before a Soviet attack in Europe, which could lead to a general war between the Eastern and Western camps, or the outbreak of World War III. That is why, like his Norwegian counterpart, the Greek ambassador to the UK inquired in July about whether the British Foreign Office had any information concerning Soviet intentions toward Greece.[49] That is why at a rally in Skarpnack, near Stockholm, Sweden, the same month, the youth of Sweden and neighboring countries appealed to Stalin, rather than the North Koreans or their leader Kim Il-sung (Kim Il-seong), to stop the Korean War.[50] And that is why many in European countries perceived the Korean War as a warning regarding the defense of Europe in the face of another world war, a way of thinking that opened the door for the rearmament of West Germany.[51]

In line with this viewpoint, a daily newspaper in the Netherlands, *Het Binnenhof*, editorialized in mid-July:

> The conclusion is that the West will have to direct all its energies to the strengthening of its defences, even though the war is not yet warm in the West. The people of the West, in their peace illusion, have dwelt too much on the past, with the result that Bonn and Tokyo still have no armies of their own with which if the necessity should arise to assist in the defence of Western democracy.[52]

Observing the development of discussions concerning European defense, a special correspondent for the Japanese newspaper *Asahi Shinbun* reported from Paris on July 29 that the war in Korea had been dominating the front pages of French newspapers for more than a month, adding that it had been a long time since Europeans had paid such careful and continuous attention to the Far East, if they ever had before. The correspondent concluded, "With the incident occurring in a remote peninsula in the Far East, Europe is keeping step with the world, and opened a new page of postwar history."[53]

Just across the sea from the burning peninsula, Japan, too, opened a new page of postwar history. Immediately following the North Korean attack, some experienced soldiers reportedly volunteered to support South Korea. Radical leftists, on the other hand, responded by happily spreading rumors that the people's army was approaching and would conquer Japan in a few years.[54] A renowned intellectual, Takeuchi Yoshimi, nicely captured the climate of the period: "In 1950, war and revolution was not prediction but reality. The People's Republic of China was established in the previous year, and the Korean War occurred in that year. Many believed a revolution in Japan was inevitable. No one at that time expected tranquility ten years hence."[55]

As in Europe, such a turbulent mood boosted discussions of Japan's rearmament, which became the central issue in the years that followed.[56] Within weeks of North Korea's attack, a renowned international legal scholar, Yokota Kisaburo, wrote an article titled "The Crisis of World War III and National Security of Japan," arguing that the attack should not be seen solely as actions by North Korea, that World War III was possible, and that Japan would need to establish a concept of national defense in a "realistic" manner.[57] Yokota's view was backed by conservatives, such as Baba Tsunego, president of *Yomiuri Shinbun,* who wrote frankly: "The roar of gunfire in Korea awoke us from a five-year dream of peace in Japan. . . . Nobody can guarantee that Japan will not experience the same fate when we see the North Korean army's surprise attack, as well as wartime chaos in Korea today."[58]

Amid such a radicalization and polarization of political viewpoints in Japan, those disappointed were a group of people, including both conservatives and leftists, who had been advocating for the unarmed neutrality of Japan, based on a comprehensive peace treaty that would conclude World War II. Some, of course, continued to argue, or even sharpened, the same position, but many thought that this line of thinking would no longer hold up. For them, a world war between the Soviet Union and the United States—the possibility of which they had been advocating to avoid through negotiations—was already occurring a stone's throw from Japan. One popular intellectual, Shimizu Ikutaro, lost patience, writing only few words in his diary on the day following the attack: "What nonsense."[59] He later recalled that he felt absurd because all his efforts in support of the unarmed neutrality of Japan and its comprehensive peace treaty had come to nothing because, he believed, the basic premise of U.S.-USSR coexistence was undercut by the outbreak of the Korean War.[60]

Yokota and Shimizu's statements appeared neither peculiar nor out of sync with the "common" view at that time. In Tokyo, in Shanghai, in Taipei, in New York, in Sofia, in Paris, in The Hague, and in many other places throughout the world, millions of people agreed that they were witnessing the opening shots of a general war between the USSR and the United States, which meant, for many, the beginning of World War III. "We are already in the initial stage of World War III," the Nobel prize–winning British philosopher Bertrand Russell, thus, felt able to declare in a solemn prophecy at the end of June 1950: "If World War III became an actuality, it must happen in Europe and Asia more or less simultaneously." He even added confidently, "Russia will go to war, and World War III will last for ten years."[61] It was such certitude in World War III discourse at the time of the Korean conflict that compelled numerous people to confirm this period as a moratorium, a moment just before the advent of World War III—the era of the Cold War. It was also this particular conceptualization of the moment that silenced various disagreements and different views, making what was merely a discourse of the Cold War into the irrefutable "actuality" of the world.

"NO HYSTERICS PLEASE"

The discourse of World War III, however, was a figment of the imagination, a product of fear, more than reality, as was the Cold War world based on it. Despite popular belief in the Korean War as Stalin's test drive for future endeavors, Stalin did not, in fact, *order* Kim Il-sung to attack South Korea, although he was surely responsible for *accepting* Kim's persistent pleas.[62] As recent studies have shown, the primary propelling force, among many other factors, behind North Korea's invasion was not so much Stalin, but Kim, who for years had been advocating a concept of *Namjin* (Southward March).[63] Apart from a few ebullient rhetorical slogans, Stalin, in his actual behavior and policy-making, remained cautious about starting a war with Western forces in either Europe or Asia and, in particular, a direct confrontation with the United States.[64] President Truman, as well, despite widespread fear (and hope) in China and other places, did not consider expanding the war to mainland China, let alone planning another world war.[65] In short, the leadership of the two "camps" remained cautious about not inciting another world war. Nonetheless, with the outbreak of the Korean War, the discourse of World War III increasingly gained great plausibility worldwide, as did the imagined reality of the Cold War.

There is, however, a pitfall in this kind of globalist thinking. Although the discourse of World War III surely spread in many parts of the world simultaneously, it never became a universal idea. In other words, the proliferation of this discourse did not occur everywhere. Where did it widely circulate and where did not? How can we characterize these regions? As we have just seen, the areas in which the discourse of World War III mushroomed explosively at the time of the Korean War were, most notably, in East Asia, Europe, and the United States. Obviously, these are the locations that first firmly embraced the idea of the Cold War. And these regions have another commonality: experiences and memories of World War II.

Fear of World War III had strong appeal in the societies where World War II had left the most direct and deepest scars and relatively little in places like Africa, Latin America, and South Asia, which were not, relatively speaking, principal battlefields of World War II. Intriguingly, the "reality" of the Cold War first gained verisimilitude in the former group, while relatively not so much, at least at this point, among the latter group. Viewed in this way, we can note a sort of correlation between experiences of World War II and verisimilitude of the Cold War. To put it bluntly, cruel experiences of World War II drove many to view the Korean War as the start of World War III, and this, in turn, endorsed the "actuality" of the Cold War. In fact, the outbreak of the Korean War was often compared to the Nazi invasion of Czechoslovakia, while Stalin was similarly likened to Adolf Hitler; one Briton, for instance, explicitly used this comparison when observing the situation in 1950: "Stalin is another Hitler all over again. He uses the same methods," the man said, "The only difference is that whereas Hitler fought anybody the Russians try and always get on the side of the winners."[66] In a sense, the Cold War was based on the fear of World War III, which was largely constructed in the shadow of World War II. However shared worldwide, the "reality" of the Cold War, in essence, was an understanding of the world situation as viewed through local lenses, a product of social and historical construction, rather than the objective situation of the postwar world.

In fact, fear of World War III did not develop in areas that did not directly experience the devastation of World War II, and, interestingly, a belief in the Cold War did not take root in those regions, either. Switzerland, with its long tradition of impartiality in foreign political matters, for instance, experienced the moment at a much lower key, as the Swiss Broadcasting

Corporation observed on July 8, 1950, Swiss public opinion was moved much less easily than that in other countries.[67] Likewise, Canada, which certainly participated in World War II, yet did not experience it as a series of actual battles, air bombings, or mass killings on its own territory, had a low-key reaction compared to that of its southern neighbor. Although opinions were sharply divided, such a restrained attitude can be seen in a political cartoon published in one of the largest-circulation newspapers in Canada, the *Toronto Star,* on July 20, illustrating a man tagged "Canada" who is dealing with paperwork labeled "Plans Preparations" and "Korean Situation," while soberly saying, "No hysterics please," to a man who, in a panic, asks, "What are we doing! What are we doing—!!? What are we going to do?"[68]

The illustrator might have had the reactions of U.S. residents in mind when drawing this cartoon. In fact, the *Toronto Star* took the trouble to write an editorial on panicky reactions by its southern neighbor and proudly reported that "it is gratifying the little evidence has been found in Canada of 'panic-buying' which occurred in the United States in the past fortnight."[69] Indeed, hoarding, which was widespread in the United States, did not occur in Canada. Such a difference in reactions, however, does not necessarily mean that the population of the United States was short-tempered and hysterical and that of Canada was cool and calm. Rather, the difference in war experiences and national memories more likely had an effect on local translation processes in viewing and understanding a "similar" event occurring just five years after the previous world war ended.

Another place that experienced the moment at a lower key was India, where the impact of World War II was felt more in its legacy—the end of British colonialism in 1947—than actual war and occupation experiences. For example, on the day after the attack, the *Times of India,* the most widely read English-language newspaper in the country, editorialized about the war, urging that it be treated as a "civil war—an internal affair for the Korean people to settle."[70] Readers promptly reacted to this editorial, most favorably. "Your observation that the Korean affairs should be treated purely as an internal matter of the country is perfectly right," wrote an Ahmedabad reader to the editor.[71] Similarly, a Kandivlee reader asserted that the nations of Asia should frankly tell the Great Powers to leave them alone and allow them to choose a political set-up according to their own preferences.[72] Although differing views were occasionally expressed as well, the dominant underlying tone was that of skepticism toward foreign colonial

"No Hysterics Please." *Toronto Star,* 20 July 1950. (Supplied by Library and Archives Canada. Reprinted with permission, Torstar Syndication Services.)

powers; a Calcutta (now Kolkata) man summarized such a feeling well: "However artificially the country might be partitioned, the people of Korea have the inherent right to work for the re-union of the two parts even by the use of arms; this may require even war on the scale such as of the American War of Independence."[73]

Political debates in India evolved in this atmosphere. When the Indian Parliament met and spent two days discussing the Korean issue on August 3 and 4, Prime Minister Jawaharlal Nehru drew intensive flak for India's support of the UN Security Council's resolution condemning North Korea as an aggressor. Syama Prosad Mookerjee, former Supply Minister of India, harshly criticized Nehru, asserting that India had become a "partisan in what was really a civil war" in its decision to accept the UN resolution, and, thus, he instead urged a "hands off Korea" policy.[74] Therefore, Nehru had to tone down his characterization of the Korean War. Instead of describing it as the beginning of World War III, he called it simply "some kind of war on a relatively small scale," in which most Indians would sympathize with the Korean people but would not see as a "giant shadow" falling on India.[75] Apparently, the Korean War did not provoke among Indians the spread of World War III discourse—fears that their own country might be dragged into a full-scale war, thus, it did not lead to an explosive spread of Cold War discourse in the region at this time. Rather, it evoked anticolonial and even anti-Western feelings.

This was particularly the case for many Asian societies that had suffered (and were still suffering) from colonial rule for decades and centuries. If it was true that almost all phenomena in the postwar era developed in tandem with wartime experiences and emotions in the areas where World War II had been fought, it was also true that almost all issues in postcolonial societies evolved in tandem with colonial (and anticolonial) experiences.

ANTICOLONIAL MOMENT

"The old style empires are dead but it does not mean that they have completely ceased to exist or that they do not function in Asia and Africa," said Nehru in Parliament on August 3, 1950: "They do function."[76] This recognition of and skepticism toward colonial influences still in effect set the basic tone for postcolonial societies in Asia when viewing the outbreak of the Korean War and U.S. intervention in it. Therefore, Nehru was harshly criticized for his decision to "join the Anglo-American bloc" by supporting UN actions in Korea.[77] In a similar manner, in Indonesia, which had just achieved its independence from the Netherlands in 1949, the attitude toward the

Korean War and American involvement was nothing more than skepticism. Instead of adopting an aggressive anti-communist stance, the Indonesian government expressed an unwillingness to take any role in the matter, and the local press continued to urge maintaining distance from the Korean conflict and the East-West confrontation in general.[78] A British official in Singapore analyzed this Indonesian neutral attitude as arising from the need of a newly independent state to prove its own subjectivity to the world and to its own people.[79] The Korean War, in other words, provided an opportunity for countries to demonstrate their independence by choosing not to align with any foreign power. Being neutral in the Cold War world, thus, was useful in manifesting a nation's independent judgment and, thus, bolstering legitimacy at home. The local background was general anticolonial feelings toward the West. After all, independence was newly won, and many Indonesians were extremely sensitive to any attempt to restore direct or indirect rule by colonial powers. A reporter for the British *Observer* was keenly aware of this point: "People here think 'anti-imperialist' rather than 'anti-communist.'"[80]

This was also the case in the Middle East. Reactions in Egypt and neighboring countries, for example, might have made the Indonesian government's distanced, neutral policy look mild by comparison. On June 30, immediately following Washington's announcement of its decision to dispatch U.S. forces to Korea, Egyptian prime minister Mustafa el-Nahhas called a press conference to announce his government's decision not to support the UN Security Council resolution on the Korean issue. He criticized the United States and the United Nations in a roundabout way, saying:

> In the past there have been causes of aggression against peoples, violations of sovereignty, and of the unity of the territory of . . . members of the U.N. These aggressions and violations were submitted to the U.N., which, contrary to what it is now doing in the case of Korea, took no action to stop them.[81]

Cairo Radio was much more explicit and trenchant the following day, harshly condemning American and British attitudes: "What is the difference between injustice in Korea and injustice in Egypt and Palestine? What is the difference between freedom in East Asia and freedom in West Asia? It is not a question of arms and military strength but of right and wrong."[82]

Apparently, the situation was observed and understood through the lens of Egypt's own bitter defeat in the Arab-Israeli War (1948), which was called the Nakba (Catastrophe) in Egypt and the "War of Independence" in Israel. Cairo Radio acrimoniously queried:

[W]e ask the American gentlemen: Did you never think, when you supported Israel against the Arab states and inflicted injustice on Palestine and made hundreds of thousands of people homeless, that the aggression in Palestine was worse than that in South Korea? In Korea, the invaders of Korea were Korean people, while in Palestine the invaders were intruders—foreigners and immigrants from the United States and Europe.[83]

Behind such a feeling of injustice lay a deeper distrust toward the British, Egypt's former colonizer. The broadcast continued:

We ask our friends, the British: Did you really believe, after denying Egypt and the Sudan their rights and after their many sacrifices during two Great Wars in which they stood at your side, that Egypt would support you? Did you really think that the Egyptian people would burn their fingers a third time to pull your chestnut out of the fire?[84]

This was not the only response in Egyptian society. Some newspapers, such as *Al Mokattam*, urged the government to support the United States against communist aggression. However, many others advocated outright neutrality, with a virulent anticolonial and anti-Western tone.[85] Such an attitude was shared in other Arab countries. Almost all the newspapers in Baghdad, Iraq, for instance, supported the Egyptian position of nonalignment. In Damascus, Syria, as well, most newspapers expressed skepticism, if not outright distrust, of the "purity" of American aims, charging that Americans sought only their own interests while disregarding human rights in other areas.[86]

A striking similarity can be seen between Arab and Indian reactions in how they looked at the war in Korea with their own regional conflicts in mind. "One cannot help wondering at the sudden overzeal [*sic*] of the Security Council and, for that matter, of the Government of USA," one Jamshedpur reader, for instance, wrote in a letter to Calcutta newspaper *Amrita Bazar Partika*, "For it is not the first time that peace has been menaced, fundamental right violated, and the authority of the UN flouted." He continued: "When

Pakistani troops invaded Kashmir, the Security Council did not order Pakistani forces 'back over the border' nor did it consider the imposition of 'stringent sanctions' against the aggressor," sarcastically adding that this was "a strange commentary on the champions of freedom and democracy!"[87]

As seen in these cases, existing local lenses—anticolonial sentiments and regional conflicts—played unmistakable roles in translating the meaning of the Korean War in these formerly colonized countries outside the West, as historical experiences of World War II did in translating it as the start of World War III in the West, setting the tone for the Cold War world. Such a process of local translation was most obvious outside the Korean Peninsula and tended to presuppose different historical backgrounds and various social and political needs. But, in essence, a similar process occurred domestically in South Korea, as well, where the meaning of the attack from the north was redefined from the Cold War perspective, along with the social and political needs of nation building in the country.

NATION BUILDING DURING WAR

In South Korea, as we can tell from Kim Song-chil's diary, it was quite common to see the outbreak of a full-scale war as in line with continuing civil war struggles, and it was not unusual for a majority of the population to remain in their cities and villages, instead of fleeing southward following the evacuation of the Syngman Rhee (Yi Sung-man) regime. After all, although Kim Il-sung's assertion of *Namjin* (Southern March) had been common knowledge for years, but so had Rhee's declaration of *Bukbeol* (Northern Conquest). Ever since the Soviet and U.S. occupation following the defeat of Japan in World War II and, particularly since the establishment of the Democratic People's Republic of Korea and the Republic of Korea in 1948 (with mutual disapproval), Korea had been in a state of civil war. The peninsula had experienced guerrilla warfare and insurgency, including the Cheju (Jeju) Incident and the Yeosu-Suncheon Uprising in 1948 as well as social unrest in every province in the South and numerous skirmishes along the 38th parallel.[88]

Under these circumstances, the North Korean leaders may have considered their relative strength to the South in terms of economic and industrial power in the post-World War II period. Due in large measure to the historical legacy of Japanese colonialism, basic infrastructure in the Korean Peninsula was located north of the 38th parallel. As of January 1950, according to a British diplomat's survey, over 90 percent of Korea's hydroelectric power was generated in the north, and none of this was available to the south; 95 percent of iron and steel production facilities, seven out of eight major cement facilities, and the majority of its chemical industries (notably fertilizers), as well as its only petroleum-processing plant, were all situated north of the 38th parallel. Likewise, 75 percent of Korea's coal and 65 percent of its timber lay north of the 38th parallel, and, thus, were no longer accessible to the south.[89] The report concluded: "It seems that the balance of strength between the north and the south is now somewhat in favour of the north."[90] It is not particularly surprising that North Korea seized the initiative before South Korea was able to develop.

This is what alarmed the South Korean leadership and led Seoul to pleading with Washington for more military supplies, including long-range artillery, combat airplanes, and patrol ships, and stress the need to unify the peninsula before its northern rival could attempt to do so.[91] Rhee claimed to an American visitor just a few days before the outbreak of the war that his country would launch an offensive to take over the north within a year and that this could be completed within a few days because the people would rise up against the Kim regime. He even asserted that they would do so with or without support from Washington, adding that an attempt to unify Korea would not be an act of "aggression."[92] This meant that Rhee saw the military effort in support of the unification of Korea as part of the civil war.

If the Rhee regime had enjoyed enormous popular support and trust among the population, then the majority of the population might have evacuated their cities and villages and followed the president all the way to Pusan. However, it did not. The fact is that not only workers and peasants but many businessmen, industrialists, and intellectuals stayed in their cities and villages, at least at the outset.[93] This was partly because the regime was widely and extremely unpopular due to its oppression and corruption, as well as its undemocratic rule and abuses of power. Police control had been tightened in the daily life of ordinary people, and numerous arrests were made under the National Security Law, which was enacted in 1948 for the purpose of maintaining order and protecting the nation's safety. By 1950, in effect, 80 percent of the 60,000 prisoners in South Korea had been charged with violation of this law.[94] Much worse still, torture was regularly applied to those arrested on political and other charges, and "died under torture" became a routine entry in police records.[95]

Even U.S. officials, who had been supporting the Rhee regime, were increasingly alarmed at the abusive application of the National Security Law to deal with any critic of the government.[96] Likewise, British officials' apprehensions about the situation in South Korea deepened:

> The abuses of authority are many and seldom neglected, and the corruption and oppression of the police has become an outstanding feature of the life of the country. . . . The Government indeed finds itself in a perplexing predicament, for without employing harsh repressive measures, it cannot withstand communism, and yet these very measures . . . make new converts to the communist cause.[97]

Due to such circumstances, the regime was increasingly unpopular and did not win popular legitimacy among the population. It was no wonder that not only workers and peasants but many businessmen, industrialists, and intellectuals stayed in Seoul, and it was also no wonder that those who had been engaged in student, peasant, or any other kind of leftist movement vehemently opposed the regime and thus had been harshly repressed even cheered when the north's attack resulted in Rhee's evacuation from Seoul. "The despot Syngman Rhee has finally been kicked out of Seoul. Usurping dictatorial power by taking mean advantage of people's ignorance and inability, Syngman Rhee is the enemy of our people," one student in Seoul wrote excitedly immediately following the attack: "Syngman Rhee's country is a country of torture. We have to record his torture, so that it will be remembered by later generations."[98]

Even if not all were quite so excited and determined, many retained considerable doubts as to whether it was good or bad to perpetuate the Rhee regime. For many, the distinction between "us" and "them" was not yet clear. Kim Tae-gil, an Ewha Women's University professor, felt deeply uneasy when he heard the news of the arrival of the South Korean army with the support of U.S. forces, because it was not clear to him "which side was our forces and which side was enemies."[99] In other words, popular support for the Rhee regime was very thin, and legitimacy had not established among the population. The crux of the Rhee regime's problem in the pre–Korean War period, in short, was the lack of a sense of the "nation," characterized by fervent nationalism toward the nation-state.

This was partly due to the legacy of Japanese colonialism, which had ruled Korea for nearly four decades since the early twentieth century. Because of that, Koreans rarely had strong feelings of patriotism toward a "ruler" or "state" before the Korean War; their attachments had more to do with ethnic identification, such as being Korean in contrast to being Chinese or Japanese, than with a state such as South Korea or North Korea.[100] It is not surprising, therefore, that Rhee, immediately following the outbreak of the war, saw the situation as representing the "best opportunity for settling the Korean problem once and for all."[101] Indeed, like many wars in history, the Korean conflict, which in South Korea came to be called the "6.25 [June 25] War" or just "6.25," proved useful for inventing and consolidating the meaning of nation and nationalism.

As we have seen, the act of naming is essentially political and often functions to help users of a name follow a particular way of thinking, while preventing further thinking and discussion about the nature of things. Calling the war the "6.25 War" made it possible, as the Korean sociologist Kim Dong-choon points out, to highlight what happened on that day, separating it from what had happened previously, as if peace had been abruptly destroyed on that precise day and as if sole responsibility for the conflict lay with North Korea, which had presumably acted as a tool of the Soviet Union.[102] It was such naming that translated the very meanings of the war, from representing a culmination of a civil war struggle to representing part of an international confrontation between the Eastern and Western camps—a translation that provided an opportunity to clarify a distinction between "us" and "them" and helped mold a sense of the nation while silencing various opposition groups and differing views, thus, contributing to nation building in South Korea.

Seen in this way, adopting a Cold War logic had its own merit to a locality. Such a process of translation was not fundamentally different from those in other societies; in essence, it was not a process through which understandings were shaped through observation of reality; rather, it was one in which "reality" was constructed in accordance with frameworks of understanding. In effect, reality was imagined, and, imagination became reality.

Briefly examining the years between 1945 and 1950, we have seen in Chapters 1 and 2 that many societies went through profound transformations in this postwar period. What erupted amid chaotic situations were new emotions, new demands, new ways of thinking, and new ways of life, which unavoidably provoked conflicts, and which, by nature, remained difficult to name. Old terms like "communism" and "anti-communism" came into vogue and were now given new usage in many parts of the world, in a way that made it seem as if different societies shared the same problem when, actually, they connoted locally distinctive meanings and hopes. Likewise, new vocabularies, such as a "cold war," were invented and expanded in their scope, from describing situations in Europe to more broadly referring to world situations or even social conflicts at home. In short, the immediate postwar era was a historical moment when unnamable things were gradually given new names and meanings. At the same time, as the act of naming in essence means the suspension of further inquiry concerning the substance of the things being named, it was a moment when various possibilities disappeared and the range of possible futures narrowed.

One event that hastened such a process was, as we have seen, the outbreak of the Korean War, which was witnessed simultaneously across the world yet interpreted in widely different ways. On the one hand, the outbreak of the conflict and American intervention added verisimilitude to the discourse of World War III, worldwide. With memories of World War II still fresh, the war in Korea did not appear to be simply a local struggle between North and South Korea. Many assumed that superpowers had to be behind them. Against the backdrop of such a discourse, the moment was now conceptualized and periodized as a moratorium, or a transitional period, before the advent of World War III—the era of the Cold War. It was such a particular mode of recognition of the present that made what was merely a discourse of the Cold War into the actuality of the world.

However, the "reality" of the Cold War was more a reflection of local imagination, a product of fear, based on intense experiences and memories of World War II. In fact, the areas that observed the spread of fear of World War III and Cold War fantasy were, more or less, limited to the societies that were involved in the previous world war or those in which the war experience formed national memories, such as those in East Asia, Europe, and the United States. In other words, however much it was shared worldwide, the concept of the Cold War was, in essence, a series of local understandings of the world. In other areas of the world, the Korean War did not look like the start of World War III, nor did the Cold War discourse take root, at least at this point. In those areas, a variety of different local lenses—from colonial experiences and anti-Western sentiments to the social and political needs of nation building, among others—served an almost identical function, translating the meanings of the Korean War in accordance with the frameworks of existing systems of knowledge.

This happened because of the nature and problem of "translation," in a metaphorical sense. Any work of translation between two languages, for example, has to creatively interpret the meanings of foreign words in terms of one's native language and express them through the form of the native language, leading to imaginative understanding or even the creation of new meanings. Likewise, observation of foreign events and phenomena is always accompanied by the risk that they will be viewed in terms of spectators' local experiences, contexts, and political languages and needs, even though they might have different contexts and historical backgrounds. This is almost always unavoidable because any context is a matter of the "here," based on local experiences and memories; it is something that the majority of the population in a particular area takes for granted, and no one really has doubts about. However, physical distance makes it difficult, if not impossible, to share such local knowledge and emotions, and gives local people enormous power to translate and localize foreign events in terms of their own domestic experiences, memories, and needs, resulting in the formation of multiple different versions of the "reality" of the world. Such locally interpreted "reality" cannot be ignored because it is this reality that lays the foundation on which people and policymakers see their societies and choose particular policies. In the following chapters, we will look into how such locally produced reality actually functioned in the processes of policymaking in Washington and Beijing in the fall of 1950.

II

The Social

CHAPTER THREE

Cold War Fantasy

LORRAINE HENDERSON, A high school student in Connecticut, probably never imagined that she was creating the Cold War in the summer of 1950. She might have thought that such a war was brought about by an evil Russian ruler, Joseph Stalin. Yet, in actuality, she was indeed creating the Cold War, as one of numerous participants in the imagined reality of the conflict, when she adopted a particular worldview, convinced herself of that worldview, and reproduced it as she expressed her opinion in a letter to President Harry S. Truman. "I am only a high school student and you most likely won't even read my letter but if you would try to understand how a 15 year girl wants the chance to live [*sic*]. If we, the United States could only make a sneak attack on Russia before they get the chance to make one on us," she wrote and explained why she reached such a conclusion:

> One night when I was laying in my bed and could [not] sleep, I heard a plane over head and a streak of fear went through me, afraid any minute we all would be killed. . . . Why don't we take a chance and sneak up on them

even if we lose the war (which I doubt it if we do something about it) at least
we can say we tried. We are a wonderful nation, let's keep it that way.[1]

Lorraine was not alone in believing and expressing such a fear. Joel Brinkley, a schoolteacher, who was a child in the 1950s, recalled a similar feeling
during this era: "It seems surreal now. Every summer, when I heard heat
lightning over the city and the sky would light up, I was convinced it was
all over. My whole childhood was built on the notion that the Soviets were
the real threat."[2] Their feelings were not unique nor did their beliefs origi-
nate with them. They may have simply echoed what many others told them.
However, in the making and maintenance of the Cold War, what really
mattered was not so much who began it as who believed it and how many
did so. In other words, what mattered was the fact that millions of people,
like Lorraine and Joel, embraced such a worldview and reproduced it, contributing to the authorization of a particular version of reality, which, in
turn, solidified the world of the Cold War.

Such a "reality" was not simply an ephemeral mirage; rather, once it was
shared widely and maintained among a majority of the people, it constituted
the social context of the time. Although the literature of U.S. diplomatic
history is particularly rich and dense in terms of the role of policymakers
and of realpolitik during the Korean War, what remain less well understood
are the functions of such social contexts and locally specific realities, which
often made some political actions more probable while making others unlikely.[3] Likewise, although there has been a surge of literature that explores
ordinary people's daily lives in and cultural aspects of the Cold War, much
of it has tended to describe the Cold War as a given phenomenon—like the
weather—rather than constructed reality, and, thus, it has tended to focus on
the *effects* of the Cold War on culture and daily lives of ordinary people.[4]

Looking at these two major trends in Cold War studies, therefore, one
might gain the following impression: policymakers' calculations and miscalculations brought about the Cold War, which, in turn, had enormous
aftereffects on society, culture, and daily lives of ordinary people. This impression has been shaped and maintained through the collaboration of diplomatic historians and social and cultural historians as well as scholars of
cultural productions. The former, in general, have been in charge of investigating the *origins* of the Cold War, and the latter have explored the *effects* of
the conflict, without bothering each other. Yet much more needs to be writ-

ten, because the relationship between policymakers and ordinary people, as well as culture and politics, was far more interactive and complicated than we usually think.

A perfect example to use in examining such interplay can be seen in the ways in which Washington stepped into a new phase of the Cold War by choosing an offensive strategy in the Korean War in October 1950—a choice to cross the 38th parallel northward. In retrospect, because the conflict began with the North Korean army's invasion of the southern half of the peninsula, it could have ended with the restoration of the prewar situation. In fact, the official stance of the U.S. government in July 1950 was that the United States "had no intention to do more than to restore the *status quo ante* and no intention to proceed to the conquest of northern Korea."[5] The Truman administration, thus, could have stopped U.S. troops at the 38th parallel and declared victory in early October 1950, possibly avoiding China's full-scale entry and averting a prolonged war. There was, in fact, heated discussion within the government, and the administration did not necessarily see the policy of crossing the 38th parallel as appealing. Yet members of the Truman administration believed that, as the veteran diplomat Averell Harriman recalled, there would be "no way to stop it."[6]

Despite this opportunity to terminate the war at an early stage, the war went on until July 1953, when a ceasefire was finally reached, almost precisely at the 38th parallel, after huge numbers of American, Chinese, Korean, and other military casualties as well as millions of civilian casualties on the peninsula. Why was Washington not satisfied with recovery of the prewar situation? How was the initial strategy of stopping at the 38th parallel challenged and modified in the summer and fall of 1950? Why did Washington stick to the notion of crossing the 38th parallel, a line that the Truman administration saw as unimportant in a military and economic sense?[7] In examining these questions in a specific case, we will raise a much broader, more fundamental question: How did ordinary people participate in making reality and history?

"REAL" WAR AT HOME AND ABROAD

Looking back from the standpoint of the twenty-first century, numerous ordinary people, as well as American society as a whole, appear to have had a peculiar interpretation of "common sense" in 1950–1951: fear of World War III and atomic attacks was prevalent; many housewives hoarded commodities due to fear of another general war; many children had to practice air-raid drills in elementary school, learning the song, "Duck and Cover"; many also had to wear identification tags in case of death from an atomic attack; stories of communist spies were popular and ubiquitous in fiction and nonfiction; communist organizations everywhere, including those in China and North Korea, in addition to socialist and leftist groups and individuals in the United States, were believed to be monolithic under the tight control of Joseph Stalin; and the Korean War made Senator Joseph McCarthy look more like a prophet than a demagogue.[8]

Because of progress in the war in Korea, ordinary people were not just sitting back; many began fighting in their own capacities and neighborhoods. Longshoremen in New York and Boston, for instance, began refusing to discharge tons of Soviet "red" crabmeat.[9] In another case, irate parents in Glendale, near Los Angeles, began a fight against "red propaganda" when they found a child's playing card depicting a Soviet soldier standing with smiling children in front of the Kremlin, with the red hammer-and-sickle communist banner over their heads; eventually, they forced the superintendent of a local elementary school to ban bringing card collections to school.[10] Similarly, concerned citizens in San Francisco touched off a heated debate as to whether a series of murals in the lobby of the main downtown post office represented art or communist propaganda, partly because the murals included scenes of a maritime strike, with a pro-labor tone.[11]

These examples might appear strange, or even funny, from today's viewpoint, but, at that time, that was not the case. They were reported and taken quite seriously. These small neighborhood battles were, after all, parts of the "real" war. With memories of World War II still fresh, Americans in 1950 were fighting not only in actual combat in Korea but also imaginary battles at home that were generated, to a large extent, by their own imagination—a "Cold War fantasy."[12] Of course, many at that time did not see it as fantasy; it was "real." Such imaginings of real situations were maintained through daily participation and practice, taken up not only by politicians and government and military officials but by millions of ordinary people, old and young. Yet the meaning of these ordinary people's swift and spontaneous participation, in contrast to Washington's response, has not been sufficiently discussed.[13]

Local people's active involvement of this kind appeared most clearly in their everyday behavior. For instance, hoarding was one of the most noticeable phenomena in American society following the outbreak of the Korean War. More interesting, however, are people's reactions to hoarders. An interesting case was observed by an *Atlanta Journal and Constitution* reporter, who in August 1950 posed as a hoarder, walked into a local supermarket, and ordered twenty-five cartons of cigarettes. Although the reporter might have conducted this experiment lightheartedly, the resulting article was quite thought-provoking; it described how the "angry salesgirl glowered" at him and then "slowly began to stack up the cartons, counting each one in a voice that could be heard in every corner of the store."[14] The article also illustrated how other customers raised their eyebrows at the reporter's excessive purchase. What is most interesting is that hoarders were increasingly seen as not merely selfish but unpatriotic. As a number of popular magazines' political cartoons depicted, criticism of hoarders and support for the U.S. intervention in Korea were unmistakably connected.[15] Ordinary people's reproachful reactions to hoarders imply that these people felt as if they knew how to behave and act when their country was committed in battle overseas. In a sense, many ordinary people mobilized of their own free will to preserve the interests of the nation.

In the midst of strong, even fanatical, support and participation in the nation's war efforts, an interesting phenomenon occurred. One might expect that the public would oppose tax increases, price controls, and cooperation with a strict mobilization plan. Nonetheless, many Americans in the summer of 1950 informed government officials and newspaper editors that they would gladly accept such obligations and went even further in urging an increase in taxes and a systematic mobilization of society for war. "If [price] ceilings are for our country's best interest, we are for ceilings," wrote one Minnesota businessman to Congress. A laundry owner in Colorado entreated, "Permit me to urge the Government confiscation of all profits from industry." A woman in Illinois wrote a letter to President Truman on July 17: "Let's have complete mobilization now—to win in Korea as soon as possible, and to deter the Russians from attacking anywhere else in the world."[16] A man in Michigan adamantly supported U.S. military intervention in Korea

SHAKEDOWN FOR DECENCY

"Shakedown for Decency." *Saturday Evening Post,* 19 August 1950. (The *Saturday Evening Post* illustration © SEPS licensed by Curtis Licensing, Indianapolis, IN. All rights reserved.)

but was growing irritated with the slow pace of U.S. action. In a letter to the president on August 16, he asserted:

> From the conversation I have with men on the street, it would appear that the American citizen is farther ahead in his thinking than you in Washington. We are ready and anxious for controls, rationing, priorities and all the other measures to help our poor boys in Korea. Let us put aside business-as-

usual and show Russia that Communism is not the answer—that the American people willingly will work and sacrifice to retain their freedom.[17]

Along these lines, 70 percent of poll respondents supported higher taxes to build a larger army and navy, according to George Gallup.[18] Responding to the question of how to pay defense costs, 60 percent suggested raising taxes and 19 percent proposed borrowing. Republican Representative from New York Jacob Javits was probably right to comment, "I think the American people are way ahead of their leaders in the things they are willing to do to defeat this communist menace as we see it in Korea."[19]

DEADLOCK IN WASHINGTON

Washington was keenly aware of this intense political mood. Were it not for the discourse of World War III and its impact on domestic politics, the administration might not have felt the need to dispatch troops to Korea. In fact, many strategists and military officers, such as the director of the Policy Planning Staff, Paul Nitze, as well as the secretary of the Army, Frank Pace, and General Bonner Fellers, did not see U.S. involvement as necessary.[20] After all, the Joint Chiefs of Staff (JCS) had decided a few years earlier that South Korea was not within the area that was essential for the defense of the United States, and, thus, for them, the crisis represented simply a military event on the distant Korean Peninsula, one detached from American security interests and one to which Americans would not need to react, they thought.[21]

Secretary of State Dean Acheson, in his meetings with the Canadian minister for external affairs, Lester B. Pearson, on July 29 and 30, repeatedly pointed out that, strategically, Korea was not important and that the decision to meet the challenge in Korea was "a purely political one."[22] Pace also clarified that the dispatch of U.S. troops was based not on the wishes of the Department of Defense but its support for the "political policies" of the government.[23] In short, from the beginning, the Truman administration's choice to intervene in the war was more about political decisions than military and strategic needs. Of course, this might apply to any administration's decision to go to any war, but it was particularly the case for the Truman administration in 1950. And the administration's decision to cross the 38th parallel northward was no exception.

It is important to note that the Truman administration at the outset maintained a cautious attitude that was far from aggressive or reckless. "I don't want any implication . . . that we are going to war with Russia," said President Harry S. Truman at a National Security Council (NSC) meeting on June 29, 1950: "We want to take any steps we have to to push the North Koreans behind the line but I don't want to get us over-committed to a whole lot of other things that could mean war [with Russia]. . . . We must be *damn* careful."[24] White House staff member George Elsey attended this meeting and took handwritten minutes, determinedly underlining the word "damn," perhaps signifying that the president raised his voice, emphasizing the need to be cautious. At the same meeting, Pace inquired whether U.S. actions would be kept south of the 38th parallel; Acheson immediately confirmed this and did not make any suggestion for any action across that line.[25] Acheson repeated this position a few days later, affirming that U.S. actions were taken "solely for the purpose of restoring South Korea to its status prior to the invasion from the north."[26]

As these conversations suggest, in closed-door communications, policymakers remained cautious at the beginning of the Korean War. The Truman administration did not see crossing the 38th parallel as appealing and, thus, did not plan to pursue a hard-line policy.[27] Reflecting this initial posture, a U.S. Army spokesman in Korea reportedly stated that U.S. troops were only involved in fighting "to drive the North Koreans back to the 38th parallel and would stop there, and use force if necessary to prevent South Korean troops from advancing beyond the 38th parallel."[28]

This initial stance, however, was questioned and challenged throughout the summer of 1950 and eventually abandoned by the end of September. Some of the earliest challenges to the initially wary attitude came from key officials within the administration, including Truman's personal advisor Clark Clifford, director of the Office of Northeast Asian Affairs John Allison, and Assistant Secretary of State for Far Eastern Affairs Dean Rusk.[29] A special adviser to Secretary of State, John Foster Dulles, more than anyone else, believed that it would be "folly" to return to the division of Korea at the 38th parallel because, he thought, there would be neither peace nor successful government in a divided Korea.[30] A similar view was explicitly put forth in the Defense Department's analysis of the implications of the Korean situation:

> The situation in Korea now provides the United States and the free world with the first opportunity to displace part of the Soviet Orbit. . . . The estab-

lishment of a free and united Korea and the elimination of the North Korean Communist regime . . . would be a step in reversing the dangerous
strategic trend in the Far East of the past twelve months.[31]

As this memo expressed, hardliners viewed crossing the 38th parallel and
the successful unification of Korea as an attractive chance for Washington to wipe out the disgrace of "losing ground" in the Cold War—an
early advocacy of what later became known as the "rollback" policy of the
mid-1950s.

Nonetheless, this hardline viewpoint was not prevalent. Truman thought
Clifford's idea was "a little premature." No consensus for broader action
north of the 38th parallel existed even in the State Department, let alone
other branches of the government. Some of the most vocal arguments came
from George F. Kennan and his staff in the Policy Planning Staff (PPS).
They consistently maintained that U.S. forces stop at the 38th parallel,
warning that, if U.S. forces were to carry military action north of the line,
"the danger of conflict with Chinese communist or Soviet forces would be
greatly increased."[32] The Central Intelligence Agency (CIA) also opposed
crossing the 38th parallel, arguing that, although a successful invasion of
North Korea would have some merit in terms of increasing the prestige of the
United States, it might bring "grave risk of general war" with China and the
Soviet Union.[33] Omar Bradley, chairman of the JCS, similarly disagreed
with crossing the line, but in a different light: arguing that military ground
operations north of the 38th parallel "should be conducted by South Korean forces since it [is] assumed that the actions [will] probably be of a guerrilla character."[34]

Furthermore, warnings about the 38th parallel came from European
allies. French officials cautioned that, until the UN Security Council
passed a further resolution on the subject, UN forces should not cross the
parallel, as this would create a new situation and might bring the USSR
and China into the war.[35] British officials, too, doubted whether crossing
the parallel could be justified under the original UN resolution, because
it was aimed only at repelling attacks from the North, and were concerned that fighting north of the 38th parallel would increase the risk of
Soviet intervention. They did not believe that the USSR wished to provoke a major war, but were concerned that the Soviet Union might dispatch a volunteer force or significant military supplies, which would create a situation full of explosive possibilities. In this way, these European

allies tried to put on the brakes on the conduct of the United States.[36] "The United States' reactions to the Far Eastern situation are at present highly emotional, with the result that reasoned arguments may prove to have little appeal," wrote a British official in the summer of 1950. Worrying that the conflict might spread to China or elsewhere, the report wrote: "The main aim [of the British government] should be to try to convince the United States that their policy should be directed wholly toward the solution of the Korean problem."[37]

In the midst of such division of opinion inside and outside the government, President Truman was reluctant to make a decision and expressed "considerable worry" concerning the matter.[38] On July 17, he asked the NSC to prepare a report as to which course U.S. forces should take after reaching the parallel. Yet the divide was so deep and wide that, throughout the summer, the administration lacked a clear, unified opinion on the question. This unusual situation continued until early September. Philip Jessup, a State Department staff member, complained on August 24 that he "could hardly understand how, in the light of the President's specific request, we could reply to the President merely stating that we have no policy recommendations at this time."[39]

On September 1, 1950, the NSC finally produced the government's official viewpoint, although it was not a clear-cut, unified opinion. The document (NSC-81) suggested that U.S. forces could invade North Korean territory across the parallel in order to compel the enemy to stay behind the 38th parallel. But it also warned that crossing the 38th parallel "would create a situation to which the Soviet Union would be almost certain to react in some manner" and suggested that, if only South Korean forces were to operate north of the 38th parallel, the risk of general hostilities would be reduced.[40] Although this document was the first to officially authorize the possibility of U.S. forces' advancement north of the parallel, it remained ambiguous in suggesting two policies at the same time. This vagueness implies that there was still strong opposition to such a course of action. In short, discussions among State Department bureaucrats were deadlocked, as were those in the CIA and Defense Department. The JCS and European allies were issuing serious warnings. Furthermore, the NSC's suggestion to the president did not really provide a clear answer. Why, then, did the Truman administration decide to cross the 38th parallel?

PUBLIC PERCEPTIONS

Beyond the government level, the discussion over whether U.S. forces should cross the 38th parallel was not so complicated. Although dissenting voices surely existed, as we will see below, intriguingly, serious debate did not develop among the public in the summer of 1950. The major, commonly held view was that Washington should be expected to take a tough stance in foreign policy. In fact, as early as late July, attention among leading commentators had already turned to the question of what to do *after* crossing the parallel.[41] For instance, Walter Lippmann of the *Washington Post* argued that a return to the status quo was impossible.[42] Even the left-leaning *New York Compass* supported the unification of Korea, rather than halting U.S. forces at the parallel.[43] The *Dallas News* asserted, "One thing is clear. Before this thing is over with, we shall have to drive the North Korean army and its Russian staff past the 38th parallel and clean out of North Korea."[44] A local newspaper, the *Ithaca Journal*, also insisted that the United Nations had never recognized the division of Korea, and declared, "Its aim from the beginning has been a united Korea. Why not declare firmly now that a united, free Korea will result from military operations there?"[45]

By the end of July and early August, a growing number of observers believed that U.S. forces should press their offensive into North Korea. The *Kansas City Star*, Truman's home state newspaper, asserted, "It would be intolerable if, once the tide of battle turns definitely against the aggressors they should be permitted to break off hostilities and simply retire behind the 38th parallel to await a better opportunity to strike again."[46] Other newspapers were in lockstep with this view. According to a State Department survey in August 1950, the *Providence Journal,* the *Watertown Times,* the *Detroit News,* the *Christian Science Monitor,* and the *Washington Post* supported carrying the offensive beyond the 38th parallel in order to unite Korea under the United Nations.[47]

In effect, while opinions of government officials continued to be divided concerning U.S. war strategy throughout the summer, popular attitudes seemed to reveal a clear and united viewpoint. The Office of Public Opinion Studies (OPOS) in the State Department summarized this plainly in August:

> There is substantial agreement that the Korean problem cannot be satisfactorily solved short of reuniting the nation under a government freely elected

by the people of the north and south. Those endorsing this view are prepared
to see the UN force carry the offensive north of the 38th parallel, if necessary, to achieve these objectives, and they reject any thought of returning to
the status quo.[48]

The "substantial agreement" that this report describes needs a bit more explanation because such a consensus did not actually exist; there were, in
fact, significant disagreements, with dissenting voices demanding that U.S.
forces halt at the 38th parallel, as we shall see below. Still, such a frenzied,
aggressive social climate could not be irrelevant to the course of politics and
policy-making processes in the fall of 1950. This was particularly the case in
1950, because it was a midterm election year, with Republicans angling to
stage a comeback.

DOMESTIC POLITICS 1950—REPUBLICANS

Although bureaucrats in Washington had as yet been unable to form a solid,
unified strategy, many Republican members of Congress were avidly paying attention to political currents in society and swiftly taking advantage of
the situation. Vividly remembering their bitter defeat in the presidential
election of 1948, Republicans were now on the offensive with powerful slogans with which to attack Democrats: "Soft on Communism," "Who Lost
China?" and "Liberty against Socialism." Although Congress was often described as a weak branch during the Cold War period, its election campaigns in 1950 had a significant impact in terms of pressing the Executive
Branch to adopt a more aggressive policy. Actually, the Korean War was the
major issue in the midterm elections; the *New York Times* observed in August that the elections would be decided "almost wholly by public reaction
to the Korean War and its multiplying problems at home."[49]

The strongest critic of the Truman administration's Korean policy was the
powerful Republican senator from Ohio, Robert A. Taft, who was position-
ing himself for the Republican nomination in the 1952 presidential election.[50] While generally agreeing with the administration's decision to send
troops to Korea, Taft sharpened his criticism in a speech on the floor of
Congress on June 28, 1950, pointing to the "bungling and inconsistent
foreign policy of the administration."[51] At the same time, Taft presented a

heated critique of the administration's refusal to announce an intention to cross the 38th parallel. As early as July 6, Taft urged U.S. forces not to stop at the parallel.[52] Asked about this in a radio interview, Taft announced: "I don't understand that the administration has decided this question [concerning the parallel]. Personally, I should think we would have to march right on [over the parallel] and at least occupy the southern part of North Korea so that a unified Korea can be set up."[53]

Taft's tough stance on foreign policy issues should be seen in the context of his re-election campaign that year, rather than as deriving from his political philosophy, which tended toward isolationism. In the postwar period, the Ohio senator adapted to a contingent political culture, transforming his political rhetoric from isolationist to internationalist. This was particularly the case during the period between the fall of 1949 and the summer of 1950, when Taft reshaped his stance on foreign policy and anti-communist issues, at least publicly. The background for this change was that he was already seen as a possible candidate for president in 1952, and Taft himself positioned his senatorial campaign in 1950 as a test case for this future plan.[54] He had to win and by a large margin. Then, the outbreak of the Korean War provided him with an opportunity. In a private letter to the chairman of the Minnesota Republican Party in mid-August, Taft forecast that the effects of the Korean War would be an "asset for the Republicans" in their election campaigns that year, indicating that they should not hesitate to point out the weakness of the administration's foreign policy in their campaigns.[55] Although Ohio was seen as Taft country, his re-election campaign was not particularly easy. In fact, the Republicans had lost Ohio to the Democrats in the 1948 presidential election, by a slim margin. He needed to take any advantage that he could, and he did.

Yet Taft's shift caused some confusion regarding his stance on foreign policy issues, even in his own mind. When he received a letter that advocated being aggressive and firm on foreign relations issues, Taft replied emphatically, using strong words to the effect that he was not an isolationist. But when he received another letter insisting that the United States not be so involved in foreign matters, Taft replied reassuringly that he had been cautious and critical of the Truman administration's overly internationalist approach. His judgment also wavered, depending on to whom he was writing, with regard to recognition of the People's Republic of China. In some private letters, he appeared flexible, even asserting that he was not opposed to recognition, while, in other situations, he maintained a strictly anti-communist tone.[56] Taft's adaptation to appearing to be a "Cold Warrior" in his public image exemplifies the point that political figures often change their stances due to shifts in the popular political culture surrounding them, rather than adhering to their own political philosophy or beliefs. In the case of Korea in the summer of 1950, Taft's choice was to be tough and aggressive, urging a "rollback" policy.

Such a transition can be clearly seen in modifications that Taft made to his speeches between 1949 and 1950. For instance, a draft written in 1949 read: "Today's major domestic issue is whether we shall remain in this country a free people in full control of our government, or whether we shall delegate to an all-powerful government the right to direct our local communities, agriculture, industry, labor, and the daily lives of our citizens."[57] The tone in this speech was vintage Taft, an anti–New Deal politician who focused mainly on domestic issues, with a strong aversion to statism. The same speech draft evolved during his 1950 campaign with the addition of sentences that gave a new context to the original line; it read:

> *Today's major issue* is whether we shall remain in this country a free people in full control of our government, or whether we shall delegate to an all-powerful government the right to direct our local communities, agriculture, industry, labor and the daily lives of our citizens. *This is the struggle between socialism and liberty. It is a conflict that rages not only in this country but throughout the world. On the world stage the battle is between free government and Communism—the most extreme form of socialism denying most affectively the liberty and responsibility of the human soul. This is the root of the "cold war." In this country the struggle is no less intense, and it promises to be the principal issue of the 1950 election.*[58]

Taft deleted the word "domestic" from the first line and added five new sentences, italicized here. The message was the same, but the context had changed radically from domestic to international. It is important to note that Taft's opinion remained the same but was simply connected with and projected onto international issues. In other words, his international view was not based on studying international relations or local situations in foreign countries; his domestic views simply extended to the global arena. In short, Taft's tough stance had more to do with electoral campaign tactics than with strategic and military considerations.

Such a tendency was not exclusively Taft's. Although scholars have focused on the Cold War's impact on domestic politics, the opposite tendency—the impact of domestic political context on foreign policy-making—needs to be further examined.[59] The "politicalness" of foreign policy issues in the summer of 1950 was unmistakable. Indeed, the Korean War and its multiplying problems at home were expected to be the central issue of the 1950 midterm elections, as seen in reports and cartoons of the *New York Times* and *Saturday Evening Post.*[60] Keenly realizing this, many Republicans took full advantage of the situation. Richard Nixon, then a rookie senatorial candidate in California, for instance, made ample use of foreign policy issues in his election campaign. He knew that wages were growing, employment was up, and farmers and small businesses had prospered since the previous elections and that, therefore, it would be difficult to attack Democrats on domestic issues. Thus, as a supporter advised, foreign policy issues became an appropriate topic for criticizing the Truman administration.[61]

Similar tactics were adopted nationwide, as Republicans in other states declared the central issue of the election to be "the tragic [foreign] policy pursued by the [Truman] administration for five years that culminated in the war in Korea."[62] By the end of the summer, the Republican National Committee had created and circulated a fifty-nine-page pamphlet, *Background to Korea,* summarizing historical events leading to the war and emphasizing the administration's "failures" in foreign policy toward East Asia.[63] The same strategy was evident in a Republican's one-minute radio advertisement: "In 1950, when the free world has been challenged in Korea by the totalitarian forces of international communism, it is the responsibility of every registered American voter to go to the polls. The eyes of freemen and those who hope to be free all around the world will be upon us on November 7," it announced. In the end, it skillfully appealed for voters' patriotism by framing the election not just a matter of domestic and party politics but of the survival of the nation and its position in the world: "Regardless of partisan affiliation, American citizens have an opportunity on November 7 of serving notice on the forces of international communism that they are wrong when they speak of decadent democracy."[64]

With the growing imagining of "real" situations in the summer of 1950, a politician who had been criticized and was fading away suddenly came back to center stage: Joseph McCarthy. Indeed, it was the Korean War that made McCarthy a national star.[65] "Today American boys lie dead in the

THE THIRD MAN

"The Third Man." *Saturday Evening Post,* 23 September 1950. (The *Saturday Evening Post* illustration © SEPS licensed by Curtis Licensing, Indianapolis, IN. All rights reserved.)

mud of Korean valleys," claimed McCarthy, stepping up his offensive on July 12, "Some have their hands tied behind their back, their faces shot away by Communist machine guns." After critiquing the Truman administration's management of the Korean situation, McCarthy went on to question the presence of alleged communists in the State Department:

Today Korea is the crisis area. Where will it be tomorrow if the same men act as your advisors and mold your thinking, Mr. President? . . . There are those who say we should not spend time searching for those responsible for the disasters of the past few years. Common horse-sense dictates, however, that in order to protect America in the critical weeks, months and years ahead we must determine who in positions of trust seek to betray us, and then act to get them out of government. If allowed to remain, they will undoubtedly tip the scales for disaster and against victory for this nation.[66]

Although he had been criticized for his wild attacks, riding a tide of war scare and anti-communist feelings, McCarthy launched a counterattack. Against Millard Tydings, Democratic senator from Maryland, whose senatorial committee's report had criticized his charges as groundless, McCarthy struck back, saying, "[Tydings] sought to assure communists in the government that they are safe in their positions."[67] Now, it was Tydings who was driven into a difficult position. According to a Gallup Poll taken immediately after the outbreak of the Korean War, 41 percent of those respondents believed McCarthy's charges, while only 20 percent did not.[68] A full-page editorial in the *Washington Times–Herald* declared in early July that nobody would believe the Tydings report, calling it "large bucket of whitewash."[69] In this way, McCarthy's charges appeared increasingly plausible, in view of the Korean War and the dominant perspective in American society.

However, it was not McCarthy who created the red scare of this period nor did the Korean War create that phenomenon. Actually, it was a domestic version of "anti-communist" logic that conditioned many Americans to view the Korean War as part of Moscow's communist aggression, which, in turn, increased the verisimilitude of McCarthy's charges. In a climate as highly charged with domestic politics as the summer of 1950, the usually cool-headed Senator Taft heightened his criticism of the administration and the State Department, joining in McCarthyite attacks and arguing that the U.S. government had been unprepared diplomatically and militarily to meet communist aggression and that communist sympathizers in the government needed to be gotten rid of.[70] By the early fall of 1950, the Ohio senator was asserting repeatedly that U.S. forces would have to prepare to go north of the 38th parallel not only "to bring [about] the unification of Korea" but also "to punish the aggressor."[71] By the crucial month of September, Republicans had gone fully on the offensive, demanding an aggressive policy in Korea.

DOMESTIC POLITICS 1950—DEMOCRATS

Democrats and members of the Truman administration were keenly aware of and sensitive to the potency of Republican charges. As early as June 27, 1950, Joseph O'Mahoney, senator from Wyoming and a member of the Democratic Senatorial Campaign Committee (DSCC), warned President Truman that foreign policy would "undoubtedly be used to support a charge that our policy was soft toward the Communists in Korea."[72] As O'Mahoney pointed out, more failures in foreign relations would give people a negative view of the administration, which would subsequently hurt Democrats. They hoped, however, that the opposite would be true, as well. One observer wrote late in the summer of 1950: "If the counteroffensive in Korea is successful . . . , if Russia does not throw her air [force to Korea], then that will greatly help the Democrats. They can go to the country with good news."[73] In short, a more favorable picture of the Korean War, Democrats anticipated, would help them in the November elections.[74]

Knowing the potency of foreign policy issues as double-edged swords, the DSCC made a full effort in the campaigns by publishing a variety of pamphlets, as well as educating candidates on how to respond to questions concerning foreign policy issues. Some questions were along these lines: "Is it true that the Truman Administration has been 'soft toward communism?'" The answer provided was: "No. Rather than being soft toward communism, the Truman Administration has taken the lead in opposing communism and strengthening freedom in the world." This answer then proceeded to list the administration's "achievements," such as economic and military aid to Greece and Turkey as well as creation of the Marshall Plan and the North Atlantic Treaty Organization (NATO).[75]

This use of foreign policy issues in domestic campaigns was noteworthy because domestic politics, in turn, had begun demanding a certain direction in U.S. "foreign" policy. Looking back, the Truman administration's first "anti-communist" policies were announced in March 1947—the Truman Doctrine and the Loyalty Security Program—in an attempt to roll back Democrats' defeats in the midterm elections in November 1946. Then, Truman's renewed anti-communist stance in foreign policy issues appeared in late February 1950 in response to McCarthy's (in)famous anti-communist and anti-State Department speech he made at Wheeling, West Virginia, early in the same month.[76] Two months later, the president adopted further strong language in denouncing the Soviet Union, particularly stressing that Americans "must make ourselves heard round the world in a great campaign of truth."[77]

Seen in this way, it is clear that President Truman increasingly toughened his "Cold War" rhetoric and policy in response to domestic political and social situations more than military and diplomatic considerations. Such a pattern continued following the outbreak of the Korean War. The fighting in Korea and McCarthyite attacks at home made international and domestic affairs appear interrelated. This was not considered negative at that time but was described as consistent. It was formally articulated in Democrats' election campaigns, as one pamphlet declared that U.S. foreign policy abroad and domestic policy at home were "two sides of the same coin. Foreign policy is a logical and necessary *extension* of our program at home."[78]

Professional diplomats and military officers might have argued that diplomatic and military affairs were special and should be considered by experts. Yet, in practice, these affairs were seldom isolated from politics at home. The Truman administration was no exception. Vice President Alben Barkley, who had been responsible for the 1950 midterm campaigns, suggested at an NSC meeting in August that the forthcoming document on the Korean situation (NSC-81) needed to take into consideration possible congressional reactions.[79] This suggestion was telling, because it revealed the essence of the 38th parallel question: it was not just a distant military concern but also a domestic political issue.

Throughout the campaign, in fact, younger Democratic members of Congress were itching to defend the conduct of U.S. foreign policy and refute some of the wild charges against the administration and State Department. The trouble, as one freshman representative complained, was that "the State Department does not give us enough equipment and ammunition with which to answer these charges."[80] The DSCC sent a memorandum to White House staff on September 2, 1950, requesting that they provide "a clear, affirmative statement of the *achievement* of American foreign policy, including our entire policy in the Far East."[81] In the critical weeks between late August and September, as midterm elections drew near, domestic politics demanded that the administration have a clearer and tougher foreign policy, along with concrete achievements abroad.

AFTERMATH OF THE INCHON LANDING

The sweeping victory of U.S. forces in the Inchon Landing Operation on September 15, 1950, further complicated the entanglement of domestic and foreign affairs, as well as political and military issues. The Inchon Landing was not necessarily either a bolt out of the blue or MacArthur's miracle, as was believed at that time and since. In fact, the operation was based on a blueprint prepared prior to the war by U.S. and South Korean military officials as a contingency plan.[82] In addition, Chinese military officers and Mao Zedong had foreseen an American counterattack at Inchon, and Kim Il-sung, too, had given orders to begin preparation for the defense of Inchon by late August.[83] Thus, as the historian Wada Haruki puts it, the operation itself was, militarily, quite a normal strategy for counterattack.[84]

Nonetheless, political effects were undoubtedly dramatic. Many Americans took an even more optimistic view regarding the ability of the U.S. forces to reunify Korea, accelerating demands for more aggressive American action. The approval rate of U.S. intervention in Korea jumped; according to a study taken in October by the National Opinion Research Center, 81 percent of respondents believed that the United States was right in entering the war, while 13 percent thought it was wrong, compared with 75 to 21 percent, respectively, in July.[85] As this shift shows, those who previously disagreed with Truman's policy had changed their attitudes and began showing their support. A Baltimore man, for instance, wrote to the president in early October expressing profound gratitude for the military action in Korea, even though he had never voted for Democrats before and still found many of the administration's actions and policies at home and abroad mistaken.[86]

With the rise of this optimistic climate, demands for crossing the 38th parallel significantly increased among newspapers and commentators. The *Denver Post,* for instance, maintained that UN forces should "march above the 38th parallel and occupy the whole of Korea until new elections under U.N. supervision [could] be held."[87] An NBC commentator asserted that stopping at the parallel would offer "no satisfactory solution."[88] The *Boston Post* even argued that it would be "folly" to keep UN forces below the parallel. The *New York Herald–Tribune* likewise insisted:

> To imagine that it is now possible to go back to the fictitious 38th parallel, to sit down and negotiate the freedom and unification of Korea across that

passion-charged line, is to imagine an absurdity. . . . [Korean unity] is the test of the [UN] assembly's ability to live up to its principles.[89]

This kind of hard line was shared by other newspapers, including the *Washington Star,* the *Pittsburgh Post-Gazette,* the *Baltimore Sun,* the *Rochester Democrat and Chronicle,* and the *Detroit Free Press.*[90] Major news magazine articles also urged U.S. forces to cross the 38th parallel and destroy the North Korean army. Among these, even the pro-Democratic *Newsweek* insisted, " 'Keep going' was the motto for all the U.N. forces" on the front.[91]

Many members of Congress lined up to advocate for a more aggressive policy as well.[92] A notable example was California Republican Senator William Knowland, who charged that failure to cross the 38th parallel would be "appeasement" of the Soviet Union. By the same token, Pennsylvania Republican Representative Hardie Scott accused the State Department of seeking to "subvert our military victory" by calling for a halt at the parallel.[93] It is no wonder that the ABC and MBS (Mutual Broadcasting System) broadcasting networks felt able to declare in late September that sentiments in Congress were "overwhelmingly in favor of going through with this job [to cross the parallel and unify Korea]."[94]

A significant number of dissenting voices remained, even after the sweeping victory of the Inchon Landing. Some major newspapers took a firm stand in favor of stopping U.S. forces at the parallel. The *Los Angeles Times,* for instance, wrote that UN forces should not attempt to cross the line, arguing: "Such a job will have to be undertaken by the South Koreans alone at some time in the more or less distant future."[95] In a similar tone, the *Chicago Tribune* warned: "We shall be face to face with the hordes of Russia and red China with a new line more explosively dangerous than the 38th parallel ever was."[96] The *Atlanta Constitution* and the *New York Post* agreed, both contending that there was no need to go beyond the line.[97] Frank Edward, a radio commentator at MBS, expressed a similar viewpoint succinctly immediately after the Inchon Landing:

> It seems probable that our troops will not penetrate into North Korea. If we crush the Communist armies in South Korea and then stop at the 38th parallel it would amount to a double-barrel victory for us. First, we would then have shown the world we are not to be pushed around, and we would give

the lie to the Communist charges that we are imperialists out to gobble up
the world.[98]

As these examples show, there was much disagreement. In fact, popular attitudes were not monolithically in agreement. A Gallup Poll taken immediately after the Inchon Landing suggests that, while 64 percent of respondents
urged U.S. forces to cross the parallel and continue fighting until the North
Koreans surrendered, 27 percent thought that U.S. forces should stop at the
parallel.[99] In view of the political culture at that time, and in view of the
phenomenon later termed the rally-'round-the-flag effect, it is rather surprising that more than one-quarter of those surveyed opposed carrying the war
into North Korean territory.

Nonetheless, these oppositional voices were becoming less and less audible in the fall of 1950, not because there was a consensus but because those
who disagreed restrained themselves from expressing their views in public
and kept silence in view of an increasingly charged climate. As a result, the
number of dissenting voices seemed smaller than it actually was, while aggressive voices seemed more numerous than they really were.[100] In this situation, which the German sociologist Elisabeth Noelle-Neumann would
call a "spiral of silence," the seeming "consensus" was established, and it
was broadly and commonly perceived that the public was unanimously
calling for U.S. forces to advance beyond the 38th parallel in the natural
course of things.

Several professional diplomats were uncomfortable with this development. Characteristically more concerned with international strategy and
realpolitik than domestic politics and election campaigns, George F. Kennan believed that it would be far beyond U.S. capabilities to keep Korea
permanently out of the sphere of Soviet influence. He frankly admitted that
it was not essential for the United States to have an anti-Soviet Korean regime in all of Korea for all time. He even added: "[W]e could even eventually tolerate for a certain period of time a Korea nominally independent but
actually amenable to Soviet influence."[101]

Kennan's strategic thinking might have been well justified. After all,
crossing the 38th parallel, occupying North Korea, and having a 900-mile
border with the PRC and the USSR on land would create far more difficult
military tasks than a defense line at sea, where U.S. forces had a far greater

advantage. Even a defense line at the "waist" of the Korean Peninsula, Kennan argued, would be far shorter and easier to hold than a long border with China and the Soviet Union.[102] A similar view was presented by the Canadian diplomat Escott Reid, who believed military action north to the parallel unnecessary and even "nonsense."[103] Hoping to put the brakes on Washington, Reid wrote to Canada's External Affairs Minister Pearson, arguing that crossing the parallel and occupying the north would lead, at best, to the prospect of maintaining large forces at the Chinese and Soviet borders and, at worst, would involve a continuing risk of clashes with the Soviet Union in North Korea.[104] Yet these diplomats' views were far removed from the charged climate in American society and domestic politics in 1950.

The more politically astute Dean Acheson, on the other hand, rejected Kennan's view: "Such was national interest in the abstract. In view of public opinion and political pressures in the concrete, ideas such as these could only be kept in mind as warnings not to be drawn into quicksands."[105] According to Kennan's recollections, Dulles refused his advice on the same grounds. From a politician's viewpoint, Dulles argued, it would confuse American public opinion and weaken support for the president's programs for strengthening American defenses.[106] A reaction of this kind was, indeed, not surprising in view of the social and political climate in American society in the summer and fall of 1950, with foreign policy, and Korea in particular, rapidly becoming the major domestic election issue.[107]

Observing this situation, foreign policymakers who had attempted to temper U.S. conduct must have sensed the limits of diplomatic measures. All diplomatic efforts having been exhausted in vain, British Foreign Secretary Ernest Bevin resignedly lamented in early September 1950:

> The atmosphere is very highly charged in the U.S. at this moment and with the elections coming on in November the administration is going to find it very difficult to take any step which does not have popular support. It is most unfortunate that the Far East should have become a party political issue in the U.S. but I am afraid we have to accept that this is so.[108]

Based on this acceptance of the American domestic-political situation, the British government modified its stance on the 38th parallel issue, from cautious and skeptical to more optimistic and even casual. Now, London kept in step with Washington and ceased criticizing its policy as reckless, newly arguing that the unification of Korea had been the primary objective since 1948 and that the "imaginary line" had never received recognition internationally as a boundary.[109]

Seen from Asia, particularly from China and India, which had suffered Western colonialism for nearly a century, however, such a dramatic shift in Britain's foreign policy stance, along with Washington's aggressive policy in Korea, was nothing but careless and unthinking act. Beijing had been carefully observing Western responses as well as the situation in Korea, and, immediately after the Inchon Landing, it quickly issued a series of warnings. On September 25, the acting chief of staff of the Chinese army, Nie Rongzhen, told the Indian ambassador to China, K. M. Panikkar, that China would not "sit back with folded hands and let the Americans come up to the border."[110]

Having received reports from Panikkar and recognized the firm tone of Beijing's leaders, the Indian Prime Minister Jawaharlal Nehru warned London that UN/U.S. forces should not cross the 38th parallel. "That any decision or even suggestion that UN forces will move beyond [the] 38th parallel is likely to precipitate what might well be world catastrophe is, I fear, more than probable," argued Nehru in a message to Bevin in late September 1950: "If . . . Peking is envisaging military action, [an] announcement that UN forces are going to advance beyond [the] 38th parallel will add fuel to [the] fire."[111] In this message to London, Nehru conveyed Beijing's attitude, delivered through Panikkar, and forcefully argued against the idea of crossing the parallel northward. In fact, he repeated his objection *four* times, asserting: "I would, therefore, urge with all the emphasis at my command, that NO action be taken by the UN that would involve crossing the 38th parallel."[112] Nehru could not have been any clearer or more straightforward than this.

Very few, however, took Nehru's warning and the Chinese messages seriously.[113] The British Foreign Office, for example, quickly concluded on September 29 that it would be "unlikely" that China would intervene in Korea, on the grounds that Beijing still faced a mountain of difficult problems at home and that China lacked the basic military capability to fight the United States.[114] It was too late for China to enter the war, they thought.[115] Observing the situation in a similar manner, a large majority of officials in Washington also refused to take Beijing's warnings seriously, viewing them, as Acheson put it, as merely a "bluff."[116] Instead of taking India's warning seriously, a joke circulated in Washington: "Panikkar is panicking."[117]

THE DECISION TO CROSS THE 38TH PARALLEL

Throughout the summer of 1950, opinions about crossing the 38th parallel were divided in various branches of the government, as were those of Truman's top advisors. However, newspaper reporters asked the same questions again and again: "Will U.S. forces cross the 38th parallel?"[118] This question became more urgent after the success of the Inchon Landing, as UN/U.S. forces came closer to the 38th parallel day by day. Recalling those days, one State Department official described the mood: "It was felt in Washington, particularly in the State Department, that we were completely justified in throwing the North Koreans back into their own country, but to occupy it raised many questions."[119]

During this period, government officials exchanged quite a lot of interdepartmental correspondence and correspondence with foreign ambassadors. Nevertheless, none of these documents suggests a critical decision because the core of the issue had less to do with a particular foreign policy or military tactics than it did with politics. In fact, many documents presented a similar line: the decision would be made at the highest level of government.[120] Even as late as September 26, 1950, a State Department staff member, James Webb, composed a directive to U.S. officials in Korea to "make every effort [to] discourage [Syngman] Rhee or other ROK spokesmen from making pronouncements regarding ROK's unilateral extension of authority north of the 38th parallel" because the matter was "being considered at a higher government level."[121]

Yet officials at the highest levels of the administration did not have a clear policy, either. They did not necessarily see the policy of crossing the 38th parallel as attractive and were extremely concerned about possible consequences. Rejecting Kennan's advice, Acheson did recognize the high level of risk involved in crossing the parallel. At Princeton Seminars held in 1954, former policymakers, including Acheson, Kennan, and Harriman, gathered and discussed their foreign policy decisions in the Truman administration. At one session, Harriman recalled the situation that they faced with respect to the 38th parallel issue and addressed Acheson:

> Dean, I think I remember—if I'm wrong, correct me—you are talking in my presence, and I think perhaps to me personally, about the concern that you had when we went over the 38th Parallel; you recognized that of course because

of . . . the success of the Inchon Landings that there would be no way to stop it. But as I recall it, you were concerned over the possible effects of our going beyond the 38th Parallel, and I got the impression that you would have been happier at that time if we hadn't gone across. Although you fully recognized that the military situation as it was, and (with) the possibility of destroying the North Korean army [*sic*], that it was not possible to stop.[122]

In Harriman's observation, Acheson would have been "happier at that time" if the U.S. Army had not crossed the parallel. In response, Acheson said succinctly: "That is true, Averell." Recalling his agreement to the decision to cross the 38th parallel, he added, "It was a very worrying thing and I was very worried about what the Indians and Chinese were saying as to what would happen."[123]

As Harriman's and Acheson's recollection shows, even top officials were not necessarily in favor of an aggressive policy. But, with initial defeats in Korea, the American public became more or less irritated, if not about to lose confidence, with the administration's lack of preparedness. The Truman administration had already been attacked as being "soft on communism." The president could not accept any more criticism of this kind and desperately sought opportunities to show his "toughness." What the administration really needed in the late summer of 1950 was not to "scare" or "deceive" the American people in order to "sell" its hardline defense program.[124] American domestic sentiment was already ahead of it in that sense. What the Truman administration desired was to catch up and to have "some affirmative action," as Dulles described, "in the field of foreign affairs which would restore the *confidence* of the American people that the government had a capacity to deal with the Communist menace."[125] As its election campaign committee had persistently demanded, the administration needed "achievement."

Such an entanglement between domestic and foreign affairs, and between political and military issues, could be seen clearly on September 29, 1950, a day that marked one of the most critical watersheds in "Cold War history," not only because the administration finally approved the decision to go north of the parallel at the highest-level meetings but also because it shifted the basic stance of U.S. foreign policy.

That morning, at 10 a.m., a Cabinet meeting was held at the White House. At the outset, European defense was discussed briefly, followed by, for the most part, domestic issues. First, Secretary of Agriculture Charles F.

Brannan discussed consumer prices, reporting that the prices of meats, such as pork, beef, and lamb, had held steady or gone down, while those of woolen goods had increased appreciably. Responding to this report, Secretary of Commerce Charles W. Sawyer suggested a greater use of substitutes, such as nylon products for woolens, and took a new tack, reporting that employment was holding steady, that housewives' hoarding had calmed down, and that any hoarding problem now was at a retail level. Then, Secretary of Labor Maurice J. Tobin shifted the conversation, reporting on a serious labor shortage in Arizona and California. Following this, Vice President Barkley talked about the election campaign tour that was ongoing on the West Coast and other parts of the country, raising the question of whether personal attacks should be made on Republican candidates. To this question, President Truman replied that they should instead emphasize the record of the Democratic Party. Tobin further insisted that they should stress the successful achievements of the administration in fighting communism in Greece, Iran, Turkey, and Europe.[126]

Then, Acheson cut in. "Korea will be used as a stage to prove to the world what Western Democracy can do to help the underprivileged countries of the world," he explained. "Plans are being developed to set up a commission to go into Korea and start rehabilitation." The secretary added, "The 38th parallel [will] be ignored."[127] This was the first and last time that the Truman Cabinet officially acknowledged its decision concerning the advancement of U.S. forces into North Korea. It is symbolic that the issue was brought up in relation to the topic of domestic political campaigns. It is also profoundly interesting that Acheson linked this opinion about crossing the 38th parallel to the issue of America's credibility in the world—rhetoric that would be repeated in the years that followed.

At around noon, Truman, Acheson, and Secretary of Defense George Marshall had lunch together at Blair House. After lunch, the dishes were cleared away, and a large map of Korea was brought in. Over the map, they discussed, at this highest level, the details of crossing the 38th parallel—what should be done and how far the troops should go, and so forth—and, finally, agreed to give General Douglas MacArthur the green light to cross the parallel northward. Although Truman had received a briefing on this plan two days earlier and generally accepted this policy with some conditions, with this final decision, the invasion of North Korea by U.S. forces for the purpose of unifying the divided country was formally authorized.[128]

That afternoon, Marshall sent a telegram to MacArthur, stating, "We want you to feel unhampered tactically and strategically to proceed north of the 38th parallel."[129]

At 3 p.m., the three returned to the White House, attended an NSC meeting, and officially approved NSC-68, which, at first, in April, had been rejected by the president, and had been pending throughout the summer. Since the discovery of that confidential document in 1975, diplomatic historians have emphasized its significant role in promoting a massive military build-up in the 1950s, as well as justifying far more aggressive and confrontational attitudes toward the Soviet Union. The historian Ernest May, for instance, writes, "NSC-68 laid out the rationale for U.S. strategy during much of the Cold War," and Walter LaFeber describes it as the "American blueprint for waging the Cold War."[130] However, the document was not seen this way when it was written. Paul Nitze, its chief writer, described it at that time as "a statement of [U.S. foreign] policy to be followed over the next four or five years."[131] Even Nitze gave up on it when the document was flatly rejected and had no prospect to be adopted. In other words, it would have gone nowhere had it not been for the Korean War and multiplying problems related to the war at home. The war increased its "importance," and so it was finally approved on that Friday afternoon, the day that the administration formally decided to cross the 38th parallel.

The two decisions made on September 29, 1950, one concerning the 38th parallel and the other concerning NSC-68, not only represented the militaristic escalation of the Korean War but also signified the solidification of the "Cold War" framework, destroying any possibility for meaningful diplomacy between East and West. It is important to note that these policies emerged less from Cold War thinking or geopolitical considerations as from their judgments concerning domestic political circumstances and popular sentiment. Throughout this period, and particularly just before the elections, the administration had to avoid being seen as "soft on communism" at all costs. The discussion about the 38th parallel had less to do with a particular military policy than symbolic political struggles to maintain the government's and administration's credibility in the hearts and minds of millions and billions of people at home. This was when the notion of "containment," which had been advocated by Kennan since the late 1940s, was replaced with a more aggressive, militarized, and socially constructed strategy of "rollback," which would be popularized from then on, leading to the height of the Cold War. Having made such crucial political decisions on that Friday afternoon, President Truman left the White House for a planned week of vacation. The war, he may have thought, was over.

In Tokyo, General MacArthur similarly believed that the war had been won and declared that the "Chinese commies" would not attack and U.S. troops could be withdrawn from Korea by the end of the year.[132] In line with this belief, on October 19, U.S. troops entered Pyongyang, and, on the next day, MacArthur was on a tour from Tokyo, inspecting airborne landings at the front lines and visiting the newly reached northern capital. According to the United Press International correspondent Earnest Hoberecht, who accompanied him on the tour, MacArthur was in a cheerful mood, jokingly asking General Walton H. Walker, who greeted him at Pyongyang Airport, "Any celebrities here to greet me?" He scornfully added, "Where is Kim Buck Too?"[133] Such an optimistic attitude was not limited to the general and policymakers in Washington; even the *New York Times* devoted a great deal of space to two sensationalist articles, "Toward V-K Day" and "U.N.'s War in Korea Enters Its Last Phase; MacArthur's Forces Now in Position to Wipe Out Last Communist Units."[134] Many, indeed, were already declaring the war over.

However, the situation on the ground was changing rapidly. At almost the same time, in Shenyang, in northeastern China, extensive air raid precautions were suddenly begun, pillboxes erected, trenches dug in the streets, many factories dismantled, and machinery moved to the north, and many residents began evacuating. British diplomats in Beijing collected scattered pieces of information, from sources such as travelers from Shanghai who testified that they saw CCP armies in Shanghai moving up to Shenyang, or a foreign businessman who affirmed that Shenyang was in a mood of "considerable panic" and concluded: "It is clear that the measures may portend some new move on the part of the Chinese Government in connection with Korea for which they fear severe retaliation."[135] This observation was accurate. On exactly the same day that MacArthur was dismissing the possibility of China's entry and ridiculing the North Korean leader at Pyongyang Airport, roughly 120,000 Chinese officers and soldiers began crossing the Yalu River at the Chinese–North Korean border. Within three days, a total of 260,000 troops had entered North Korean territory, marching southward to redraw the map of the war.[136]

CHAPTER FOUR

Politics of Impression

IN MID-NOVEMBER 1950, a letter arrived at the Beijing municipal office of the Chinese Communist Party (CCP). Although the office had been receiving hundreds of letters, particularly following the public announcement of the entry of the Chinese People's Volunteers (CPV) into the Korean conflict, this letter, written by a young worker at the Beijing Municipal Bureau for Cleaning, might have drawn special attention from local cadres. To begin with, unlike many other letters that were labeled *zhiyuanshu* (letter for enlisting), this one was labeled *yijianshu* (letter of opinion). In addition, instead of supporting the official line and enthusiastically volunteering for the army, the worker straightforwardly expressed his concerns and opinions and, in the end, refused to go to war. It read:

> When I learned about the Korean issue, my understanding was still inaccurate, and I was thinking that the Korean War was not deeply relevant to us. Through some study, however, I have realized that such a view was merely a narrow ethnic notion.

Now I am not viewing the Korean problem as an isolated issue. I see it as part of American imperialism, which follows the path of the Japanese imperialism of the past, using Korea as a stepping-stone to invade China. Today they have been already realizing it.

Based on this understanding, I am joining the Resisting America and Assisting Korea movement for the defense of our country and people, and for the protection of my own security, peace, and daily life.

Nevertheless, what I have done so far is just to mobilize other people, and I have not thought about my own action. I have a concept of action. But how can I express it?

That's a big problem! Ordinary people have participated in the Volunteer Army and gone to Korea. How about myself?

Also join the Volunteer Army?

No, I cannot!

My mind is messed up. I don't have such a high level of resolution. I don't have such a sense of self-sacrifice. However much I continue to discuss this matter, I cannot overcome my contradictions. . . .

Why cannot I equally carry out this duty as other people of the proletariat have been doing?

It's hard for me.

It's really painful to me.[1]

While refusing to go to war, this worker promised in the latter half of his long letter that he would voluntarily reduce his salary by 5 percent, and extend his working hours by one hour every day.

Letters of this kind—or popular attitudes, in general, in the early years of the People's Republic of China (PRC)—have not been well examined until recently.[2] Voices and behaviors of ordinary people have rarely been even referred to in the existing literature that deals with politics and policy-making during the Korean War.[3] This is due, perhaps, to our conventional images of the powerful CCP, which was believed to be manipulating and suppressing people's thinking. The communist authorities conducted propaganda and political campaigns on a massive scale, and, thus, people must have lacked any choice but to obey. Although such a view might have some merit, much more needs to be examined and explained. Simply put, what we can see in the letter above is not only how news of the Korean War forced even a worker to connect a foreign war to his daily life and to reflect on his behavior but also how an individual observed and thought about the situation, suffered anxiety, and made decisions about his own behavior.

Close examination of people's letters as well as communist authorities' internal reports reveal that popular sentiments were not at all monolithic and that ordinary people's diverse attitudes—support, cooperation, and enthusiasm, as well as doubt, perplexity, and objections—were not irrelevant to the CCP's politics and policy-making. This was because, at its core, Beijing's foreign strategy during the Korean War was not merely a matter of military tactics or merely part of the Cold War; rather, it was connected to domestic politics and, most importantly, to the very basis of the newly established regime: legitimacy. Let us examine this point by looking into the voices and daily lives of ordinary people, social and historical contexts, and domestic politics, as well as Beijing's foreign strategy during the early phase of the Korean War and, specifically, China's entry into the Korean War and its decision to cross the 38th parallel southward.

BEIJING'S ATTITUDE OF RESTRAINT

Immediately following the outbreak of the Korean War, what was unmistakable in China was the prevalence of fear of World War III, as well as rising doubts and skepticism regarding the CCP. After all, this was a rare opportunity for those who had been opposed to the communist regime to fight back, with the United States on their side. Equally noticeable was a surge in anti-American and anti-Western sentiments, to a degree that often went beyond the official Party line. In contrast to such a polarization of popular sentiments, however, Beijing remained remarkably cautious in its stance toward the Korean War, at least publicly. As the Chinese historians Shen Zhihua and Niu Jun point out, while paying significant attention to the progress of the situation, the communist leadership, at first, maintained a restrained attitude following the outbreak of and U.S. intervention in the war. Although Beijing, in principal, supported North Korea's effort and began preparing for establishing the Frontier Defense Army in defense of the northeast border as early as July and, it carefully avoided direct involvement.[4]

Such a stance by the CCP was observable in its official and semiofficial newspapers. The CCP's official newspaper, *Renmin Ribao*, for instance, maintained a relatively moderate position from the war's outbreak until November 1950. Several political cartoons published in the paper between July 19 and 23 displayed the CCP's initial attitude. One depicts General Douglas MacArthur and Syngman Rhee hurriedly running away from the giant hands of the "Korean People's Army" and "Korean guerrilla forces," which are about to catch them from both sides. Another cartoon illustrates Americans being run over and killed by a North Korean army tank.[5] The common theme in these cartoons was that the war was *Koreans'* fight against American imperialism; Chinese soldiers, or other Chinese people, never appeared.

Along similar lines, a poem in *Renmin Ribao* on July 23 included the line "Salute the Brave Korean People's Army!" A headline concerning a student demonstration against American intervention read: "Beijing Students Unfold Various Campaigns, Cheer on the Korean People, Oppose the American Invasion."[6] These articles also implied that, although the Chinese people were opposed to U.S. intervention and thus respected North Korea's struggle, the Chinese people were still a third party in the war. In fact, among thirty-five slogans for the yearly celebration of the establishment of the People's Liberation Army (PLA) in early August, "Oppose the American Invasion!" and "Salute the Korean People's Army!" appeared only as twentieth and twenty-first, tagged on far behind domestic slogans such as "Prepare to Effectuate Land Reform!" and "Suppress Rebels and Reactionaries!"[7] This attitude indicated that, during the early summer of 1950, Beijing was carefully avoiding an open, direct confrontation with the United States.

In a similar manner, *Guangming Ribao*, a semiofficial newspaper published by the China Democratic League, a group of pro-CCP but noncommunist political parties, followed *Renmin Ribao*'s official line, although there were still differences in degree of enthusiasm. For example, on August 6, 1950, *Guangming Ribao* carried a photo essay titled "Unite Whole People, Liberate Taiwan, Liberate Tibet." On the same page, another small headline read "Salute the Brave Korean People's Army!"[8] A subtle implication, here, was that Korea was still carefully differentiated from the Chinese people's initiative. Although *Guangming Ribao* took a slightly more aggressive stance, using harsh words regarding the Korean War and expressing anti-American feelings, the paper seldom walked out of step.

By the same token, *Jiefang Ribao*, CCP Shanghai committee's official newspaper, was even more reticent in terms of Chinese commitment to

"A Pincer Attack." *Renmin Ribao,* 19 July 1950.

"American Bandits' Miscalculation." *Renmin Ribao,* 19 July 1950.

Korea. The headline of an article on the yearly celebration of the establishment of the PLA in August read "We are waiting for an order to march on Taiwan!" but there was no mention at all of Korea.[9] A political cartoon on August 30 was more revealing, with the lightning of "protest" piercing the *Mei-di* (American imperialism) of General Douglas MacArthur.[10] Here, the lightning is labeled simply "voices of protest"; there is not even a sword or spear. In short, in the early summer of 1950, official and semiofficial newspapers carefully depicted China as a third party in the Korean War, suggesting a reticent stance on the part of CCP.

Much more interesting than the contents of these official newspapers is that various regional and local newspapers tended to publish articles and political cartoons with much more aggressive language, conveying anti-American attitudes that went far beyond *Renmin Ribao*.[11] These papers, particularly those issued by local committees, tended to deliver more detailed reports and stories, including readers' responses, with stronger anti-American and anti-Western sentiments. For example, the CCP's regional newspaper in Wuhan, *Changjiang Ribao*, published a letter in early July from local high school students who criticized American intervention and asserted that they would not surrender in the face of enemy attack.[12] Another reader, on July 20, even appealed to countrymen to "attack our *common* enemy!"[13] Likewise, *Changchun Xinbao*, a local newspaper in Changchun, published a reader's letter to Korean soldiers on July 28, praising the North Korean war effort, saying, "When you are fighting, we will not neglect you for even a minute!"[14]

"Struck dead by Lightning." *Jiefang Ribao*, 30 August 1950. (Reprinted with permission, *Jiefang Ribao*.)

More telling is a cartoon published in *Changjiang Ribao* in early August in which a dog representing "American imperialism" is stabbed with a sword representing the "Korean people" from the left and multiple swords representing "Chinese people," "Vietnamese people," and "Filipino people" from the right (the sword representing "Chinese people" is the largest of all).[15] What is interesting is that these cartoons in local and regional committees' newspapers portrayed China as an important participant, rather than an observer, from the very beginning of the war, and that they depicted bayonets and swords, as opposed to the mere "voices of protest" in the official newspapers.

Such a surge in anti-American sentiments that began evolving even beyond the official party line can be seen on the ground in an increase in trivial local disputes in the summer of 1950 between Chinese and American residents, of a kind that previously many Chinese most likely had to endure in silence. For example, on July 15, a male American teacher at a middle school in Wuchang was exposed to ridicule for homosexual activity with his students.[16] On August 5, an American in Jiangxi Province was accused of "letting" his dog bite a Chinese student on the thigh.[17] In September, a female American professor at Jinling University in Nanjing was pilloried for her "distortion" of modern Chinese history.[18] To be sure, incidents like these had occurred occasionally since the late 1940s, but what is interesting is that they were being exposed all at once in this short period.

What is more intriguing in these instances is that communist authorities in July devoted themselves to putting out fires. In the first case, the Foreign Ministry sought to end the dispute by expelling the accused teacher and directing local authorities not to prolong the matter.[19] In the second case, the Foreign Ministry urged a local court, which had given the man a three-month jail sentence, to mitigate this punishment.[20] In yet another case, concerning American Christian missionaries, Beijing issued a directive to local committees at the end of July, urging them not to interfere with missionaries' daily activities and not to confuse China's anti-imperialist stance with policies concerning religion.[21] These examples give us a glimpse of anti-American sentiments, in some cases, emerging and developing rather spontaneously alongside the development of the Korean conflict, without the central authority necessarily needing to play leading roles in shaping them. As we will see in greater detail below, there was a rise in skepticism and doubt toward the CCP, while, at the same time, a surge in anti-American sentiments that went beyond the Party line was observable. The evolution of these paradoxical feelings soon posed a dilemma for the Beijing leadership with the question of whether China should enter the Korean War in the fall of 1950.

RUMORS AND FEARS AFTER INCHON

One major factor in Beijing's change of attitude, as the historian Chen Jian points out, was the American victory in the Inchon Landing on September 15, 1950.[22] On the Korean Peninsula, almost instantly, North Korean armies, as well as the Kim Il-sung regime were on the verge of the collapse. Suddenly, a broad array of anti-communist organizations in Korea returned to life and began retaliating against Kim's supporters and sympathizers.[23] Observing such a swift turn from Taiwan, Chiang Kai-shek was exuberant, writing in his diary in late September: "I feel as if I should thank God."[24] For Chiang, it was a turning point not only in the Korean War but for politics in East Asia, as a whole. This new situation in Korea suggested to him that something similar could occur in China—once Taiwan's counterattack began, with the support of U.S. forces, the Chinese people would rise up and the communist regime would fall.

Not surprisingly, therefore, the Inchon Landing had a profound impact on the course of the CCP's foreign (and domestic) policy-making. Mao Zedong seems to have begun changing his mind on China's stance in the war almost immediately, writing to the Northeast Bureau Secretary Gao Gang, "It seems that not sending troops would be inappropriate, and that we need to prepare in earnest."[25] Yet no consensus existed among the CCP leadership, and any decision to enter the war was yet to come. What became critical for Beijing leaders' final decision in early October to enter the war were serious social and political ramifications of the Inchon Landing, as well as Beijing's observation of these factors, which have not been well understood in the existing literature.

Newspapers in China at that time, to be sure, rarely delivered reports that could be viewed as portraying the CCP in a negative light. The U.S. victory at Inchon was reported several days later, and only in a short article, which described not an American victory but North Korean forces' "fierce defensive battle," in which the Korean People's Army caused "serious damage" to U.S. forces.[26] Similarly, North Korean forces' retreat from Seoul was described as a "planned withdrawal" and "victory."[27] News of the war then sharply decreased in late September and October.[28] It might appear strange, thus, to think about social and political ramifications of the Inchon Landing in Chinese society. One might ask: How could the operation have had an impact on the public with so little information?

Yet the fact that newspapers stopped reporting on the war situation provided enough of a sign to let readers sense the changing tide. We can see the development of such skepticism in internal reports that surveyed rumors in society. "Editors of newspapers must have racked their brains to figure out how to say People's Army's 'victory' to describe their retreat from Seoul!" sarcastically remarked one traffic police officer in Beijing.[29] Another police officer, Li Guozhong, was even more critical: "Newspapers report how many Americans died, and how many Syngman Rhee soldiers died. But did no one die on the Korean [People's Army] side? The news is nothing but propaganda."[30] Another internal report similarly informed Beijing that many people no longer trusted *Renmin Ribao,* viewing it as reporting only good news for the CCP, as the Nationalist Party's newspaper had done for it formerly.[31] The internal report, thus, concluded, "After Inchon, a sense of disappointment is spreading."[32]

In contrast to the marked decline in the quantity of war news, what increased rapidly following the Inchon Landing were rumors, from the verisimilar and credible to the wild and fantastical in retrospect. "America is not a 'paper tiger'; it is an 'iron tiger'!" "North Koreans can do nothing about it," maintained whispers in Shanghai and neighboring cities.[33] Another typical story involved the fate of Kim Il-sung; one rumor in Beijing had it that Kim had already been captured and taken prisoner, and another that he had evacuated to Beijing or, possibly, Moscow.[34] The changing tide in Korea increased concerns about its neighboring region, Northeast China; one student at Youzhen Junior School in Beijing, Ma Lilan, heard that all schools in Shenyang had moved to Harbin. Another, who had been accepted at a university in the northeast, decided not to go, because his family feared the outbreak of war in the north.[35]

Such imaginings concerning the prospect of war were not limited to the northeast. "American airplanes are attacking the northeast. What should we do if they come to Beijing?" "The United States will, without doubt, use an atom bomb in Shanghai," maintained rumors in Beijing and Shanghai, respectively.[36] Because of these rumors and fears, commodity prices increased again in many cities in late September, and the price of gold jumped again. In Wuxi, Jiangsu Province, for instance, gold prices increased by 125 percent immediately following the U.S. victory in Inchon.[37] Such an atmosphere also sparked another concern—the recurrence of civil war, specifically, the Nationalist Party's counteroffensive.

Whispers circulated that "The Nationalist Party has already begun landing at Guangdong and Dalian"; "GMD armies, 2 million strong, are already heading for Changsha." Another story even claimed, "[A renowned CCP military leader] Lin Biao was already killed in an air raid on August 8, and his coffin has already arrived at Changsha."[38] In such whispers, even the weather provided a rationale for the fate of the CCP; one rumor maintained that World War III had just begun and that the people now working for the CCP would be killed, soon, adding, "When Japanese armies came here we had a long spell of dry weather, and the Japanese were routed within a year. Now the communist armies have come and we have a long drought, too. They will not be here so long, either."[39]

After the U.S. forces' landing at Inchon and North Korean army's setbacks, along with rumors of the GMD's counteroffensive on the mainland, came a sea change in popular attitudes. According to internal reports, some local, village-level cadres became half-hearted, some who had claimed interest in registering with the CCP suddenly evaded commitment, members of the Communist Youth League began planning to withdraw, or had already withdrawn, their names from membership, and peasants became reluctant to provide provisions.[40] Such half-heartedness became quite common. A staff member of the Beijing Police Department, Liu Baomin, while publicly advocating his "determined support" for the stance of the Beijing government, reportedly purchased a pedicab after the Inchon Landing, in secret, preparing to flee Beijing in case of the outbreak of World War III.[41]

Such an attitude was a sort of self-protection for ordinary people at a time of uncertainty and unrest and not at all unreasonable in view of an increasingly deteriorating social order. In fact, anti-communist and insurrectionary activities became more and more common after the United States entered the Korean War, and it was particularly the case in the weeks following the U.S. victory at Inchon. Various "counterrevolutionaries," for instance, attacked factories and railways, set fire to warehouses and private houses, and even organized riots and battles against local communist governments.[42] Reactionary slogans were ubiquitous; graffiti in a public convenience at Beihai Park in Beijing read: "Defeat Mao Zedong!" "Mao Zedong is the head of rebels," and so on. Similar slogans appeared even in front of army camps.[43]

Such rumors and doubts about the CCP's legitimacy were partly due to the fact that, in some remote areas, local communist governments had difficulties in managing, or even lost ground, against "local rebels." A local official in Zhejiang Province, south of Shanghai, for example, informed Beijing at the end of September 1950:

> In August, [our] military achievements against rebels were not so large, and our attack on them was not strong enough, giving them opportunities to take advantage of. The activities of rebels have now tended to become rampant. . . . They spread rumors, deceive people, frighten people, and kidnap people. They send foodstuffs and money to people as they wish, and, at the same time, conduct looting, thus destroying and damaging our organization in villages. They assassinate our active supporters in villages, block traffic, and destroy electric cables, thus disturbing order in villages.[44]

Such situations were not limited to this area in the eastern part of China. Another report, from Hubei Province in Central China, similarly described instances of local resistance, which became particularly rampant in late summer of 1950. These instances included dozens of robberies every month, destruction of crops, and demolition of traffic routes and electric cables.[45] Likewise, a report from Hunan Province detailed activities of counterrevolutionary groups, such as the "Chinese Self-Rescuing Army" in the area.[46] It was said that, in the western part of the province, where around 300,000 people lived, there were more than "70,000 rebels." A far more remote corner, Guizhou Province, might have been the most troubling from Beijing's perspective, because 80 percent of the province had been captured by local insurgents.[47]

CCP leaders were acutely aware of widespread unrest and noted associations between counterrevolutionary activities and America's intervention in the Korean War. With America's entry into the war and its dispatch of the

Seventh Fleet to the Taiwan Strait, Beijing feared for the survival of its new government. This fear was increased by the prospect of counterrevolutionary pressures from within and without and was not at all groundless, particularly in view of the continuing civil war.[48]

CONTINUING CIVIL WAR

In fact, at the time of the establishment of the PRC, one-third of Chinese territory was not yet under CCP control. In addition to Hainan Island, Tibet, and Taiwan, all or most of Guangdong, Guangxi, Sichuan, Guizhou, and Yunnan, as well as portions of Shanxi, Hunan, and Hubei had yet to be "liberated." By the time of the outbreak of the Korean War, most of these regions had come under control, yet Tibet and Taiwan remained thorns in the CCP's side. In addition to this, even in "liberated" areas, resistance remained powerful. In Guangxi Province, for example, the local branch of the CCP announced that more than 7,000 people had been killed by reactionaries in 1950.[49] At a glance, this number may seem high, but, in response, the local PLA unit suppressed 143,000 insurgents the same year.[50] More specifically, in only five days in early December 1950, about 4,560 "reactionaries" were reportedly killed in Guangxi.[51]

This large-scale purge was not an isolated event. According to a speech by Premier Zhou Enlai, the PLA had eliminated about 8 million dissenters since 1946, and, in one year, between 1949 and 1950, more than 2 million "reactionaries" were killed.[52] These massive numbers announced by the CCP may have been exaggerated in order to impress their audience, but, even so, the essence of the problem—the existence of social unrest—was certain. They indicate, in short, not only the strength of CCP rule but the existence of a deep-rooted disavowal of the legitimacy of the communist regime.

After Inchon, in particular, the prospect of counterrevolution wore an aura of "reality" as the Nationalist Party heightened its anti-communist propaganda campaigns in Central and South China, particularly from late September to December 1950. On September 26, for instance, ten airplanes originating from the Nationalist government in Taiwan flew over coastal and central areas, including Hubei, Hunan, Anhui, Jiangxi, Zhejiang, Fujian, and Guangdong Provinces, dropping bags containing rice, books, and leaflets. A letter to "fellow countrymen who suffer from famine" told readers that North Korean forces had already been defeated, and that the Nationalist Party was preparing a counterattack, adding, "Our fellow countrymen on the mainland! Stand up, and support the GMD's counteroffensive!"[53] The tone heated up throughout the fall; in addition to airdrop operations, the Nationalist Party continually appealed to the mass public on the mainland through radio broadcasts, saying:

> Our soldiers and compatriots on the mainland! . . .
>> Refuse to participate in the army!
>> Refuse to contribute foodstuffs!
>> Refuse to go northward! Refuse to fight abroad!
>> Oppose the invasion of the Soviet Union in Korea!
>> If you find yourself on the front of the Korean War, refuse to attend operations and gather under the flag of the United Nations![54]

The claims of such anti-communist campaigns across the Taiwan Strait did not necessarily appear implausible, especially in view of the American presence on the Korean Peninsula and Taiwan Strait, and particularly in view of the U.S. victory at Inchon. In fact, even after China's victories on the battlefield, some simply did not believe the news, ominously anticipating that the United States would plan a direct landing, like that at Inchon, on the coast of Qingdao or Shanghai.[55]

In short, feelings of uneasiness did not disappear, even following China's entry into the Korean War and its victories on the battlefield. Such popular attitudes lingered as an issue that officials had to address. Unbelievable as it might sound, at this point even a solar eclipse became a source of anxiety for communist authorities; the local committee's newspaper in Shanxi Province, for instance, explained the scientific mechanism of the eclipse, appealing to readers not to believe any rumors that might take advantage of worries among the masses at the time of the sun was obscured.[56] This suggests that the communist authority paid attention to any small incident that had the possibility of damaging its legitimacy. Given such a situation, it is reasonable to say that the CCP in the fall of 1950 was still far from establishing popular authority and credibility. Recurring counterrevolutionary activities and the continuing civil war, thus, were not simply military issues but, essentially, political issues, which could have fundamental and negative ramifications for domestic social programs—including those at the core of the CCP's legitimacy, such as land reform.

SOCIAL ISSUES VIEWED THROUGH INTERNATIONAL CONFLICT

In fact, for the CCP, land reform was not really "agrarian" reform but, rather, a political campaign, because its aim was the destruction of the political power of the gentry-landlord class and the establishment of legitimacy in thousands of villages throughout China. In the countryside, where more than 70 percent of the population of 500 million consisted of poor peasants, the heart of agrarian reform was building a sense of trust toward the CCP. Yet this basis of the program began to deteriorate with the progress of the Korean War. An internal report written in November 1950 summarized this critical situation:

> After the American intervention in Korea, landlords and rich peasants appeared to be planning mischief, and, particularly after this fall, there have been more than a hundred cases of various kinds of reactionary activities. In particular, in the areas of Shangdu and Kangbao, there were more than fifty such cases. For example, some landlords threatened peasants and recaptured their land, and others seized their crops. In other cases, they ejected peasants through threatening them or starting rumors, saying, for instance, "World War III has started. The land [allocated to peasants] will be returned to its original owners." Peasants are afraid of a change of government. There was a case in which landlords merged with local gangs, killing communist cadres and active peasants. Such landlords' counterattacks have attracted the attention of the local communist government, which has decided to suppress these actions. Many cases of intense conflicts between peasants and landlords are emerging everywhere.[57]

Evidence indicates that conflicts of this kind were much more persistent and deep-rooted than this report described. In fact, these problems existed and were being exacerbated before the outbreak of the war but finally surfaced in light of America's entry into the war and landing at Inchon.

The crux of the problem was the CCP's initially moderate stance toward land reform, which was adopted in the early months of the PRC, in the spring of 1950. It promised that land reform would be conducted in "an orderly manner through a step-by-step process."[58] Radicalism was avoided, and less revolutionary policies—such as preservation of rich peasants—were chosen. Such a mild, gradualist course was taken to make it possible to sustain production levels and avoid social and economic disorder. Yet, at the same time, such policies could lead to the continuation of "reactionary" forces, keeping the lives of peasants as they were.[59] In short, moderate policies could have benefits economically but negative effects politically.

In fact, *Xin Hunan Bao*, a local newspaper in Hunan Province, received letters from readers raising questions and expressing doubts about such moderate land reform in the early months of the PRC: "Is this policy not contradictory to a previous one that aimed at eradicating the land-owning class?" "How could peasants live without confiscating lands of rich peasants?" "How was the previous land reform policy changed as such?" "What kind of attitude should we take toward former landlords?"[60] Lower-ranking officials in villages as well expressed puzzlement. "The policy of protecting prosperous farmers cannot satisfy peasants' demands, and land reform would be rendered meaningless." Fearful of a decline in peasants' spirits, some cadres intentionally did not convey this policy in the spring of 1950, and others even deliberately misrepresented the content of recent land reform policies in an attempt to win peasants' hearts.[61] It is no surprise that the CCP had so little success in collecting taxes and foodstuffs; Deng Xiaoping, who was in charge of the southwest at that time as first secretary of the Southwest Bureau, reported that the Party collected only 11 percent of expected taxes and 40 percent of expected foodstuffs. The main cause of this difficulty, Deng pointed out, was the resistance of the land-owning classes.[62]

Much worse than the tax problem was the stalled progress of land reform, an issue at the very basis of the credibility of the regime. In fact, landowners made desperate efforts to survive the revolution. Some provided feasts for peasants, some repurchased land and farming equipment from peasants, and others threatened peasants by saying, as noted above, that the Nationalist Party had already returned to the mainland and that communist rule would not last for very long.[63] In the south, where clan organizations were strong and local communist parties relatively weak, the gentry used kinship ties to protect themselves.[64] In many of these southern regions, CCP officials were considered "outsiders," who had come abruptly from the "north," with little knowledge of local situations, often not even speaking the native dialect, and thus provoking resentment among local people.[65]

In these areas, the CCP had not yet achieved social control at the local level, and, thus, residents often followed local rules of indigenous "gangs and bandits" who had been dominant for a long time, because they feared these local forces more than the CCP. As Frederick C. Teiwes points out, ordinary peasants still had little confidence in whether CCP rule would be irreversible.[66] In rural areas of Hunan, for instance, residents avoided talking to communist officials publicly for fear of revenge by "local bandits," reportedly saying, "The government would release bandits just two or three months after they arrested them. What can we say?"[67] "I do not fear the Heaven or Earth, but I am only afraid that the people's government will be too tolerant."[68]

IMAGES OF AMERICA

Such doubts and fears gained the ring of truth as U.S. forces landed at Inchon and advanced to the north. According to an internal report, "unlawful" landowners resumed making their presence felt in rural communities, often bringing together a variety of anti-communist forces to form armed resistance groups.[69] Peasant leaders lost enthusiasm, village cadres grew reluctant to conduct programs, and peasants did not dare to attend meetings. In fact, one meeting in Shanghai in early November that was supposed to include more than twenty participants only had ten.[70] Fearing the return of the Nationalist Party, some peasants refused to take possession of lands and houses allocated to them. "Landlords will stage a counterattack. Our peasant leader cannot be reliable," one peasant on the outskirts of Wuxi said. At this point, an elementary schoolteacher's comment appeared plausible: "Peasants cannot do anything well for ever and ever. If they want to do something, they must rely on landlords."[71]

Popular images of the United States were combined with those of the landowning class because it was viewed as backing Chiang Kai-shek and, by extension, the landowning class in China. Even though landowners in rural China had nothing to do with U.S. intervention in Korea, images of *Mei-di* connected them in a symbolic sense. If Beijing did not take an aggressive stance toward the United States in Korea, how could local Party members logically convince peasants to confront landowners at home? How could peasants believe in the CCP's land reform program if Beijing was soft on "American imperialism," which was said to be backing landlords in China? In this way, domestic and foreign issues were seen as connected, and American involvement in Korea became an undesirable factor for CCP supporters at home, which could cause the destabilization of domestic order and erosion of confidence among the people.[72]

Viewed in this way, it is no surprise that some of those who had been enthusiastic and supportive toward the CCP grew impatient with its cautious stance at home and abroad. In early September, for instance, a local committee in Zhenjiang, eastern China, was informed that people were saying, "Why don't we go and fight? What is the point of just issuing protests in writing?"[73] A committee in Beijing received similar letters: "The U.S. Army invades Korea at full strength. That's too much for the Korean people. Why doesn't our Democratic side send troops?" "*Mei-di* has already come over our head." "American imperialists openly invade [Korea]; why don't we support Korea in open ways?"[74]

However, this aggressive stance remained only one of several viewpoints and did not represent the majority.[75] According to local cadres' observations in Beijing, many expressed reluctance at the idea of entering the war. Some said, "To be sure, it is a good thing to send troops to Korea, but it would be difficult to do so because many people now dislike any war, many don't have hatred toward the United States, and thus morale is very low." Similarly, one low-ranking Party member said, "China has just emerged from the horrors of war. We need enough rest and preparation."[76]

In addition, some college students, intellectuals, and businessmen simply remained sympathetic to the United States. "I simply don't feel hatred toward the United States," one female student at Yanjing (Yen-ching) University in Beijing said.[77] Another high school student in the northeastern city of Jilin asked, "What's wrong with the United States? I love to have American bread and milk."[78] A similar opinion came up in a discussion class at a junior school in Beijing; one student voiced his opinion that: "Americans are good. They came to help us before. Giving us foodstuffs can be called an 'economic invasion,' but not a 'political invasion,'" and further inquired, "If this is an invasion, why do not we think the support from the Soviet Union an invasion?"[79]

Still another kind of attitude was common and widespread: apathy. "It's not my business whether we go to war or not. I just do my job. That's it," said one police officer in Beijing in late August 1950.[80] A similar view could be observed everywhere; a local committee in Nanjing observed that some people were saying: " 'Opposing America' is just something Mao Zedong is doing. If we can just continue to eat, for us, anything would be fine. If Americans come, it's all right, too."[81] In Shanghai as well, a significant number of students were saying, "Who cares?"[82] From the perspective of many ordinary people, it mattered little. Such an attitude can also be found in the words of a Shanghai factory worker:

> Today, Taiwan is conducting its land reform, and Chiang Kai-shek has also begun criticizing himself. They now understand that they need to serve the general public and people. Why should we attack them now? Is it impossible for Mao Zedong and Chiang Kai-shek to issue a joint statement that neither is going to participate in World War III? We common people just need to eat and survive. We don't need to say, "You are a supporter of Mao!" or "You are a supporter of Chiang!" Who cares?[83]

From the perspective of the CCP, however, such a lack of interest was, in a sense, most threatening of all, because it could undermine the *cause* of the communist revolution and government. In other words, a point of contention was the reason for their existence. Such elements of indifference could be dangerous because people could easily switch positions depending on the course of current events.

This is why the communist leadership paid significant attention to popular attitudes. The municipal committee in Beijing, for example, studied public reactions concerning China's stance on the Korean War, classifying people into four categories: those who urged Beijing to enter the war, those who opposed entering the war on the basis of China's lack of ability, those who opposed entering the war on the basis of a lack of just cause, and those who did not find any fault on the American side.[84]

A similar investigation was conducted with a portion of the PLA in August 1950. It focused on soldiers' attitudes toward the United States, dividing them into three categories: 50 percent had strong anti-American sentiments and firm confidence in communist programs; another 40 percent understood the CCP's programs and the meaning of the war but were less confident; and the remaining 10 percent had a tendency to "fear

America," "admire America," or "sympathize with America." This last 10 percent, reportedly mostly youth from newly "liberated" areas, lacked confidence in CCP programs.[85] While we cannot gauge the reliability of this study, its results suggest that, although the majority had confidence in the CCP's programs, nearly half still remained more or less dubious about them. What is more interesting than the accuracy of this ratio, however, is the fact that communist authorities were paying attention to popular attitudes.

In fact, policymakers in Beijing were attentive to the balance among these categories: the majority, made up of supportive elements; another large portion on the fence; and a small portion that remained doubtful toward the communist cause. Because of the supportive majority, the CCP would be able to conduct its programs at home. Yet the discontented faction remained, and the large portion of politically "on the fence" elements could easily falter, depending on circumstances, particularly in wartime.

Although Beijing was still relatively cautious about the Korean War and America's involvement throughout the summer of 1950, the complexity of popular attitudes created a difficult situation: if Beijing chose not to confront the United States abroad, the majority of supportive elements could become reluctant about or lose confidence in CCP programs, and at the same time the undesirable elements in society could rise up, possibly damaging CCP legitimacy at home. At the early stages of the Korean War, thus, the communist leadership had to deal with foreign issues in conjunction with domestic matters because achieving one goal could possibly promote other goals, while failing to attain one goal could have a harmful influence on others, whether at home or abroad. Such considerations weighed heavily when Beijing faced the question of whether China should enter the Korean War in early October 1950.

CHINA'S ENTRY INTO THE KOREAN WAR

On October 1, 1950, the PRC celebrated its first anniversary. Newspapers printed pictures of Mao Zedong and Sun Yat-sen (Sun Wen) side-by-side and carried articles and letters extolling the achievements of the "people's victory." In Beijing, Tian'anmen Square was filled all day long with thousands of people; a review of the troops began in the morning, followed by waves of demonstrations and parades in the afternoon, which Mao and other CCP leaders observed from the top of Tian'anmen Gate. Similar events were held all over the country, with tens of thousands of people celebrating the first anniversary of the new government.

Mao, however, might not have been in the mood to celebrate, as he had received two urgent messages that day, one from Kim Il-sung and the other from Joseph Stalin, both soliciting Beijing to enter the war in support of North Korea. The situation in Korea was grave. North Korean armies were on the verge of defeat, and the Kim regime was facing imminent collapse. Worse still, Beijing had received an intelligence report indicating that U.S. forces had crossed the 38th parallel, though, in retrospect, this report was inaccurate.[86] Having received these letters and information, Mao held an urgent meeting that evening with CCP's top leaders, including Zhu De, Liu Shaoqi, and Zhou Enlai, in which he insisted that China needed to enter the war. Perhaps due to the lingering feverish atmosphere of the anniversary, Mao's view prevailed.[87]

In that spirit, Mao stayed up late and wrote two telegrams, one to CCP's Northeast Bureau and the other meant for Stalin. It was already around 2 a.m. on October 2. Mao instructed Northeast Bureau to complete preparations for the Northeast Border Defense Army and put it on standby, and specifically directed its secretary Gao to come to Beijing.[88] To Stalin, he wrote:

> We have decided to send a portion of our troops to Korea under the name of Volunteers in order to assist Korean comrades in fighting the troops of the United States and its running dog Syngman Rhee. If Korea were completely occupied by the Americans, the Koreans' revolutionary potency would be fundamentally destroyed, and the American invaders would be more rampant, and [such a situation would be] very unfavorable to the whole East.[89]

In this long telegram, Mao further explained a possible worst-case scenario, involving domestic concerns and possible repercussions of the war among the most unfavorable elements at home. He wrote:

> We consider that the most unfavorable situation would be that the Chinese forces fail to destroy American troops in large numbers in Korea, thus resulting in a stalemate, while the United States openly enters the war against

China. [That situation] would be destructive to China's economic construction already under way, and would cause discontent toward us among the national bourgeoisie and other sectors of the people (they are afraid of war).[90]

This telegram, however, was not sent to Moscow.[91] That afternoon, a meeting of the Politburo Standing Committee was held at Zhongnanhai, and, to Mao's surprise, virtually everyone expressed skepticism, pessimism, and even opposition to his idea of entering the war. Lin Biao, then commander of the Fourth Field Army in the northeast, expressed reservations as well and refused Mao's request to become the commander of Chinese forces.[92]

Faced with such unexpected opposition among the CCP leadership, instead of sending his draft to Moscow, Mao met with N. V. Roschin, the Soviet ambassador to China, late that night, orally informing him that China was not ready to enter the war. He explained that China's entry would entail "extremely serious consequences"; first of all, U.S. forces would overpower China, since China's military capability was nowhere near that of the United States. Second, China's entry could bring about open warfare between China and the United States, which could lead to the possibility of pulling the Soviet Union into the war. Much worse, such a situation would cause the entire program of building the country to weaken, possibly provoking broad discontent toward the communist regime among the people. Thus, Mao recommended that North Korea take on a guerrilla warfare strategy and, while adding that the final decision had not been made, concluded that it would be better to show patience, refrain from advancing troops, and prepare for action at a time more advantageous to China.[93]

Roschin was surprised by Mao's reply, informing Stalin the following day, October 3, that the Chinese leadership had changed its stance. Stalin, who had been carefully avoiding a direct confrontation with the United States, may not have been particularly surprised. In fact, in the first draft of his reply to Mao, Stalin acknowledged Mao's reservations. To be sure, Stalin continued to urge China to send troops to Korea on the assumption that the United States was not yet fully prepared for a large-scale war and that the Japanese had not yet recovered and would not provide any military support for the United States.[94] Yet, at the end of the draft, Stalin referred to domestic situations in China and accepted Mao's position:

Your reply contains a consideration that is new to me, the one on the domestic situation of China, which, in my opinion, is of decisive significance. You assert that, in case of a new war with regard to Korean events there will be very many malcontents in the country, that there is strong longing for peace in the country. This means that China, with regard to its internal situation, is not ready for a new war. In such a big country as China, the future of the people is decided not by foreign policy factors, but by the factors of domestic situation. Of course, you should know the domestic situation in China better than anybody else. If the internal situation in China does not allow you to risk such steps that might lead to a new war, then one should think in general if one should undertake such a risk. Therefore I fully understand you and your position.[95]

Stalin, however, did not send this draft on the spot. Instead, he revised and sent the revised version on the following night, October 5. In the final draft, Stalin's tone urging China to send troops intensified, with the addition of his own interpretation of China's domestic situation and possible consequences. Instead of simply accepting Mao's explanation that the new war against the United States would cause a rise in discontent, Stalin pointed out that, in this emerging war situation, the bourgeois parties that were part of the Chinese coalition would exploit discontent in the country against the CCP and its leadership.[96]

Mao and the Chinese leadership probably did not need Stalin's analysis. It was already clear. They were keenly aware of and paid attention to such possible ramifications for domestic politics. In fact, Beijing did not wait for Stalin's reply. Before the message was orally conveyed to Mao on the night of October 6, Beijing's leadership had already confirmed China's entry into the war. The decision was made in a series of CCP Central Committee Politburo meetings, held on October 4 and 5 in Zhongnanhai.

DISCUSSION AND WAVERING IN BEIJING

At the first meeting, on October 4, the mood was not conducive to making a decision to go to war. As in the meeting on October 2, virtually everyone other than Mao expressed reservations.[97] From their viewpoint, there were five primary objections. First, wounds from previous wars had not healed and the Chinese economy remained weak. Second, land reform had not advanced and the newly established regime was not yet consolidated. Third, Taiwan and many other areas had yet to be captured, and there were still about a million "rebels" and "counterrevolutionaries." Fourth, China's military arsenal was far behind that of the United States, and China had command of neither the air nor sea. Finally, soldiers and civilians shared a feeling of war-weariness.[98] Scholars have not yet agreed on whether Lin Biao, who was Mao's first choice to be commander of the CPV, attended this meeting on October 4, but some have argued that he did and raised a strong objection, along with Gao Gang and Liu Shaoqi, by pointing out domestic and military concerns.[99]

The tide of discussion changed during the meeting on October 5. Peng Dehuai, who had been asked by Mao to become the commander of Chinese forces that morning, delivered an impassioned speech, asserting that China would need to enter the war for three reasons. First, if U.S. forces stayed in Taiwan and Korea, they could find an excuse to invade China at any time. Second, if Americans occupied the Korean Peninsula, future problems could be more complicated. Third, China could strike a serious blow to "domestic and international reactionary spirits" and "*Qin-Mei* [sympathizing with America] elements" at home.[100]

Peng developed the last portion of this argument several days later in speeches before high-ranking military officials in the northeast, saying that, if China did not actively dispatch troops to support the Korean revolutionary government and its people, domestic and international counterrevolutionaries' spirits could begin to rise, and *Qin-Mei* elements in society would be able to become active.[101] For these reasons, he insisted, attacking earlier would be better than having to do so later. His powerful assertion made a strong impression on other participants in the meeting, eventually persuading the Politburo to back Mao's stance.[102] It is important to note that, although Lin and other Politburo members used domestic and military arguments to oppose China's entry into the war, Peng listed different sets of domestic and military reasoning to advocate it.

The Politburo's decision, however, remained in flux for another two weeks due to Stalin's ambiguous stance. In a ten-hour-long meeting with Zhou Enlai and Lin on October 10–11, Stalin clarified that the Soviet Union would not be able to provide air support for Korea in short order.[103] The Chinese meeting participants felt betrayed by this statement, as they had made their decision on the assumption that the Soviet Union would provide air support for Chinese land forces. This assumption derived from correspondence between Moscow and Beijing in July 1950, in which Moscow recommended that Beijing move Chinese divisions to the Sino-Korean border in case U.S. forces crossed the 38th parallel and vaguely promised that the USSR would "try to provide air cover for these units." Thus, it may have been that, from Moscow's perspective, Stalin's promise of air cover was, from the beginning, limited to Chinese forces on the Sino-Korean border and did not include air support over the Korean Peninsula.

Because of this discrepancy, Zhou and Lin viewed sending troops to Korea as simply impossible. While Stalin continued to counsel them to accept China's entry into the war, he could not convince them. Eventually, Stalin and Zhou agreed that China would not send troops to Korea and that they would give up North Korea, letting Kim Il-sung and his troops evacuate to Northeast China.[104] A telegram under the joint signature of Stalin and Zhou was sent to Beijing on October 11, to which Mao replied on the next day, confirming that he agreed to this arrangement and had already given instructions to halt the plan to enter Korea. Mao also immediately canceled the movements of divisions stationed in Shandong, in the northeast.[105] Receiving Mao's reply, Stalin telegraphed Kim on October 13, informing him that China would not enter the war and recommending guerrilla warfare in Northeast China. Stalin also ordered foreign minister V. M. Molotov, on that day, to assist with Kim's evacuation. The Korean War, thus, might have ended at this point, with the defeat of North Korea.

To Stalin's surprise, however, Beijing ignored Moscow's advice and decided to send troops to Korea, even without Soviet air support. After receiving Stalin's telegram on the afternoon of October 12, Mao, on the one hand, notified Moscow that he had halted the plan to send troops and, on the other, summoned Peng and Gao to Beijing for an emergency meeting on October 13. We still do not have a detailed account of this meeting, but, through discussing the pros and cons of not sending troops, the Beijing leaders eventually reached the conclusion that they had no choice but to enter the war.[106] After the meeting, Mao wrote to Zhou, who was still in Moscow:

> As a result of discussions with Gao Gang, Peng Dehuai, and other comrades on the Politburo, we all recognize that it is still advantageous to send our troops to Korea. . . . The active policy we adopted would be extremely

beneficial to China, Korea, the East, and the world. If we do not send troops, and let the enemy reach the banks of the Yalu River, domestic and international reactionary spirits will rise up, which would be detrimental to all of these aspects. It would be particularly unfavorable to the northeast [of China]; the entire Northeast Border Defense Army would have to be tied up down there, and the electric power plants in south Manchuria would be under the enemy's control.[107]

As shown in this telegram, Beijing had multiple considerations. It was surely concerned with border security but also apprehensive about more vague and far-reaching effects of U.S. forces' victory in Korea, that is, a possible increase in "reactionary sprits" at home and abroad.

The examination of Beijing's reasoning in this series of discussions sheds light on several important historiographical issues. First, it is clear that Beijing did not enter the Korean War because of "intense pressure" from Moscow.[108] To be sure, Stalin had been encouraging Beijing to assist North Korea; in particular, Stalin's message, dispatched at 11 p.m. on October 5, has been well known among scholars because of Stalin's famous declaration that the communist camp should not fear war against the United States, adding, "If a war is inevitable, then let it be waged now."[109] However, the arrival of this message did not affect Beijing's policy-making; it was delivered at 10:30 p.m. on October 6—that is, one day after the CCP Politburo reached its conclusion—and this was the same meeting at which Mao conveyed the Politburo's decision to send troops to Korea.[110]

Furthermore, as the historian Kathryn Weathersby points out, Stalin remained cautious, making every effort to avoid a military confrontation with the United States.[111] In fact, when the controversy over air support loomed and the Chinese leadership refused to send ground troops at the meeting on October 10–11, Stalin gave up on North Korea, instructing Kim Il-song to evacuate to China. It was the Beijing leadership that declined Stalin's suggestion and informed Moscow that China would send troops regardless of the Soviet stance.

By the same token, it is reasonable to say that the U.S. crossing of the 38th parallel was only one of a number of factors that lead Beijing to choose war. If the American actions had been the primary factor, China's decision would have been made afterward, and Beijing would not have wavered in its stance after that. But Beijing's decision was contemplated before the event and then reversed and reconsidered again and again until the moment of Chinese forces' actual crossing of the Yalu River. The prospect of U.S. forces' presence on the other side of the Yalu posed a threat to the security of the border region. Yet what concerned Beijing was more the *meaning* of that presence than the presence itself. In other words, we can see that the notion of "security" included not only the physical threat to the northeast but far-reaching repercussions of impressions by people at home. This way of thinking reappeared when Beijing faced the issue of whether to cross the 38th parallel southward at the end of 1950. From the framing of the issue to the implementation of the plan, Chinese leaders were concerned not just with military strategy but with the politics of impressions.

ADVANCING TO THE SOUTH

In the middle of the piercing cold night of December 31, 1950, the CPV began their third offensive and crossed the 38th parallel southward.[112] This offensive marked a symbolic watershed in the Korean War, signifying China's counterattack and America's retreat. In retrospect, Beijing could have terminated the war at this point by halting CPV forces at the parallel and declaring victory over the United States. Strategically, the CPV had already recovered most of North Korea's lost territory, and China's strong resolution and abilities had been clearly demonstrated to the world. Moreover, Chinese troops were approaching their combat and logistical limits.[113] In fact, Peng Dehuai, the CPV's field commander, had been reluctant to conduct this offensive. He understood the difficulty of the war situation and viewed Chinese forces as already fatigued and in need of rest. Furthermore, he had seen a lack of food and clothing supplies at the front. In his telegram to Beijing on December 8, 1950, Peng actually suggested that Chinese armies halt north of the parallel and conduct another offensive the following spring. Zhou Enlai backed Peng's proposition and similarly suggested to Mao that the offensive be postponed until March.[114]

This was expected by many in China, particularly those who had considered the dispatch of the CPV useless or dangerous and were surprised at the news of CPV's capture of Pyongyang in mid-December. Some businessmen in Fuzhou, for instance, reportedly expressed the hope that the war would end immediately if Chinese armies stopped at the 38th parallel.[115] Foreign observers expressed similar hopes; a major Japanese newspaper, *Asahi Shinbun,* for instance, stated that the PRC would not need to worry about border security because no country in the Western camp had ambitions to invade China.[116] Beijing was not concerned about this, either; Chinese policymakers did not think that the United States would attack the mainland.[117] Why, then, did China take an aggressive course, ignoring opportunities to end the war at this moment?[118]

Although scholars have generally emphasized military and diplomatic considerations, as well as Moscow's pressure on Beijing, it might be hasty to attribute China's decision to cross the parallel solely to these factors. Another possible explanation for Beijing's decision involves domestic concerns regarding the political consequences of stopping CPV armies at the 38th parallel and postponing their attack on U.S. forces. As the historian Chen Jian insightfully points out, Beijing had been concerned about the withering of revolutionary passion among the majority of the population and worried about the fading of the inner dynamics of the revolution.[119] Thus, it is not surprising that Mao turned his attention to domestic popular impressions while dealing with international issues. Such a tendency can be seen in correspondence between Beijing and the battlefront. In a telegram to Peng on December 13, for instance, Mao wrote:

> The United States, Britain, and other countries are requiring our armies to halt to the north of the 38th parallel, in order to reorganize their forces for another offensive. Therefore, our forces must cross the 38th parallel. If we were to arrive and stop to the north of the parallel, it would cause us serious political disadvantages.[120]

Receiving Mao's telegram, four days later, Peng once again replied with a long telegram, warning of difficulties on the battlefield. In particular, he was worried about the rapid growth of "an unrealistic optimism for a quick victory" following the CPV's two major victories. In his view, U.S. forces would not retreat soon, and the war would be "protracted and arduous." Peng wrote, "If our attack does not go smoothly, we will stop fighting right away. Whether we can and will control the 38th parallel will depend on concrete conditions."[121] Receiving Peng's message, Mao responded immediately, trying to explain the symbolic and political meaning of the third offensive to cross the parallel. He wrote:

Your assessment of the enemy's situation is correct. We must be prepared for a protracted war. Now the United States and Britain are taking advantage of the old impression of the 38th parallel in the people's minds for their political propaganda in order to force us to accept a cease-fire. Therefore, our forces must cross the parallel now and rest afterward.[122]

Mao, thus, tried to explain the political impact of crossing the parallel in terms of public impressions. In another telegram, Mao wrote that, after crossing the parallel, the CPV could return and rest north of it.[123] Peng accepted Mao's instructions but remained ambivalent, complaining mildly:

In the mobilization for this offensive we have stressed the political significance of the crossing of the 38th parallel (it is actually not that important politically). It will be more difficult for us to explain to our troops why we seized the 38th parallel and gave it up afterward. Once [it is] occupied, we may as well retain it if there are no other particular concerns involved.[124]

The next day, December 29, Mao again sent a telegram to Peng, attempting to clarify the political purpose and symbolic meaning of the third offensive in order to reassure a seemingly dissatisfied field commander:

The so-called 38th parallel is an old impression in the people's minds and will no longer exist after this campaign. It therefore does not matter whether our troops rest and reorganize south or north of the 38th parallel. [However], if we do not launch this offensive, and if our forces spend the entire winter resting and reorganizing, it will arouse the capitalist countries to speculate a great deal [on our intentions] and cause the democratic nations to disdain us; should we gain another victory in early January . . . , we will greatly impress the democratic front and the people of the capitalist countries, thereby striking a new blow at the imperialists and enhancing pessimism among them.[125]

In a purely military sense, Mao's directions to Peng might have been nonsense, because he was suggesting that, although he had ordered the crossing of the 38th parallel, it would not matter whether the CPV retained it after the campaign. From a military commander's perspective, an offensive would not be necessary if the parallel were strategically unimportant.

Nevertheless, Mao's concerns were not simply about military tactics. Rather, his focus was on *political impressions*. More specifically, he was contemplating the campaign's symbolic impact—a victory for communist

China and a defeat for "American imperialism"—in the minds of people at home and abroad.[126] Mao seemed to view the crossing of the parallel as not only a military strategy but a symbolic political—in a sense, public relations—victory. For Beijing, halting the Chinese armies at the parallel would have meant concession to the enemy, the image of which would create, in Mao's words, a "serious political disadvantage," possibly hindering the progress of China's land reform, economic reconstruction, and anti-counterrevolutionary programs, as well as possibly causing actual withering of popular support for the newly established government.

In 1950, the PRC was less than a year old, had yet to build a strong foundation, and faced several critical issues. The Chinese economy had to be reconstructed along communist lines. Land reform, which had only begun nationwide that summer, had already produced serious problems. The Anti-Rightist movement was about to be launched. The civil war had finally come to an end in southern and western China only in the spring of 1950, yet forces of resistance and counterrevolution were still active all over the country. In addition, Tibet and Taiwan were not under CCP control. Last but not least, although revolutionary enthusiasm was strong among some portions of the population, a significant portion remained doubtful, if not overtly hostile, of the CCP's legitimacy.

Although such domestic problems were the primary reasons for the CCP leaders' reluctance to enter into large-scale warfare, they also weighed heavily on their decision to enter the war. This is because the image of "America" had been symbolically connected with the "enemy" in *all* communist programs at home since the late 1940s, including reconstruction of the economy, land reform, the Anti-Rightist movement, suppression of various counterrevolutionaries, and, most of all, continuation of the civil war. Therefore, America's intervention in Korea in the summer of 1950 created a dilemma: entering into the war might be a great burden for China, slowing CCP reconstruction programs, but, at the same time, all of those programs might be damaged, if not destroyed, if Beijing did not engage in an aggressive policy in the war.

Viewed in this way, Beijing's aggressive posture does not seem like a mere reflection of Cold War strategy by Moscow or simply Beijing's concern over border security. If any of these were the case, the decision could have been made much earlier, with little hesitation, and would not have fluctuated after the decision was made. Yet, as we have seen, Beijing oscillated back and forth, tilted by changes in circumstances. What Beijing sought in this sense was not merely border security but holding on to favorable popular impressions and domestic social equilibrium at home by maintaining border security. In a sense, the Korean War was a test case for the CCP's legitimacy and identity in the turbulent, uncertain period following the establishment of the new regime. It would be reasonable to say that Beijing's decision was built on the leadership's constant observation of social attitudes, its fear of withering revolutionary support at home, and its practical needs concerning the consolidation of CCP legitimacy, given unpredictable and precarious domestic situations. In this way, Beijing's decisions were not isolated from domestic matrices, popular political culture, and the daily lives of ordinary people, and thus can be seen as part of a massive public relations campaign meant to solidify the identity of the newly established government in minds of millions of people at home and abroad.

In exploring the ways in which Washington and Beijing contemplated and formulated policies about the Korean War in the fall of 1950, what is striking is the emergence of a situation that can be called the encroachment of the social into the sphere of high politics. Here, the term "emergence" might be misleading, because this historical tendency had been developing throughout the first half of the twentieth century. The point here, however, is not to discuss the origins of such a situation but to suggest that it became an unmistakable and unavoidable precondition by the time of the mid-twentieth century. Looking back, nineteenth-century diplomats and statesmen might have been able to dismiss various social actors and factors because they were not the basis of government legitimacy. However, because of the experiences of total war in many parts of the world, it became increasingly difficult, if not impossible, to conduct politics without considering the desires of a nation's population. Simply put, the nature of politics had changed. To be more precise, in the contemporary era, it was not necessarily the participation of citizens but the satisfaction of the population that became a primary factor in government legitimacy.

In such a society, political leaders pay significant attention to the currents of popular attitudes and often change stances, rather than stubbornly sticking to their own political philosophies. In other words, contemporary "leaders" have to be skillful "readers" of their societies and popular attitudes.

Therefore, we must look carefully into how they adapt, in addition to what they believe. We need to examine not just policymakers' personal traits and beliefs but also society, culture, values, norms, and people's reactions, with which they regularly have contact. This is because their conduct and decisions are shaped through interactive, spontaneous communications with all of these.

In other words, however trivial they might appear—from a Connecticut high-school student's fear of World War III or a New Jersey housewife's hoarding, to a Beijing police officer's purchase of a pedicab or Shanghai students' and workers' conduct in writing letters of enlistment—tiny everyday occurrences, even in remote corners of the world, were not irrelevant to the making of the Cold War world. It was such small but numerous "fights" on the ground that constituted social and political contexts in each region, contributing to the configuration of locally specific realities that shaped the directions of politics in each location. In this way, the Cold War was not necessarily a product created through policymakers' conduct and misconduct; numerous nameless people were, more or less, also participants in the making of such a world.

When the tendency toward the encroachment of the social into the sphere of politics became unavoidable, another tendency grew even more conspicuous: the intervention of state politics into society and the private sphere. By now, the topic has been relatively well researched, and it was not a particularly new phenomenon in the mid-twentieth century. The point, however, is not so much its origins as its solidification by the middle of the century. This was the kind of politics that characterized the materialization of the Cold War and that can be observed not only in China but in the United States as well as other parts of the world. In Chapters 5 and 6, we will explore such politics of "truth-making," carried out from both above and below, in the fall of 1950 and early 1951.

CHAPTER FIVE

The Truth-Making Campaign

IN THE FALL of 1950, Jeanne Cole, a housewife living in Los Angeles, found that something strange was going on with her eldest son. He normally liked to go to school, but, recently, he seemed to be reluctant to leave home in the morning. Jeanne, thus, questioned him as to what was wrong. The little boy said, "Well, Mom, I'm not afraid at home, and I'm not afraid at school, but what if the bomb drops at my feet when I'm on my way there?" Realizing that his primary school had just begun atom bomb drills, Jeanne immediately joined a regular meeting of the Los Angeles City School Board of Education and made an appeal to stop practicing air drills at school: "Now they are learning to fear [the] sky over their head. Now they are learning to cry in the night."[1]

She was not alone in expressing such a protest about atom bomb drills at school; a group of mothers in the same district similarly disapproved, seeing the practice as senseless, futile, and excessive, causing the children great mental and physical harm.[2] A similar concern was expressed by Jack Moore, the father of a five-and-half-year-old boy, in Tujunga, Florida:

My son attends primary at the Pinewood School in Tujunga. He has been worried about war since the teachers have been giving atom bomb drills. It has been quite a job to convince him he is in no imminent danger of destruction each day he goes to school. Every time I get him quieted, along comes another drill; and I have it to do all over again.[3]

In his view, the twice-weekly drills at schools were not just senseless but deleterious, as they would damage his son's nervous system as well as impress young minds with the inevitability of war and acceptance of war as a way of life.[4]

Such ripples of protest came to the surface with the consolidation of a particular kind of "consensus" and "reality." The fact that such protests were conspicuous, however, does not mean that they represented the majority; rather, they stood out because they were relatively rare. In other words, many others silently cooperated with such air drills, as well as various mobilization and civil defense programs, whether enthusiastically or half-heartedly. In fact, the Los Angeles City Board of Education could reject Jeanne's protests even without much explanation.[5] Fear was real and convincing enough to drive many to embrace such practices. But how did the "truth" behind this fear attain such verisimilitude, and who created it?

Another interesting point is that quite a few people did not really change their opinions, at least at the early stages and, instead, heightened their criticism, as in the cases of Jeanne and Jack, despite the prevalence of a particular version of reality and despite its penetration through schools, films, and even fiction, as well as a wide range of state propaganda and mobilization programs. This raises questions about the real effectiveness of such state propaganda programs and media influence. Were they really effective? Thanks to a rich literature on the subject, we have relatively detailed accounts of the roles of official programs and cultural productions in shaping reality and mobilizing people.[6] Less well understood, however, are the roles of society and, more precisely, of ordinary people. After all, we cannot evaluate the effectiveness of propaganda and mobilization programs without looking at its recipients—the people. What kind of power relations were observed between state and society and between elite policymakers and ordinary people in the making of truth?

"WORLD WAR III IS HERE NOW"

"I've had conference after conference on the jittery situation facing the country," wrote President Truman in his journal on December 9, 1950. "I've worked for peace for five years and six months, and it looks like World War III is here. I hope not—but we must meet whatever comes and we will."[7] Like many Americans, the president had just learned that the Pyongyang region had fallen into the enemy's hands and that U.S. forces were outnumbered in Korea. A cable from General Douglas MacArthur had informed him that the number of Chinese soldiers was estimated at 300,000, while that of U.S. troops was merely 135,000.[8] Following news of China's entry into the Korean War, what was widespread in American society in December 1950 were fears and rumors of World War III—particularly of already losing it.[9]

Sharing Truman's viewpoint, one U.S. military official wrote to a friend in mid-December: "We must recognize publicly that World War III is here *now*. We must take all appropriate action to win; universal war service, industrial mobilization, the build-up of not only American forces but also the forces of Nationalist China, of Japan, of Free Korea, of Germany, and Franco's Spain."[10] MacArthur, who might have already shared such a view of World War III as a reality, urged Washington to take far more aggressive action, advocating a blockade of the Chinese coast, an attack on China's industrial capacity to wage war, and the use of Chiang Kai-shek's armies in the war in Korea and, possibly, in mainland China.[11]

While not accepting MacArthur's demands, President Truman made a declaration of national emergency by radio on December 15, with a similar sense of crisis. "I am talking to you tonight about what our country is up against, and what we are going to do about it. Our homes, our Nation, all the things we believe in, are in great danger. This danger has been created by the rulers of the Soviet Union," said the president, briefly summarizing the chronology of recent events by pointing out that, in June, the communists had commenced open warfare in Korea and, in November, had thrown their Chinese armies into the battle, showing, according to Truman, that they were willing to push the world to the brink of general war. "This is the real meaning of the events that have been taking place in Korea. This is why we are in such grave danger," asserted the president.[12]

In this speech, the president's use of "they"—referring to the communists and the "rulers of the Soviet Union"—stands out. In using "they," he
connected different events in various places in the world as a single-thread
narrative of a communist attack conducted under the direction of Moscow.
It was this third-person pronoun, suggesting an unspecified large number
of people, that made it possible to view different events as part of a larger
imaginary story of the Cold War. This grand narrative, of course, was not
Truman's creation; it was simply a repetition of a familiar narrative. Yet, in
the development of the so-called Cold War, it was not particular *origins* that
generated and led to the formation of such a world. Rather, what was more
important was *repetitions* that consolidated the logic and, eventually, the
world of the Cold War, while silencing and marginalizing various opposition viewpoints.

In this version of "reality," Moscow's intentions and abilities were often
overestimated; the Kremlin was believed to be in control of China and North
Korea, as well as all communists and "pinks" in American society. Sharing
this widespread perspective, the head of a Christian organization in California sent a long letter to his senator, William Knowland, asserting that North
Korea's attack was due to the machinations of Stalin, that the CCP was also
without a doubt under the control of Moscow, and that the Kremlin was
hoping to break up American society via networks of communist agents living in the United States. He concluded: "Russia plans a controlled, deliberate provocation of America, chopping at us with small but steady internal
blows when possible, throwing blocks at us with her satellites, all the time
readying her forces for that day when it may be necessary to strike."[13]

Like this letter, great speculation concerning the Kremlin's intentions circulated widely, in contrast to a relatively small amount of conjecture about
Beijing's intentions. For many, Beijing's intentions did not really matter;
what counted were those of the Kremlin. Some thought that the Soviet aim
was the occupation of Japan, and others that the entire campaign in Korea
and East Asia was a large-scale feint operation to distract attention from
Europe; the ultimate design, this thesis maintained, must be the occupation of Western Europe.[14]

Based on such a perceived reality of World War III, in the winter of 1950
rumors of war and fear of atomic attacks escalated. According to a nationwide opinion poll, an overwhelming majority—more than 90 percent—
agreed that everyone should be required to wear an identification tag in case

of a bomb attack.[15] (In fact, all children in New York State had to wear identification tags). The increase in such imagining of enemy atom bomb attacks
led some to embrace extremism. "Please pour Atom-bombs on Russia before
they do it to us some bright Holiday Morning! . . . Please mobirize [sic] completely!" a man from Plainfield, New Jersey, pleaded with the president.[16] In a
similar tone, a man from Santa Barbara, California, wrote to his senator, asking him to help give the green light to MacArthur to carry out an atom bomb
attack on Northeast China.[17] These opinions were, to be sure, from some of
the most extreme hardliners, but they were not in the minority.

Keenly aware of such fear of World War III, many political figures and
government officials continuously adjusted their posture and took aggressive stances. At a meeting between the president and several members of
Congress, Colorado Republican Senator Eugene Donald Millikin expressed
his irritation in a similar tone: "Nobody abroad would be scared by anything we did unless we had 'massive' strength. Just issuing a declaration [of
national emergency] wouldn't scare anybody abroad unless we had an army
to go along with it." Pounding the table with his fist, the senator advocated,
"We ought to make ourselves as strong as possible as fast as possible."[18]
Keeping step, Charles Eaton, Republican Representative from New Jersey
and chairman of the House Foreign Affairs Committee, escalated this critique, saying: "There [is] only one thing to do: to strip off our peace clothes
and to show our muscle to the world. This [will] not slow down the Russians because they are determined to destroy us but it [will] make it clear to
the rest of the world that we [are] determined to stop them and we are going
to stop them."[19]

Such a hawkish tone was not limited to Republicans. Democratic Senator from Maryland Millard Tydings, who had recently lost his bid for
re-election, primarily because he was labeled as too soft on communism,
similarly adopted the toughest attitude: "The United States is in deadly peril.
The question now is whether we can survive. . . . The war in Korea has
shown us how weak we are, and how strong the enemy is. The war is Korea
has shown us how well-equipped communist troops are and how well they
can fight. We still have some time left, but damn little."[20] His grave tone
was unmistakable.

Quite a few people, of course, did not agree with these popular versions
of "common sense." Fred Stover, president of the Iowa Farmers Union, for
instance, observed that anti-communist hysteria in the United States was

becoming ridiculous, sarcastically noting: "Americans are trying so hard nowadays to be different from Russia and communists in every way that it shouldn't surprise us if a lot of Americans develop such a case of neurosis that they will become nudists simply because they found out that communists wear clothes."[21] Like Stover, foreign observers who did not share in this "reality" and "common sense" grew concerned about aggressive attitudes in the United States. The anti-communist socialist Norman Thomas, for instance, traveled to India, reporting that he read and heard considerable criticism of American "war hysteria" and encountered much fear of the United States as a "war monger."[22] Observing the hardening of popular attitudes and politicians' tones in the United States, by December 1950, even America's allies were becoming uneasy. U.S. Ambassador to France David Bruce, for example, reported that there was a feeling among French officials that "some brakes should be put on the 'impetuous' leadership of the U.S."[23]

Sparks of this kind flew as British prime minister Clement Attlee hurriedly visited the White House in early December 1950. Because he came immediately following Truman's "statement" about the possible use of the atomic bomb in Korea, the media focused sensationally on that issue.[24] Yet, in the more than nine hours of six meetings between Truman and Attlee over five days, the most controversial and recurrent issue involved how to evaluate China's actions.[25] The real focus was on whether Chinese communists were subservient "satellites" and whether China's intervention was a part of "Moscow's game"—a part of the Cold War. Attlee pointed out, "The Chinese don't owe [the USSR] very much. . . . There is a strong mixture of Chinese nationalism in their communist attitude." Alluding to Marshal Tito of Yugoslavia, the British prime minister concluded, "They may wear the Red flag with a difference."[26] Urging Truman to treat China as a Chinese issue and Korea as a Korean issue, instead of viewing both as parts of the Kremlin's scheme, Attlee opposed the spread of war against mainland China and insisted on the recognition of the PRC, suggesting that it be given a seat at the United Nations.[27]

For Acheson and Truman, however, such a suggestion was out of the question. "[I am] far less optimistic about China," said Secretary of State Dean Acheson, "Chinese Communists were servient [sic] to Moscow. All they do is based on the Moscow pattern, and they are better pupils even than the Eastern European satellites."[28] In this comment, Acheson's usage of the term "pupil" in characterizing China in comparison to Eastern European countries is suggestive. Like MacArthur, who in 1951 described Japan as a "boy of 12," compared to the Germans and Anglo-Saxons, who were "45 years of age," Acheson compared Chinese and Eastern European communist countries; the former, in his mind, was a better "pupil"—a metaphor that fit well with conventional prejudicial views of the Chinese as more passive, submissive, and dependent than Europeans.[29]

Acheson's observation was not surprising in view of the American popular version of perceived reality. For many Americans, it was "decadent" Europeans who continued to "close their eyes to the danger [rather] than squarely face it."[30] The president of a trading company in Detroit, Michigan, opposed Attlee's suggestion in his letter to the White House, saying:

> We all know that Russia is behind the moves in Red China. We know that Russia knows we are not prepared. . . . [N]ow is the time to get tough. Now is the time to tell Stalin that, if he doesn't see that Red China gets out of Korea at once, we will use the [atom] bomb, not only on Chinese concentrations but on the Kremlin as well. . . . I believe if we were to drop a couple of [atom] bombs on the Kremlin and pour it on them we might start a revolution within.[31]

A San Francisco man similarly insisted, "Appeasement is a backward step. It did not work with Hitler; it will not work with Stalin. Americans will fight and fight alone if necessary."[32] A New Yorker asserted: "The people seem to understand better than the diplomats that there is no difference between the Russian and Chinese brands of communism."[33] What is important about these expressions of displeasure about Attlee's attempt to convince Truman is not their rarity but their prevalence in American society. An editorial in the *Pittsburgh Press* concluded: "To assume that the American people will accept what appears to be Britain's attitude toward those Red aggressors is a fantastic absurdity."[34] It was a "fantastic absurdity" because the danger appeared to be so clear and present for many Americans. Fighting communism at home and abroad seemed to be of vital importance in protecting Americans.[35] It was such widespread fear of World War III and the fantasy of the Cold War that impelled many Americans to support and even initiate various kinds of mobilization and civil defense programs, thus participating in the politics of truth-making on their own.

PEOPLE'S PARTICIPATION IN MAKING TRUTH

"Why do we fight in such a distant place?" asked the narrator of a film titled *Why Korea?*, produced by Twentieth Century–Fox in December 1950. Showing unfamiliar images of rice paddies and mountains, the narrator asked again, "Why do we fight in Korea, a faraway place we barely know? Why?" Instead of answering this question immediately, however, the film provided a "history" of the recent past, stringing together kaleidoscopic images of the prewar and postwar periods—Japan's invasion of China after the Manchurian Incident, Adolf Hitler's and Benito Mussolini's marches in Europe, parades at the Kremlin, communist expansion in Eastern Europe, as well as East and Southeast Asia, followed by heroic images of the Berlin Airlift. Describing the outbreak of the Korean War as part of Moscow's worldwide schemes, the film warned that there would be "no more geographical boundaries." Showing pictures of Paris, London, New York City, Washington, DC, Chicago, San Francisco, and, finally, Seoul, it concluded: "Today this is Korea, but Korea is an example. We are fighting not for geographical borders but for a way of life. If we don't fight there, we will fight here. We have no other choice."[36] This film was screened in hundreds of theaters nationwide, from New York City and San Francisco to Des Moines, Iowa, and Dallas, Texas, and eventually won the Academy Award for best documentary in 1951.

Many viewers might have recalled Frank Capra's *Prelude to War,* a masterpiece of wartime propaganda, released during World War II, in May 1942, which, similarly, won the Academy Award that year. There were, however, a couple of important differences. First, *Why Korea?* was designed and produced at the initiative of a private corporation, Twentieth Century–Fox, in contrast to Capra's *Prelude to War,* produced, commissioned, and supported by General George Marshall and the then–War Department. Second, unlike Capra's film, *Why Korea?* produced an undeniable controversy. Although many theaters ran the film, and some did so enthusiastically, quite a few theater owners refused, calling it a "war mongering film."[37] The Independent Theatre Owners of Ohio, for instance, protested to the White House, which had authorized and urged theater owners to show the film, insisting that the government make another film titled "Why We Should Get Out of Korea."[38] The existence of such controversy reveals the contested nature of the "reality" of the Cold War, as well as the malleability of "reality" and "truth." In fact, while largely accepted at that time, the "truth" that *Why Korea?* provided contained certain preconceptions held by American society, rather than the actuality of Korea and East Asia. In other words, such a "reality" did not exist out there and, thus, had to be boldly addressed, widely shared, and unquestioningly supported to maintain its prestigious status as "reality." Because such a consensus regarding "truth" did not exist, it had to be created and sustained, initiating waves of truth-making campaigns in American society.

Such truth-making programs were nothing new in 1950. Many similar programs had already been developed as wartime mobilization campaigns during the administration of Franklin D. Roosevelt. Most, however, were terminated in the early postwar period due to government budget cutting. The development of the Korean War re-energized these programs. Immediately following the outbreak of the Korean War, the "Campaign of Truth," aimed at rolling back Soviet versions of "truth," obtained financial and institutional support from Congress.[39] At the end of 1950, President Truman issued an executive order to establish the Federal Civil Defense Administration within the Office for Emergency Management, which was quickly elevated to an independent government agency in the Executive Branch.[40]

As several historians have examined in detail, this agency played an active role in the years that followed in initiating various propaganda and mobilization campaigns through publishing numerous pamphlets and leaflets, broadcasting various programs, holding a variety of exhibits, and even helping to establish a college, National Civil Defense College, in Olney, Maryland, which aimed to instruct citizens in various rescue techniques as part of the nation's civil defense effort.[41] Among the largest and best-known campaigns were "Operation Skywatch" and "Alert America," in which, according to a speech by Truman, 2 million Americans voluntarily participated.[42] Throughout these campaigns, civil defense officials continuously warned that the Soviet Union had atom bombs and airplanes that could drop those bombs on American cities, stressing that every city, factory, office, and home must be prepared and organized for civil defense.[43] Even in the middle of the prairies in Kansas, the need for civil defense was advocated: "There is no one in Kansas who will not be affected by an enemy attack on any part of Kansas," warned a local civil defense bulletin.[44]

Many Americans did not really need such warnings from officials. Less well known than the relatively detailed accounts of official propaganda and civil defense programs is the sort of bottom-up formation of such programs through the active participation, or even initiative, of ordinary people. In the fall of 1950, many had already gone ahead with engaging in various kinds of social mobilization and civil defense efforts out of their own motivations and for their own purposes. A superintendent of the Los Angeles City Board of Education, Alexander Stoddard, for instance, wrote to Secretary of Defense George Marshall, proposing that the school system's facilities be used for the training of civilians and workers for defense programs. He believed that such projects, once begun from his district, would be duplicated in many other school systems throughout the country. Unfortunately for him, Marshall turned down the offer on the grounds that such training had to be done under the jurisdiction of the Labor Department.[45] Although the proposal was unsuccessful, what is interesting here is that it came from a private individual, not from government officials.

Such instances were, indeed, common. In a similar way, a Houston housewife wrote a letter to Marshall to report the lack of mobilization efforts in her neighborhood, telling him that she was ready to find a housewife's place in the atom bomb defense plan and asking what she could do for this purpose.[46] Not surprisingly, some found job and business opportunities in civil defense programs; a 33-year-old firefighter in Huntington Park, California, sent his résumé to a newly appointed head of civil defense programs in the hope of becoming an instructor for civil defense training, and a New York car dealer developed an innovative ambulance trailer-truck for the use of civil defense agencies, which, according to his proposal, could be used as a small auditorium or lecture room in peacetime, as well as an emergency and operating room in wartime.[47]

Still others, particularly those with military experience, emphasized the need for and importance of voluntary civil defense programs. A veteran living in a rural community, 100 miles north of New York City, for instance, wrote the White House:

> There are too many men in this land with excellent military experience who are forced to stand on the side-lines of war, helpless to assist because of age, infirmities and lack of up-to-the-minute training. . . . They all want to be identified as being active in the defense of their country, but not on an "air raid

warden" basis. . . . I know that our defense potential can be greatly increased
if these veterans are asked to serve and if they are given recognition of a sort
for a specialized type of defense work.[48]

This man's letter attracted an army official's attention. Responding to the
official's request for more details, the man enthusiastically introduced his
own plan for organizing and defending his community, envisioning active
roles for "citizen soldiers," who would work eight hours per day at their
regular civilian jobs and serve twelve hours at night for their country—
including four hours on active duty for air interceptor defense, and eight
hours on reserve at a local headquarters—which would enable citizens, the
man suggested, to carry on both civilian and military duties.[49]

Unfortunately for this man, and, perhaps, fortunately for the rest of his
community's citizens, neither the president nor the Army adopted his demanding scheme. Nevertheless, the basic idea that he proposed was not far
out of step with the core ethos of civil defense ideology: individuals voluntarily serving the state, as epitomized in a pamphlet drawing, illustrating
society as a pyramid structure, composed of individuals, families, neighborhoods, communities, cities, states, and, finally, the federal government,
in that specific order. The aforementioned veteran's proposal simply took this
idea to an extreme, as if creating a militarized society.

Most, if not all, the proposals that ordinary citizens made were simply
turned down. Indeed, having received hundreds of such offers and proposals, local and national officials did not necessarily respond as quickly as the
public demanded. As the historian Guy Oaks properly points out, behind
closed doors, quite a few authorities were skeptical of the practical useful-
ness of civil defense programs at the time of an actual atom bomb attack; in
public, however, they optimistically maintained the need for such programs.
The reason to continue such mostly useless practices was, as Richard Nixon
later pointed out, "because the country demands it."[50] In this way, the illusions and irritations concerning the "reality" of the Cold War emerged and
grew in a bottom-up manner.

After all, it was numerous, nameless citizens who developed the Cold War
fantasy and demanded countermeasures. "I am disgusted with the whole situation insofar as it regards both city of Los Angeles nor county of Los Angeles officials and administrations," angrily wrote a man in Los Angeles after
spending practically all of his time in the summer of 1950 trying to set up and

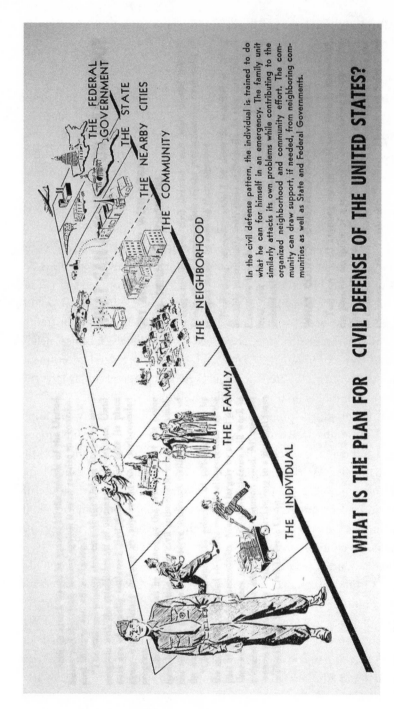

In the civil defense pattern, the individual is trained to do what he can for himself in an emergency. The family unit similarly attacks its own problems while contributing to the organized neighborhood and community effort. The community can draw support, if needed, from neighboring communities as well as State and Federal Governments.

THE FEDERAL GOVERNMENT

THE STATE

THE NEARBY CITIES

THE COMMUNITY

THE NEIGHBORHOOD

THE FAMILY

THE INDIVIDUAL

WHAT IS THE PLAN FOR CIVIL DEFENSE OF THE UNITED STATES?

Boy Scouts of America, "Civil Defense: A Guide for Council and District Planning." (Harry S. Truman Library, Truman Papers, OF1591, Box 1842. Reprinted with permission, Boy Scouts of America.)

mobilize a coordinated and effective civilian defense organization. The man believed that the authorities were too slow and lazy, replying with stock answers, such as: "We have no need for volunteers"; "You people out there will have to be on your own"; "We're waiting for instruction from higher levels"; "We have our plan on paper; we'll make some announcements later;" and so on. Denouncing the authorities' idleness, he claimed that the public should be gravely concerned that local authorities had not put into operation any efficient civilian defense organization, asserting: "Our need for civilian defense right now is far greater than it was at any time during World War II."[51]

In short, the evolution of a variety of mobilization and civil defense programs during the Korean War was not necessarily the end result of official propaganda or policy. Rather, numerous everyday people mobilized themselves, often taking the initiative and urging local officials and policymakers to take on much more rigorous stances, thus contributing to the production of a particular version of "truth."

PREJUDICE MASQUERADING AS FACTS

Observing such zealous popular support for and participation in civil defense and propaganda programs, one would notice an interesting characteristic: the absence of mention of the Chinese and Korean people. This was also true of the aforementioned film, *Why Korea?* Capra's masterpieces of propaganda, such as *Prelude to War* and *Know Your Enemy,* depicted the Japanese and the Nazis as primary enemies from beginning to end, however clichéd and stereotypical these depictions were. On the contrary, *Why Korea?* barely showed Koreans at all, whether from the north or south, nor did the Chinese appear. Except for a few shots of refugees, the Korean people were almost completely absent.

This was because the outbreak of the Korean War and the Chinese intervention were assumed to be merely results of the Kremlin's worldwide scheme, signs of the beginning of World War III, which, for many, supposedly provided concrete "evidence" of the validity of the Cold War. Nonetheless, the cornerstone of such fear of and prospects for World War III was the assumption that the Chinese and North Koreans were acting in service of Moscow's global scheme. After all, if North Korean and Chinese actions were viewed as deriving from their own decisions, the logic of World War III could not have been maintained. The questions that this raises are: Why did so many people in American society find the Chinese and Koreans so devoid of agency? What was the basis for that understanding of the world?

It is worthwhile to recall how Chinese intervention was perceived at the outset. General Douglas MacArthur described the situation as he perceived it on December 3, 1950, as follows: "We are in an entirely new war against an entirely new power of great military strength and under entirely new conditions."[52] Receiving disturbing news from Tokyo, President Truman lamented: "Unfortunately for us, the Chinese Communists had entered Korea without any provocation and they had come in for the purpose of driving out General MacArthur's forces."[53] By mid-December, the news of China's entry had been widely acknowledged at home, inciting rampant criticism of the Truman administration's failure to predict China's decision.[54] Thus, it was understandable for MacArthur and Truman to emphasize the newness and abruptness of the situation, in view of their misjudgment in promising the public that China would not attack and that the war would be over by Christmas.

However, the situation was not really as "new" as MacArthur asserted nor was China's intervention "without any provocation" as Truman alleged. Beijing had issued warnings repeatedly.[55] Intelligence reports warning of China's moves had arrived in Tokyo and Washington.[56] The British and French governments had conveyed their concerns to the Truman administration as well.[57] These warnings, however, had not been taken seriously. Chinese premier Zhou Enlai's warning was simply seen as a bluff and ignored, as was Indian prime minister Jawaharlal Nehru's persistent admonition.[58] Intelligence reports calling for caution were delivered but dismissed as containing "no firm evidence."[59] Much worse, MacArthur's subordinates often altered contents of intelligence information, because the general did not like to hear reports that contradicted his conviction that China would never intervene.[60] A self-appointed authority on "Oriental psychology," MacArthur *knew* that Asians were "obedient, dutiful, child-like, and quick to follow resolute leadership."[61] Because he held such preconceptions about "Asians," the general remained reluctant to publicly accept China's full entry as late as December 1950, showing a clear contrast to Chiang Kai-shek, who wrote in his diaries as early as October that China's full intervention was "without a doubt."[62] Therefore, it was not so much lack of information as common prejudice concerning "China" and "Asians" that hindered U.S. policymakers in Tokyo and Washington in connecting pieces of information that would have predicted China's actions.

The pattern that appeared in the fall of 1950 was strikingly similar to the one observed during the Pacific War in the early 1940s. As the historian John Dower discusses, before World War II Japan was not considered a military threat. Many Americans *knew* that the Japanese could not shoot, sail, or fly because it was believed and "scientifically" proven that they had poor vision. Likewise, the high performance of Japan's fighter plane—the Zero—was reported before Pearl Harbor but simply ignored. In Dower's words, "prejudice masqueraded as facts."[63] Then, at the time of Japan's attack on Pearl Harbor and the Philippines, MacArthur at first refused to believe that the Japanese were responsible, insisting that there must have been "white mercenaries." Such a reaction was not MacArthur's alone. During the war, a common rumor maintained that "German experts are directing the Jap artillery."[64]

Likewise, in 1950, as Harold Isaacs's classic study describes, the Chinese had been widely thought to be "hopelessly backward and incapable of marshaling military power"—a nineteenth-century idea that had been rampant in the United States.[65] Isaacs's study found that typical terms associated with the "Chinese" were: "inert," "submissive," "servile," "slow," "illiterate," "superstitious," "ignorant," and so on.[66] One publisher in the Midwest told an interviewer: "I never thought of the Chinese as belligerent. I never thought we would be risking war with them. A peasant country! It would have been inconceivable to me even five or ten years ago that we could have a war with China."[67]

Such an attitude was not so much a result of individual traits as of social construction. In fact, leading officials, such as Dean Acheson, George F. Kennan, and the president, shared similar views. As the historian Thomas Borstelmann observes, Kennan tended to lump the peoples of Africa, Asia, the Middle East, and Latin America together as impulsive, fanatical, ignorant, lazy, unhappy, and prone to mental disorders and other biological deficiencies—a surprisingly mediocre preconception for the peerlessly intelligent diplomat to hold.[68] The feelings of surprise that many Americans experienced when facing China's entry into the Korean War did not truly result from its coming from out of the blue; it simply did not fit well with existing dominant preconceptions about the Chinese.

After China's intervention became undeniable, conventional images of China had to be modified. But this modification did not occur as a reconsideration or correction of conventional images of China and the Chinese, but merely as extension and adjustment of existing preconceptions: China as a tool of the Soviet Union. Indeed, Beijing was rarely seen as a decision-maker; it was widely supposed that the attack was made under orders and with support from Moscow. One of Isaacs's interviewees, who later became a high-ranking official in the administration of President Dwight Eisenhower recollected:

> I was brought up to think [that] the Chinese couldn't handle a machine. Now, suddenly, the Chinese are flying jets! The American idea was that Asiatics are nonmechanical, except the Japanese, and the Japanese were freaks, not really mechanical, just copied what others did. In practically everything one ever read . . . the Asiatic is always plowing with his fingernails and the European is handling the machine. Now the Chinese is flying jets! Disturbing, especially since you have several hundred million of them teamed up with the USSR. I always thought the Yellow Peril business is nonsense. . . . Now I can visualize that Asiatics teamed up with the Slavs could indeed conquer the world![69]

In a similar tone, *Life* asserted, "China's Red Army, a guerrilla rabble 20 years ago, had been built into a menacingly Russianized fighting force."[70] An underlying belief was that the Chinese could not have done so by themselves. They were merely "rabble" who could not fly jets by themselves.

To make sense of this dramatic change, a new common narrative, instead of correcting prejudice, claimed that there must have been significant support or a push from a foreign power—the Soviet Unions.[71] This modified "common sense" maintained that the Kremlin forced and supported China in entering Korea on behalf of the Soviet Union—an idea that matched perfectly with existing knowledge in the United States of the global Cold War, however misleading it was.

One illustrative example of this perspective is a fake "translation" of the Sino-Soviet Treaty of Friendship and Alliance and an image of it that began circulating in the summer of 1950. Although different versions existed, such a "translation" typically maintained that China had permitted Soviet troops to be stationed in China; that Beijing had agreed to place the PLA under direct Soviet command, to be turned into an international communist army; that China had also agreed to provide 10 million laborers to the

"The Sino-Soviet Friendship: This Is Mao Zedong's Method to Fawn On." (Center for the Study of the Korean War, Paul Wolfgeher Special Collection, SP. 3.3.)

USSR, and so on.[72] None of this was true.[73] These items reflected, more than anything else, conventional American views of China as a colonized country, a tool of the Soviet Union, and a place with a large number of submissive manual workers.

AN IMAGE OF "CAPTIVE MILLIONS"

American propaganda during the Korean War reflected the same traits, depicting the Korean and the Chinese as subordinates. Such a projection of domestic images of China over "reality" was not a new phenomenon; as the historian T. Christopher Jespersen observes in his study of American perceptions of China between the 1930s and 1940s, "[American] images and conceptions of China have been . . . more the product of domestic forces than the result of anything else."[74] However twisted it was, after it was accepted and took root among the population, this domestic perspective was no longer imagination; it became "reality."

Policymakers in Washington reflected this socially constructed worldview. John Foster Dulles, for example, personally warned Truman: "Developments in Asia confirm that there is a comprehensive program, in which the Soviet and Chinese communists are cooperating."[75] Assistant Secretary of State Dean Rusk was more brazen: "The Peiping [Beijing] regime may be a colonial Russian government—a Slavic Manchukuo [Manchuria] on a larger scale. It is not the Government of China. . . . It is not Chinese."[76] In Rusk's view, thus, China was a passive, colonized country, and what was happening in China was, therefore, far from the will of the Chinese people.

The tendency to separate the Beijing government and the Chinese people was common not just among mainstream policymakers but among leftists, who voiced their dislike of the corrupt Chiang Kai-shek government and sympathies with the Chinese people. Henry A. Wallace, who had just resigned from the presidency of the Progressive Party, for example, viewed Beijing as a satellite regime of Moscow and stated: "The danger we face today comes from the common man of Asia and Russia falling into the hands of men who are determined to dominate the world." Wallace continued, "Ninety-nine percent of the Chinese people are not communistic in any but the most superficial sense."[77] Although superficially sympathetic, Wallace's attitude was one of mingled paternalism and contempt, dismissing the possibility that the Chinese possessed proactive agency. This was another way of maintaining conventional images of the Chinese as passive, weak, and miserable.

Wallace's view consisted of another prevalent image of "reality": millions of Chinese captured by a handful of communists. As political cartoons in the *Saturday Evening Post* depicted, a peasant-like Chinese slave in chains was threatened by a communist with a rifle.[78] It is worth paying attention to how conventional prejudice toward the Chinese endured; the foreign, communist "Mao Tse-tung" was depicted as small but aggressive, while the "Captive Millions" of the Chinese were illustrated as gigantic but weak, pitiful, and submissive—a stereotypical image of the Chinese as in need of help. In contrasting Mao and the captive Chinese people in terms of size, this cartoon conveyed the message that the majority of the Chinese had simply fallen into the hands of a few communists against their will.

Many believed this, and some advocated the need to support counterrevolutionary movements in enemy lands. A man in Colorado, for instance, said, "There is much unrest in Russia. There is in every satellite country an intense dislike for Russia if they could only voice the dislike. Why haven't we cooperated with their underground? (This includes China.) Why don't we use the people of the underground and resistance movement?"[79] The assumption here

HARVEST TIME FOR THE "AGRARIAN REFORMER"

"Harvest Time for the 'Agrarian Reformer.'" *Saturday Evening Post,* 16 December 1950.
(The *Saturday Evening Post* illustration © SEPS licensed by Curtis Licensing, Indianapolis, IN.
All rights reserved.)

was that the large majority in communist-governed areas did not support communism and that they would revolt against communists and welcome Americans, as soon as the United States offered serious support.

Official and informal reports from the Nationalist Chinese might have bolstered the verisimilitude of this sort of narrative. In effect, Nationalist officials, who had found a golden opportunity for counterattack, had been arguing that, in mainland China, passion for the CCP had evaporated, and eagerness for a counteroffensive was ripening, while the strength of guerrilla forces was increasing in rural areas, particularly in southern and southwestern China.[80] Likewise, it was widely believed that many Chinese soldiers were sent to the front against their will and, thus, would surrender if U.S. forces appealed to them in the name of Chiang Kai-shek.[81] The Nationalists' newspaper, *Zhongyang Ribao*, similarly claimed that there were 1.6 million anti-communist guerrillas in mainland China and that their countrymen on the mainland were enslaved by the Soviet imperialists and waiting to be rescued.[82]

These images, of course, were not entirely illusory. As we have seen, a portion of the population too large to be ignored expressed doubts and distrust about the CCP. In addition, counterrevolutionaries were still active within China, and the legitimacy of the communist government was not yet consolidated.[83] For millions of Chinese who had been repressed and forced to evacuate from the mainland, the image of "Captive Millions" did represent reality. That said, these "facts" alone cannot explain other kinds of "facts," such as enthusiastic popular support for social change and anti-colonial movements among millions of Chinese, through which the CCP had gained popularity.[84] By the same token, Beijing and Moscow certainly maintained close contact regarding the Korean War.[85] Yet this "fact" does not mean that Beijing entered the war under Moscow's orders as we have seen in the previous chapter.[86]

From the dominant American perspective at the time of the Korean War, however, the logic of Moscow's controlling Beijing and Pyongyang seemed obvious enough that some people expressed wonder, if not irritation, that others did not see this "reality" and act accordingly. One military officer lamented: "If [other countries] are really aligned with us in 'putting a stop to aggression'— which is an actual threat to all alike—why in hell do they not come in, contribute their share to the common cause?"[87] Irritation of this kind was not seen as hysterical, panicky, or aggressive, at least not in the United States. Rather, it was considered legitimate against the backdrop of fear of World War III and increasingly popular Cold War logic. The world, according to this view, should have been more closely united, as symbolically illustrated in the *Kansas City Star*'s cartoon, in which countless people from many different nations rally to the side of the UN and the United States.[88] Although this reflected a desire based on domestic and historical preconceptions—more straightforwardly, prejudice—in American society, it appeared natural, realistic, and even essential for the nation's defense in light of a particular version of "reality."

"If There Ever Was a Time for the Free World to Rally!" *Kansas City Star,* 16 December 1950. (Illustration by S. J. Ray. Supplied by Harry S. Truman Library. S. J. Ray Papers, Box 4. Reprinted with permission, PARS International Corp.)

CLARIFYING DIVIDES WITHIN

With the advent of such a "reality," dividing lines were further clarified within American society. China experts, among others, had been warning repeatedly against the dominant images of China. The Harvard historian John King Fairbank, for instance, argued that the Chinese Revolution was fundamentally a matter for the Chinese people to decide and that Americans "must put the Communist victory in China down as a case of self-determination, not of outside aggression."[89] As a China specialist, he paid attention to the inner dynamics of China, and this made him much more conscious of the limits of foreign influence. He wrote:

> The greatest error that Americans can make is to look at China but think only of Russian expansion. . . . It is incredible that Modern China . . . could be brought into the orbit of any foreign power—Russian, American, or any other—except insofar as China's own inner development *itself* conduced to such an orientation.[90]

Other China experts, such as Owen Lattimore of Johns Hopkins University, Thomas A. Bisson of the University of California at Berkeley, as well as John Paton Davies, John Stewart Service, and O. Edmund Clubb of the State Department, expressed similar viewpoints, which could have deepened and diversified various conceptions of China. Of course, that did not happen. Most of these experts were silenced and suppressed in the early 1950s, and, instead, two popular images of China—"China and Korea as a tool of the USSR" and "Captive Millions"—become pervasive. Why? Why were some particular "facts" magnified so that they became the dominant views of "reality," marginalizing other kinds of facts and realities?

To answer these questions, we need to look at the dynamics of local translation in the United States. When Americans observed foreign affairs amid a sea of information, domestic preconceptions functioned as filters, sorting what would be considered "factual" and what would not be. As the historian Akira Iriye astutely points out, "All realities in a way are imagined realities, products of forces and movements that are mediated though human consciousness."[91] In other words, only a version of "reality" that was consistent with the popular imagination and acceptance could survive and prevail. As such, images of a submissive China became prevalent not necessarily because they properly reflected the real situation in China but because they were well suited to existing prejudices in American society. By the same token, the aforementioned China experts were marginalized in the McCarthy era—all but Fairbank lost their jobs—not because they told "lies" but because their perspectives did not fit with dominant views and, thus, came to be considered dangerous. In other words, reality somewhere else did not shape understandings; rather, the frame of understanding defined what would be considered "facts" and "reality."

Because of the prevalence of such a "reality," those who had disagreed became more and more conspicuous in their communities, looked upon as "enemies" from within. A Gallup Poll in the summer of 1950, for example, indicated that 90 percent of respondents agreed that all members of the Communist Party in heavy industry should be removed from their jobs.[92] In addition, 40 percent insisted that, in the case of war with the Soviet Union, members of the Communist Party of the USA (CPUSA) should be put in internment camps or prisons.[93] Such a tense climate reflected fear of losing the war, not just in Korea, but everywhere, including in the United States—a feeling succinctly expressed in a fierce warning in the anti-communist newsletter *Counterattack*: "If we lose the war . . . , the whole earth will be governed by Moscow. . . . Every possible step to eradicate Communism abroad and at home must be taken. Communism and fellow travelers are . . . 'traitors to the UN and US.'"[94] Such rigid attitudes might appear strange, even absurd, from today's vantage point, but, at that time, that was not the case. One Ohioan wrote an angry letter to the president in mid-September:

> We should have a law to hang every spy in peace time as well as war time. We should have laws made especially to deal with them. They are given too much protection here under our ordinary laws, and they should not have that protection. And there should be a law saying that any kind of criticism from them would be reason to banish them from this country. They don't have to live here and are not wanted if they don't like the kind of treatment they get here.[95]

In such a climate, it is no surprise that, in September 1950, Congress overturned President Truman's veto of the Internal Security Act of 1950—often called the Anti-Communist Act—which required the registration of "communist" organizations in the United States, blocked members of these organizations from citizenship, and established an investigative board to examine persons suspected of engaging in subversive activities.

Behind such congressional support for the act was the large proportion of the population that detested "communists," whatever that meant. Under this particular "reality," those who had inclinations toward Marxist thought, or even those who were related to those who did, began having a difficult time. "When I was in my first year in high school, the Korean War was going on. In a social studies class, I said something about it being a civil war and [that] America should stay out of it," Becky Jenkins, whose father was a member of the CPUSA in California, recalled, "The teacher responded with 'That's the position of the Communists!' and the class started to laugh and scream and hoot at me, yelling 'Commie!' I ran home from school sobbing, just humiliated."[96]

By the fall of 1950, not only members of the Communist Party but also various leftists, social democrats, progressives, and labor activists began to be viewed as enemies from within, or "traitors" at home.[97] By this time, even those who had proudly called themselves "liberals" began to fear being described in such terms.[98] President Truman also stopped portraying himself as "liberal," preferring to be called "forward looking."[99]

Because of the prospect of being publicly assaulted, many people finally began changing their behavior. Many who had previously signed petitions for the Progressive Party, for instance, began asking local branches to remove their names from those petitions. Some asked to withdraw from membership. Other asked to stop receiving any publications that might attract attention from their neighbors.[100] One Wisconsinite wrote to the secretariat of the party: "Please do not send me any more letters or papers of the Progressive Party. I am not interested. So please discontinue any mail dealing with the Party."[101] Another similarly wrote: "You will save yourself time and mailing costs if you remove our names from your mailing list. You will also save us the trouble of receiving and opening your political literature."[102] Some wrote in a more apologetic tone that their decisions to withdraw were made to defend themselves. One Denver woman, for instance, explained the reason she had to resign from the Women's International League for Peace and Freedom: "I have my job to consider and my place in the community life."[103]

In such an overwhelmingly hawkish and repressive atmosphere in the second half of 1950, a broad array of dissenters and nonconformists came to feel inhibited, hesitating to express their opinions in public. An anonymous progressive lamented: "The war fever is running so high in this country, and the Left is so intimidated that everything to talk for peace with reason and calmness is almost as useless as shouting in the teeth of a hurricane."[104] Faced with such a situation, many, not surprisingly, suffered from neurosis; a California psychologist observed in the summer of 1950:

> A great many young men are approaching me professionally with questions, in a mood of extreme anxiety. . . . [T]hey feel that the United States has become a police state, in which citizens are no longer free to speak frankly, and where to desire peace is considered subversive, almost unlawful. Life in the United States has become a sort of a nightmare to them.[105]

Because this environment of surveillance was so pervasive, promoted not just by the government but ordinary people's efforts, the clarification of dividing lines in society between "us" and "them"—friends and foes—became apparent. The primary function of official propaganda and civil defense programs, thus, had less to do with forging a consensus than with clarifying who "enemies" were. Such phenomena were not particularly unique to American society; they were quite common, as can be seen even in Chinese society at that time. In order to "overcome" such divisions, and to "solve" such internal disagreements, much more brutal societal measures followed: domestic purges and social punishment around the world.

CHAPTER SIX

Between Mobilization and Participation

ALL NEWSPAPERS in Shanghai appeared five hours late on the morning of Sunday, November 12, 1950. It turned out that CCP officials had arrived at each newspaper office around 4 A.M. that day and closely scrutinized every news item.[1] Just a day earlier, there had been a clear harbinger for this tightening of news censorship. The Chinese business manager of the *North China Daily News,* a British-owned English-language newspaper in Shanghai, was summoned by telephone to the Foreign Affairs Bureau. In the interview that followed, two senior CCP officials conveyed to him an order of the Military Control Commission to the effect that there could no longer be reports "against" either the People's Republic of China or countries friendly to the PRC and that publication of reports from news agencies or radio stations operated by "unfriendly imperialist countries"—by which they meant Reuters and the Associated Press and UPI—had to cease immediately.[2] Following this notification on Saturday, and surprise inspections on Sunday, the communist authorities on Monday, on November 13, sealed Reuters's receiving apparatus used by the *North China Daily News,* ruling out any hope for a relaxing of censorship. This, in a practical sense, was the moment that the historic newspaper, established in Shanghai by a British millionaire in 1850, ended its century-long history.[3]

On the next day, Tuesday, November 14, all theaters in Beijing and Shanghai stopped screening American films, altogether. In Beijing, the interiors and exteriors of all sixteen theaters were decorated with slogans written in eye-catching yellow characters on red cloth. All the theaters held exhibitions of cartoons and photos, and most set up megaphones in front for chanting slogans out loud.[4] In the following weeks, these theaters showed thirty-one films—seventeen Chinese, thirteen Russian, and one North Korean, with titles like *Defend the Country, Preserve Family, Warriors in White Robes*, and *A Chinese Girl*.[5] Each showing was interrupted frequently with cheers and shouts from the audience for "Chinese People's Volunteers!," "Chairman Mao!," and "Generalissimo Stalin!" In no time, newspapers in Beijing began publishing advertisements for and reviews of these films every single day, and more than 50,000 large posters for them appeared all over the city. According to a summary of the campaign, submitted by the Beijing Cinema Guild, during this period, more than 400,000 people watched films in the sixteen theaters in Beijing. Similarly, in Shanghai, the Cinema Guild declared that the city had been suffering a cultural invasion from the United States since its first screening of American films in 1926: "American films, which have inundated China like a flood, have raised a portion of our young people to be pro-American, and disarmed them psychologically," asserted the Shanghai Cinema Guild. "These films brought young people up to be idlers who don't make honest livings, reared them as weaklings, trained them to despise women, and made them decadent and degenerate, rotten and spoiled."[6]

Along with the elimination of Western media and films, a notable and rapid change appeared in the tone of *Renmin Ribao* in November 1950, from cautious and relatively low-key, as had prevailed since July, to more aggressive and harshly anti-American. "Who has been feeding Chiang Kai-shek? Who has spent $6 billion in support of reactionaries in China? . . . Who has destroyed world peace? Who has raped our sisters? Who has been our worst and deadliest enemy?" asked a poem titled "American Killer" in late November. "That is American imperial invaders! American demons!"[7] This aggressive tone heightened following the Chinese and North Korean forces' initial victories and, in particular, the capture of Pyongyang on December 6. The following day, *Renmin Ribao* published a three-frame cartoon,

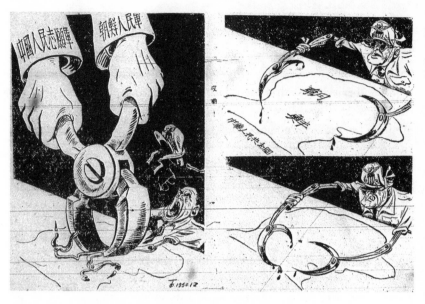

"Failure of MacArthur's 'All-Out Attack.'" *Renmin Ribao,* 7 December 1950.

depicting MacArthur almost succeeding in capturing all of Korea in the first two frames but being blocked in the last frame by giant shears in the hands of the "Chinese People's Volunteers" and "Korean People's Army." This was the first time that *Renmin Ribao* featured the "Chinese" who, previously, had been characterized simply as supportive observers, now as important participants in the war.[8]

Such a noticeable shift can be seen in the newspaper's eight-line poem, which was published along with a photo of gift bags for soldiers:

> Thousands of comfort bags
> Thousands of comfort letters
> Thousands of Chinese people's respect and love
> Devote them to the heroic soldiers on the Korean front
> Bravely advance to the south
> Continuously advance to the south
> To Seoul, to the seacoast
> Our hearts are with you forever.[9]

The poem clearly displayed an aggressive stance by evoking Chinese forces' crossing of the 38th parallel and the unification of the Korean peninsula, with its emphasis on "Seoul" and "the seacoast." Clarification of this attitude, with a strong sense of determination to drive U.S. forces from Korea, was a significant departure for *Renmin Ribao,* which had been making a cautious effort to differentiate the Korean War from Chinese people's business and continued to obscure China's aims in the war.

In November and December 1950, all of these developments—the tightening of censorship in the news media, spread of propaganda campaigns in the film industry, and noticeable changes in *Renmin Ribao*'s attitude—came alongside the beginning and development of the "*kang Mei yuan Chao* (Resist America and Aid Korea)" movement, which swept China and extended to every corner of people's daily lives during the Korean War period, involving both men and women, old and young.[10] Within a couple of weeks in late November, various events and programs unfolded rapidly, including marches and demonstrations, conferences and speech-making contests, study groups and meetings at teahouses, and exhibitions of political cartoons and slogans, as well as various gatherings to discuss imperialists' past crimes.[11]

With this rise in patriotism, tens of thousands, if not millions, of people became involved in this movement, forming a particular kind of consensus and reality in the newly established communist-revolutionary country, which

A demonstration against anti-American imperialism at the Sixteenth Cotton Spinning Factory in Shanghai, 1951. (Shanghai Municipal Archives, H1-31-6-20.)

eventually and effectively marginalized various dissidents and minorities. To be sure, all of these campaigns were the result of officially designed top-down programs, which were often coercive and brutal.[12] And yet, to understand the spread of this movement and the solidification of a particular reality, more explanation is needed. In examining this subject, we will pay close attention to everyday people's whispers and rumors. As the historian James T. Sparrow discusses in his study of rumors in wartime America, truly absurd tales were not remembered nor were they able to spread.[13] However small people's actions might be, telling stories and listening to rumors were meaningful ways through which people perceived and constructed their world and through which we can catch a glimpse of their logic as to how such a large number of people came to participate in and eventually shape this national movement, and why. Let us begin our exploration by looking at how ordinary people reacted to CCP propaganda campaigns in the fall of 1950.

OPPOSITION AND FEAR

First, it is important to note that popular attitudes were not merely products of CCP propaganda, nor were they monolithic. Because we know about the severe repression under communist rule in later years, it might be difficult to imagine open and bold criticism of the CCP. Yet, in the fall of 1950, such mass suppression was yet to come, and voices of head-on opposition to Beijing's policy were audible. Among those objections was the lack of a just cause. One elementary school teacher in Beijing, for instance, raised a question in November 1950: "We have been proclaiming that we support peace. Is it not contradictory if we send troops now?"[14] Another said, "Dispatching troops to Korea is interference in Korea's internal affairs, which clearly goes against the UN Charter."[15] Others even grew concerned that China would become an imperialist power if its troops remained in Korea.[16] Business circles shared such concerns; a senior executive for an electric company in Tianjin, for instance, said in late November, "China and Korea are, after all, two separate countries. Korea is not like Henan or Hebei Province, where we can send troops and help them out. When we were fighting a civil war, did any countries come to China to help us? We should liberate Taiwan before going to Korea."[17]

In addition to such straightforward objections, feelings of distrust and fear were widespread, in spite, or, perhaps, because of CCP propaganda campaigns. "The Communist Party's propaganda deceives people," said one worker in a factory in Shanghai, "It has been said that the United States is a paper tiger. But now the lie comes to light. In fact, American forces defeated North Korean armies and they are almost arriving at the Yalu River, aren't they?"[18] A local communist official in Changsha began to grow desperate, because many workers, shopkeepers, teachers, and students in the area happily read Hong Kong editions of *Da Gong Bao* and *Wenhui Bao* and did not trust communist newspapers, because they believed that those papers carried only "good" news for the party.[19] Another official in Hangzhou informed Beijing that many merchants in the city listened to and trusted an American radio network Voice of America.[20] A manager of the Zhongnan Bank in Nanjing reportedly spewed out, "Nothing good will happen for China after entering the war. China's shoreline is so long, and the Americans can make a landing offensive anytime. The Communist Party said that American forces are worn out, but actually it is Chinese armies that are dead tired."[21]

Such doubts provided countless topics for conversation, producing numerous rumors. In Xi'an, for instance, rumor had it in November that the United States had already dropped an atomic bomb on northeastern China two weeks earlier and that the communist government was going to move to Lanzhou in the interior, more than 1,000 miles west of Beijing.[22] Other rumors, in Jiangxi Province, maintained that the North Korean government had already escaped to Chinese territory, that U.S. forces had occupied Hainan Island, and that Chiang Kai-shek would began a counteroffensive immediately.[23] Similar rumors related to the Nationalist Party were particularly abundant and tended to contain details that made them appear "truer," however wild they might have been. One, in Changsha in November, asserted that the Nationalist Party, led by prominent generals Chen Cheng and He Yingqin, would attack the South and Central China, Okamura Yasuji, an ex-commander of the Japanese military, would attack North China, and General Douglas MacArthur would be in command of the entire force.[24]

Intriguingly, such rumors reflected a myth widely held in Chinese society: Nationalist, Japanese, and U.S. forces were cooperating in an effort to attack China. This kind of rumor usually proceeded as follows: World War III had already begun, and Chiang, with the support of Japanese and U.S. forces, would return to the mainland by the following year; Americans would land near Shanghai, the Japanese would attack from Korea, and Chiang would make a counteroffensive from the south; and then it would be the CCP that would have to retreat to Taiwan.[25] These rumors often contained sequels, as well; the Nationalist Party would then cede the Beijing-Shanghai railways to Japan, Shanghai would go to Britain, and Tianjin and Qingdao to the United States; and these countries would dispatch their troops and quickly seize these territories.[26] Another version added France to this list of foreign powers, adding that the French would take Guangxi Province, located next to Vietnam.[27]

Behind such rumors and fears, it is not difficult to find certain historical preconceptions concerning both foreign countries and the Chinese people. As we have seen in Chapter 5, many Americans at that time had particular images of China, including one depicting China as an incapable child, and such prejudice helped them to form a certain pattern of "reality" from an American perspective.[28] Interestingly, many Chinese held similar biases about themselves. One local communist official in Beijing, for example, said, "China is like a child, while the United States is like a wall. How can a child move a wall? We should wait for a while until the child becomes an adult."[29] Another senior official in Shenyang made a similar comparison: "If the United States is a paper tiger, you know, China is less than a cat!"[30] One low-ranking police officer in the city, Zhao Wei, also lamented, "Who can match the United States? Who can stop Japan if it returns? The Soviet Union is not so strong. Once they were severely defeated by the Japanese. I am a northeasterner myself and I know it very well."[31] In a mood of deep pessimism, resignation, and desperation, a strange phenomenon emerged in many places in November 1950: people throwing parties, eating and drinking heavily. One internal bulletin reported on such parties in the northeast, describing one as including a lot of freshly butchered pork and chicken.[32]

Yet fear was not the only reaction. Although names of foreign countries and their imagined acquisitions varied, many of these rumors and their preconceptions were rooted in historical experiences and memories of Western and Japanese colonialism. And it was this association of historical memories with contemporary events in Korea that led to another pattern of popular reactions that eventually contributed to the extension of the "Resist

America and Aid Korea" movement: a surge in fierce anticolonial sentiment, as well as patriotism and sense of pride, particularly among the youth.

CONSENT AND PARTICIPATION

After hearing news of battlefield victories in early December 1950, excited
students gathered in front of foreign embassies and consulates in Beijing,
loudly shouting "Defeat imperialism," scribbling "Defeat American imperialists" on walls, and, eventually, even getting into fights with foreigners.
The Beijing Municipal Committee later excused such incidents, asserting
that they resulted from simple enthusiasm from the mob, having nothing to
do with the CCP, though promising the Central Committee that it would
prevent the recurrence of events like this.[33] Concerned about such events,
Liu Shaoqi, one of the CCP's top leaders, forwarded a memorandum to all
provincial and municipal committees nationwide, requiring them to prevent incidents like these, which were excessively antagonistic to foreigners.[34]
As is clear from these incidents and the CCP's response to them, anticolonial and anti-American sentiments grew explosively in the fall of 1950, to a
degree that often exceeded the Party line.

By this point, numerous broadsides and posters had appeared at schools
and universities in many cities. At Peking University, for example, broadsides on the current news were renewed every day, one after another, with
estimated character counts at more than 60,000 a day. In addition, an anti-
America signature-collecting campaign in Beijing reportedly received 7,460
signatures in only three days. Some students and workers even wrote in
blood, to which the Beijing Municipal Committee responded by ordering a
stop to such practices.[35] Surprised by such a result, an official on the Beijing
Municipal Committee wrote: "Student attendance is ardent. The number
of signatures exceeds our original estimation. Moreover, this is not an event
that is organized by force."[36] Such a rise in patriotism was unmistakable. A
senior director of the Jardine Engineering Corporation in Hong Kong,
H. Y. Hsu, visited Guangdong in the fall of 1950 and observed: "The tide of
neo-patriotism has swept high, especially in the minds of young people.
Everywhere in China one hears young people singing anti-American songs,
and notices them rushing for military training, as they feel that they are
fighting for a righteous cause and in order to defend their nation."[37] As Hsu

Anti-American imperialism posters at the Sixteenth Cotton Spinning Factory in
Shanghai, 1951. (Shanghai Municipal Archives, H1-31-6-8.)

observed, the extent of such feelings was particularly evident in the daily
lives of young people.

Let us take a look at one earnest student's day in Shanghai, based on the
observations of an anonymous British man in the city: at 10 a.m., the student participated in reading and discussion of current events as reported in
the newspapers; from 2 p.m. to 4 p.m., the student attended a class discussion
meeting; from 4 p.m. to 6 p.m., he attended another meeting of students who
were planning to go to the Military Academy; finally, after supper, he went
with classmates to see a Russian World War II film, titled *Berlin: An Im-
pregnable Fortress*.[38] In addition to all the above extracurricular activities,
course work in the classroom was also associated with the "Resist America
and Aid Korea" movement. A high school history course, for instance, introduced the history of American invasions of China since the mid-
nineteenth century; a science course discussed how empty the threat of
the atomic bomb was; an art class contributed to the production of anti-
imperialist and anti-American drawings and cartoons; and a literature ses-

sion provided students with opportunities to read newspaper and magazine articles on current events.[39]

These activities and programs in schools, of course, were spread as part of the CCP's "Resist America and Aid Korea" movement. Yet, at the same time, their daily practice and implementation was dependent on and conducted by numerous local actors, such as devoted students like the one described above as well as their classmates, teachers, and parents. The enthusiastic participation of such local people is undeniable if one wishes to understand the scale and extension of these movements. One teacher in Shanghai, for example, expressed his sense of mission as an educator: "We have to convey to our youth and children the crimes of American imperialism. We need to work on letting all of the Chinese people love our motherland, and to let them participate in this patriotic movement."[40] Such a call for patriotism did not appear out of place at that time. Many students and parents acted in concert. The aforementioned British man in Shanghai observed:

> Many very fine students are actually volunteering to leave their high schools and colleges to respond to "the call of the fatherland." It is a tragedy and a fact of great importance that such a large number of these young patriots are volunteering with their major motive that of resisting the U.S.A. Frequently one reads that it is a "sacred task to resist the U.S.A." When I asked one student what he was joining, he replied immediately, "The Air Force to bomb Americans."[41]

He lamented, then, that many students who were, academically speaking, the best in class willingly stood up to volunteer, concluding that "the movement to 'answer the call of the fatherland' is definitely growing."[42]

We can catch a glimpse of such determination among young students and workers in the hundreds of letters sent to local communist offices. Many of these letters, preserved in the Beijing Municipal Archives, allow us to explore the various reasons and emotions that drove many to participate into the war. One such letter, written by Yang Tiwei, a student at Peking University, reads:

> Today I have read articles in *Renmin Ribao,* reporting that many workers and students have expressed their willingness to enlist in the army to fight in Korea, and I was very much impressed. I realized that I should not stay out

anymore, and that I just need to make myself into a volunteer soldier. Thus, I request the Party to dispatch me to Korea in order to participate in the battle against American imperialism, and to make their forces disappear. . . . I have been thinking about this issue since yesterday, and I think my thoughts are ripe enough now. I have no reason to stay here and not go to Korea. I have thought about my mother . . . and I believe she should think that my enlistment is an honor. My volunteering is not something I can decide on by myself; it is the requirement of the era and revolution. I was born to a well-to-do family, and need to toughen myself. Let me be dispatched to the place where the battle is most fierce.[43]

One might suspect that such a quick evolution of anti-American sentiments was originated and orchestrated by the CCP. Nonetheless, while the Party certainly exerted enormous influence through its propaganda, censorship, and a variety of political campaigns, and while it was definitely an important *part* of the story, the CCP did not necessarily *create* such a trend.

We can see this point in the way popular critiques of American motives developed in China. One such story begins with the publication of an article in a hawkish American weekly magazine, *Collier's,* which advocated direct attacks on China, with a cartoon depicting a possible strategy for U.S. forces to attack China from three directions: Korea, Taiwan, and Vietnam. The cartoon was reprinted on November 20 in Tianjin's *Jinbu Ribao,* one of China's oldest nonpartisan newspapers, which had changed its name from *Da Gong Bao* in late 1949. The illustration was reprinted again in neighboring regional newspapers, *Henan Ribao* and *Shanxi Ribao,* on November 23. Then, it was republished in *Renmin Ribao* on November 24. Finally, Premier Zhou Enlai referred to the cartoon in his talk on November 25, saying:

> We don't need to search for proof of America's scheme for invasion. Let us look at and quote Americans' own voices. Pictures published in [American] newspapers and magazines can prove this. In all of these pictures, drawings of arrows are all directed at mainland China, via Taiwan and Vietnam. . . . In fact, after the outbreak of the Korean War, the United States immediately began its invasion of Taiwan and Vietnam.[44]

It is interesting to note the direction of movement of this image. It did not go from central to local; rather, it appeared first in Tianjin, then in neighboring local newspapers, and, finally, in *Renmin Ribao* and, ultimately, in

Zhou's adaptation in his speech. Moreover, this story indicates the malleable and constructed nature of "reality." Beijing's observations, as well as those of the local newspapers were, from a historian's hindsight, inaccurate. The Truman administration was concerned about the spread of the war and never seriously considered the idea of war with China, let alone a world war. The cartoon that appeared in *Collier's* was not representative of Washington's viewpoint. It was simply an expression of one of many different opinions, and, actually, one of the most hawkish, in American society at that time.

Yet, because *Collier's* aggressive stance fit neatly with a dominant Chinese perception of America's motives, its cartoon was picked up and understood as revealing the "real" motives of the United States. Only these hawkish voices seemed to be "real," while dovish voices were viewed as hypocritical, as sarcastically described in a set of two cartoons in *Renmin Ribao*, in which, seen from the front, an American gentleman and lady were smilingly announcing that the United States has been always friendly toward Chinese people and has never invaded and will never invade China's territory, while, seen from the back, they revealed their real intention of attacking China from the Korean peninsula, with the man hiding a pistol at his lower back.[45] Such a skeptical attitude was considered thoughtful,

American double-dealers (1). *Renmin Ribao*, 29 November 1950.

American double-dealers (2). *Renmin Ribao,* 29 November 1950.

intelligent, and realistic, even though it was not based on factual information or reliable communications. Whereas a dominant American narrative
described China's entry into the Korean War as part of Moscow's strategy
against the West, a growing narrative in China viewed American intervention in Korea as a prelude to an attack on China. Thus, one low-ranking
communist cadre's observation did not seem illogical in November 1950:
"The war in Korea is expanding. The war is not merely a civil war in Korea;
it is a part of a world war that the United States has been pushing forward."[46] The question is: Why did such an interpretation become dominant
in China? Why did so many people take this particular perspective?

Such an interpretation of events, in effect, was, perhaps, more important
than the events themselves, because it was these perceptions, not the events
themselves, that shaped "reality." In other words, how events were observed
and understood was more influential than what the events actually were. And
no events were observed in a vacuum; they were seen through observers' particular historical, cultural, or even linguistic conditions. In China in the fall
of 1950, one dominant historical context provided a basis for understanding
the outside world and current events: experiences of the War against Japan.

MEMORIES OF WAR AND THE CONSOLIDATION OF "TRUTH"

Such a historical context can be seen in daily practices of the "Resist America and Aid Korea" movement on the ground in the fall of 1950. Although the name of the campaign was clearly anti-American, principal discussion topics at actual meetings had less to do with "American" intervention in Korea than with the War against Japan. For instance, at a meeting in Beijing, one teacher revealed that she had been raped by Japanese soldiers during the war, recalling her experiences and her hatred of imperialism.[47] At another meeting, a police officer shared his wartime experience: "When I was working as a police officer at a train station, I was often beaten and humiliated by the Japanese, Americans, and British. Now they are coming again. And I can go and fight them. Let me be sent to the front lines immediately."[48] In a similar manner, the Taxi Trade Guild resolved in November 22:

> Now, war is approaching the border of our northeastern region. American imperialists are following the same path the Japanese took before: first invading Taiwan and Korea, then northeastern China, and eventually attempting to invade China. Let us remember when the Japanese occupied the northeast. What did they do? In terms of our business, for instance, long-distance buses had to be stopped. . . . We should remember such a history of national ruin.[49]

By the same token, at a meeting organized by a Beijing branch office of the People's Bank of China, participants primarily discussed their experiences during World War II. "Today American imperialists follow the same path that the Japanese imperialists took before, seeking to take Asians and Chinese back to the days of colonialism and make them their slaves one more time," declared one participant. He further went on to expound on Chinese people's suffering during the War against Japan, connecting it to his criticism of the contemporary conduct of the United States: "We have suffered the invasion by Japan; fathers and mothers and brothers and sisters were killed and violated. How much did our hearts hurt when our men were hung and beaten by the Japanese? I cannot even express it. We will never accept the same thing happening again."[50] Accusations of Japanese war crimes during the Anti-Japanese War were so common at Resist America and Aid Korea meetings that some participants questioned whether there were too many stories about Japan.[51]

Shanghai banking staff and workers demonstrating against America's rearming of Japan, March 1951. (Shanghai Municipal Archives, H1-23-6-45.)

It turned out, however, that this approach was extremely efficient and influential. The conventional wisdom maintained that American imperialists were copying Japanese imperialists and that their plan was to conquer China, Asia, and the entire world. In this way, memories of the War against Japan were, indeed, everywhere, providing many people with a lens through which to view U.S. intervention in Korea. One photo that captured a moment at a Resist America and Aid Korea demonstration shows such a tendency quite well; the banner raised high illustrated a scene in which an American (MacArthur) orders a Japanese soldier with a rifle to attack Korea. Similarly, a cartoon in *Changjiang Ribao* depicted an alleged American plan to invade China, devised by Harry S. Truman, Douglas MacArthur, and Dean Acheson, and described their plan as a "plot in the same old way," comparing it to the Japanese empire's expansion in East Asia, beginning with the Sino-Japanese War of 1894–1895, the Russo-Japanese War of 1904–1905, and the Manchurian Incident and the Second Sino-Japanese War in the 1930s.[52]

It is interesting to look at the interplay between the reproduction of memory and shaping of "reality." On the one hand, cruel experiences of the Anti-Japanese War created a basis for many Chinese to perceive contemporary situations through the lens of World War II, contributing to the production of the "reality" of Americans' scheme to invade and enslave China. On the other hand, such a "reality" contributed to the renewed reproduction of a certain kind of historical narrative concerning experiences of the War against Japan. These parts of this reciprocal cycle reinforced one another, reproducing *both* certain images of "reality" and certain kinds of memories of the Anti-Japanese War, which in turn formed particular "truths" about "us" and "them." Such truths typically maintained that the United States was launching an all-out attack on mainland China from three directions, such as Korea, Taiwan, and Vietnam, as often depicted in cartoons, and that "we" must fight against the enemy.[53] These truths provided a foundation for a whole set of mechanisms of state mobilization and people's genuine participation, while being constructed and reproduced anew through these state and grassroots activities.

In sum, the rapid rise of anticolonial and anti-American sentiments and movements as well as the ardent participation of thousands of people in such movements cannot be understood without looking at memories of the War against Japan and the version of "reality" that was built on them. Official propaganda, of course, had certain effects in the shaping of such imagination, but much more fundamental were people's ability to imagine and embrace such narratives as "reality." In a sense, while we often focus on the roles of propaganda to "shape" and "lead" popular attitudes, we should not dismiss followers' intentions to follow such propaganda.[54] After all, propaganda cannot be successful unless it is embraced by the large portion of the population. Equally or, arguably, far more important than state propaganda were social and historical contexts, interpretations of the progress of the war, and individuals' numerous choices concerning their behaviors. What state propaganda actually did, then, was not necessarily to *create* consensus but to *clarify* dividing lines within society.

SUPPORT AND PARTICIPATION

After a series of Chinese victories in Korea, the "Resist America and Aid Korea" movement continued to develop in the winter of 1950. This was particularly the case following the capture of Pyongyang on December 6, 1950, which came almost out of the blue for many Chinese people, who largely doubted that Chinese armies had any chance of defeating U.S. forces.[55]

"Resist America and Aid Korea" movement: female workers giving flowers to cadres,
January 1951. (Shanghai Municipal Archives, H1-23-6-6.)

Thus, it had an enormous impact on a large portion of the population,
changing the current of popular emotions in society. We can see such a sea
change in numerous internal reports sent from many parts of China. A local communist cadre in Fuzhou, for instance, observed that peasants were
delighted by news of the CPV's victory, while many landlords reportedly
found it discouraging.[56] Likewise, another report recorded that passions for
participating in the volunteer army quickly increased in rural areas of Hunan Province and that the local committee received more than 2,000 ap-

Mass of people seeing off the Fourth and Fifth Voluntary Medical Groups going to Korea, July 1951. (Shanghai Municipal Archives, HI-11-3-19.)

plicants by the end of December.[57] Similar scenes were witnessed in northeastern provinces, including Rehe, Jilin, and Heilongjiang. News of the CPV's victory aroused enthusiasm among many people: Peasants reportedly began submitting taxes and foodstuffs more earnestly and punctually; many students began volunteering to be soldiers and to attend the Military Academy; and medical students began joining the army to go to Korea.

Against this background, Chinese people's views toward their own country began changing. One high school student reportedly said that he had previously looked down on his country because it had only a lot of people but no airplanes or artillery, however, now, after hearing the news of China's victory, he had come to love his fatherland.[58] Liu Hongsheng, a well-known Shanghai businessman, had similar feelings; initially dubious about China's campaigns against the United States, he changed his view after China's victorious advances on the battlefield, recalling later, "For the first time in my life, I am proud to be Chinese."[59] Because of the development of such a fervent attitude, numerous people now embraced and participated in the movement; countless storekeepers in major cities competed to make further donations, many shoemakers declared their intention to repair soldiers' shoes for free, rickshaw coolies signed or provided their names for anti-American signature collecting campaigns, and students and workers participated in various kinds of mobilization programs, some even volunteering for the army.[60]

Like their counterparts in the United States, many Chinese knew how to behave when their country was committed in battle. Like Americans, they mobilized themselves to protect the interests of the nation. These were the people who surprised a tax office clerk in Beijing, who, previously, had experienced the perpetual problem of nonpayment of overdue taxes in his district, because now taxpayers were taking initiative in paying taxes.[61] These were the people who cooperated and made it possible to put the CCP's mobilization programs into action. Viewed in this way, the CCP's campaigns were not necessarily always forcefully and brutally imposed; to some extent, they were welcomed and supported by certain portions, if not a majority, of the population. This feeling of cooperation and sense of unity are evident in a report compiled by an official of the Beijing Cinema Guild:

> On the morning of December 13, 1950, about seventy elementary school children walked more than three miles to the Beijing Theater from the outskirts of the city, but found not a single free seat when they arrived. For these children fully soaked in sweat, the theater wanted to give them a rest, thus making an announcement to the audience—"These children came from far away but could not find any free seat; can we take care of them, offering seats and letting them take a rest?" As soon as this announcement finished, everyone stood up; some held their children on knees; some offered their seats; and others shared seats. And then, quickly all of these seventy children could sit down. The theater was filled with a warm and kindly air; it was like a big family.[62]

Aside from such a degree of enthusiasm and mood of cooperation among the people, the most interesting point of this report is the way in which the author illustrated this scene using the metaphor of a "big family." This is because this notion of "family" indicates why so many people welcomed and participated in the "Resist America and Aid Korea" campaigns in the fall of 1950. After all, the tightening of censorship in the news media, the escalation of propaganda campaigns, and the spread of nationalistic education were not disdained. Rather, they were in many ways *embraced* as means of bringing order, unity, and a sense of national pride to the country, which came to be commonly and proudly proclaimed as *"Xin Zhongguo* (New China)." Indeed, without understanding this aspect of "attractiveness," we cannot comprehend the spread and function of the movements. This was the moment when patriotism and pride developed in China swiftly and profoundly, both from top down and bottom up.

DOUBTS AND OPPOSITION

The Chinese communist leadership would have been satisfied and happy if this sort of attitude had been unanimous. Needless to say, it was not. Far from it: an undisputable portion of the population remained doubtful, indifferent, or hostile to Beijing's policies, even after China's entry into the war, even following the CPV's victories over U.S. forces, and even amid the massive propaganda campaigns that swept China in the fall and winter of 1950. "On the surface, many people agree with the idea of the 'Resist America and Aid Korea' campaigns, but many bear doubts about the future of the war, and the majority is afraid of the American forces in their hearts," pointed out one internal report from Shanxi Province. "Many do not trust our newspapers, always listen to the Nationalist Party's radio programs, and hastily believe in wild rumors, thus remaining unstable. Even in public, there have been a lot of behaviors of boldly abusing the people's government."[63] The Beijing municipal office similarly observed that "quite a few people" maintained a negative attitude toward China's entry into the war and that intellectuals and businessmen, in particular, expressed "'yes' in mouths 'no' in hearts" to the CCP's efforts at home and in Korea.[64]

The ominous tone in these reports cannot be considered as mere exaggeration in view of the chaotic domestic situations in China. In Shanghai, a statue of Mao Zedong at the Meixi Elementary School was destroyed in early November, with a flyer left on it that said "Defeat Mao Zedong!"[65] Throughout November, graffiti and handbills suddenly appeared in many places. Anti-communist slogans, such as "If Mao Zedong and Zhu De stay, the war will never end," were written in the bathrooms and on walls of the Dongji High School, Minli Female School, Qingxin Female School, and Jiangnan Shipbuilding School.[66] Furthermore, Jingye High School had two alleged incidents of arson, leading officials to conduct an investigation.[67] In

Dalian, similar slogans, like "Defeat Moscow," and "Defeat Traitors, Communists," appeared in the bathrooms of the Bo'ai Market and on the wall of the Dalian Transportation Company—just some among a total of thirty-nine incidents.[68]

Such sentiments were not limited to urban areas. Many rural areas experienced an increase in anti-communist activities, including poisoning of the food supply, arson, and murder. In a rural area in western Sichuan, for instance, incidents of untraceable food poisoning occurred frequently in early November. The actual cause of these incidents is unknown, but it was reported that a former landlord poisoned a well, perhaps, in retaliation against a communist program that confiscated his land.[69] In the same period, "reactionary" slogans often appeared in rural areas, as well: "Welcome the Nationalist Army back to the Mainland" and "The Communist Party is reducing the rich to poor and then slaughtering the poor."[70]

In newly "liberated" areas in southern and central regions of China, kinship played a role in undermining communist programs and unity. For instance, in Guizhou Province—one of the poorest regions and farthest from communist control—kinship relationships proved to be effective in cutting communist ties. According to an internal report sent from Guiyang, a Nationalist sympathizer who was trying to influence a CCP sympathizer said the following in a typical case relying on kinship: "Why don't we reunite our family group again? You and I had a good relationship before, didn't we? You are now being deceived by the communists and are following a different path, but, if you think it over again and regret it now, we can forget about your past, and assure you a future position and work."[71]

In addition to such "gentle" persuasion, more direct measures—threats and assassinations—were taken. In Guiyang, untraceable letters were sent to local chiefs of communist agricultural associations, threatening and urging them to surrender with promises of amnesty. Furthermore, rumors spread that one could receive a ton of white rice in exchange for the murder of an association leader. In fact, a local leader's entire family was reportedly killed near Chengdu, their bodies thrown into a river, though we do not know whether the killer actually received a ton of white rice.[72] In this situation, it is not surprising that former landlords felt a bit heartened, while newly "liberated" peasants were frightened. According to an internal report sent in November 1950, a peasant named Liu Chongyi refused to take possession of land distributed through communist land reform, and another moved out of a house that had been allocated through a communist program, saying, "My former landlord will come back and I will be killed if I stay here."[73] Local cadres in villages had trouble arguing with such views because the amount of news and reports had been radically reduced, so they did not know how to refute rumors.[74]

REALITY STILL UNCERTAIN

The situation in the fall of 1950 was, indeed, chaotic. During this period, there was a rapid development of support and confidence, on the one hand, and doubt and dissatisfaction, on the other. The achievements of the newly established government against the backdrop of a colonized past undoubtedly inspired a sense of pride, but, at the same time, there existed a strong undercurrent of dissatisfaction, doubts, hostility, and apathy.[75] Government officials were keenly aware of such a climate in society. "Chaotic" is the best term for describing the situation, rather than "state controlled" or "monolithic." It would be a mistake to view the communist regime as strong, consolidated, or lacking in conflict.[76]

Facing such turbulence, a communist official in Shenyang wrote a lengthy internal report concerning the social situation and public order based on his own observations and materials from the local police department. The report appeared on November 30, in *Neibu Cankao* (Internal Reference), the CCP's internal bulletin, issued daily and circulated among only an extremely limited number of high-ranking governmental officials.[77] It read:

> A large majority of the population (workers, peasants, students, and so on) in Shenyang recognizes the justice of our volunteer army in the war for the liberation of the Korean people, and believes in our victory, thus strictly observing law and order and positively participating in their work. . . .
>
> However, a small portion of the people is afraid of American weapons and ravages of war, leading to unrest and fear. In the Wuyi (5.1) Factory, for example, more than 1,200 workers were absent from work for several days after October 19. At another plant, about 450 workers—roughly 28 percent of the total—deserted their jobs in the two weeks following October 10. At

the Medical University, eighteen students ran away, and these kinds of sentiments are already affecting our party and organization members, especially
those from Southern China. . . . Our enemies' destructive activities are
growing. Reactionary groups—remnants of Chiang Kai-shek's troops and
landlords—recognize that now is the time to change the government, and
they are feeling extremely excited, becoming active, and spreading rumors
and making trouble. . . .

Given the increase in enemy activity, we now see reactionary slogans everywhere; in October alone, we have found about thirty reactionary slogans
and graffiti in twenty-nine locations, including elementary and middle/high
schools, the Sanitation Department, Army Hospital, an iron mill, rubber
plant, machine manufacturing plant, chemical factory, and electric paper
manufacturing plant, all in the city of Shenyang. Among these, thirteen
were scribbled on bathroom walls, and others appeared on blackboards in
schools, on street walls, and telephone poles, and even on the surface of a
water pot and the insides of dishes. Their contents usually involve cursing
the Communist Party, intimidating party and organization members, or
sowing discord within the Sino-Soviet relationship. For instance, "Defeat
the Soviet Union," "Party and Youth League members, guard your skull,"
and so on.

On October 17, sixteen bills and posters labeled the "Youth Association
for Opposing Communism and Saving the Country" appeared in three alley-
ways in Haichang, Nenjiang, and Andong, as well as on Nansi Street in the
Heping District, which is under the jurisdiction of the Kaiming Police
Branch. On October 20, another four reactionary posters were found in the
bathroom of the paint processing plant; On October 23, twelve reactionary
leaflets were found in a mailbox on Taiyuan Street, all urging the youth
to conduct counterrevolutionary activities and propagate military victories
against the United States.

Facing the aforementioned situation, in order to consolidate social order,
maintain economic development, and prevent destruction by enemies, each
factory and organization should conduct and deepen security education,
heighten vigilance, tighten various rules, clarify and distinguish each responsibility to avoid suffering any loss. [78]

This report includes several interesting points. First, it clearly demonstrates
the existence of extensive doubts about the ruling communist party. Second,
its meticulous manner indicates the capability of the CCP's organization,
even at the local level. Third, it reveals the depth of local communist officials'

concerns about social order, as well as the degree of their emphasis on the role of education and propaganda in maintaining the desired social order.

Finally, the locations where "reactionary" slogans and graffiti were found—schools, hospitals, factories, and a local administrative building—suggest that quite a few discontented and hostile elements existed actually within the "governing" system. Those working in these locations included lower-ranking local government officials, local police officers, public school teachers, doctors, and professors, as well as various kinds of technocrats and engineers. These were the local elite and professional class in society, who had worked for the Nationalist government and remained in their positions under the Communist government. In other words, the most menacing threat to the legitimacy of the Beijing government actually resided within its own headquarters.

We can catch a glimpse of such dissatisfaction among a certain portion of the population in one memorandum, scrawled on a piece of paper, now held by the Beijing Municipal Archives. The memo recounts a brief conversation between a rickshaw man and his female customer, a doctor. According to this note, their chat went as follows. When the rickshaw approached Beihai Park in Beijing, the two saw propaganda cartoons of the "Resist America and Aid Korea" campaign, and the doctor said to the puller: "The Communist Party is trying to deceive people by using these 'Resist America and Aid Korea' cartoons. Now Chiang Kai-shek and the Americans are united in the war. The Russians are now actually chasing and violating women in northeast. Moreover, they took over six power plants there." The doctor went on to say, "Today, all men between eighteen and fifty years old are conscripted; on the surface, it is, of course, called 'volunteering,' but in fact it is forced. Alas, China will get nowhere. Mao Zedong must know that Stalin is hoping to ruin China."[79] When the rickshaw man asked the doctor if the story was really true, she replied, "I am a northeasterner. I saw it myself."[80] This story is intriguing not so much for its information but because it shows the existence of individual observation and judgment, in spite of the massive scale of propaganda campaigns all over China during this period.

These various examples suggest that what propaganda campaigns in the fall and winter of 1950 really did was not necessarily to forcefully *change* people's minds. As we have seen, although certain portions of the population embraced and participated in the CCP's campaigns, quite a few remained dubious, if not hostile, to CCP rule. Seen in this way, the primary effect of such extensive campaigns was to *clarify* where the divides existed in society. On the one hand, active communist sympathizers became more enthusiastic and aggressive, while, on the other hand, those who had been dubious about the communist regime became further confirmed in their distrust. At schools, for instance, such divisions were conspicuous, with devoted students staying up all night to write letters to Mao, some even writing them in blood to show their dedication, while other, dissatisfied students told enthusiastic classmates: "Just go to Korea as soon as possible, or I will see your heads at the execution ground when Chiang Kai-shek returns."[81] Still other students who were not excited about either side held their ground, simply saying to passionate classmates: "Well, let's talk about it after the exam."[82] As such, the waves of propaganda campaigns did not dispel confusion. Nor were they able to convince nonconformists. Nor did they form a consensus. Rather, they brought hidden divides to the surface.

An examination of the "Resist America and Aid Korea" movement sheds new light on the movement's actual dynamics and functions. All campaigns, to be sure, resulted from officially designed programs, which were often top down and coercive. Throughout the movements, the CCP's focus was on persuading people to participate. The point at issue was how people saw themselves, their history, and the outside world and how they behaved accordingly. It was reasonable for the CCP to begin these campaigns in the news and film industries as well as education, literature, and history. Nevertheless, the CCP's propaganda campaign only half-succeeded, because it appealed mostly to those who were already supportive and sympathetic toward their programs. The real implementation of the campaigns, thus, actually depended on more diverse actors and factors—namely, the existence of countless devoted followers and historical memories that provided a rationale.

This point raises questions about images of powerful manipulation by the communist regime. In short, the sweeping manner of the extension and materialization of the campaign cannot be understood if we look solely at coercion and control by the communist authorities. On the contrary, it was made possible by a significant degree of consent, initiative, and participation by local people on the ground. In other words, the widespread penetration of the campaign was possible only at a crossroads of coercion and willingness, of mobilization and participation. The primary function of state propaganda thus had less to do with forging a consensus than locating and clarifying dividing lines between "us" and "them." To "resolve" such disputes in society, more direct, more brutal, and more socially based processes were required—that is, social suppression and punishment conducted among ordinary people, which took place in many parts of the world in the years that followed.

III

The Simultaneity

CHAPTER SEVEN

Social Warfare

ON THE KOREAN PENINSULA, war situations shifted at a dizzying pace between the summer of 1950 and spring of 1951: the North Korean armies' attack on the south, the American intervention and crossing of the 38th parallel northward, and China's entry and crossing of the parallel southward, followed by a fierce seesaw until the war reached a stalemate near the parallel. With such rapid turning of the tables, atrocities occurred in many parts of Korea. One of the best-known incidents happened in Nogunri (Noguen-ri), south of Taejun (Daejeon), in July 1950, and involved American soldiers' indiscriminate killing of several hundred civilians, including infants and the elderly.[1] Another case, occurring in Gwangju immediately following the Inchon Landing, involved the North Korean forces' killing of 600 political prisoners.[2] Furthermore, near the Jirisan region in the spring of 1951, South Korean soldiers indiscriminately massacred 1,500 local residents suspected of helping the enemy.[3] In addition to these mass killings conducted primarily by state militaries, however, recent studies have begun revealing many different patterns of massacres, which occurred in areas where regular armies were absent. For example, in the Yeonggwang region, 35,000 local residents—one-fifth of the area's population—were reportedly murdered at the hands of local residents, with little involvement of the regular army.[4] In another case, in the village of Sedeung-ri on the southern island of Jindo, various indigenous struggles flared up, eventually leading to mass killings.[5]

Such massacres, which have come to light in recent years, were indeed diverse, defying simple classification and labeling. Still, we can discern a number of common characteristics among them. First, most were conducted under Cold War terms, such as "rounding up Communists" or "class struggle." Second, nonetheless, quite a few contained elements of local struggles in social, cultural, and historical settings, including conflicts not only between leftists and rightists, but also between landowners and sharecroppers, wartime collaborators and noncollaborators, and Christians and non-Christians, as well as among clans, families, friends, and neighborhoods. In many cases, these were the struggles that had existed long before the outbreak of the Korean War but remained "unresolved" and reignited and escalated with turns in the war situation. Third, many mass killings functioned, in a way, to "resolve" such local conflicts, though they were commonly carried out under rubric of the Cold War, in terms of "class struggle" or "anti-communism." Last not least, such struggles often involved the participation of local people, in some cases quite directly, and, in other cases, more indirectly through rumors and mutual surveillance among residents, all of which exacerbated the degree of violence.[6] In short, in addition to massacres conducted by state military forces, many large-scale massacres in Korea contained elements of what we might be able to call "social warfare"—social suppression and punishment of local people, based on existing conflicts that were rekindled at the time of the Korean War.

Interestingly, this kind of situation was not unique to Korea. Although degrees of violence differed widely, similar patterns of social purges appeared in many parts of the world almost simultaneously during the Korean War period: China cracked down on counterrevolutionaries; Taiwan implemented the White Terror; the Philippines suppressed "un-Filipino" activities; Japan conducted its Red Purge; Britain launched vigorous anti-labor initiatives; and the United States allowed McCarthyism to take root. Each instance of domestic suppression has its own local history, and, thus, each has generally been treated separately. Also, each phenomenon has been viewed through a Cold War lens. However, if we raise questions about this Cold War framework itself, and if we view them together as parts of global history, instead of separate local issues, these events appear quite different. Why did such similar suppressions occur simultaneously all over the world? What were the implications of this worldwide phenomenon? Let us first look at the one that peaked in the United States during the Korean War period: McCarthyism.

RECONSIDERING MCCARTHYISM

Helen MacMartin's life was nearly ruined in the waves of McCarthyite attacks that peaked during the Korean War period. A local member of the Progressive Party in Burlington (pop. 33,155 in 1950), Vermont, Helen, fifty-nine years old, experienced a typical five-step suppression. The first step was a change in human relations in her community. Just a few days after she expressed her disapproval of U.S. military actions in Korea in a local newspaper in July 1950, Helen began receiving letters from old friends. One read:

> I cannot believe that you have personally sold out to the Communist Cause—though everything you have said in the article [in the local newspaper] would indicate so. I am writing because I do believe that you will listen to what I have to say, and because I hope there is still some hope for saving a person for the good of peace and democracy in which I think you believe, and because I hate to see a person persecuted.[7]

Helen replied immediately:

> No, I am not a Communist, have not "sold out" as you put it. If my convictions lead me more and more to know that Fascism and monopoly capitalism and imperialism of the U.S. is the great threat of our day and of many years back, it does not mean that I embrace Communism. Unfortunately for me and for many like me, just because the Communists believe this also, we are called Communists. . . . I wish I could talk with you. But I don't suppose you would be seen having lunch with me again.[8]

No further reply came from the friend.

The second step came in the form of a public attack in a local newspaper, the *Burlington Daily News,* which devoted an entire editorial in early August 1950 to censuring Helen. It read:

> Her ranting against "American imperialism" when American soldiers are dying on Korean battlefields is disgusting. . . . The wild bleating of Mrs.

> MacMartin marks her as a woman gone too far in her political thinking, as one who has been carried away by ideological confusions. . . . The political aims and aspirations of Mrs. MacMartin are detestable in this time of grave crisis.[9]

As in many such cases in this period, a local newspaper took initiative in fueling anti-communist sentiments.[10]

The third step was a general boycott in the community. In the fall of 1950, Helen tried to fight back, sending letters to local newspapers, hoping they would be published. She also continued to write to her friends, asking them to stand up for her. These letters, however, were ignored.[11] The fourth step was estrangement from family members; she was harshly condemned by her sister as a "dupe" and "fool" who wanted to "wear a martyr's crown." After a contentious conversation, Helen realized that it was almost impossible to talk with her.[12] Even her daughter sent her a somewhat distant letter, simply saying "I hope you are forming the prospect for yourself realistically."[13] Finally, in the fifth and last step, in early 1951, she lost her job caring for an elderly man in her neighborhood.[14] The simple question that we ask here is: Why was she shunned in her community?

Considering her leftist stance and objection to the U.S. intervention in Korea, this does not seem like a difficult question to answer; at first glance, her case appears to represent one of numerous false charges that accompanied reckless anti-communist attacks in the era of McCarthyism.[15] A popular interpretation of the Korean War as the start of World War III made it possible to revive the notion of "wartime" in postwar America, which, in turn, made it easy to hunt "enemies" within.[16] Thus, first and foremost, it seems to make sense to see Helen MacMartin as a victim of McCarthyism or, as the historian Philip Jenkins puts it, the "Korean War Red Scare."[17] However, much broader and more fundamental struggles were going on beneath such ostensible attacks over ideological beliefs. The primary aim of this chapter is to shed light on a less-well-understood aspect of the era of McCarthyism: social warfare.

Battles of such warfare can be found in much writing of the period. "Why must our boys die fighting Communists in Korea [when] they are allowed to roam freely among us and go on with their fight against us?" asked a West Virginia woman in early August 1950. She contended that Congress was not protecting the rights of "true citizens" in being too careful about observing the constitutional rights of "traitors," urging, "Let's drive these traitors underground and then dig them out like rats. Let's make America safe for Americans."[18] She was not alone in heightening the "anticommunist" tone at that time. In a similar manner, a Wisconsin woman wrote to the president: "As a devoted and hundred percent American citizen, I feel that I cannot stand by and do nothing while our country is being overrun by Communists." She continued:

> [E]ach and every person who does not care for American ways of living in freedom and liberty, but prefers Russian ways should be made to go and live there. . . . May the Good Lord, give you strength and courage to discharge those who are not 100% True American.[19]

In a similar tone, a father of nine children in the tiny village of McGrath, Alaska, wrote that he would not hesitate to make any sacrifice in fighting communism and that this was because he wanted his nine children "to grow up in a lawful and orderly society."[20] Such a desire to defend the way of life to which they were accustomed was quite natural and should not be dismissed as a hysterical or irrational attitude. In fact, these opinions were considered righteous and patriotic, and thus many Americans embraced such a position to protect their communities and families.

In the letters excerpted above, what is evident is an enormous affection for "America," as well as sheer hatred of "communists." What is *not* so clear is what precisely "America" was and who exactly "communists" were. These are taken for granted. The authors of these letters did not spell them out, not because they did not know, but because, perhaps, the definitions seemed too obvious to mention. The meaning of "America," for them, was part of common sense. Similarly, the meaning of "communism" had less to do with political ideas or a regime than anything deemed unharmonious with common images of "America." The crux of the matter, thus, was less about political ideology or types of institutions than a state of social order and custom—or, simply, a way of life.

Nevertheless, here existed the politics of inclusion and exclusion. The less clear points are: What kinds of communities and families did people want to defend? What kinds of communities and families did they *not* want to protect? What kinds of things should be considered "American," and what should not be? Answers to these questions were actually more difficult to articulate than many letter writers would have assumed. This was because the definitions and realities of community, family, and society were radically changing in the United States in the postwar period, primarily because of various social changes that resulted from the Great Depression and World War II.

These two monumental historical events altered social relationships, particularly in the areas of racial, gender, and labor relations, generating social conflicts in the wake of the war. In brief, many African Americans and civil rights activists who intensified their struggles in the 1930s and advocated a "double victory" during wartime—over not just foreign enemies but domestic discrimination—did not want to return to their previous inferior status. Quite a few women who had acquired new jobs and social status in wartime wanted to retain social positions beyond the conventional "mother" and "wife." Many workers who had obtained new authority during the New Deal period fiercely fought management in the early postwar period. Similarly, homosexuals, who found fellows in the army and did not return to their rural hometowns after the war, began creating a new subculture in urban areas.

These were the areas in which repression was the most severe in the McCarthy era. What these groups represented was not a single political ideology but, rather, elements of wartime and postwar transformations in American society. Observing such transformations and suppressions from a social point of view, thus, we can pose the following hypothesis: the true nature of McCarthyism, often viewed as the Cold War at home, was not really that of an anti-communist campaign but waves of grassroots conservative backlash under the name of anti-communism, which functioned to pacify social upheavals in postwar America. The battle line, therefore, was less about particular ideological beliefs than about individuals' social behavior, manners, and attitudes about life.

Seen in this way, Helen MacMartin's case looks different. A 1913 graduate of William Smith College, in Geneva, New York, she had been active in Vermont social, civil, educational, and political organizations since the late 1920s. She was a member of the American Association of University Women, active in the Burlington League of Women Voters, and a chairman of the Burlington Zonta Club, an organization of business, executive, and professional women that aimed to advance the status of women. In the 1930s, she completed her graduate work at Simmons College's School of

Social Work, worked for the U.S. Employment Service in Vermont for more than a decade, and was active in labor and civil rights campaigns in Vermont.[21] In brief, she embodied a new type of woman, active beyond conventional images of mother and wife, whose lifestyle typically encouraged some while irritating others. Viewed in this way, her persecution can be seen not simply as an incidental false charge; she may have really been a target of social repression of new elements of social change.

In viewing McCarthyism merely as anti-communist politics, we have tended to describe those who were oppressed even though they were not communists as innocent victims of false accusations. This view characterizes the period as a time of groundless attacks and malicious slander, which the Wisconsin senator was later believed to personify. However, seeing McCarthyism as the politics of social screening and repression of nonconformists, dissenters, and malcontents in an attempt to protect desirable order and harmony in society, we can see that the diverse groups suppressed were the real targets, rather than being innocent victims. In short, they were "guilty" of causing, or potentially causing, social disorder. In a sense, the entire phenomenon of McCarthyism can be seen as a social mechanism of inclusion and exclusion, functioning to identify and eliminate "un-American"—or simply unconventional—activities and to restore and defend "American"—or conventional—values. Briefly, it was a backlash of grassroots social conservatism aimed at the restoration of "normal" social order and relations, through purging thousands of nonconformists at home, carried out by innumerable, nameless ordinary people.

In fact, Helen's persecution was conducted mostly at a social level. Nothing was truly official, and persecutors were not necessarily politicians, lawyers, or agents of the Federal Bureau of Investigation (FBI) but neighbors, friends, family members, and employers. With regard to method, there was no formal prosecution, no hearing, no trial. She was "punished" through rumors, slander, and a boycott in the community. Her case was simply the tip of the iceberg; there were numerous "Helen MacMartins" at that time. Even in cases in which people were summoned to official hearings such as those held by the House Un-American Activities Committee (HUAC), a large majority was not sentenced; many, however, immediately found that their private employers fired them.[22] In sum, many were not convicted officially and legally but condemned socially in unofficial publicity trials.

In examining various areas in which McCarthyite attacks were most severe, we will see such social repression and will explore the true nature of conflicts behind the wall of "anti-communist" campaigns. The primary focus here is not on the centers of power. This is because, in primarily examining intentions and decisions of powerful policymakers, such as Harry S. Truman, Joseph McCarthy, Pat McCarran, or J. Edgar Hoover, often considered primarily responsible for the development of anticommunist politics in the postwar period, we tend to pay little attention to the fundamental meanings of social phenomena. Meanings, in this approach, are assumed to be self-evident, as they are often confused with policymakers' intentions, as if a social phenomenon were a result of these intentions and as if the political center were the origin of social and cultural changes. Instead, our focus is on reassessing the meaning of this repression by examining society, looking at what happened on the ground. The simple questions to be raised here are: Who purged whom, and for what purpose? What were the functions, mechanisms, and implications of such repression and punishments carried out in society?

COLD WAR REPRESSION AS SOCIAL STRUGGLE

First and foremost among the people severely repressed during the McCarthy era were African Americans and civil rights activists who became active in the postwar period. Although the effects of the Cold War and anti-communist attacks on these groups have been well researched, recent scholarship has tended to focus more on the "beneficial" aspects of the Cold War for the civil rights movement.[23] However, this was a later development; in the late 1940s and early 1950s, anti-communist politics was, indeed, a force that was destructive toward civil rights groups and, more broadly, the black community.[24]

In fact, many African Americans' attempts to challenge racial hierarchy in the immediate postwar period were not successful; their hope for a "double victory" was not fulfilled but crushed, not necessarily in the form of blunt racial discrimination but in the name of security risks. One 34-year-old African American in New York, for instance, lost his job at the post office, for which he had been hired during the war, because his records revealed that, in the 1930s, he had joined a group that criticized racial discrimination and prejudice. This was a problem because this group was now labeled a "communist-led" organization. Then, he found another job as a truck driver, at a lower salary, but soon lost it when his employer found and used these records to fire him. It was not necessarily an exaggeration for an African-American leader in New York City to recall: "It was all but impossible for a black person to avoid the Communist label as long as he or she advocated civil rights with any degree of vigor."[25] During the Korean War, a segregationist discourse that communists were behind integration solidified into verisimilitude, contributing effectively to defeating African Americans' ongoing challenges to the existing racial hierarchy.[26]

Similar hardships befell progressive whites, particularly those living in the South, who had advocated the abolition of segregation.[27] In the Korean War period, in fact, both elites and grassroots Southerners escalated their critiques of civil rights activists as "communistic" and "un-American," contributing to the defense of the Southern way of life—segregation—under the banner of patriotism and to the marginalization of those engaged in social conflict in the name of national security. It is reasonable to see the Southern red scare, as the historian Jeff Woods notes, as a byproduct of "massive resistance to integration."[28] Indeed, it worked; few Southern whites dared to stand up against segregation at the cost of being ostracized, being "pariah[s] in their society."[29]

Similar sentiments appeared in growing Northern cities, where the influx of African Americans and Mexican Americans during and after the war created racial tensions among residents. In Detroit, for instance, more than half of respondents polled expressed unfavorable attitudes toward integration, and only 18 percent expressed favorable views toward the "full acceptance of Negroes."[30] Such racial tensions flared over public housing programs for lower-income households in Detroit, as well as other cities, like Milwaukee and Los Angeles. In the late 1940s, white residents criticized a public housing program as a "Negro housing project," expressing their concern over the "colored problem"—or "black invasion"—in their traditionally white neighborhood because, they thought, "Eighty percent [of blacks] are animals" and "They think they own the city."[31] According to the historian Thomas Sugrue, one irate housewife in Detroit wrote: "What about us, who cannot afford to move to a better location and are surrounded by colored? . . . Most of us invested our life's savings in property and now we are in constant fear that the neighbor will sell its property to people of a different race."[32] As seen in these comments, the housing developments in large cities were points of dispute primarily in terms of racial struggles in the late 1940s.

Then, against a backdrop of the "reality" of the Cold War during the Korean War, opponents of public housing programs reframed their attitudes and rhetoric. Now, opponents increasingly adopted a new logic and condemned the same programs not in terms of racial conflicts but of the Cold War struggle. One resident of Los Angeles, for instance, wrote a letter to a local council member, describing the city's housing program as the "Russian Communistic Socialistic Housing Project, which is trying to destroy our freedom, liberty, and our free enterprise system."[33] Amid this sea change, one city council member and former supporter of the housing program changed position, attacking it as the "creeping cancer of socialism which will bring us to socialism and social decay."[34] The application of this new Cold War logic to existing racial conflicts can be found with regard to the housing projects in other major cities nationwide, where criticism successfully slowed and trimmed the speed and size of projects. In these cases as well, white neighborhoods applied Cold War logic to "resolve" social and racial conflicts.[35]

In a similar manner, opponents of a national health-care program adopted a Cold War rhetoric. Many doctors and nurses had already criticized the program because, they argued, it would lower the quality of medical services, science, and institutions in the United States.[36] With the progress of the Korean War, however, they now used a Cold War logic to "resolve" an existing conflict. Immediately following the outbreak of the war, for example, the president of the American Medical Association delivered a speech broadcast on radio networks nationwide, harshly condemning state-controlled medical care: "American medicine has become the focal point in a struggle which may determine whether America remains free, or whether we are to become a Socialist State."[37] Such a critique was effective. In the face of mounting criticism, fashioned according to Cold War logic, Democrats abandoned talk of a national health-care program in 1950.

Another kind of social conflict effectively silenced in the Korean War period was labor disputes.[38] The use of anti-communist attacks on labor movements was already quite prevalent in the late 1940s, particularly following the critical strike year of 1946, when there were nearly 5,000 strikes—a record high in American history in terms of scale and number.

In Hawaii, with memories of the 1946 Sugar Strike still fresh, such red scare politics became rampant as early as the spring of 1947. Hawaii's governor Ingram Stainback, for instance, warned that there was a communist plan to take over Hawaii and that there were communists in labor organizations as well as universities and schools. "We are facing a struggle for the very survival of our nation," Stainback claimed.[39] This kind of attack, thus, was already common even before the notion of the Cold War became ubiquitous.

That said, what happened during the Korean War was not merely an escalation and extension of existing trends. The war, and, more importantly, popular interpretations of the war, made the verisimilitude of anti-communist claims conclusive, turning what were merely opinions about "a cold war" into the "reality" of the Cold War. Having been imagined and shared widely, such a reality provided a wartime context, which, in turn, supplied a logic that made it easy to adopt a definite and conclusive attitude against dissidents. Amid this war fever, a judge at a Hawaiian court, in fact, refused to grant bail to a leading labor activist in Hawaii because he was a security risk. The judge claimed: "The Army and Navy and Marine Corps will hold the beachheads in Korea. Our duty at home is to protect the beachheads that involve internal security."[40] The Cold War logic made it possible to connect two distinct subjects, war in Korea and labor activism at home, which, normally, would be considered separate. It is no coincidence that, in the midst of the Korean conflict, a major newspaper in Kansas published a political cartoon, portraying a scene in which "Management," "Labor," and the "American People" agreed on Uncle Sam's "Defense Program."[41]

Needless to say, the actual situation was not so neat. The "consensus," if it existed, was created not necessarily through actual agreement but, often, through brutal coercion. At a Buick plant in Flint, Michigan, right-wing union workers purged "radical" and "communistic" workers amid war fever. At a Ford plant in Linden, New Jersey, workers who tried to pass out "Hands Off Korea" leaflets were rounded up, beaten up, and literally pushed out of the factory. In this way, various tensions and disagreements in workplaces, which had been mounting since the late 1940s, between employers and workers, and among right- and left-wing unionists, were forcibly silenced and resolved.

In a similar way, another social issue—immigration problems—suddenly loomed large when those who had been concerned about the increasing presence of immigrants adopted a Cold War logic to renew their attacks.

"We Owe It to Our Fighting Men." *Kansas City Star,* 13 September 1950. (Illustration by
S. J. Ray. Supplied by Harry S. Truman Library. S. J. Ray Papers, Box 4, Folder: "July–December
1950." Reprinted with permission, PARS International Corp.)

One notable example was Democratic Nevada senator Pat McCarran, who had previously been known for his stubborn opposition to the increase of immigrants in American society. Even before the late 1940s, McCarran had been concerned about the deterioration of "Americanness," and arguing that the United States should accept immigrants only from Western Europe, not from Southern or Eastern Europe, let alone Asia or Latin America.[42] Then, in 1950, following the spread of popular interpretation of the Korean War as the start of World War III, McCarran increasingly adopted "anti-communist" logic, claiming that the admission of newcomers would invite communist subversion and espionage.[43] He said:

> The time has long since passed when we can afford to open our borders indiscriminately to give unstinting hospitality to any person whose purpose, whose ideological goal, is to overthrow our institutions and replace them with the evil oppression of totalitarianism.[44]

He eventually penned the Internal Security Act of 1950—the so-called Anti-Communist Act—and became known more as a dogged anti-communist than as a staunch immigration restrictionist. His goal—restricting immigration and maintaining alleged domestic tranquility—remained the same, though the change in logic made his claim more plausible and effective against the backdrop of the "reality" of the Cold War.

COLD WAR SUPPRESSION AS GENDER STRUGGLE

Another group suppressed through the application of Cold War logic was homosexuals, who increased their visibility in postwar America following the nationwide "coming-out experience" during wartime, thus, posing a challenge to conventional gender norms.[45] Denunciation of such "sexual perverts" existed during and after the war, but there was a change in the Korean War period, in terms of both quantity and quality. Dismissals of "sexual perverts" from civilian posts in the federal government, for instance, averaged only five per month from 1947 to the early months of 1950 but increased twelvefold in the second half of 1950.[46]

Interestingly, the logic behind expelling "sexual perverts" changed somewhat as well. Previously, the logic attacking "sexual perverts" was simply that they would attract more of their own kind. It was thus nothing more than simple hatred.[47] Because of the progress of the Korean War, however, another reason was added; the point of contention now was a perceived security risk. The logic maintained that sexual aberration made homosexuals "pressure prone"—that is, that they might leak classified information if a communist took advantage of their fear of exposure. Eventually, more than 800 people were fired from government jobs as a result of "investigation into allegations of homosexuality."[48] With the addition of this new, seemingly incontrovertible logic, one of the growing conflicts in postwar America in terms of sexuality was effectively silenced.

Similar repression was enforced on a much larger scale with regard to another element of change in gender relations: women, particularly working mothers, who increased their presence in the 1930s and during the war. The fact that many women found employment outside the home had already posed a certain challenge to conventional norms, but much more direct in igniting postwar conflict were, first, women's daily experiences of tense relations with men, and, second, working women's disagreements with another large group of women who believed in traditional roles for mothers and housewives.

First and foremost, many working women experienced disappointment that an increase in women's presence in the workplace did not in itself mean that they had achieved what they had hoped for. As Betty de Losada, a leading labor activist in San Francisco, recalled, a woman in the workplace was often treated as simply a "showcase woman" or expected to be "the woman" who could articulate the "woman's viewpoint." In addition, in her experience, men's attitudes were particularly defensive and stiff when women argued with them.[49] However, such frustration, in addition to the mass layoff of women in the immediate postwar period, did not dampen women's and feminists' enthusiasm for improving their social position but, rather, gave further vigor to their movement. For example, a group of leftist women in 1946 formed the Congress of American Women, an umbrella organization for the advancement of female equality and social reform. "Until the day when the American woman is free to develop her mind and abilities to their fullest extent, without discrimination because of her sex, . . . her long struggle for emancipation must continue," the group declared.[50]

Such a proclamation no doubt encouraged many women and feminists who had been radicalized through their wartime experiences but, at the same time, irritated many others who deemed it a "threat" to existing gender relations. Thus, women—particularly working mothers—began facing harsh criticism in the immediate postwar era and were told that their jobs really belonged to men, that real happiness lay in marriage and raising children, and that a "good" mother would not seek fulfillment outside the home.[51]

Such an assault on working women and feminists further escalated with the progress of the Korean War and the rapid spread of civil defense programs at home. One promotional film produced amid the war fever, for instance, proudly told viewers that the civil defense program revived old American traditions. "When the Indians struck, the man would run the stockade, the woman would load the rifles, the older children would take care of the small," the film claimed. "Each member of the group had an assigned job to do in the common defense of his community." The implication was that a man works outside, and a woman stays at home, helping with men's work. This notion of "family" imposed certain social roles, such as father, mother, and children, as given categories, implicitly discouraging individuals from crossing role boundaries.

This kind of "traditional American family" was more like an invention of the 1950s than one rooted in actual past experience.[52] But the fact that it lacked substance does not mean that the image was powerless. After it was conceived and disseminated widely, it restrained people from deviating from it. This gendered discourse of the "traditional" family became widely circulated and popular not because such a family was the norm but because the experiences of the Great Depression and World War II had diversified the forms of families and the roles of members, and there was no consensus on what a family was and should be.

The Congress of American Women, which had been challenging conventional gender and family norms, thereupon came under attack. The organization was targeted by the HUAC, which claimed that the organization's aim was "not to deal primarily with women's problems, as such, but rather to serve as a specialized arm of Soviet political warfare."[53] The group ended its short life when it officially disbanded in 1950. In a similar manner, women working in high-level government positions frequently came under attack. Landon R. Y. Storrs's study shows that women made up only a small percentage of high-level positions but comprised a disproportionately high percentage of those who faced loyalty cases.[54] It is reasonable to say, as the historian Elaine Taylor May suggests, that the logic of national security functioned not simply as containment of communism at a global level but containment of women at home.[55] Seen in this way, we can get to the heart of the matter. Despite its name, "anti-communism" was not really a goal; it was more a means, a discursive social device used for restoring and maintaining conventional (however imagined) order domestically, that assigned men and women specific roles and discouraged them from trespassing on each other's territory.

It is important to note that attacks against women, particularly against feminism under the banner of anti-communism, were not limited to conflicts between men and women. There was also a growing conflict among women over conflicting images of women. In the immediate postwar period, not only did progressive women and feminists heighten their demands for better and equal treatment, but another large portion of women with more conventional viewpoints similarly raised their voices, initiating the emergence of conservative movements in postwar America.[56]

On the one hand, progressives radicalized their criticism. In an article titled "Women Are Household Slaves," a housewife, Edith M. Stern, denounced the institution of housewifery in perhaps intentionally provocative and offensive tone, calling it a "brain-dribbling, spirit-stifling vocation" and contending bluntly that "only a psychology of slavery" can lead women to assume such a position. "As long as the institution of housewifery in its present form persists, both ideologically and practically, it blocks any true liberation of women," she argued.[57] Simultaneously, as the historians Michelle M. Nickerson and Nancy C. Brennan have pointed out, there was a surge in women's conservative movements intended to protect family, home, school, community, and, by extension, the national interest.[58] These two trends did not represent distinct tendencies; rather, the latter evolved rapidly as the former became conspicuous. In other words, both embodied major historical trends that emerged during and after the war in many parts of the world, one representing profound social change, the other a large-scale backlash.

For conservative women who began finding and raising their voices in the postwar era, home and housewifery were not despicable. "The first and original governor in our democracy is the women," Republican senator from Maine Margaret Chase Smith declared. "There is not a finer role that you can play in the defense of democracy and our American way of life than that of wife, mother, and homemaker."[59] Conservative women's campaigns to defend the "American way of life" extended over a wide range of

"Anti Red Housewives": A group of women in New York City protesting against the
Soviet regime, August 1951. (Photograph by Keystone. Getty Images, Hulton Archive,
2694860.)

subjects, from protesting labor strikes to opposing desegregation, criticizing
"bad" mothers, and participating in anti-communist demonstrations in the
streets. In one high-profile school controversy, which broke out in Pasa-
dena, California, a community-wide campaign by conservative women
ousted the city's progressive superintendent, who had tried to promote desegregation in schools, as this effort was seen not just as fomenting social
upheaval but as "subversive" and even "un-American."[60]

COLD WAR SUPPRESSION AS GRASSROOTS
SOCIAL CONSERVATISM

The other side of the harsh criticism of "subversive" and "un-American" elements was the call for "America for Americans" and the "American way of
life," which was celebrated in 1950.[61] This explains the enormous popularity

of self-proclaimed "100 percent American" Senator Joseph McCarthy in the second half of the year. At this time, he received 2,000 invitations to talk, more than all other Republican spokesmen combined.[62] Richard Nixon, a rookie candidate for the United States Senate in the midterm elections of 1950, did not miss an opportunity to fashion himself as an "All-American senator," accusing a rival candidate, Helen Gahagan Douglas, of "[fighting] everything which has made America great" and "[fostering] everything we consider un-American."[63] His tactics worked; Nixon made his debut as a freshman senator from California the following spring.

The "communist" label was convenient for many elite and grassroots conservatives because it was vague enough to use to attack anyone who had been critical of society's conventional norms. Republican senator from Minnesota Walter Judd even claimed: "Communists emphasize all the bad conditions in our country—Jim Crowism, the discrimination, the slums, inadequate education or medical care."[64] Logic of this kind was versatile, as it was often used in reverse; someone who emphasized bad conditions and tried to change them must be a "communist." One anti-communist pamphlet, in fact, included a series of typical Q and As: "How can you tell a Communist?" The answer read: "Get him in an argument about the United States. He can tell you plenty of things wrong with this country."[65] Not surprisingly, quite a few progressives, as well as labor and civil rights activists, withdrew from their movements, at least for the time being.

Seen in this way, the silencing accomplished through "anti-communist" Cold War politics during the McCarthy era was more multifarious than we usually think, targeting African Americans, civil rights activists, labor unionists, gays and lesbians, working women, feminists, and immigrants, as well as advocates of public housing programs and national health care, and others. What they shared was not a communist ideology but a tendency to challenge conventional social values in the aftermath of World War II, implicitly or explicitly, and this made them appear to be "un-American" elements from a standard viewpoint. In other words, the actual nature of Cold War repression had less to do with "anti-communism" than with a more general conservative backlash, not necessarily in terms of political conservatism, but social conservatism. The battle line was not so much ideology or international politics as social customs, common sense, gender and sexual norms, and way of life.

This tendency shows up clearly in an analysis of what the attackers cared about. One example is *Militant Truth,* a Christian fundamentalist, anticommunist newspaper, published bimonthly in Chattanooga, Tennessee (and later in Atlanta, Georgia). On the issue of race, the paper asserted, " 'Keep the whites white and the blacks black' is the slogan which is spreading across the nation." It argued: "Christian people, who hold no hatred or prejudice in their hearts, believe [that] it will wreck our nation if we do not do something to curb the left-wing, pro-Communist program to destroy race purity by intermixture and intermarriage."[66]

On the issue of labor, the editor of *Militant Truth,* Sherman A. Patterson, wrote a long article, "Red Treachery Exposed," arguing that "good Americans" knew that their first loyalty as wage earners was to their employer, not to some outside organization. It further argued that labor unions were developed through "Communist propaganda," stirring up class hatred and driving an "iron wedge of suspicion, mistrust, and disloyalty between employee and employer."[67] Furthermore, on the issue of homosexuality, the paper characterized the problem as "filthy mess" and harshly blamed "sex perverts" at government offices because they would attract subordinates like themselves, warning: "The shades of Sodom and Gomorrah are upon us."[68]

Finally, on the subject of family, *Militant Truth* continually emphasized the importance of traditional values. In an article titled "Fathers, Mothers, and Their Children," which reported on the increase in family attendance at churches in the postwar era, the author described a "daily" family gathering at home: "All members of the family—baby in mother's arms, the little tots toddling around the room, the older boys and girls trying to sit still in their chairs—all gathered together around the table or in the living room while father opened the big book and read."[69] Here again, as in a civil defense promotional film, the implication was that the man is the center of the scene, leading other members, while the women and children obediently follow. Moreover, each is described as having a specific role, making up an orderly, harmonious family. A woman, in this description, would not lead the discussion nor would children resist their parents. In fact, the article contended that teaching children obedience was important because otherwise they would not learn it at school or in the community. In this sense, the article argued, obedience at home would lay the foundation for good citizenship. "Good citizens do not break the laws of home, school, state, or nation. . . . Godly homes are the Nation's first line of defense."[70]

Because of its consistent emphasis on issues of defense and security, with harsh criticism of "Communist programs," one might gain the impression that the *Militant Truth*, first and foremost, was a staunch anti-communist newspaper at the height of the Cold War. Yet, close examination shows that the newspaper's principal criticism was not necessarily about geopolitics or ideology but more toward newly arising social changes in terms of race relations, labor-management relations, gender relations, and so forth, which threatened, from its perspective, harmonious and orderly society. These were the problems which were ongoing throughout the postwar period, and which were finally "resolved" through the application of anti-communist logic after the "reality" of the Cold War increased verisimilitude during the Korean War.

Loyalty hearings emerged at such a crossroads of "anti-communist" logic and social and cultural conflicts, exemplifying the multifaceted nature of Cold War repression. Indeed, the topics covered included not only political ideology, the Korean War, and the Cold War but also religion, church attendance, race relations, and sexual morality.[71]

> Have you ever danced with a white girl?
> Have you ever had dinner with a mixed group?
> Have you ever had Negroes in your home?
> Did you ever write a letter to the Red Cross about segregation of blood?
> Do you go to church?
> What do you think about sex before marriage?[72]

Those being questioned could avoid answering by citing the Fifth Amendment right against self-incrimination, as many did. Nonetheless, quite a few found that their employers arbitrarily dismissed them or urged them to resign. Waves of mass terminations increased in the spring of 1951 following President Truman's announcement regarding the Loyalty Program. After his announcement, a dismissal that previously had to "show reasonable grounds" now had to indicate only "reasonable doubts." This change had the effect of broadening grounds for dismissals and repression.[73] A female employee at the State Department, for instance, was urged to resign because "her first child arrived too soon after her marriage," and, likewise, several male officials were dismissed on grounds of "fornication" and "[keeping] a mistress while on remote station" and so forth.[74]

The case of Esther and Stephen Brunauer was even more mysterious (and, thus, it is suggestive about what actual factors were behind ostensible McCarthyite attacks). Born in California in 1901, Esther graduated from Mills College in Oakland, received her PhD in history from Stanford University, and then studied in Switzerland and Germany. She built most of her career as an international relations secretary at the American Association of University Women, and in this capacity she gave lectures, led discussions, and wrote international study guides for newsletters and so on. During the war, she was employed by the State Department and continued to work after the war as a specialist on international organizations.[75] In short, she exemplified a sort of "new woman." Stephen, who was born and grew up in Hungary, immigrated to the United States in 1921 at the age of seventeen, and studied chemistry, in which he earned a PhD from Johns Hopkins University. During World War II, he served in the Navy, and after the war he continued to work in the Department of the Navy.[76] In today's terminology, they might be called a "power couple."

Attacks began in 1947 with Illinois Republican Representative Fred Busbey's smearing of Esther as "anti-American" for having pointed out illiteracy, poverty, and monopolistic practices in society. Lacking a decisive blow, attackers in the late 1940s turned their attention to her husband, accusing him of having communist connections through his Hungarian friends. Like many others who were subjected to loyalty hearings, the Brunauers were face with repeated rounds of new charges and clearance for years. Although their case bogged down in 1950 because of the lack of proof of disloyalty or communist tendencies, the decisive blow finally came in regard to their attitudes about life, particularly about sex.

One accuser wrote that she kept her distance from the Brunauers because, she thought, they lacked moral conduct in terms of American standards. "They had a 'European' attitude toward such things as sex and were most loose in thoughts and actions," the accuser wrote. "By a 'European' attitude I mean that their moral code was very different than the average American, and [being] unfaithful between husband and wife was common."[77] The accuser pointed out that the couple even "lived together as man and wife" a year before they were married. Another informer even pointed out that the couple "advocated free love, had sex orgies."[78] After such criticism, a new accusation, "moral turpitude," was added.

Accordingly, Esther and Stephen had to explain their private lives in public, specifically that Stephen had engaged in two or three extramarital affairs during their twenty years of marriage; that they had twice discussed divorce; that he was not a "woman-chaser" or "philanderer" by inclination; and that, despite these problems, they trusted each other and had kept the family together and so on.[79] Despite their efforts, however, criticism and harassment continued, with anonymous telephone calls, accompanied by threats, such as "Get out of this neighborhood, you Communists, or you will be carried out in a box."[80] In the end, despite their attempts to fight back, both were suspended from their positions in 1951. Stephen resigned, and Esther, while trying to appeal, was dismissed in 1952.

For the most part, these cases during the McCarthy era—Esther and Stephen Brunauer, Helen MacMartin, and numerous others in various fields who fell under suspicion—have been considered examples of false charges: tragedies, certainly, but an epiphenomenon, which coincidentally accompanied the reckless attacks characteristic of the era of McCarthyism.[81] Because they have been seen in this way, not much attention has been paid to exploring what these "false charges" really meant. To begin with, these thousands of "misrepresentations" look like an epiphenomenon only because we assume that McCarthyism was about anti-communist red-hunting, therefore, those who were persecuted even though they were not communists appear to have been innocent victims of reckless charges. But, in labeling and perceiving the phenomenon in this way, we tend to miss other diverse incidents of social repression that silenced social conflict under the banner of anti-communism. These local struggles involved racial, labor, gender, and other tensions. As we have seen, many targets were neither communists nor fifth columnists, but African Americans, civil rights activists, labor unionists, working and professional women, and gays and lesbians, as well as advocates of New Deal programs, such as public housing and public health care.

These groups represented not communist ideology but newly emerging social conflicts, which had developed because of experiences of World War II. Viewed in this way, the phenomenon commonly called McCarthyism looks quite different. Numerous cases of "false charges" were not simple and incidental mistakes but incidents of social repression, enacted on elements of social change, effectively pacifying chaotic postwar situations through purifying society and stifling dissenting voices, eventually bringing a more "harmonious" and "orderly" society to postwar America for decades to come—a sort of social mechanism that necessitated the imagined reality of the Cold War. Looking at McCarthyism in this way, we avoid describing it as a peculiar American phenomenon that occurred in the abnormal climate of the Cold War. Instead, the phenomenon can be seen as something that could develop at any time and place under similar social and historical conditions.

Indeed, this observation can be made about other parts of the world as well. Although the degree of violence differed widely, similar patterns of social repression emerged simultaneously outside the United States during the Korean War. In China, in Taiwan, in the Philippines, in Japan, and in the United Kingdom, local people similarly adopted the bipolar logic of the Cold War in stifling various kinds of social and cultural conflicts at home. Conventionally, each has been treated as a separate phenomenon, viewed largely through a Cold War lens, and, thus, often described as an end result of the global confrontation on the ground. Thus, the existing literature has tended to consolidate, rather than question, notions of the Cold War. However, in an effort to raise questions about this Cold War framework itself, we consider each of these domestic purges, reconsidering the meaning of such phenomena that escalated in this short period. Why did such similar repressions occur simultaneously across the globe? In Chapter 8, we look into the phenomena that culminated in the fall of 1950 in Japan and the United Kingdom.

CHAPTER EIGHT

"Expose Enemies within Our Gates!"

ON THURSDAY, SEPTEMBER 14, 1950, nearly half the buses in London were off the road. Traffic was a mess throughout the city, but the most congested spot was Victoria Station, where thousands of people arriving from the suburbs and beyond found that bus routes had been canceled. It was an unofficial strike, carried out by a portion of the membership of the Transport Workers' Union, which demanded an increase in wages and nonemployment of women conductors. The next day, the strike spread from thirteen bus garages in the city to twenty, with more than 11,000 drivers and conductors out and nearly 2,000 buses standing idle. In addition, some tram drivers and port workers, mostly men, joined in the strike.[1] Such strikes were nothing unusual in postwar Britain. Demands for additional pay were not strange in view of rapid increases in the cost of living since the end of the war, particularly around 1950, and the demand to exclude women reflected ongoing social and gender conflicts, unleashed through the experience of World War II, during which thousands of women for the first time entered the workplace outside the home. These issues were in contention throughout the postwar period, so nothing was really new in the fall of 1950.

However, what was unusual at that time was the degree of criticism concerning such disagreements in society, with the application of a new logic. The Korean War had begun only a few months earlier, and widespread fear and an interpretation of the war as the start of World War III provided the context for a change in the logic used to justify criticism of labor movements. "Anyone who goes on strike now will do so knowing that he is helping traitors," declared the popular *Daily Graphic:* "He will range himself with the enemies of Britain—with the fifth column within this country that takes its orders from foreigners who seek to destroy us."[2] The London bus strike happened to coincide with the release of the first British casualty list in Korea and was increasingly seen not as merely one of the many constant social battles but as part of a global confrontation—the Cold War at home.[3]

The minister of labour, George A. Isaacs, for example, began his speech at the House of Commons on September 15 by introducing the Cold War context even before discussing the bus strike or the employment of women. "I am speaking at a time when our men are facing serious risks in Korea, and when it is essential that there should be no danger of interference with their supplies and support," he stated:

The plot is for workers on the docks, road transport, meat-carrying and the markets to strike in key places. The ultimate purpose is to slow the rearmament drive and hold up reinforcement and supplies to the fighting front in Korea. None of the strikes may be big, but the total effect is intensified to cripple industrial activity and spread discontent.[4]

The minister insisted that this attempt to create "trouble" would not succeed if the workers refused to be pawns, adding, "I earnestly appeal to them to be on their guard against all attempt to drag them into the struggle which will be to the detriment of the nation and their fellow workers."[5]

Popular newspapers, likewise, criticized the strikers as "traitors," "plotters," and "wreckers." Britain's best-selling newspaper, the *Daily Express* in London, warned in an editorial: "No one knows when the enemy will strike next; maybe it will be in bloodless fashion in the ports of Britain."[6] The *Daily Graphic* ran an article complaining that the minister did not provide names of leading strikers and insisting, "Name the traitors! Name the plotters who seek to use British workers as tools in their dark design. Expose these enemies within our gates!"[7]

BRITAIN'S COLD WAR AT HOME

As seen in these comments, aggressive anti-communist campaigns were not limited to the United States, and they shared not just their appearance but the ways in which they marginalized existing social problems. On September 16, the *Daily Mail*, a popular London newspaper, published a lengthy editorial, "Moscow's Mission," that embodied this development of logic, warning, "What are the intentions of these traitors? The London bus strike may prove to be only the start of their wretched scheme." It argued that workers' grievances at the moment were "of little real importance" compared with the danger that the whole country faced and described the strike as merely Red agents' attempt to foment discord throughout key industries and services in the country. These strikers were traitors to the nation, it continued, and needed to be detained until all danger was past, however long that might take. The paper even recommended the establishment of laws necessary to detain them, saying: "This is not a matter of punishment but of protection."[8]

As suggested in this editorial, legal measures against strikers and members of the Communist Party became a hot topic in Great Britain in the fall of 1950.[9] To be sure, such anti-communist bills were not introduced in Parliament, but National Arbitration Order No. 1305—a wartime regulation originally introduced as part of the Emergency Powers Act during World War II in 1940—was invoked to curb labor activism for five years after the end of the war. When some 1,400 London gas workers walked out in late September, actually, ten leading figures in the strike were summoned, arrested, and imprisoned for a month under the terms of this wartime regulation.[10]

Although we usually think of postwar British society as relatively free of a McCarthyite red-baiting climate, this was not the case. Echoes of McCarthyism did emerge, and the rise of anti-communist campaigns was conspicuous, with popular newspapers consistently attacking the Labour government, labeling it "socialist" and "communist."[11] Moreover, the intensity of conservatives' criticism was remarkable. For instance, *Popular Pictorial*, a bimonthly publication issued by the Conservative Party, devoted its entire February–March 1951 issue to the communist menace, meeting with an exceedingly good public reception, with early sales reaching 100,000 copies above normal circulation.[12] The magazine warned: "Of course, the cost of

Cover illustration of the *Popular Pictorial* (February–March 1951). (Supplied by National Library of Australia. Reprinted with permission, The Conservative Party of the U.K.)

living, shortage of houses, and breakdown of coal supplies are matters of grave concern to all of us, but there is one factor that could make these other worries comparably unimportant." The most vital issue, it wrote, was the communist threat, declaring: "The theory and practice of Communism means the end of personal liberty, the end of spiritual values, the destruction of the British Constitution and of family life."[13]

Faced with the explosion of criticism toward strikes in the fall of 1950, participants were bewildered. "Who, me, an agitator? Don't talk silly," a 39-year-old member of the Merseyside Port Workers' Committee said, "I am a member of the town's Liberal Party executive." Another 24-year-old man, likewise, asked a reporter, "Do I look like a saboteur? I am happily married. I am a supporter of the Labour Party." A 32-year-old man added, "We were all democratically elected by the dockers for this job."[14] These members argued that such an allegation that they all were communists would not solve any wage or working-conditions problems on the docks.

Nonetheless, strikes were rapidly losing support from within as well. To begin with, labor leaders gave them the cold shoulder. After all, the London bus strike was an unofficial, wildcat strike; such strikes were quite common in postwar British society, where grassroots workers' claims were mostly blocked by the unions. The leadership's attitude, indeed, was not simply distant but even hostile. At an official meeting of the Transport Workers' Union, which was held only a few days before the beginning of the London bus strike, one of the top officials described the situation as "dynamite," condemning an attempt to carry out the strike as an effort by "subversive elements" to create chaos and confusion.[15] Even a somewhat more sympathetic labor union leader recommended that the bus strikers pull back before it was too late: "I have had my share of strikes. But on this issue I appeal to all trade unionists here to accept the guidance of their officials," he said. "A strike now would be a blow at our boys fighting in Korea."[16]

This was a familiar logic. As in many other societies, in Britain at the time of the Korean War, discussions of social issues were replaced with those of alleged global conflict and national security. Asked about the labor strike, one respondent said: "I don't think the strike should be on. Had enough. Now they should help the country a bit more."[17] In the fall of 1950, participants in strikes were keenly aware that they were increasingly viewed as serving foreign, communist interests, and this compelled them to go back to work, according to one union leader's observation.[18] In the case of the London bus strike, a planned mass meeting was aborted because no speaker arrived and very few attended.[19] Faced with this mounting criticism fashioned in Cold War logic, and with the deterioration in support from union members, the London bus strikes collapsed both from within and from without.

In Britain's national politics as well, the winter of 1950–1951 marked a dramatic swing in popular attitudes away from the Labour Party, which had been in power since 1945. With the country at war, and with mounting criticism toward strikers and leftists in general, a Gallup Poll found a sharp rise in popular opinion in favor of the Conservative Party; furthermore, throughout the winter, the party's lead widened more than ever before.[20] Eventually, in the national election of 1951, the Conservatives came to power for the first time in the postwar period.[21] It may appear, at a glance, that the Korean War ignited a flare-up in anti-communist sentiments in Britain, which, in turn, spelled the end of the Labour government.

CONSTANT WAR OF LIFE

However, beneath seemingly apparent Cold War politics, here again existed local and social struggles concerning what should be considered "normal" and "orderly" in postwar Britain. In order to explore this point, let us take a micro view of the London bus strike once again, following diary entries of Frances Berner, a housewife living in South London. On the day the strike began, she was at the hairdresser's and got caught up in a mess on the way home. At Raynes Park terminus, where the bus usually arrived every five minutes, a crowd of people was waiting for more than twenty minutes. Recognizing that the strike advocated excluding women from the work-place, she thought: "When war is in progress women are asked to do their domestic chores in their leisure time and work in factories, engineering shops, and the transport services. But they are not to be allowed to have the freedom of doing these jobs because [men] would like to do them."[22] After the bus came and disgorged its passengers, it quickly filled again with housewives, who began to talk while waiting for the bus to depart. Some criticized the strike's demand for women not to work as bus conductors, saying, "They were glad enough of the women during the war." Others tried to defend the strikers' cause by explaining the complex situations confronting bus drivers. "I mused on the constant war of life," she wrote, "Men against women, groups of workers against other groups, employers versus employed, the growing power of the unions."[23]

This was an accurate observation. Although loud anti-communist attacks increased on the surface, what was going on in the streets was an outburst of social and cultural disagreements—or, as she put it, the "war of life"—which had been growing continuously in postwar Britain. In fact, on the ground, strikers were criticized not because of the content of their demands for higher pay, let alone their ideological inclinations or political beliefs, but the manner in which demands were made: by striking, which disturbed order and daily life. Asked about strikes, one respondent, for example, said, "Not against strikes, if [for a] good cause, but [it] causes too much upheaval."[24] Another person pointed out the negative effects of the strategy: "The strikers will not get what they want by striking because the public will go against them and it will do more harm than good."[25] In this sense, the *Daily Mail*'s cartoon captured popular dissatisfaction about strikers; it depicted an uncontrollable black cat, labeled "Workers," rushing wildly on a dining table toward a dish of "Higher Wages," as if stating that strikers were unruly and disobedient elements—that is, enemies of society.[26] In other words, beneath the Cold War rhetoric that was utilized in putting down strikes was a distaste for uncertainty and confusion in society. Following the turbulent years of the war and postwar periods, and following the Labour Party's various experimental policies, such as nationalization of the coal, electricity, and gas industries since 1945, what became increasingly conspicuous was a desire for a return to an "orderly" and "normal" way of life.

Five years after the end of the war, postwar Britain was still far from peaceful or orderly. More than anything else, the cost of living was skyrocketing, particularly around 1950. Increases in costs of electricity, gas, and coal, as well as general consumer goods was evident. Transportation and lodging expenses were high as well.[27] The food—particularly meat—situation was deteriorating. "The meat situation is worse. . . . [Two years ago] we could have a meat meal once a day without having to worry unduly where it was coming from," a 52-year-old woman said; "Everything is constantly going up in price and down in quality."[28] Such economic hardship forced many to alter their daily habits. "In no way is my standard of living

"Desire Caught by Tail." *Daily Mail,* 11 October 1950. (Illustration by Leslie Illingworth. Supplied by Llyfrgell Genedlaethol Cymru/National Library of Wales, Leslie Illingworth Cartoon Collection, ILW 1793. Reprinted with permission, Solo Syndication, London.)

better. It is worse in every aspect," another 44-year-old woman told an interviewer in February 1951, complaining:

> The prices of everything in the shops is up [*sic*]. To buy the necessities is exorbitant. The cost of taxi's is more. That means to go out is now even more expensive. My life grows more and more quiet. It is like living in wartime. . . . I just don't do anything and yet the money flows away.[29]

Gone was the rosy image of the postwar era, and emerging instead were the realities of social problems and various conflicts arising with them.

By the same token, the housing shortages forced many families to change their way of living, compelling entire families to live in a single room, couples to live with their parents, or multiple families to share a house, and so on.[30] In brief, a long-standing dispute over what should be considered normal life was bubbling over beneath the Cold War rhetoric, and Labour and strikers were seen as blocking the return to ordinary life or preventing the creation of a route toward the restoration of such a life.

Furthermore, these issues were often connected with another common social conflict in the postwar era: struggles over what women should and should not do. During World War II, many British women found employment outside the home for the first time in their lives, and many continued to work after the war ended. In fact, more women were at work in the spring of 1951 than during the peak period of the war in 1943.[31] Naturally, this provoked controversy. On the one hand, the women hoped to improve their social position. On the other hand, there was a backlash that involved efforts to maintain gender distinctions and family values and to exclude women from the workplace. In fact, as in American society and elsewhere, working women in postwar Britain faced various difficulties in continuing to work; as we have seen, the London bus strike in 1950 actually originated with efforts by male drivers to exclude women from the workplace. Popular newspapers made fun of working women, portraying them as working outside the home due to "loneliness."[32]

Not surprisingly, such criticism, directly and indirectly, was an underlying subject in conservative publications in the postwar era. *Popular Pictorial's* one-page cartoon, "You can fight Communism without a tin hat," exemplified this conservative backlash. In the cartoon, the protagonist, Bill, at first chose not to attend a union meeting and instead went to a movie with his girlfriend, Sally. At the movie theater, a newsreel was shown, including a scene of Korea. Bill said, "Our boys in the Far East are having a tough time. Wish I could be out there giving the commies what for." Sally, whose head was leaning on his shoulder, replied, "But Bill, surely the fight's on in this country, too! Doesn't your union fight communism in industry?" At the end, when Sally asked Bill to dance, Bill apologetically but firmly turned her down because he had decided to go to the union meeting to fight communists. Asked if she minded, she replied, "No, Darling! Because you will be fighting for me and our future."[33] The implication is that while supporting the man and playing a decisive role in changing his attitude, and in fact becoming his motivation and cause, the woman remains someone who needs to be protected and does not participate in actual politics—which is man's business—suggesting a conventional image of women while keeping the gender line distinct and stable. In short, behind an ostensibly anti-communist facade, this cartoon portrayed two "enemies within" in postwar Britain that had been upending conventional systems of order and harmony: labor unions and working women.

The crux of popular resentment was disappointment over the fact that "normal" life had not been restored even five years after the end of the war. One man described this situation as the reason that he turned his back on Labour: "I was Labour until my wife went away for [work], and I had to do the shopping. That was enough!"[34] It was not just men who felt dissatisfied. Quite a few British women also seemed to desire a return to normalcy. According to research by the Conservative Party, many female workers remained reluctant about, or even opposed to, taking part in labor movements, and, actually, middle-class women were considered pivotal in the victory of the Conservative Party in 1951.[35] Such a longing for a return to "normalcy" can be seen symbolically in an editorial in the *Daily Mail* on New Year's Day 1951. It urged Britons: "Let us get back some of the silliness of life, returning to the giggle, and to an abandonment to the fun of the moment."[36]

Viewed in this way, the upsurge in anti-communist attacks, as well as the swing to the Conservatives in 1950–1951, was not due simply to the progress of the Korean War and the materialization of the Cold War but to domestic desires for the restoration of the "normal" social order and ordinary life of peacetime, which had presumably been interrupted only during World War II. Many members of the working and middle classes were fed up with restrictions on small pleasures that they had enjoyed before the war, and those in the middle class were increasingly resentful of the Labour government's experimental policies and imposed austerity, thanks to the increasing cost of living, food shortages, and housing problems.[37] What they hoped for was, as the historians Robert Taylor and Alfred H. Havighurst have pointed out, the improvement of their lives within an existing framework, not the radical transformation of society.[38] For them to realize such a normal life, the social tensions especially evident in the chaotic postwar era had to be quelled. Doing so required the wartime logic of national security, and maintaining this logic necessitated the "reality" of the Cold War. Intriguingly, this situation was not limited to Britain. A similar dynamic was unfolding on the other side of the world, in Japan.

RECONSIDERING THE RED PURGE IN JAPAN

At 3 p.m. on July 28, 1950, thirty-one workers at *Mainichi Shinbun* in Tokyo were called to their bosses' offices, most of them individually, and told that they were fired, on the spot. The only reason that they were given was that the news media had an important responsibility in driving out communists and communist sympathizers from the company. Similar notifications were conveyed simultaneously at other major newspapers, such as *Asahi Shinbun* and *Yomiuri Shinbun*. This was the beginning of the waves of mass dismissals, conducted first through General Douglas MacArthur's directive to remove communists from the newspaper industry.[39] Based on this directive, fifty newspaper companies nationwide unilaterally notified a total of 704 employees that they were being terminated. These ranged from major newspapers like *Asahi Shinbun* (104 dismissed out of 5,200 staff), *Mainichi Shinbun* (49 of 5,000), and *Yomiuri Shinbun* (34 of 2,200) to small local newspapers such as *Nihonkai Shinbun* (9 of 90) in Tottori, as well as *Shinyo Shinbun* (1 of 50) in Matsumoto.[40]

This wave of mass dismissals in the newspaper industry then spread to other companies on a much larger scale. In the fall of 1950, roughly 13,000 people were fired from industries including coal, steel, shipbuilding, chemistry, railways, and mining—a phenomenon commonly known in Japan as the "Red Purge."[41] As the name suggests, these waves of mass dismissals have conventionally been viewed through a Cold War lens. The traditional understanding is that this was a purge of communists, conducted primarily under orders from the U.S. occupation forces. Under such a presumption, there has not been much discussion of *who* actually planned and conducted this so-called Red Purge. In the existing literature, the answer has almost been taken for granted.[42] It was the Americans. It was the GHQ and Washington. Their reason for the Red Purge was, it is commonly argued, to make Japan a fortress against the threat of Soviet expansionism in East Asia. By the same token, not much attention has been paid to who the actual victims were; that they were communists and communist sympathizers or innocent victims dismissed due to false charges has also been taken for granted. In short, the Red Purge has been commonly understood as an aftereffect of the Cold War—an inevitable end result of the global confrontation.

However, this grand narrative has prevented us from inquiring further into the meaning of the Red Purge and the Cold War. Once we raise questions about the Cold War framework itself, the mass firings of 1950 seem more than just a Red Purge. Rather, they look more like part of a global phenomenon of domestic purges that raged in many places during the Korean War. To begin with, we need to make a distinction between the mass firings in the newspaper industry and those that followed in other industries on a much larger scale. The first wave was based on MacArthur's statement, developed in the context of the Korean War and aimed at picking off "communists," however vague the meaning of that term might have been—a series of mass dismissals which can be justifiably called the Red Purge. By contrast, the following and larger waves of the mass firings, which all got lumped together as the Red Purge, were carried out based on the judgments of each company, targeting not just communists but anything deemed "destructive."[43] There was no single order issued by the GHQ. William Murcutt, chief of the Economic and Scientific Section, actually, told Robert Amis, chief of the Labor Division in August 1950, that the "GHQ must not be involved in dismissals."[44] Recalling the situations surrounding the Red Purge, Amis told an interviewer years later:

> It is a mistake to believe a criticism that I directed the Red Purge. I did not begin it. I believe that it came out from the inside of Japan's labor unions . . . for they wanted to exclude communist factions. It came neither from the Government Section (in the GHQ) nor MacArthur; it came from the Japanese themselves. . . . I got embroiled by leaders of the management and labor.

They often invited me to dinner, took pictures, and used it to show that they were close to me and that I was hoping to implement the Red Purge.[45]

Many historians of the Red Purge have been skeptical of Amis's remarks, seeing him as feigning ignorance, because scholars have firmly believed in the absolute rule of U.S. occupation power in Japan.[46] This view, of course, has a certain merit; after all, the GHQ intervened at various critical moments, such as the dismissal of "communists" at newspapers. Nonetheless, Amis's recollection does not seem like a mere fraud, considering that this is when the GHQ gradually lost its special aura in the occupation of Japan. Over the course of the Red Purge, American officers experienced being ignored and used by Japanese actors, and many realized, as Valery Burati, a GHQ official in the Labor Division, wrote in a personal letter, that "the Occupation [had] gone to seed."[47] Japanese politicians and labor leaders likewise had been learning about this tendency and realized that they could negotiate, or even flatly reject, the GHQ's "orders."[48] In sum, the large portion of mass dismissal cases which we now commonly consider part of the Red Purge was, in essence, planned, conducted, and maintained through judgments by each company, with each using its own reasoning and criteria for who should be let go and why.

LOCAL DYNAMICS OF THE RED PURGE

Let us take a look at one long list of criteria, compiled by the largest mining company in Japan, the Mitsui Miike Coal Mine, to examine how diverse the targets of their "Red Purge" were. This list, comprising twenty-two itemized categories, targeted not only communists, communist party members, and those who had left or been removed from the party, but also various "sympathizers" who, for example, had tried to help those who were fired. It targeted even those who might behave in such a way or might hinder the company's operations.[49] With criteria so broad and vague, how did this second wave of mass dismissals function on the ground? Observing the expansion of the Red Purge, the Labor Division of the GHQ warned that it must not be mixed up with the rationalizations of companies.[50] Various archival documents show, however, that the actual practice of this Red Purge was not limited to the termination of "communists"; more often, it was used in various and local ways, as an excuse to dismiss certain kinds of people.

Take one case as an example: that of Nippon Kokan (Nippon Steel Tube Company), which fired 190 workers in the fall of 1950. The dispute began with an announcement by the company president, Kawata Shige, on October 23, that he was compelled to discharge workers "who hindered the smooth operation of the company's business or refused to cooperate with the company."[51] Even GHQ officials, often considered operators of the Red Purge, were alarmed; one staff member in the Labor Division, for example, described this mass firing as an "abuse of the Red Purge."[52] As the chief of the division, Amis warned the Nippon Kokan management:

> What I have said before is not being followed by the management. It seems to me that the management is taking advantage. Concrete reasons for dismissal should be given. If reasons for dismissal cannot be cited correctly, defer the discharge. When a dismissed employee does not fall under the reason, he should be returned to his post, and wages during his dismissal should be paid.[53]

The company simply ignored this warning.

Meanwhile, Ishijima Seiichi, a 27-year-old worker at the company's Tsurumi Plant, wrote a lengthy petition to Amis, asking for help and explaining that, although he was an active union member at his plant, he had never been a communist or a communist sympathizer. He argued that the company disliked him because, as a union member, he had "found many defects in the way the management of the company [was] carried out" and because he "submitted his opinion about the improvement of the management."[54] Ishijima's letter, which contained a detailed counterargument to the company's charges, was translated and taken seriously. Amis, then, examined the letter's legitimacy with the help of Japan's Labor Ministry, whose officials interviewed Ishijima and concluded that he was not a communist. Based on this information, Amis met with company officers and urged them to give Ishijima his job back.

This time, the company reacted. It invited Ishijima to a dinner and told him that the company admitted he was not a communist. Yet it still refused to re-employ him and asked to make a deal, offering him a sum of 250,000 yen—more than the average yearly income at that time—on condition that he did not challenge the management again before the GHQ or the public.[55] Ishijima was in a tough spot. Having a wife and children, and without any possibility of returning to the company, he apparently accepted this offer. We do not have any further records involving him. GHQ officials were confused and disturbed by the company's refusal to rehire Ishijima, in spite of GHQ's repeated warnings. One Japanese official at the Labor Ministry explained to them that, even though he was not a communist, he might be considered some kind of a "troublemaker" at the company because as one of the founding organizers of a union at his factory in Tsurumi he had actively criticized the management.[56]

In fact, it was Japan's Labor Ministry, not the GHQ, who, in early October 1950, presented a "guideline" for the Red Purge at companies and accepted the dismissal of not only members of the communist party and fellow-travelers but also "those inveterate active trouble makers, taking leadership roles in activities, inciting others, or being original planners of incitation, thus causing real injury to the safety and peace of the enterprise."[57] Relying on this vague definition of "troublemakers," numerous companies took advantage. One such case is that of Niigata Tekkosho, a small ironworks in Niigata Prefecture, where three dozen workers, mostly active union members, were fired as "troublemakers" for being "uncooperative," "disturbing," and "undesirable" elements at the company. One worker noticed that dismissals of workers were especially numerous where labor-management negotiations had been contentious.[58]

Similar conduct can be seen in the case of Japan's major transport company, Nittsu, where 800 "reds" were fired. Many were, actually, guilty only of participating in wildcat strikes earlier in the summer of 1950. In the case of Dai Nippon Boseki (Dai Nippon Spinning Company), this tendency was so conspicuous that a GHQ official Burati described the company as "one of the worst offenders in the field of textiles in taking advantage of [the] 'red purge' to dismiss anti-communists who were, in fact, aggressive union officers."[59] As this comment shows, the implementation of the Red Purge went far beyond the control of the GHQ and, in practice, covered up what were, in reality, labor and social disputes.

Nevertheless, it is still simplistic to describe the Red Purge simply as a phenomenon in which the management took advantage of the anti-communist climate to solve labor disputes. This is because struggles were waged not only between management and labor but also within labor unions. In the case of Densan (All-Japan Electrical Workers Union), for example, a dispute between, at least on the surface, "communist" and "non-communist" factions had been developing since 1947. This internal dispute culminated at the union's annual conference in Nara in May 1950, which was eventually canceled due to a violent clash between the two factions. Following this incident, the mainstream "noncommunist" faction of the union circulated a communiqué, requiring the full membership of approximately 130,000 to reregister, which was approved by 110,000 members and rejected by 20,000. When the management announced the dismissal of 2,137 "key figures" among those who had refused to reregister under the climate of the Red Purge in late August, the labor union acquiesced, because those dismissed were no longer "union members."[60]

In other words, behind the image of ideological struggle between "communist" and "non-communist" factions, the point of contention was less over ideology than a sense of belonging within the company. As we have seen, Nippon Kokan president's criticism was about "uncooperative" attitudes by a "few" workers, who allegedly were acting according to "directions given by the outsiders."[61] Likewise, as for the labor activists, what became the battle line was a sense of solidarity, not between workers across companies or nations but within employees of a specific company. One labor leader, in fact, recalled "strong attachment to the company" as a common tendency among mainstream union members, while not even trying to hide his dislike of those who did not have such feelings of intimacy for their company.[62] In other words, the actual battle line was more about whether members "loved" their companies.

Similar tendencies were observed outside of private enterprise, such as at schools and universities. At an elementary school in Gunma Prefecture, for example, several teachers were fired for diverse, basically non-ideological reasons, such as "uncooperative attitudes," "discord with colleagues," and "criticism of local and national politics." As is apparent in these examples, many cases of the so-called Red Purge actually involved a screening of nonconformists, dissenters, and malcontents at workplaces. In other words, the actual dynamics of the mass firings around 1950 were not necessarily about ideology but about a desirable style of order and harmony at workplaces and in society.

Many, of course, refused to accept sudden terminations and continued to fight. Some simply went to their workplace but were forcefully removed by security guards and plainclothes police. Others sought help from the union at their companies but, in many cases, were almost completely ignored. Still others took the matter to court, but many of their cases were refused, as most courts concluded that they did not have jurisdiction over MacArthur's orders during the occupation.[63] But what most severely and effectively discouraged those who had been discharged, according to many people's recollections, was the abrupt change in the attitude of their colleagues, union members, and personal friends. "I felt as if I suddenly became a person with an infectious disease. Everyone stopped talking to me," recalled Kuboi Mitsuko, a female employee at *Asahi Shinbun,* about the period after she was dismissed. She recalled that her colleagues literally turned their faces away when she happened to run into them.[64]

As seen in these examples, with the solidification of the Cold War framework against a backdrop, the Red Scare climate not only began functioning within companies and unions, but began affecting ordinary individuals' ways of thinking and daily behaviors. This climate further spread to employment in the fall of 1950, and many companies, particularly banks and department stores, which typically cared about image and reputation, began systematically using private investigators to check applicants' backgrounds and political attitudes. This climate reminded some people of wartime Japan under the tight control of the Public Security Preservation Law of 1925, which provided a legal basis for the imprisonment of communists and socialists, as well as liberals and Christians, and later laid the groundwork for the repression of any kind of opposition that did not join in Japan's war effort. It was this sense of a return to wartime that precipitated the anti–Red Purge agitation among high school and college students.

STUDENT ACTIVISM AND GRASSROOTS CONSERVATISM

Although the student movements had been growing since the early days of the postwar period, it was the period between 1950 and 1953, in particular, that marked their full zenith.[65] On September 29, 1950, for instance, 1,500 students gathered at Waseda University in opposition to the firing of "red" professors at Waseda, Hosei, and Tokyo Universities.[66] Anti–Red Purge movements spread quickly among students, and, a week later, in October 1950, about 3,000 students rallied at Tokyo University.[67] The student movements became widely known to the general public on October 17, when a riot erupted at Waseda, during which police arrested 143 students en masse for the first time in Japanese history.[68]

Students' demonstration opposing the Red Purge at the University of Tokyo. *Mainichi Shinbun*, 5 October 1950. (Reprinted with permission, *Mainichi Shinbun*.)

Kobe Mitsuo, one of eighty-nine students eventually suspended from the school for an indefinite period, wrote: "I am not a member of the Japanese Communist Party, nor am I a communist. Needless to say not a 'tool' of it. I am just an everyday sort of a student. I just feel extremely angry with a powerful force that suppresses freedom. I am sure all of us remember the ravages of war."[69] This statement indicates that his opposition to the Red Purge was less based on his ideological and political belief than his wartime experiences during World War II. This feeling was shared widely among many participants in student movements. The evolution of such student activism is worthy of study, but our interest here is not so much student movements as social reactions to these movements.

In brief, the general reaction toward anti–Red Purge movements was one of disinterest. The primary concern of the general public was less the "Red Purge" than the seeming threat to social order. For instance, major newspapers remained critical of the student movements. Describing them as an "unprecedented scandal," an editorial in *Mainichi Shinbun* asserted: "College students should not behave like spoiled children." The newspaper went on to say that the "scandal" was taking place under the "guidance of a small and peculiar group of students," that student activism was nothing more than a "kind of sport among certain happy people," and that the youth and women were particularly vulnerable to communist propaganda.[70] *Asahi Shinbun,* similarly, warned that such "extreme actions" should be stopped to ensure social order.[71]

Even college newspapers, like *Waseda Daigaku Shinbun* (Waseda University Newspaper), which had supported student political activity, changed its tone, stating, "Students must not be rioters at any time. The incident was by no means orderly behavior."[72] From their perspective, the anti–Red Purge movement was bad not because of its point of view but its violation of social order. For many, whatever the content of their arguments, the students needed to be punished because they violated public order and security. In order to restore order—and to pacify the students—two measures were taken: first, a number of the leading figures of the student demonstrations were detained, and, second, the Cold War logic, which effectively provided a context for marginalizing disagreements and restoring order at home, was even more widely disseminated.[73]

Such a desire for conventional order clearly played a part in the 1952 national election—the first following the end of the U.S. occupation, which returned a conservative party to national politics. Observing the election results, the literary scholar Togawa Yukio wrote:

> The fact that the Liberal Party obtained a majority after all demonstrates the popular will. It suggests the wish of the voiceless people, which seems to be: "No more reform." People are finally able to live like decent human beings seven years after being defeated in the war. Of course, they have grievances and anxiety, but for now people want to preserve the status quo. After drastic reforms, one after the other, people usually feel, for better or worse, "It's all right as it is. Don't change anything anymore." I think now is the time for such a period.[74]

Togawa's observation was, perhaps, too restrained, because the victory of the conservatives did not mean the maintenance of the status quo of the postwar period. Their victory clearly supported the restoration of the traditional, accustomed order in Japan, which was disrupted, from the conservatives' perspective, only during the wartime and occupation period.[75] However, Togawa had a sharp eye in pointing out that society had come to dislike dramatic social change.[76]

To get a feeling for the social atmosphere, one can read hundreds of letters and postcards in the National Diet Library in Tokyo, written by ordinary people and sent to various local and national politicians from the fall of 1950 through 1951. One is from an anonymous resident in Kyoto, sent to a local politician in 1951. This letter is interesting because it expressed an aversion to social change in the postwar period and because it advocated limiting such change in the name of national defense. It read:

> I believe the course of action we have taken since the defeat in the war in every field, particularly politics and education, must lead to the destruction of our nation. Such a way simply won't work to fight communism at all. . . . I don't want to turn our mother country into a battlefield. I don't want to turn our country into the Balkans in East Asia, nor another Korea. I want to save our country by our hands, and, no matter what, to protect it from a foreign invasion.[77]

At the end of this long letter, the author got to the crux of his concern over the lack of *chusin* (center) in postwar Japan:

> We, the people of this nation, wish to have the center. The solidarity of the nation is of vital importance. Nobody in our country will accept lines of argument such as "for freedom," "for peace," or "for the improvement of the standard of living." Most importantly, we don't want to throw away our long tradition. Nor do we want to give up our history. Only in this manner will we be able to achieve independence and to cooperate with the anti-communist front on the Western side.[78]

In stressing the "threat" of communism, what this anonymous writer longed for was to reassemble a shattered social order—or, broadly, a conventional and desirable national identity. For this author, however biased his interpretation, foreign events and the war in Korea provided a chance to effectively address his concerns on domestic issues.

Indeed, like other societies, Japanese society had changed a great deal during and after the war. The center seemed to be "lost," and traditional order seemed "disturbed." Students were rioting, women were increasingly working outside the home, and workers also were expanding their influence.

The rise of new actors in postwar Japan made a large portion of the conservative population of Japan anxious, and even resentful. One of the angriest men might have been a 58-year-old doctor, named Hidaka Hiroshi, in the small city of Yonago, Shimane Prefecture. He was worried about the postwar emergence of women, who, he believed, were "ignorant and uncomprehending." He wrote in April 1951:

> I feel gloomy about the superficiality of Japan's national character and its society today when I see such women, jumping on the bandwagon of the current of the times, getting positions in important posts such as mayor or congressman. Women who put forth practically impossible arguments against rearmament are virtually traitors to our country. It is no exaggeration to say so in view of today's world situation.[79]

This letter is interesting because of his use of the "real world situation" to express his disgust about the rising status of women in postwar Japan. He continued:

> From old times, the saying "There are women behind history" always means tragedy and collapse. Women's participation in politics rarely produced positive results, and, whether in the East or the West, there are many examples of the saying "A woman who shows her cleverness fails to sell the cow." While we cannot take legal measures to ban women's political involvement, we should seriously question the appointment of women to important and practical posts in politics. The anti-rearmament argument is, after all, a purely empty theory that ignores the real situation in the world. I seriously doubt the existence of their conscience.[80]

At the end of his long letter, he expressed opposition to conducting a referendum on amending the constitution on the grounds that the majority of "ignorant" women might cause an unfavorable result. This letter is interesting because of its clear expression of grassroots conservatism opposing social change in the postwar period, and because of its use of the East-West confrontation in an attempt to contain such social conflict. Of course, this letter was not written as a representative voice of a particular group, but it conveys the feeling of people who quietly supported the social purges of 1950 and who supported silencing anti–Red Purge movements. It was such people who directly and indirectly repressed various "troublemakers" under the name of the Red Purge. Indeed, the legacy of this social suppression and punishment lasted for years and even decades. According to memoirs, many who were purged experienced difficulty in getting jobs and were ostracized in their hometowns for years, which resulted, in extreme cases, in family estrangement, divorce, and suicide.[81]

A large majority of the existing literature on the Red Purge suggests that it was the GHQ and Washington that ordered the purge of communists and communist sympathizers in order to create an anti-communist country in East Asia. However, what we have seen here does not fit neatly into such a Washington-directed model. First and foremost, many dismissals at ordinary companies actually resulted from ordinary employers' own decisions, and factional disputes in labor unions facilitated the mass dismissals of certain groups of people. Second, most of those expelled were not necessarily communists or fifth columnists. Third, in some cases, the Labor Division of the GHQ even tried to stop "abuse of the Red Purge," and many were, nevertheless, fired for disturbing the conventional order and harmony of their workplaces. Finally, opposition to the Red Purge was muted among the majority in society, who chose to say: "No more reform." Therefore, it is reasonable to suggest that the Red Purge was carried out not so much by the GHQ and Washington as by tens of thousands of local people in Japan.

This re-examination of agency leads us to reconsider the nature of events. In some cases, events fit well with the conventional Red Purge model, but a large majority of other cases are better conceived broadly as social repression conducted by nameless and numberless local people in attempts to restrain social disagreements that came to surface following the defeat in the war. Viewed in this way, the Red Purge does not seem like a mere end result of the Cold War; rather it was part of a conservative backlash among a large portion of the population that silenced disagreements and created domestic tranquility, for which the imagined reality of the Cold War was necessitated.

Examining the individual waves of domestic repression circa 1950–1951 in Japan, Britain, and the United States, Chapters 7 and 8 shed new light not only on the dynamics of the purge in each occurrence, but also on the meaning of their occurring simultaneously as parts of a larger whole. Most existing literature has suggested that each was an example of Cold War repression aimed at the elimination of communists and communist sympathizers, thus viewing them as consequential events at home—ultimately, aftereffects of the global Cold War. Yet this conventional view appears plausible only when we view these events from a perspective that accepts the "reality" of the Cold War.

Stripping away Cold War imaginings and re-examining local and social disputes on the ground, these situations look different. What these waves of domestic purge commonly represented, instead, was a backlash of grassroots social conservatism whose goal was the restoration of "normal" order and social relations, by repressing thousands of nonconformists at home. During the Korean conflict, a previously disputable Cold War discourse solidified its verisimilitude and proved increasingly effective in each society at helping to silence various social and cultural disagreements in the name of safety and security.

In these chapters, we have examined three former colonizer countries—Japan, Britain, and the United States—but strikingly similar situations can be found as well in a number of postcolonial societies, such as the Philippines, Taiwan, and the People's Republic of China. In 1950, these countries were in the midst of nation building, with an urgent need to create order and unity at home, often by eliminating thousands of "others" within each society. Before discussing the meaning of this global phenomenon of social repression during the Korean War, let us explore these latter subjects, beginning with the large-scale purge of "counterrevolutionaries" in China in the fall of 1950.

CHAPTER NINE

People's War at Home

ON THE MORNING of April 28, 1951, the atmosphere was heated at Shanghai's famous Canidrome, a once fashionable and dazzling greyhound-racing stadium, originally built in 1928. Squeezed against the oval of the immense greensward was a crowd of 10,000 people. A stage was set up in front of the central platform at the center of the sea of humanity, and on stage were the accused, bound by ropes or chains, with heads down, awaiting judgment, and listening to speeches by Party officials, witnesses, students, and peasants. According to a British newspaper *Manchester Guardian*'s reporter, the masses of the people sang songs, waved red flags bearing the slogans of the regime, and howled imprecations against the accused. It was one of countless mass accusation meetings in Shanghai, conducted as part of the *Zhenya fan geming,* or *Zhenfan* (Campaign to Suppress Counterrevolutionaries), a wave that swept Shanghai and numerous other cities nationwide from the late fall of 1950 through the summer of 1951. Such a mass meeting was reportedly preceded by a series of accusations and confessions, in each case followed by a customary question and answer between official prosecutors and the crowd. "Shall we shoot them?" asked a prosecutor, in one instance.

"Death to them! Death to them!" answered the crowd, "Take them back to the scene of their crime and kill them."[1]

On that day at the Canidrome in Shanghai, the crowd sentenced to death more than 200 with such shouts, which local newspapers described as "a unanimous roar." These sentences were reviewed and confirmed the next day by the Shanghai Military Control Commission. According to court documents, Zhang Wanjin, a 31-year-old former police officer, who retained his position following the change of regime, was sentenced to prison for the crime of spreading a rumor in 1950, allegedly saying, "Chiang Kai-shek will counterattack this year, and the U.S. forces will land at ports nearby, attacking Shanghai from three directions—land, sea, and air."[2] Likewise, Lian Zhenan, a 33-year-old former military doctor, was sentenced to prison, charged with allegedly having disrupted a *fan MeifuRi* (Oppose U.S. support of Japan) demonstration in Shanghai on March 4, 1951, by shouting "reactionary" slogans.[3] Cheng Wei, 39-year-old man, was sentenced to death, charged with allegedly having spread "reactionary" rumors, such as "The Nationalist Party is coming back." According to a judgment, available at the Shanghai Municipal Archives, he retorted, "Now everyone shouts Chairman Mao. But in the era of Chiang Kai-shek, everyone shouted Generalissimo Chiang, Generalissimo Chiang. Why did nobody say Chairman Mao at that time? We don't need to be honest!"[4]

As soon as their sentences were confirmed, such "criminals" were transported to public execution sites. Let us take a look at an example of a public execution, observed by Norimura Kaneko, a Japanese girl who witnessed a mass execution in the small city of Haicheng, near Shenyang, in the late summer of 1951. Norimura's family continued to live in the area after Japan's surrender in World War II because her father was a doctor and he worked for the CCP during the civil war, and, at that time, Norimura was a student at a local middle school. It was a sweltering day. Norimura and her schoolmates walked to the beach along the Haicheng River to attend an event, even though she did not know specifically what kind of event would be held there. When they arrived in the late afternoon, a crowd of people had already assembled. Children were playing nearby. Many students from other schools arrived at the site, and there was a joyful mood in the air. As usual at this sort of gathering, the crowd began singing, and Norimura and her classmates joined in. Within an hour, a chorus of people began yelling: "Crush the invasion of American imperialism!" and "We will never allow spies' subversive activities!" Innumerable fists were raised in the air as the slogans were repeated. "What on earth is going to happen?" Norimura wondered.[5]

Before long, appeared a progression of men, their hands tied behind their backs. The first was a thin, middle-aged man; he looked poor, his hair a mess. The second was a fair-skinned young man, in tears, nose running, chin dripping with slobber. The next one surprised Norimura, because his loose-fitting trousers slipped down to his ankles, exposing his body below the waist, as he was dragged along by soldiers and walked awkwardly. The children laughed at him as he passed by. The rest of the crowd—men and women, young and old—likewise laughed derisively and convulsively, pointing, booing, and pouring ridicule and scorn on the man. These "counterrevolutionary" prisoners passed by Norimura's eyes one by one and soon came to a stop about 100 feet from her, where they knelt as if bowing to the sun. Norimura suddenly noticed that there was a hole in the ground in front of them. "Shh! . . . Shh! . . . Quiet!" people said to one another. Soon the sound of a rifle being cocked could be heard, and, then, a soldier held the muzzle of the rifle against a prisoner's head.[6]

Bang!

With a crack, the man who had been crying fell silent and disappeared from Norimura's sight. The executions continued, one by one. Even after they were finished, the crowd remained excited. Some people tried to look into the hole, where the bodies of the prisoners had piled up.[7]

In this way, scenes of denunciation and execution were repeated in numerous locations all over China between the fall of 1950 and the summer of 1951. In Beijing and Tianjin, a variety of mass meetings were reportedly carried out, 29,629 and 21,400 times, respectively, and, in Shanghai alone, more than 33,000 people were denounced and nearly 29,000 were charged with being "counterrevolutionaries."[8] It is not surprising that, in this period, reporting the number of executions week after week became routine for foreign diplomats.[9] In addition to reporting the number of deaths, some British diplomats in Shanghai stated that their servants had suddenly disappeared or had been arrested for being "running dog[s] of the imperialists."[10] Although we still do not know the precise number of those executed and imprisoned during this period, the historian Yang Kuisong indicates that it was officially acknowledged that roughly 712,000 people had been executed nationwide, 1,290,000 were imprisoned, and 1.2 million were at some point under house arrest.[11]

The Campaign to Suppress Counterrevolutionaries has generally been considered, with good reason, a top-down, coercive, political cleansing campaign by the CCP, aimed at repression of former members of the Nationalist Party and party sympathizers.[12] In particular, scholars have paid great attention to the role of the CCP—in particular of Mao Zedong—in the movement. While disagreements surely exist in terms of political stances and evaluation of the phenomenon, most scholars approach this subject through the lens of traditional political history, that is, looking at a political event (the "*Zhenfan* movement") largely as a result of the intentions of policymakers ("Mao Zedong"). To be sure, this approach has a certain merit. The campaign initially developed as a result of Mao's directive issued on October 10, 1950, the so-called "double-ten directive," and further escalated in late January 1951 under his instruction, and, thus, it makes sense to emphasize Mao's responsibility for it.[13] Nonetheless, this approach has tended to confirm our traditional understanding of the movement, describing it as if Beijing's leadership had a consistent intention and policy, as if the CCP controlled the expansion and contraction of the phenomenon, as if ordinary people were merely passive followers—or victims—of the campaign, and as if the campaign followed a communist path peculiar to post-1949 China. These points need to be further examined, as they contain quite a few myths.

RECONSIDERING THE "CAMPAIGN TO SUPPRESS COUNTERREVOLUTIONARIES"

First of all, Beijing did not necessarily have consistent intentions or beliefs in supervising the *Zhenfan* movement from beginning to end. As Yang Kuisong traces in detail, Beijing's policy followed a zigzag course even in this short period. For example, within just two months of the announcement of the double-ten directive, Liu Shaoqi sought to slow down the escalation of the *Zhenfan* movement, and Mao agreed, suggesting that an "excessively nervous atmosphere" must not be created. And yet, a month later, in mid-January 1951, Mao endorsed a number of large-scale executions in western Hunan as a "completely necessary step," an example that, he now thought, should be followed by all other provinces, whether urban or rural.[14]

In addition, although the *Zhenfan* movement surely evolved under the direction of the central authorities, the CCP did not necessarily control the course of the phenomenon. When Beijing sought a comprehensive retrenchment of the campaign after May 1951, for instance, the waves of arrests and executions did not actually diminish in many parts of China. On the contrary, they continued to grow, despite the change in Beijing's policy. In East China, for instance, an additional 110,000 people were arrested and nearly 40,000 were executed after Beijing tried to limit large-scale and unofficially sanctioned arrests and executions.[15] A similar pattern in which Beijing sought to scale down aggressive local sentiments appeared in dealing with foreigners living in Chinese cities. Beijing was criticized as cowardly when it set a policy of deporting foreigners who committed "counterrevolutionary" acts; according to one local official's observation, some even accused the government of being weak-kneed and incompetent toward foreigners and foreign countries.[16]

Why did Beijing not have a consistent policy, and why did it not exercise greater control over the campaign? In the first place, the direction of the *Zhenfan* campaign was always linked with the war situation in Korea. For Beijing, the progress of the Korean War was an uncertain variable that could harm the CCP's domestic programs. For instance, a report from a regional CCP office argued that a lukewarm attitude in the *Zhenfan* campaign would be blamed if the war situation radically changed and the tide turned against China, since such an attitude might cause the CCP to be on the defensive and bring a difficult time once the advantage was lost.[17] As is clear in this report, the *Zhenfan* campaign was seen as being of a piece with progress in the Korean War. In fact, changes of policy in the movement coincided with changes in the war situation.

Related to this, another uncertain, arguably more fundamental variable for CCP officials was the state of popular attitudes at home, which could easily shift as a result of any change in the war situation. As a matter of fact, the question of how the masses would react was raised frequently at moments of policy change in the campaign. For example, when Beijing sought to lower the temperature of the *Zhenfan* movements in December 1950, it was reasoned that "indiscriminate and multi-directional strikes [should] be avoided lest the overall situation become too tense and we ourselves become isolated." Mao supported this view, emphasizing: "If our cadres do not have a clear idea . . . and do not stick strictly to it, . . . the people will not support us."[18] Then, when Beijing decided to implement a more aggressive and harsh policy in late January 1951, it was justified by Mao as follows: "If we are irresolute and tolerant to this evil [of counterrevolutionaries], we will alienate the people."[19] As we can see in these comments, consideration of popular attitudes constituted an important part of Beijing's policy-making logic.

Put simply, the course of the *Zhenfan* movement was often swayed by circumstances and Beijing's day-to day observations concerning them, rather than by the CCP's ideological tendencies or Mao's personality. The unbridled spread of the *Zhenfan* movement further suggests that the phenomenon was not simply the end-result of the CCP's political repression but was perpetuated because of its own dynamics—that is, the Campaign to Suppress Counterrevolutionaries as social repression and punishment.

SOCIAL SUPPRESSION IN COMMUNITIES

Let us briefly look at how the *Zhenfan* movement functioned at the local level. Beyond ideological slogans and dramatic spectacles at mass meetings, ordinary practices in the movement were less concerned with ideology and political struggles. For example, when members of the Association of Street Vendors in Beijing implemented the campaign in their markets, they used it for their own purposes to tighten morals and order among the membership. Their slogans in this anti-counterrevolutionary campaign were:

> "No delay in making tax payments."
> "No cheating of customers."
> "Always issue receipts."
> "Use standardized measuring instruments."
> "Do not charge an artificially raised price."
> "Keep street stalls clean."[20]

In addition, "Do not pee or shit by the roadside or at indoor vendors" was a slogan that the Vendors' Association advocated in its campaign against "counterrevolutionaries."[21] Many of these topics had no apparent connection to the CCP's struggles against "counterrevolutionaries," but, interestingly, this campaign was framed, conducted, and worked efficiently in the name of "Suppression of Counterrevolutionaries." It was claimed that street vendors were fighting a different kind of war against counterrevolutionaries on the home front, that cooperation among vendors could stabilize the Chinese economy and public order, and that their tax payments would support the fight against American imperialism on the front lines.[22] In short, local people utilized the foreign war and adopted the banner of the Campaign to Suppress Counterrevolutionaries for their own purposes.

Such local use of East-West confrontation was ubiquitous. As in other places, those living in the neighborhood of the Dong'an Market in Beijing adopted a guilt-by-association system during the campaign; under this system, five households formed a group, in which each household would monitor another, and, if one member of a group violated this agreement, all members would be punished.[23] Such a mutual surveillance system functioned quite efficiently. In one instance, when a street vendor tried to make money by cheating a customer, it was reported that the other vendors all informed on him.[24] In another case, local residents in Beijing participated in the *Zhenfan* movement by forming district patrol groups, though their primary aim, in addition to searching for "subversive" activities, was to prevent fires and thefts.[25]

In another case, a neighbors' group interceded in the case of a husband's engaging in domestic violence, accusing him at a community meeting, at which the man in question offered a self-criticism and promised not to commit domestic violence anymore.[26] A resident of this district described the spirits of the neighborhood as radically improved after the establishment of the neighbors' group; the area became cleaner, thefts were eliminated, bumpy roads were repaired, and residents' disputes were settled by the neighbors' group.[27] Clearly, as in the case of the Street Vendors' Association, the Dong'an Market campaigns had almost nothing to do with ideological and political struggles against "counterrevolutionaries." Rather, when it came to daily practice, locals adopted and developed the campaign in a much more commonplace manner, which functioned not merely as political cleansing but as a mechanism of "social cleansing" in order to restore and maintain order in communities.

These local campaigns on the ground show historical continuity with the past. What local people aimed to achieve was a set of certain norms, such as cleanliness as opposed to filthiness, unity as opposed to disorder, precision as opposed to laxity—or even corruption—and so on, which, actually, had all been familiar concerns in Chinese history since the late nineteenth century. Therefore, seen from a social point of view, the *Zhenfan* campaign was not particularly unique to the post-revolutionary period. It even had some similarities to the Nationalist Party's failed campaign, "*Xin Shenghuo Yundong* (the New Life Movement)," in the prewar period. According to the historian Arif Dirlik, from the viewpoint of Chiang Kai-shek and GMD leaders in the 1930s, traditional life for the Chinese could be summed up in a few words: filthiness, hedonism, laziness, self-indulgence, and so on. That is why the GMD's New Life Movement specifically delineated eight criteria to be pursued: orderliness, cleanliness, simplicity, frugality, promptness, precision, harmoniousness, and dignity—some of which were identical to what was sought in local practices of the *Zhenfan* movement in the communist era.[28] The crux of these values was, in sum, an effort to achieve modernity, or even blatant Westernization, in a way that rejected the traditional way of Chinese life, which tended to be described only in negative terms. Viewed in this way, the GMD's and CCP's movements did not seem fundamentally different. Although, of course, the terminology was different, both aimed at achieving modernity—a long-standing task, which had been a goal for decades—through mobilizing and uniting the scattered and disorganized people, whom Sun Yat-sen (Sun Wen) once bitterly described as "a heap of loose sand."[29]

The fundamental differences between the two were in terms of agency rather than content. In the *Zhenfan* campaign, informants and investigators were not necessarily official or secret police, as in the GMD era, but largely ordinary people. In fact, various "counterrevolutionary" acts were identified and reported less through official investigations than unofficially through rumors and private accusations among individuals at workplaces, at schools, in communities, in neighborhoods, and in families. Many, to be sure, remained skeptical or critical of the campaigns, particularly the mass executions. "It was too lenient before, but now it is too harsh," some reportedly said. Others likewise lamented, "It is pitiful to execute the old, and regrettable to kill the young." Still others were more sympathetic to those accused: "They committed their accused acts perhaps due to the pressure from their livelihood; everyone would do the same if their living become strained." Some even expressed doubts: "There have been too many executions. There must be some false charges." Nevertheless, these skeptical and critical views remained the minority, and these opinions were quickly responded to in retorts by others around them: "Well, do you really know how they murdered the people before? Those who were killed by these persons died in much more miserable ways."[30]

Clearly, the campaigns could not be fully implemented without the participation of a great number of people. In Shanghai alone, the authorities received more than 70,000 written denunciations.[31] Young people, in particular, were extremely active as informers; a box set up at Fudan University in Shanghai, for instance, received more than 700 reports in a few months in the spring of 1951.[32] Reportedly quite a few cases involved children and wives informing on their fathers and husbands, and vice versa.[33] An official in Shanghai stated:

> During the Campaign to Suppress Counterrevolutionaries, a lot of young people actively joined in the movement, often informing on their own fathers, sisters-in-law, and even close friends, who were counterrevolutionaries. Such cases are too numerous to mention. A multitude of people cooperated with the Public Security Bureau to collect information, participate in surveillance, and arrest counterrevolutionaries.[34]

Surveillance among the people, among students and workers, and among neighbors and family members, was so intense that many individuals internalized the campaign, restricting their own behavior. Some who came under suspicion voluntarily appeared at public security bureaus, describing their acts and associations, while others simply shut themselves up in their houses, stopped going out, and became isolated from society. In addition, some who possessed small weapons quietly left them at the doors of public security bureaus at night.[35]

More tellingly, a massive number of people decided to end their lives. Statistical data collected in the summer of 1951 shows that the ages of those who had committed suicide ranged from the early twenties to the early sixties, with those in their thirties the most numerous, and that quite a few wives of those executed as "counterrevolutionaries" were also compelled to kill themselves.[36] Those who committed suicide comprised a diverse group of people—not only landlords and former members of the Nationalist Party but also those categorized as drifters, local rebels, collaborators, and members of secret societies and religious sects, as well as those deemed "feudalistic" and "uncooperative."[37] Such heterogeneity suggests that we reconsider the nature of the *Zhenfan* movement.

Exactly the same point can be made concerning those who were executed during this period. If the Campaign to Suppress Counterrevolutionaries was purely a movement of political repression carried out by the CCP aimed at the elimination of adversaries, those who were executed and committed suicide should have been mostly political and ideological enemies, such as landlords and businessmen, as well as former GMD members and sympathizers. Yet, to the contrary, a large number, particularly those who worked for the GMD government, such as bureaucrats, police, teachers, and lower-ranking officials, retained their positions and continued to work. Those actually condemned and eliminated during this campaign involved a much broader and diverse group, comprising those who fit more neatly into the category of "social enemies" than that of "political enemies." They included, for example, members of religious sects such as *Yiguandao* (Persistent Way), powerful gangs such as *Huangniu Bang* (Yellow Ox Gang), and secret societies such as *Sanhehui* (Triads), *Qing Bang* (Green Gang), and *Gelaohui* (Elder Brothers), as well as common criminals and those involved in what were considered social evils, such as bandits, murderers, thieves, local bullies, low-level hoodlums, brothel keepers, and prostitutes.[38] A British official in Beijing observed that many of those executed were not really "counterrevolutionaries" but "little more than common criminals."[39]

Apparently, what these diverse people shared was not a single ideology. They were, rather, symptomatic of the dramatic social confusion and disorder that evolved in the midst of social chaos in the turbulent years during the 1930s and 1940s. These were years in which internal battles among warlords, the War against Japan, and the Chinese Civil War were fought, and in which social and moral standards seriously deteriorated, if not collapsed, causing massive increases in crime. This was also the time when various kinds of religious sects and secret societies wielded stronger presence, though surely they all had their own long histories.[40] Viewed in this way, thus, the *Zhenfan* movement in part was a movement of "social purification"—a backlash against social disorder.

A similar point can be observed in regard to the *Sanfan wufan* (Three-Anti and Five-Anti) movements, which developed in 1951–1953, following the Campaign to Suppress Counterrevolutionaries. Originally, the three antis referred to the CCP's fight against three "evils"—corruption, extravagance, and bureaucratism—which supposedly represented the evils of capitalism. When actions in the name of this ideological slogan were carried out, however, actual conduct criticized was less ideological and more related to personal characteristics and social behavior, such as going to a dance hall, driving a car, or engaging in a sexual affair outside marriage.[41] One document included a lengthy explanation of typical targets of this movement:

> Pursuing personal and selfish pleasure, disliking cotton cloth, buying new leather shoes to replace [ordinary] low-cut shoes, dining out on [costly] noodles instead of having breakfast in a factory, avoiding sitting around a one-pot meal together and preferring a sumptuous meal, accompanying dishes with rice, smoking a cigarette, wishing to live in a Western-[style] house, envying American bedclothes as comfortable, shunning a train as crowded and desiring to use a car or, at least, a pedicab, ride a pedicab just to go one kilometer, never negotiating price, avoiding cheap articles, and hoping to get things with high quality even though they are expensive.[42]

The items in this list were not primarily concerned about individuals' ideological tendencies so much as attitudes and behaviors on a daily basis. What they shared was, rather, an antipathy to things considered non-Chinese or, simply, overly Westernized attitudes and tastes—a sort of nativist backlash against conspicuous foreign influence, most notably in large cities such as Shanghai and Tianjin.

Simply put, the CCP's mass movements, such as the *Zhenfan* and *Sanfan* movements, were not merely political campaigns under the aegis of the Party. Rather, as they spread and escalated on the ground, they seemed to attain other dimensions—that is, first, they were parts of a long-standing goal of modernization, and, second, they were parts of a contingent, large-scale, nativist backlash, whose goal was the creation of a "harmonious" society through the elimination of tens of thousands of nonconformists and various elements of social disorder, including those deemed to have been overly influenced by Western cultures.

PEOPLE'S WAR FOR SECURITY AND PEACE

In October 1951, Luo Ruiqing, the minister for public security, praised the Campaign to Suppress Counterrevolutionaries, saying that it "brought a stable situation nationwide that China has never had before in its history."[43] Solely in terms of the level of social stability, unprecedented "peace" and "harmony" had come to China. In Nanning, for instance, the number of criminal cases declined from 4,314 in 1950 to 1,318 in 1951 and 455 in 1954.[44] Likewise, in Jiangxi Province, which was known for a low level of public safety and where even CCP officials had to travel with large numbers of heavily armed guards, public security was greatly improved, making it possible for them to travel with only a few guards.[45] Purely in terms of the number of crimes, Chinese society, indeed, became more secure and peaceful, whatever that meant.

Observing this situation, the *Manchester Guardian*, which, of course, remained critical of the *Zhenfan* movement and its purges of nonconformists, accepted the "improvement" in public spirit in Chinese society, writing that "the country as whole is more unified and peaceful than at any time since 1911."[46] What the newspaper noted were, for example, a change in attitude of public officials, claiming that one no longer saw the old familiar sight of a police officer slapping and kicking rickshaw coolies and that public-spiritedness was taking the place of excessive individualism.[47]

In a sense, even if it entailed the killing of tens of thousands of people, and however cruel it was, the *Zhenfan* movement did provide a sort of "order" to an unprecedented degree through the purification of society and settlement of social confusion and conflicts that developed over the decades of wars in the 1930s and 1940s. The CCP's propaganda, to be sure, was significant, but far more fundamental was an environment in which this propaganda could be effective—that is, first, the outbreak and development of the Korean War; second, the existence and escalation of domestic conflicts at the same time as the war; and, third, more than anything else, nameless and countless ordinary people's observations, judgments, and behaviors related to both of these.

The Korean War played a significant role, creating a wartime atmosphere and forcing many people—in particular, young people—to connect a foreign war with social problems and to rethink their behavior. Against the background of the war, many storekeepers competed to make donations, many shoemakers declared their intention to repair soldiers' shoes for free, many rickshaw pullers signed their names on the Patriotic Pledge or gave their names for it in case they could not write their names, and many students and workers participated in mobilization campaigns or even volunteered to be soldiers.[48] These were the people at the grassroots level who informed on various acts of "counterrevolution" at workplaces, at schools, in neighborhoods, and in families. These were the people who sought to solve existing social and local problems under the logic of the war and under the banner of the Campaign to Suppress Counterrevolutionaries. These were the people who, as a result, cooperated in the CCP's modernization and state-making projects against the backdrop of the Korean War. Liu Shaoqi recognized that the CCP's domestic programs, particularly land reform and the repression of counterrevolutionaries, would have been difficult to maintain without the Korean War.[49]

In this chapter, we have examined Chinese society and politics during the Korean War by tracing the development and transformation of the Campaign to Suppress Counterrevolutionaries, in which millions of people were killed or sent to prisons as "reactionaries." With the opening of Chinese archives in the past decade, the literature on this topic has grown, but most recent studies have tended to share a set of assumptions, viewing the phenomenon as political and ideological repression conducted by the CCP—with an emphasis on Mao's role—and, thus, describing it as following a communist path peculiar to post-1949 China. Tracing the multifaceted development of the campaign, however, complicates conventional understandings of the nature, agency, and function of the phenomenon, showing that, in essence, it was not simply the CCP's ideologically driven one-man show but also grassroots social punishment and repression aimed at the purification of society, with the active involvement of everyday people. Viewed in this manner, the campaign was not necessarily unique to China. Rather, using a social perspective, this campaign can be seen as part of the process of social pacification under the logic of East-West confrontation, aimed at creating a harmonious society by eliminating tens of thousands of nonconformists and social minorities, who came to be particularly conspicuous in the chaotic years during and after World War II. A different but somewhat similar process of domestic purging, with the heavy use of Cold War logic, can be seen across the Taiwan Strait, as well as the South China Sea: the escalation of the White Terror in Taiwan and the crackdown on "un-Filipino" activities in the Philippines.

CHAPTER TEN

Decolonization as Recolonization

AT 6:00 A.M. ON October 1, 1950, a court-martial at the Public Security Headquarters in Taiwan sentenced nine defendants to death for jointly plotting to overthrow the government and harboring "rebels," ordering their executions to be conducted immediately. At 6:30 a.m., the nine convicts— including Liu Quanli and others, mostly in their mid twenties and early thirties—were sent immediately to the public execution grounds, called Machangding, on the banks of the Xindian River in Taipei, where their sentence was carried out quickly. According to a news report, in spite of rain, a crowd of onlookers rushed to the scene, cheering, shouting, and applauding, as they saw the nine shot to death. The remains were promptly removed and transported to a public cemetery on the outskirts of the city.[1] A public execution of this kind in the early morning became almost a ritual in Taiwan in the summer and fall of 1950. Every time an execution was held, the names, ages, and addresses of those executed were posted at train stations and markets, written in red characters. Placards and handbills soon appeared everywhere, saying, for example, "Spies live all around you," "Informing on spies is everyone's responsibility," "Knowing spies but not informing is a crime," and "Anti-communism never compromises, anti-communism requires unity."[2] Such slogans were everywhere not just in public spaces, but also in packages of household goods and gifts, from cigarette cases, calendars, receipts, and movie tickets to paper fans and even wedding cakes.[3]

Slogans of this kind were not only visible everywhere but literally audible in many places in major cities, with loudspeakers in the street and at markets repeating anti-communist slogans and songs:

> Counteroffensive, counteroffensive to the mainland
> Counteroffensive, counteroffensive to the mainland
> The mainland is our land, the mainland is our territory
> Our land, our territory
> We cannot allow the Maoist bandits to occupy our land
> We cannot let the Russians humiliate us as they wish
> We need to make a counteroffensive
> Counteroffensive to come back
> Counteroffensive to recover the mainland
> To recover the mainland.[4]

Newspapers and magazines, likewise, discussed the need to crack down on "spies," reporting arrests and executions of "subversives," and publishing articles, poems, and cartoons featuring various stories of heroic "patriots" informing on and arresting communists.[5] These were not merely slogans or stories. After the enactment of the Wartime Regulations for the Purging of Spies in June 1950, finding and informing on subversives and those suspected of nefarious activity not only were encouraged but were required by law. Individuals at government offices, military units, schools, factories, and various other organizations were required to engage in mutual surveillance.[6]

This was the moment when the storm of purges, later called the White Terror, raged throughout Taiwan, particularly in the years following the outbreak of the Korean War, in which an estimated 3,000 to 5,000 people were executed, and 8,000 were imprisoned for decades.[7] Data provided by Taiwan's Department of Defense for the first time in 2005 shows that the number of arrests jumped from 212 in 1949 to 1,882 in 1950 and remained high until 1954.[8] According to Lin Shuyang, who was jailed in 1950, arrests could be made by various entities, such as the police, the military police, and the intelligence agencies, without following any legal procedures.[9] There was no need to present an arrest warrant, no written indictment, no lawyer, no public trial, no right to appeal, and, occasionally, even the sentencing document was omitted. Torture was routine, and often confessions were extorted or fabricated.[10] Even convicts who were not sentenced to death were often imprisoned for long periods on Lyudao (Lüdao, or Green Island), an isolated small island about 20 miles off the eastern coast of Taiwan. Lin Shuyang, for instance, was jailed there for nearly thirty-five years.[11]

Studies of the "White Terror" dramatically increased in Taiwan in the past two decades. Still, a series of purges and violence in the 1950s have received relatively little attention, compared to the large volume of research on earlier incidents of repression in Taiwan, specifically, the 2.28 (February 28) incident, a series of mass uprisings against the Nationalist Party government that broke out in the weeks following February 28, 1947.[12] Furthermore, the repression in the early 1950s has generally been viewed through a Cold War lens, and lumped together as the "White Terror." The implication of this name is that the terror was conducted primarily by the state—the government under the Nationalist Party—as a way to eliminate communists and communist sympathizers in Taiwan, efforts supported by and part of the anti-communist grand strategy of the United States.[13]

The phenomenon in the early 1950s called the White Terror, however, deserves more attention and a much more fundamental reconsideration. First and foremost, as many researchers have pointed out, a large proportion of those repressed during this period were neither communists nor communist sympathizers. In fact, underground communists in Taiwan numbered only several hundred at that time, in contrast to the number of victims, which easily surpassed ten thousand.[14] Who were the targets of repression? Why were they persecuted?

Examining the profiles of victims in this period can serve as an entry point to thinking about the actual nature of the repression. Lin Yixu, a 28-year-old elementary school teacher, for instance, was arrested in 1950 and sentenced to twelve years in prison for attending meetings of a progressive group and reading magazines such as *Guancha* (Observation) and *Zhanwang* (Prospects).[15] Likewise, Lin Enkui, a 28-year-old doctor, was arrested in 1950 for an almost identical reason.[16] Thousands of students and workers who studied and worked in Japan during the war and returned to Taiwan in the early postwar period similarly suffered persecution.[17] Chen Shaoying, who worked and studied in Osaka during the war and returned to Taiwan in 1946, was arrested in 1950, even though he actually rejected a friend's invitation to join the Communist Party.[18] Furthermore, quite a few members of elites within Taiwan's indigenous populations, such as Watan Tanaga (Lin Zhaoming, in Chinese), who advocated autonomy for their populations, were arrested in the early 1950s.[19] Moreover, Deng Jinjiang, a 29-year-old teacher at an agricultural school in Taidong, was arrested for simply expressing antiwar opinions, even though he was not involved in any antiwar or leftist activities.[20]

As seen in these examples, the victims, indeed, included diverse groups of people. These were people who had hoped that postwar Taiwan would become an autonomous region in China or an independent nation of Taiwan. These were people who found an opportunity in the postwar period to achieve a long-standing hope for indigenous tribes' autonomy. They were often members of social elites, such as intellectuals, doctors, lawyers, journalists, teachers, college students, and the literati, who, after the end of Japanese colonialism, hoped for social and political change in postwar Taiwanese society.[21]

Repressions on these diverse groups of people have generally been considered examples of false charges; these were tragedies but an epiphenomenon, which accidentally accompanied the Nationalist Party's brutal repression of communists and communist sympathizers. Because they have been viewed this way, not much attention has been paid to exploring what these "false charges" meant. To the contrary, memoirs and oral histories published in growing numbers in recent years have, rather, confirmed that many suffered false charges and, thus, were innocent victims of the White Terror. However, thousands of "misrepresentations" look like an accidental epiphenomenon only because we view the White Terror as the Nationalist Party's repression of communists. Once we remove the Cold War lens and look at local situations in Taiwan at that time, the situations look different. It is possible that the cases of "false charges" were not simple and incidental mistakes; rather, many victims might have been the real targets of the repression. The questions are: Who were the victims? What did they represent? Why were they persecuted? To answer these questions, we need to turn back to the historical and social background of the White Terror.

LOCAL AND SOCIAL ROOTS OF THE WHITE TERROR

The White Terror did not suddenly begin in the summer and fall of 1950. Many victims were arrested based on behaviors and activities between 1945 and 1949, particularly during the 2.28 incident in 1947. In a sense, the White Terror was focused on questions raised and unresolved in Taiwanese society in the post–World War II period. The crux of the matter was what kind of society Taiwan would and should be following the sudden end to Japanese colonialism, which had ruled Taiwan since the end of the nineteenth century. Indeed, society and politics in Taiwan in the postwar period appeared chaotic and divided into diverse rival camps, not just between GMD and CCP sympathizers, but also among *waishengren* (who came to Taiwan after 1945) and *benshengren* (people who had been living in Taiwan, including Chinese settlers who came before 1945; often described simply as Taiwanese), and the indigenous populations in Taiwan, as well as among those advocating unification, independence, or an autonomous status for Taiwan.[22] In such a situation, the series of purges during the Korean War period functioned to settle disputes and resolve the disorder of the postwar period. Many victims, in fact, epitomized the elements that directed and aspired to various kinds of changes—in a sense, chaos—in Taiwanese society, which emerged following the end of World War II in August 1945.

As many memoirs and oral histories suggest, the end of Japanese colonialism came with much joy and optimism about the future of Taiwan. Chen Mingzhong, a 16-year-old student, for instance, had been frustrated with the discrimination between the Japanese and Taiwanese and, thus, was excited about the arrival of GMD forces in the fall of 1945, hoping for the beginning of a new era and new society in which people would be treated equally, a realization of Sun Yat-sen (Sun Wen)'s *Sanmin zhuyi* (Three Principles of the People): self-determination, democracy, and people's livelihood.[23] His hope, however, crumbled quickly as he found that many GMD soldiers and mainlanders who had just come to Taiwan tended to look down on the local population as "slaves" of Japanese colonialism, causing numerous local conflicts between the Chinese and the local population.[24] A popular saying described the disappointment of the Taiwanese people during this period as follows: *Gou qu zhu lai* (Dog has gone, pig has come).[25]

The legacy of Japanese colonialism complicated such local conflicts. In 1946, after the colonial period ended, use of the Japanese language was suddenly forbidden, and a series of policies were issued banning Japanese songs, books, newspapers, films, and literature in public. As a result, millions of Taiwanese, particularly those under fifty years old who had been using Japanese since they were born had to learn Mandarin.[26] Worse still, the fall of the Japanese empire led to the collapse of the Taiwanese economy, as well as a food crisis, a rise in the unemployment rate, and increased pick-pocketing, theft, and robbery, causing social unrest, especially in urban areas. Because of this deterioration in public security, many urban residents put up gratings on their windows, multiple locks on doors, and high walls around their houses.[27]

Popular frustration mounted as the situation deteriorated and as the Nationalist government suppressed various demands from the Taiwanese. Such resentments eventually led to the eruption of a popular anti-Nationalist revolt all over Taiwan on February 28, which began with a small quarrel on the street in Taipei on February 27 between a woman selling black-market cigarettes and low-ranking Nationalist officials who confiscated her items and savings.[28] Although it began as a minor incident, it grew into a series of clashes between Taipei residents and police and eventually evolved into popular mass revolts against the Nationalist government and, more generally, against *waishengren*. In 1947, the total population of *benshengren* was about 6.5 million, compared with about 60,000 *waishengren*.[29] Thus, in the first few days, local rebellions were quite successful; government offices were attacked, many *waishengren* were killed, and a radio station in Taipei was occupied, allowing the protesters to broadcast anti-Nationalist speeches, with slogans such as "Defeat greedy officials," "Stand against the evil of the Chinese," and "Autonomy for Taiwan." These broadcasts in turn touched off uprisings elsewhere, in central and southern Taiwan.[30] However, GMD troops arrived from the mainland a week later, brutally putting down the popular uprisings and causing the deaths of more than 20,000 Taiwanese all over the island.[31]

Nonetheless, the ruthless suppression of revolts in the spring of 1947 did not silence resistance nor did it "resolve" the conflicts in society; rather, it intensified them. In fact, the 2.28 incident marked a turning point. Afterward, anti-government sentiments rapidly spread and became more popular, and, as a result of the GMD's repression, many turned to leftist thought as a means of opposing the Nationalist government.[32] As on the mainland, young people—in particular, college students—took the lead in spreading leftist agendas in Taiwan in the late 1940s.[33] Zhang Dongcai, a 20-year-old man in Taipei, for instance, was shocked by the military suppression of revolts in 1947 and, like his friends, began avidly reading progressive magazines sent from Hong Kong and the mainland; he wrote in his diary on July 24, 1948: "I don't mind not eating any food for three days if I can read *Guancha*."[34] As student movements were spreading like wildfire at universities on the mainland, college students in Taiwan, particularly those at National Taiwan University, intensified their activities immediately following the February 28 incident. Maintaining strong criticism of the Nationalist government, student movements in Taiwan became revitalized in the spring of 1949, including students from universities and high schools not only in Taipei but also other major cities, with slogans such as "Oppose police hitting people," "Down with starvation," and "Down with civil war."[35]

Another stream of thought that gained popularity following the 2.28 incident was the call for the independence, or autonomy, of Taiwan. Huang Guanghai, a 23-year-old GMD soldier who fled to Taiwan in 1950 and came to sympathize with the Taiwanese and was later arrested, recalled: "Because it was clear by that time that the Japanese were no good and the Chinese were no good, either, then, the best way was for Taiwan to become independent. Not governed by the Japanese and not governed by the Chinese."[36] In fact, in the years following the 2.28 incident, various activities and demands relating to Taiwanese independence increased. Along with the growth of student movements, in April 1949 the newsletter *Xin Taiwan* (New Taiwan), began publication at National Taiwan University, advocating democracy and autonomy for Taiwan.[37] During this period, in Jiayi and Taizhong in central Taiwan, where some of the hardest battles were fought in the 2.28 incident, for example, many youth formed and participated in various associations, urging people to see the true nature of the Nationalist government and insisting on autonomy.[38] In a similar manner, in 1949, Watan Tanaga (Lin Zhaoming), a 19-year-old student, and his friends formed an association that insisted on self-help and a high level of autonomy for the native Taiwanese population, such as the Atayal (Taiyal), who lived in the mountains.[39]

Communist ideology undeniably played an important role in providing a vision for the future. However, it is important to look at the mechanism of local translation. In fact, many students and other people who adopted communist agendas did not do so in order to join in the interests of Beijing, let alone Moscow. When asked about his motivation for taking part in student movements, Huang Yukun, a teacher at a junior school in Tainan, in southern Taiwan, for instance, said that he was dissatisfied with the government's handling of the 2.28 incident and that he wanted to improve the lives of the Taiwanese.[40] Like him, many students and intellectuals who were arrested in the White Terror in 1950 and the years that followed participated in student activism and embraced leftist thought in order to use these as tools to address their own discontent and resolve local conflicts.

Dissatisfaction of this kind among many people in Taiwan was further exacerbated in 1949, as the Nationalist Party retreated from the mainland to Taiwan. As the arrival of the GMD armies and refugees escalated in 1949, the number of *waishengren* dramatically increased, from 60,000 in 1947 to 1 million in 1950, and 1.5 million in the following years, changing the demography of Taiwan and heightening social conflict there.[41] By the time of the outbreak of the Korean War and the escalation of the White Terror in 1950, therefore, the seeds of social conflict had reached a flashpoint, in which the slightest provocation could touch off a "war" within Taiwanese society. Considering local and social roots of the White Terror, therefore, it is clear that we cannot fully grasp the actual nature of the repression through the lenses of the Cold War (East-West confrontation), or of the Chinese Civil War (CCP-GMD confrontation). Rather, the crux of the phenomenon was the pacification of social disorder and making of a harmonious society—that is, the creation of the nation-state of Taiwan, however cruel the process.

ENDS AND MEANS IN REVERSE

The fact that the real task had less to do with global and ideological confrontation than with the practical process of overcoming social conflict becomes much clearer when we look at the actual practices in which the Nationalist Party engaged during this period, parallel to the White Terror. Let us first begin looking at the slogans the Party promoted. While commonplace slogans of "Counterattack the Mainland" appeared frequently, they were usually accompanied by other slogans, like "Build Taiwan." Such a combination of foreign issues and domestic social issues was quite common. Typical slogans urged, for example, "Return to the Mainland," "Eliminate Communists," and "Rescue Our Countrymen," while, at the same time, stressing "Stop Luxury and Extravagance," "Be Punctual," "Keep Order," and so on. The efforts with respect to domestic and social issues were depicted as steps to achieve grandiose political goals, but, actually, the ends and means were reversed. When we look closely at the party's slogans, it is apparent that the emphasis was more on domestic and social issues, such as creating and maintaining social order at home.

A list of slogans in one of the government's mass mobilization campaigns in the summer of 1950, the Wartime Life Movement, for instance, reflected this tendency. It prioritized various tasks in this order:

1. Change social atmosphere
2. Promote wartime life
3. Restrain luxury and extravagance
4. Mobilize people for production
5. Eliminate communists
6. Defeat Soviet imperialism[42]

Note that the first four slogans primarily concerned social order and ways of life, even though the Wartime Life Movement was packaged entirely in the colors of anti-communism and the Cold War.

A similar tendency can be found in *Minsheng Bao*, a local newspaper in Jiayi. On August 5, 1950, for example, the paper appealed to readers regarding the need to "Mobilize anti-communism" and "Build Jiayi." Looking at specifics, we can see that the emphasis was on the latter, with the three tasks that the newspaper listed as urgent being: (1) to make a plan of administrative districts for the city, (2) to establish schools, and (3) to reorganize the family registration system.[43] These sociopolitical tasks and campaigns essentially concerned creating social and political order at home. Another article in the newspaper might be much more telling; it touted ten tasks, all concerned with social order and individual behavior: "Maintain Order," "Be Punctual," "Maintain Cleanliness," "Encourage Production," "No Betting," "No Alcohol," "No Need for Gorgeous Clothing," "No Need for Sumptuous Parties," and so forth.[44]

These were not merely rhetorical slogans. In a manner similar to what was happening on the mainland, the Nationalist Party promoted several mass campaigns under the umbrella banner of *Fan-gong kang-E* [Oppose Communists and Resist Russians]—a set of movements ostensibly fashioned after the logic of the Chinese Civil War and of the Cold War. By looking into specific programs, here again, we can see that the actual aims largely focused on domestic problems. For example, the Wartime Life Movement in the summer of 1950 aimed at changing lifestyles, urging people to avoid luxurious clothing, food, and parties.[45] The Campaign to Promote Public Order aimed at improving the people's manners; specific tasks included forming lines at bus stops and train stations and following rules at restaurants and theaters and in public places—typical small issues that had created numerous quarrels and fights between the newly arriving Chinese and local residents.[46]

The third mass movement, which began in December 1951, is noteworthy: the Campaign to Improve Hygiene, in which the government instructed local district offices to be attentive to environmental cleanliness in their cities and towns. Specific programs included, for example, collecting trash, sanitation control in restaurants and bars, and education and inspection by officials.[47] Chiang Kai-shek took the trouble to give lengthy instruction concerning the improvement of hygiene:

> Environmental hygiene is the basis of social reform. Now, people outside Taiwan are paying attention to us, and thus we need to take special notice of social reform. From now on, police need to look out for the cleanliness of restaurants, bars, theaters, and hotels, in particular, toilets and kitchens of these places, which should be inspected from time to time to promote the improvement of hygiene.[48]

Even though all of these slogans and campaigns were primarily concerned with individual life and social order at home, interestingly, they were packaged and promoted by the logic of the Chinese Civil War and Cold War; it was claimed that these tasks at home were all necessary to build the nation, to fight communism, and to rescue those "left" on the mainland. "Everything," it was urged, "should serve the frontlines and the victory there."[49]

Logic of this kind was most useful for rulers because it could quickly and efficiently silence opponents and malcontents under the rubric of achieving a higher goal. The defeat of the Nationalist Party on the mainland was, to be sure, a heavy blow for Chiang, but as the historian Wakabayashi Masahiro points out, the retreat to Taiwan provided the GMD with an opportunity to solidify its power base, because it freed Chiang and his supporters from problematic local politics, corrupt customs, and military cliques on the mainland, all of which had tormented them for years.[50] Thus, like those engaged in nation-building efforts in other former colonies in Asia, the Nationalist Party had to create and solidify its own power base in Taiwan.

It is not surprising, thus, that Chiang's diary for this period was filled with words like "unity" and "order" as well as phrases stressing the importance of "obeying the law" and "observing rules." In the summer of 1950, he was quite preoccupied with immediate tasks to create order at home.[51] "Let's stop discussing the differences among political factions or occupational posts. . . . Let's complete the unfinished Nationalist Revolution through cooperating under the great goal of Opposing Communists and Resisting Russians."[52] Taking full advantage of the utility of this logic, the government quickly enacted a series of laws, one after another, during the Korean War: among them, the Wartime Regulation to Purge Spies in 1950, the Law to Stimulate the Arrest of Spies in 1951, the Law Concerning Self-Surrender of Communists in 1951, and the Platform for the Mobilization of the Opposing Communism and Resisting Russians Movement in 1952.[53]

Following the declaration of martial law and the enactment of the Regulation on the Suppression of Rebellion, both in 1949, these legal measures further functioned to marginalize and eliminate dissenting voices and contributed to the stabilization of social order and consolidation of the Nationalist Party rule. At first glance, Nationalist Party leaders—in particular, Chiang Kai-shek—seemed to be the primary architects and executors of the White Terror with the goal of making a "conflict-free" nation-state of Taiwan. Therefore, it makes sense that the majority, if not all, of the existing literature focuses, critically, on the role played by the Nationalist Party. Nonetheless, it would be hasty to conclude that it was the sole culprit. There were other less noticeable and, thus, less well understood actors in the White Terror: the silent masses of the people.

PARTICIPATION BY ABSENCE

The creation of "consensus" in society is not just beneficial for the rulers of the society but also agreeable and even attractive to large numbers of ordinary people, particularly those belonging to the majority. In the case of the White Terror, people's participation was observable in two ways. First, as in the case of mainland China, quite a few people actively participated in various activities, such as cooperating and joining in mass campaigns, conducting surveillance, and informing on "suspicious" persons at schools and workplaces and in neighborhoods.[54] The act of informing became common and popular in this period primarily because of huge rewards paid to informants.[55] In a similar manner, one publisher in Taipei held a contest for "anticommunist" literature, soliciting novels, articles, songs, poems, and dramas, which attracted more than 1,700 entries.[56] This, along with the existence of a large number of informants, suggests that many ordinary people were not just passive actors or victims of the terror as usually described but, to some extent, active participants.

In addition to such straightforward collaborators, there was another kind of "participant" in the White Terror, which might be more characteristic of Taiwan in this period: those who participated by absence. These people consistently attempted to avoid involvement in victims' affairs, deliberately cut off communications and relationships with "suspicious" persons, and chose to withdraw and disconnect themselves from any activities and topics related to politics, attitudes that aided, more than anything else, the continuation of a particular social order under the rule of the Nationalist Party for the nearly four decades that followed.

Family members of "suspicious" persons knew this point well. A mother of one "suspicious" person, for instance, remembered how quickly people changed their attitudes and how cold they could be.[57] Another example is Feng Shou'e, who was arrested in 1950 with her elder brother and spent ten years in jail for attending a meeting of a "suspicious" reading group. Upon her release in 1960, she still found it difficult to find a job, to become acculturated, and to find a marriage partner because she had been labeled as part of a "rebellious family." She soon learned knitting in an attempt to open a yarn store, but when her landlord found out her background, she was forced out. It was like being transferred, she later recalled, from a small prison to a large one.[58]

In this large prison called society, the guards were not necessarily GMD officials and supporters but the masses of the people—neighbors, colleagues, classmates, friends, and even oneself—who were on the lookout for words and deeds, consciously and unconsciously avoiding involvement in any political issues that might cause trouble—that is, actually, a certain manner of "participation" in politics, which constantly suppressed the seeds of social conflicts, and which contributed to the formation and maintenance of an "orderly" and "harmonious" society for a long time. Therefore, it makes much sense that, in the early to mid-1980s, when political movements for democratization spread in Taiwan, one slogan understandably involved the overcoming of the "General Headquarters of Public Security in the heart of each individual."[59]

Such internalized attitudes and political cultures might indicate the legacy of Japanese colonialism, which ended in Taiwan in 1945 after fifty years. After all, this peculiar mode of "participation" in politics—that is, participation by nonparticipation—was quite common among residents in Taiwan under Japanese rule, particularly after various methods of resistance were crushed.[60] Second, for many ordinary people, the restoration and maintenance of social order could be more palatable than the constant divisions and disputes—in a sense, war—at home that had prevailed in the aftermath of World War II. That is why, in Taiwan and other parts of Asia, the demise of the Japanese empire meant the beginning of two processes: decolonization from the former colonizers and recolonization by the local ruling circles on their own terms.

Viewed in this way, what happened in the White Terror in Taiwan in the early 1950s was not just an end result, a stationary state, caused by the Cold War. Rather, it was a continuous process of the recolonization of Taiwan in the aftermath of a chaotic postwar period, with wide and regular participation—including participation by absence—of many people in society. The Cold War, in this instance, did not appear to be a cause of the phenomenon as often described but, rather, a necessary condition that enabled the process of "overcoming" social and cultural conflicts in postwar Taiwan. Thus, an imagined reality of the global Cold War was continuously imagined and required to exist as the "reality" of the world in order to create and then maintain order at home.

Interestingly, a similar process of recolonization under the banner of East-West confrontation can be found in another postcolonial society in Southeast Asia: the Philippines, which gained independence from the United States in 1946.

RECONSIDERING THE CRACKDOWN ON "UN-FILIPINO ACTIVITIES"

On the morning of October 20, 1950, the Philippine government's intelligence officers simultaneously raided twenty-two locations in Manila, the capital of the Philippines, arresting more than a hundred "communists," including an 18-year-old girl and a 15-year-old boy.[61] They were arrested specifically for being members of the "communist-inspired" Hukbalahap, which was allegedly plotting the overthrow of the government and conquest of the world under the direction of Moscow.[62] "We are almost half-way in solving our peace and order problem," said José Aldeguer, a representative of the Congress and a member of the Nacionalista Party, after hearing the news.[63] In line with these raids, conservatives succeeded in raising voices for outlawing the Partido Komunista ng Pilipinas (Communist Party of the Philippines, or PKP). "It seems to us the best way is to outlaw the Communist Party," said the *Manila Daily Bulletin*'s editorial on the following day, "Then, there would be no difficulty in apprehending a man of known and probable connections and holding him until more serious charges can be investigated and brought against him."[64]

One factor that provoked the intensification of "anti-communist" campaigns in the Philippines was the Korean War. Shortly after the outbreak of the war, the mayor of Manila, Manuel de la Fuente, announced on July 15, 1950, "In view of the grave developments in the world situation today, it is indeed imperative for the Philippines Government to take all precautions necessary, as well as stricter measures against the world's greatest threat."[65] Amid increasing feelings of crisis and patriotism among the population, the mayor insisted on outlawing the PKP: "An extremely false and misleading ideology, communism, in the Philippines seeks to overthrow the democratic form of government that we all are enjoying now."[66]

Within weeks of the beginning of the Korean conflict, the Philippine government swiftly declared its support for the United States, and the Philippine Congress created the Special Committee on Un-Filipino Activities (CUFA), which carried out various "anti-communist" campaigns.[67] The Philippines' anti-communist wave was not unique in terms of its timing, evolving quickly in the middle of the Korean War, nor was it unique in the sense that it silenced not only communist activities but various dissident and anti-government activities, as well as social conflicts and culture wars unleashed in the aftermath of World War II. The question we ask here is: Who purged whom for what purpose? What sort of domestic conflicts were stifled under the Cold War logic?

The Philippines was under U.S. colonial rule for more than four decades following American victories in the Spanish–American War of 1898 and Philippine–American War in 1899–1902.[68] A longing for independence had been strong since the time of Spanish colonialism and, particularly, with the establishment of the First Philippine Republic in 1898, but was met with fierce crackdowns by Spanish and American forces, respectively. Dramatic change finally came at the time of World War II, when Japan attacked the Philippines, driving U.S. forces out and occupying the islands. What Japanese occupation did in these areas of Southeast Asia was, in the words of historian Albert Lau, "nothing short of a systems-level meltdown," whose aftershocks continued long after the war ended.[69] During the war, some groups received military training from the Japanese occupying forces, while others were trained by the Allies.[70] Furthermore, while members of ruling circles—including colonial bureaucrats, landlords, and many overseers—fled or hid during the occupation, many peasants for the first time obtained firearms and took opportunities to snipe at Japanese troops, who were not numerous enough to occupy the whole area.[71]

Among many anti-Japanese guerrilla forces, the largest was the Hukbalahap (People's Anti-Japanese Liberation Army, or the Huks). The Hukbalahap movement originated in agrarian unrest in the central rice-growing areas of Luzon, where typically half of tenant farmers' produce was taken by their landlords and a large portion of the remaining half by their actual overseers in the fields.[72] With agrarian discontent as a backdrop, the Huks developed rapidly during the war, appealing not only for anti-Japanese resistance but land reform and social justice and ultimately bringing together communists, leftists, reformers, professionals, intellectuals, the middle class, workers, and, above all, tens of thousands of peasants.[73]

Even before U.S. forces returned to the Philippines after the Japanese defeat in 1945, the Huks and other anti-Japanese guerrillas had succeeded in liberating many areas of the islands from the Japanese, and begun to administer cities and towns on their own terms. A British diplomat observed: "Having once tasted the joys of virtual proprietorship, the peasants were unwilling to revert to their old status after the Japanese had been driven out, and they were prepared to use their firearms to defend what they now regarded as their rights."[74] It is therefore not surprising that the Philippines, like Korea and other postcolonial societies, entered into a situation like a civil war immediately following Japan's defeat.

Thus, even after the country was granted independence from the United States in 1946, the Philippine government did not enjoy the confidence of the vast majority of the people.[75] Furthermore, amid tumultuous social change during the war and postwar periods, social and moral standards had seriously declined, if not collapsed. Graft and exploitation were common among government officials. Many businessmen, according to the observations of a British diplomat, operated on the principle of enriching themselves, with complete disregard for business ethics, the welfare of their employees, or the future of the country.[76] Even worse, the ballot box fraud of the 1949 elections, through which Elpidio Quirino won the presidency, dampened trust among the population. A Filipino attorney in Manila summarized the postwar situation as follows: "During the occupation we were trying to cheat the Japanese, now we are trying to cheat each other."[77]

The Huks' dissident movement became bolder and more aggressive during this period, touching off a large-scale revolt, later known as the Huk Rebellion, which reached its zenith in 1949 and 1950.[78] In late August 1950, the Huks carried out well-planned and coordinated attacks on constabulary and police stations north and south of Manila; according to a British report, raids elsewhere were largely unopposed, and dissidents seemed to murder unpopular officials at will, killing no fewer than forty-seven officials and injuring thirty others.[79]

LOCAL AND SOCIAL DYNAMICS

Nevertheless, behind high-profile military incidents of this kind, the Huks' challenge was not limited to the type of political regime; it enlisted broad support partly because of its bold challenge to conventional Philippine social values, particularly those involving gender. The participation of women in the Huks during the wartime and postcolonial struggles changed the traditional image and role of women, as they changed in many other societies. As the historian Vina A. Lanzona's study shows, a significant number of peasant women left behind their traditional role and participated in the struggle. At its peak, the Huk movement included 1,000 to 2,000 active female guerrillas and far more women as peasant supporters, in general, questioning traditional norms on what women should and should not do.[80] What the rise of the Huks represented was, in short, a challenge not only to the existing political order but also to dominant social values. Yet, the uprising was quickly subdued with the spread of the Cold War logic and the beginning of the crackdown on "un-Filipino" activities following 1950. Thus, it is not surprising that, at the height of "anti-communist" attacks, female guerrillas were condemned as unpatriotic, immoral, and unnatural mothers.[81]

Broader social struggles under the ostensible mantle of Cold War repression can be seen in another major issue in the Philippines: immigrant and ethnic problems. As in many parts of Southeast Asia, overseas Chinese in the Philippines were a minority group, but their predominant control of domestic economic activity had aroused Filipino resentment for years. Then, anti-communism in the Philippines worked effectively to curve their influence. In fact, the major outcome of the Philippine Congress' anti-communist effort in the first few years, according to observation by CIA officials, was legislation designed to tighten immigration restriction directed primarily against the Chinese.[82] Apparently, this was more a reflection of local conflicts and needs than any issues related to East-West confrontation.

Such local and social dynamics of the Philippines' anti-communism can be seen clearly in the ways in which the Committee on Un-Filipino Activities developed and operated. As the name suggests, the committee was modeled after the House Un-American Activities Committee in the United States.[83] Yet it was created through the initiative of Philippine officials, not Americans. In fact, in the fall of 1950, the Committee sent an inquiry to the Philippine embassy in Washington, DC, as to the procedures, functions, and activities of its American counterpart, and the staff there investigated and prepared a detailed response to this inquiry.[84] Therefore, the evolution of CUFA's activities and stance were more reflective of needs and contexts in the Philippines than those of the United States, which became clear when the committee specifically provided ten categories of "un-Filipino activities." Some were easily conceivable; one item maintained: "It is un-Filipino to adhere to, believe in, or aid . . . in the promotional propaganda of the ideas of Communism."[85] Others maintained that it was un-Filipino not to believe in God and not to believe in morality. Another simply argued that aiding crimes was un-Filipino activity. Another added that it was un-Filipino to "view the Government as an instrument of class oppression." Finally, the last category maintained that it was un-Filipino to "believe in, and aid in the hopeless attainment of, a classless society." Social classes, according to the committee's statement, were merely natural human groupings.[86] If these definitions were literally applied, almost everyone—those who had been advocating land reform, who had been trying to repeal legacy of colonialism, or who had criticized the government, and even ordinary criminals and those considered morally questionable—could be deemed "un-Filipino" elements.[87] And that is what happened.

Viewed in this way, the front line in the ostensibly anti-communist campaigns was not necessarily about stopping the expansion of the Cold War or infiltration of communists, but containing domestic challenges, unleashed through the chaotic experiences of World War II and decolonization in the postwar era, in favor of the vested interests of conventional ruling circles. As a matter of fact, the driving force of "anti-communist" movements in the Philippines consisted of a traditional grouping of ruling elites, such as government officials, businessmen, military officers, and religious groups, as well as foreign nationals such as Americans and Britons. These were the people who made up various anti-communist associations, such as the Anti-Communist League of the Philippines, which was organized in 1951, claiming to represent 90,000 members.[88] In brief, anti-communist campaigns in the Philippines overlapped with ruling circles' efforts to "re-colonize" society on their own terms. After American colonialists and Japanese occupiers left the islands, the decolonization on the islands became a process of recolonization, with the logic of anti-communism confining emerging social conflicts in the name of the Cold War.

The outbreak of the Korean War and subsequent fear of World War III created particularly beneficial circumstances for Filipino conservatives who had been ruling the society since the time of U.S. colonial rule. In the late 1940s, the Huks' appeals for land reform and social justice remained attractive because their criticism of the ruling circles, labeling them agents of American imperialism, was quite popular. At this point, the Huks appeared more indigenous, while the ruling elites in the government looked more "foreign" because of their dependence on U.S. support. However, the logic of the Cold War following the 1950s provided a foundation for describing Huks' and other groups' efforts in support of land reform and social justice as "foreign instigation" and "Moscow directed," while making the government look more representatively "Filipino."

Many participants in social, peasant, and guerrilla movements, which posed various challenges to the government and to conventional norms, hoped to realize agrarian reform, social justice, and gender equality. But when social and cultural conflicts were superseded by matters of national security and identity—that is, the question of being "Filipino" versus "un-Filipino"—many supporters stopped discussing social problems for the protection of their nation.[89] Therefore, within a short period, challenges represented by the Huks to conventional social and political conditions in

postcolonial Philippine society were silenced under the banner of protecting the nation and forging consensus.

Indeed, the logic of the Cold War marginalized domestic opposition and
called for unity. "The Philippines now stands at the crossroads," said Judge
Oscar Castelo in a courtroom in Manila in May 1951, in which he passed a
sentence of death for six accused of rebellion. "If the Philippines is awake, it
will survive the deadly communist conspiracy in its midst. If not, it will suffer the fate of all gullible and communist-indoctrinated nations in the world."[90]
Referring to the alleged international situation, the judge then called for
unity among Filipinos.

> It now becomes the duty of all loyal Filipino citizens, regardless of their
> creed and political affiliations, to bind themselves together and join the vast
> movement of freedom-loving peoples of the world in combating Commu-
> nism in its fundamental principles and purposes.[91]

The specious logic here is worth looking into carefully. Ostensibly, the
"unity" of the population was a means to an end: that is, to fight communism. However, the means and the end were, actually, reversed. "Unity"—
domestic tranquility—was the goal in itself, and fighting communism was
the means of achieving unity of the population. This reversal of logic was a
common feature in social and political repression, not just in the Philippines but also in Taiwan as well as elsewhere. In short, the ultimate end of
domestic purges was not necessarily to fight "communism," as it appeared on
the surface, but to overcome social conflicts and culture wars, thus, creating
order and tranquility at home by eliminating various dissidents and nonconformists who embodied social changes that emerged as a result of World
War II and the chaotic postwar period.

"There is an ominous trend in this nation," a 53-year-old man wrote in January 1952. "We are developing tolerance only for the orthodox point of
view . . . , intolerance for new or different approaches." Depicting the current mood, the man pointed out that, in his society, thought was being
standardized, the permissible area for calm discussion was being narrowed,
the range of ideas was being limited, and many minds were being closed. In
the end, he warned: "The great danger of this period is not inflation, nor

the national debt, nor atomic warfare. The great, the critical danger is that we will so limit or narrow the range of permissible discussion and permissible thought that we will become victims of the orthodox school."[92] The man's name was William O. Douglas, then an Associate Justice of the U.S. Supreme Court. In his article, he was talking solely about the situation in the United States, but what he described is applicable to many societies around the world that were experiencing domestic purges at exactly the same time.

This study of domestic purges circa 1950–1952 in the United States, Japan, and Britain, as well as China, Taiwan, and the Philippines from a new perspective sheds light not only on each variation but on the simultaneity of these events. Each variation had its own history and local roots and developed in its own way, with its own level of violence. Most existing literature has examined these events separately and characterized them as manifestations of the global Cold War on the ground—consequential events but aftereffects of the global confrontation. As a result, the existing literature has tended to confirm rather than question the conventional notions of the Cold War. Such a conventional view, however, appears plausible only when we accept the "reality" of the Cold War and approach each situation using that particular lens.

If we decompose Cold War fantasy and look into local and social disputes, however, the situations appear different. The primary focus here is a reassessment of the meaning of these repressions by tracing what happened within societies, rather than investigating the centers of political power. This is because if we view a social phenomenon through an examination of political elites, we are apt not to consider the meaning of that phenomenon itself, because it is often confused with those elites' intentions. Rather, we have treated the center of power, not as the *origin,* but a *part* of social and cultural events. Therefore, although the intentions of those in power have been discussed, the focus has not been on how they led events but how they reacted to them. Instead of beginning with the search for power holders' intentions, we have delved into each society, paying particular attention to the social mechanisms of repression.

One might raise doubts about the method of treating, for instance, the Campaign to Suppress Counterrevolutionaries in China and McCarthyism in the United States equally, because they were *different* in many ways. However, the notion that they were utterly and inherently distinct is exactly what we wish to challenge. Even in light of many important differences among and between these incidences of repression, certain similarities are revealed through examining their social and local functions. We have seen that the domestic purges in this period were not so much characteristic of a particular ideology, political regime, or regional cultures as related to a simultaneous and shared worldwide phenomenon. The simple questions we have explored are: Who purged whom for what purpose? Why did such similar patterns of domestic repression occur simultaneously around the world? Were there any similarities among these repressions? What were the implications of such a worldwide phenomenon?

First and foremost, all of these societies experienced World War II and various kinds of fundamental social changes, which unleashed diverse social, cultural, and political conflicts at home. Put simply, in the aftermath of foreign wars, each society entered a period of "social warfare." In these societies, the outbreak of the Korean War evoked many people's memories of World War II, producing fear of World War III, which, in turn, provided a wartime atmosphere that justified and escalated the purification of society for the security of the public. Such purification campaigns during the Korean War evolved within each local context, functioning more or less as mechanisms for resolving emerging social conflicts in the aftermath of World War II, aiming to calm chaotic postwar situations and creating a harmonious social order in each society.

It is important to note that all of these repressive purification campaigns developed at intersections of state mobilization and people's participation, to protect, or, in some cases, create unity using a binary distinction between "us" and "them." In each instance, the Cold War logic proved its utility in tamping down social and cultural conflicts in the name of the nation and perpetual security. Taken together, the wave of social purges during the Korean War can be characterized as nativist backlashes—conservative movements, but in terms of social, rather than political, conservatism—each a local phenomenon observed worldwide, aimed at the restoration of "normal" social order and relationships, through purging thousands of nonconformists at home.

Viewed in this way, what becomes clearer is the actuality of local struggles and imagined nature of the Cold War as well as the social needs in such an imagined reality to overcome "war" at home. In this sense, the actual divide of the Cold War existed less between East and West than within each society, and each, in turn, required the continuation of the Cold War to maintain harmonious order and life at home. From this angle, each instance of local repression was not so much an end result of the Cold War but part of the engine, a component, of the Cold War, each contributing to the creation and maintenance of a gigantic imagined reality in the postwar world. The architects of and participants in this world were, thus, not only power holders in the metropoles of each society but also millions of ordinary people in cities and villages all over the world, who consciously and unconsciously engaged in creating security and order at home. It was such an ascent of people's participation in and social needs of the imagined reality of the Cold War that turned a particular discourse into the actuality of the postwar period, internally functioning to sustain and perpetuate the real global Cold War for decades to follow.

Epilogue

The Cold War as Social Politics

BEFORE FINISHING OUR JOURNEY, let us move the hands of the clock back to the early months of 1944, in the midst of World War II. While battles were still going on—or perhaps *because of* cruel experiences during the war— many soldiers were already imagining and talking about their lives after the war. One British soldier, C. S. M. Fowler, entered an essay contest concerning postwar dreams in March 1944. He wrote:

> My burning desire is to return to my wife knowing that world peace has been established and will be maintained. I look forward to the right and facilities to live within an industrious community, to contribute by my labours to its prosperity and to enjoy the benefits of social security.[1]

In his long essay, he listed five items that he hoped for as postwar conditions. The primary need, listed before everything else, was for employment in which he could feel useful and happy: "A reasonable wage, congenial conditions and a decent measure of leisure will be of paramount importance," he wrote, and added: "The haunting spectre of unemployment will not, I trust, be allowed to rise." The second item listed was a home "of which I can be proud and in which I can, with my wife and family, enjoy the freedom to which we have contributed our sacrifices." The soldier specifically wrote that postwar homes must be bright, healthy, and attractive and that overcrowding and dismal slums must be eradicated. Then, he went on to list: the improvement of the education system, development of health services including free medical attention and treatment, and expansion of social security measures. "In brief," he concluded, "postwar Britain should be a haven of peace, industry, prosperity and happiness, populated by healthy, educated people."[2]

I was struck by this letter. Perhaps I was feeling overly sentimental and emotional after several weeks on a foreign research trip, but I was deeply impressed that this one soldier—not an eminent intellectual or policymaker—could have thought so seriously about and vividly depicted such a picture of postwar society. Moreover, I felt stirred because what he probably faced after the war was not a rosy, plentiful, and peaceful world. As Barbara W. Tuchman observed in her monumental study of World War I, human beings could not sustain a war of such magnitude and pain without hope—hope that the war was fought to make a better world and that war would never happen again. But, as she pointed out, when that war was over and produced a variety of results, the dominant one, transcending all others, was disillusion.[3] Such a scenario was repeated during and following World War II. Despite high hopes during the war, what this British soldier faced was, as we have seen, rampant inflation, housing problems, insufficient wages, successive labor disputes and strikes, and various social conflicts, such as those in gender relations arising from changes during the war in terms of the meaning of family and of women. The letter forced me think about how he faced such postwar situations, how he experienced such possible disillusion, and how he dealt with subsequent likely senses of loss and powerlessness in the years following the war.

The letter also made me think about the meaning and function of such hopes and disillusions not only in British society but in other parts of the world, such as Japan and the United States. Indeed, they went through similarly radical wartime and postwar transformations in terms of social, cultural, economic, and political orders and values. Newly emerging actors who had discovered and gained voices during the war continued their struggles afterward, with high hopes for a better postwar world. In Japan, with its defeat, wartime morals and values were shattered, and this made room for new values and demands, often carried and boldly expressed by youth, women, and labor movements. Leftist and communist thought, which had been harshly suppressed during the war, also came to the spotlight as means to critique wartime Japan. The United States, too, observed an upsurge of renewed demands frequently uttered by labor, women, and African Americans, among others. These, in turn, generated seeds of postwar conflicts at home, because such hopes to create a better world clashed with others' hopes and dreams to restore and maintain more conventional, normal, and orderly societies.

Similar situations can be found in many postcolonial societies that experienced World War II, including China, Taiwan, and the Philippines. For them, the end of World War II signaled, or even brought about, the retreat and demise of colonial empires, leaving local people with opportunities to recreate and reorganize their countries on their own terms; yet, since there were many different hopes and visions for postcolonial orders, many postcolonial societies went through bloody civil wars and internal struggles.[4] In short, at the crossroads of hope and disillusion, domestic societies in many parts of the world turned into "battlefields" in the aftermath of World War II. In effect, after the end of the war that shook the world, another type of "war" emerged at home, within societies, in neighborhoods, at workplaces and schools, and and among friends and family members.

As we have seen, the "reality" of the Cold War functioned quite "well," worldwide, because it was quite effective in marginalizing dissidents and elements of disorder and in containing seeds of social disagreements, thus, bringing order and harmony at home. Because we usually think of the Cold War as an event in terms of global politics, with various ramifications at home, we tend to concentrate on high-ranking policymakers and centers of power to explain its origins and evolution. Yet we need to know more about how it worked within societies and at grassroots levels and how it was accepted by large segments of populations around the world as the "reality" of the era. In other words, we need to know more about the social needs, or self-sustaining dynamics, of a fantasy Cold War world. This is because it was such social needs and acceptance that solidified the verisimilitude of the Cold War, making possible its appearance as the irrefutable reality of its time, rather than merely one of many discourses about the world. Viewed from a social point of view, thus, the Cold War does not seem like simply a geopolitical, ideological, and global confrontation between the Soviet Union and the United States but, rather, an imagined reality, a gigantic social mechanism that operated to tranquilize chaotic postwar situations, worldwide, through putting an end to a multitude of social conflicts and culture wars at home. It can be seen, in a sense, as a mechanism of postwar settlement, not in terms of state-to-state relations, but within societies.

One might ask: Who designed it? Did anyone plan such a reordering of postwar societies? This is, however, a tricky question. We tend to approach history—particularly political history—through lenses of human will and see it as resulting from human intentions. This approach, of course, is useful for an investigation of murder or arson and, indeed, indispensable in the examination of specific policy-making processes, such as those of Washington's and Beijing's decisions to cross the 38th parallel in the fall of 1950. Yet such a police-investigation approach is inadequate for the exploration and evaluation of larger historical trends, such as wars, revolutions, and various other social and global phenomena. If we apply this model to these topics, we might end up bolstering up a sort of Great Man's history or conspiracy theory, highlighting the roles played by centers of power or imagining the existence of conspiracies. Or we might have to convince ourselves of a much more structuralist analysis, ending up with economic substructure determinism or cultural determinism. What we have attempted here is different from such models. Instead, our approach is comparable to a biologists' evolutionary model. Why does a butterfly spend its early stages as a caterpillar, while its imago develops wings? Why do beetles—among the most successful insects in the world in terms of number and variety—sacrifice a graceful flying ability to develop shells? Needless to say, no individual intended to do so, nor did someone design these (at least according to many biologists today). Particular species survived when they fit better with surrounding environments, while others did not.

Odd as it might appear, the materialization of the Cold War world might be best explained through such a biological approach. To reply to the question of who designed it, perhaps the answer is: nobody. Yet, at the same time, the world of the Cold War was, indeed, useful for many because it proved effective in fulfilling the social needs of the postwar era in creating domestic tranquility. While it was not the result of particular people's or groups' calculations (or miscalculations), it had its own social dynamics, which grew through numerous people's manifold choices. As we have seen, each acted for locally specific, diverse reasons. For a street vendor in Beijing, the Campaign to Suppress Counterrevolutionaries might have been a means to maintain order and morality in his district. For low-ranking Nationalist government officials working in municipal offices in Jiayi, Taiwan, the Opposing Communists and Resisting Russians campaign might have been a practical tool for recolonizing territory. For a conservative Japanese man and for a conventional segregationist in the United States, anti-communist campaigns might have provided a powerful logic to contain newly emerging actors such as women or African Americans. None of them, certainly, intended to create the Cold War world in order to suppress their enemies within, but that was exactly how it functioned and gained broad acceptance. Viewed in this way, the crux of the Cold War was not simply about an East-West global confrontation or balance of power, but struggles within each society—everyday people's wars at home.

In a sense, the reality of the Cold War materialized in the crucible of the postwar era, in which numerous people's myriad choices and intentions, hopes and disillusion, mingled and conflicting, leading to the rise of a particular mode of Cold War fantasy that "fit" well with social needs of populations around the world. In such a dynamic of unintended chain reaction that shaped the Cold War world, two more ingredients were indispensable: the historical legacy of World War II and the outbreak of the Korean War. After all, for many people in Europe and East and Southeast Asia, as well as the United States, World War II was not simply an event in the past. Because of the massive scale of mobilization and participation, many held a broad variety of memories of the war. Furthermore, because of the shocking cruelty involved, such memories tended to be uncompromising, as if they were the only "truth," functioning, in turn, as lessons of the past, constraining the ways in which people observed and contemplated the future of the world.[5] For them, World War II was not just a tragedy in the past; it was an image of the future.

It is no wonder, therefore, that many policymakers and ordinary people alike feared the outbreak of World War III at the time of the Korean War, which many interpreted as the first instance of a "hot" war between the two superpowers—a way of thinking that, in turn, consolidated a specific pattern of recognition of the world outside Korea as barely remaining at the stage of "cold" war. Intriguingly, however, the Cold War was not a *universal* phenomenon at that time. The "reality" of the conflict, in fact, achieved a high degree of verisimilitude in places where World War II had left massive scars, including Europe, Asia, and the United States, while retaining a low degree of it in areas where damage from the war was relatively lighter, including Latin America and Africa. Many societies in the latter group, to be sure, adopted the reality of the Cold War in the late 1950s and 1960s, but did so for different locally specific reasons and were less a part of the imagined reality of the conflict as of 1950. This is because, bluntly put, the "reality" of the Cold War at this moment was largely built on the memories and experiences of World War II, and, against a backdrop of fear of another world war, many people translated the meaning of the Korean conflict through local lenses, including domestic-political languages, historical experiences, and racial prejudice, which shaped "real" situations of the world accordingly.

This leads to a final point about the meaning of the Cold War in the twenty-first century. We usually think that the Cold War ended about two decades ago. This is true if we view the Cold War as a geopolitical, ideological confrontation between the Soviet Union and the United States. With the demise of the Soviet Union, it seems apparent, at a glance, that the conflict was an event in the past. However, such is not the case if we see the Cold War world as a gigantic social construction of an imagined reality, in which many people participated in restoring order and harmony through marginalizing disagreements at home. When we look at the Cold War in this way, the phenomenon does not seem to be a peculiar event in a time long past. Rather, it can be said that such a pattern has reappeared and, in fact, has been reinforced in the so-called post–Cold War world in the name of the "clash of civilizations" and, particularly, in the decade of the "War on Terror" following September 11, 2001.

To think about experiences of the Cold War less in terms of the U.S.-Soviet confrontation than as parts of a social mechanism of restoring order at home on a global scale is, thus, to think about the imagined and constructed nature of "reality" and "history" and their social functions on the ground and among people. This recognition, in turn, forces us to reconsider the imagined nature of our reality, our history, our institutions, and the common sense to which we adhere today. To be sure, any human society, to some extent, hinges upon imagination, which assembles these social arrangements and agreements. As we have seen in our story, however, none of these is absolute and immutable; they are and always will be socially constructed and historically contingent. Therefore, what we can learn seems to be that we need to raise questions constantly, instead of being convinced by seemingly authentic reality or history. How real is our "reality"? How does "common sense" about ourselves and foreign others contain imagined elements? How is the "history" we learn at school and from the media constructed? In what ways do such reality and history work in society? It is not futile to keep asking these questions and to raise our voices when reality seems out of sync, in however small a fashion. If there is a lesson that we can learn from our experiences of the "reality" of the Cold War and its repressive functions on the ground, it is that each of us is not merely an onlooker but a power holder in choosing, changing, and maintaining the reality of the world in the crucible of our own time.

Notes

ABBREVIATIONS

AARL	Auburn Avenue Research Library, Atlanta, GA
AFSF	Administrative File of Stafford Warren
AH	Academia Historica (Guoshiguan), Taipei, Taiwan
AHP	Ashida Hitoshi Papers
BFFP	Bonner F. Fellers Paper
BLNRR	British Library Newspaper Reading Room, Colindale, UK
BL-UCB	Bancroft Library, University of California at Berkeley, Berkeley, CA
BMA	Beijing Municipal Archives, Beijing, PRC
CAWP	Charles A. Willoughby Papers
CCP	Chinese Communist Party
CKSD	Chiang Kai-shek Diaries
CLEAR-UHWO	Center for Labor Education & Research, University of Hawaii at West Oahu, Kapolei, HI
CL-NUS	Central Library, National University of Singapore, Singapore
CMCP	Clark M. Clifford Papers

CNPR	Chinese Nationalist Party Records
COH-CU	Center for Oral History, Columbia University, New York City, NY
CPP	Conservative Party Papers
CPV	Chinese People's Volunteers
CSU	Columbus State University, Columbus, GA
CUFA	Committee on Un-Filipino Activities
CUHK	Chinese University of Hong Kong, Hong Kong
CWIHP	Cold War International History Project
DAP	Dean Acheson Papers
DHL-OU	Duke Humfrey's Library, Oxford University, Oxford, UK
DMP	Douglas MacArthur Papers
DSOD	"Daily Summary of Opinion Developments"
EAP	Eben Ayers Papers
ERP	Escott Reid Papers
FMA	Foreign Ministry Archives, Beijing, PRC
FRUS	*Foreign Relations of the United States*
FSP	Fred Stover Papers
GHQ	U.S. General Headquarters in Tokyo
GJP	George Johnston Papers
GMD	Nationalist Party (Guomindang)
GMEP	George M. Elsey Papers
HAWP	Henry A. Wallace Papers
HILA-SU	Hoover Institution Library and Archives, Stanford University, Stanford, CA
HMP	Helen MacMartin Papers
HMPPP	Helen MacMartin Progressive Party Papers
HSTL	Harry S. Truman Library, Independence, MO
HSTP	Harry S. Truman Papers
HUAC	House Un-American Activities Committee
ISEAS	Institute of Southeast Asian Studies, Singapore
JEWP	James E. Webb Papers
JSSP	John S. Service Papers
LAC	Library Archives Canada, Ottawa, Canada
LARC-SFSU	Labor Archives & Research Center, San Francisco State University, San Francisco, CA
LAUSDBER	Los Angeles Unified School District Board of Education Records
LC	Library of Congress, Washington, DC

LGY	*Lengzhan guojishi yanjiu* (Cold War International History Studies)
LPP	Lester Pearson Papers
LSC-UCLA	Library Special Collections, University of California Los Angeles, Los Angeles, CA
MENC	McCarthy Era Newspaper Clippings
MJCP	Matthew J. Connelly Papers
MJPHMR-NDL	Modern Japanese Political History Materials Room
MMA	MacArthur Memorial Archives, Norfolk, VA
MRC-UW	Modern Records Centre, University of Warwick, Coventry, UK
NAI	National Archives of India, Delhi, India
NARA	National Archives and Records Administration, College Park, MD
NHS	Nevada Historical Society, Reno, NV
NLA	National Library of Australia, Canberra, Australia
NLC	National Library of China (Zhongguo guojia tushuguan), Beijing, PRC
NMML	Nehru Memorial Museum and Library, Delhi, India
NMP	Nakamura Mitsuo Papers
NNUL	Northeastern Normal University Library, Changchun, PRC
NPA	Nationalist Party Archives (Dangshiguan), Taipei, Taiwan
NRR-NDL	Newspaper Reading Room, National Diet Library, Tokyo, Japan.
NTL	National Taiwan Library (Guoli Taiwan tushuguan), Taipei, Taiwan
NTUL	National Taiwan University Library, Taipei, Taiwan
OHR-OPL	Oakland History Room, Oakland Public Library, Oakland, CA
OISS-HU	Ohara Institute for Social Studies (Ohara shakaimondai kenkyusho), Hosei University, Tokyo, Japan
OKL-CU	Olin & Kroch Libraries, Cornell University, Ithaca, NY
OPOS	Office of Public Opinion Studies
PHNP	Paul H. Nitze Papers
PMP	Pat McCarran Papers
PPP	Progressive Party Papers
RATP	Robert A. Taft Papers
RFP	Raymond Feely Papers
SCUA-SU	Special Collections & University Archives, Stanford University, Stanford, CA
SCUA-UI	Special Collections & University Archives, University of Iowa, Iowa City, IA
SC-UV	Special Collections, University of Vermont, Burlington, VT

SIF	Security Investigation File
SKP	Stetson Kennedy Papers
SLA-GSU	Southern Labor Archives, Georgia State University, Atlanta, GA
SMA	Shanghai Municipal Archives, Shanghai, PRC
SMML-PU	Seeley Mudd Manuscript Library, Princeton University, Princeton, NJ
TK-US	The Keep, University of Sussex, Brighton, UK
TNA	The National Archives, Kew, UK
UA-UCLA	University Archives, University of California at Los Angeles, Los Angeles, CA
UHM	University of Hawaii at Manoa, Honolulu, HI
USNWR	*U.S. News and World Report*
VBP	Valery Burati Papers
VHS	Vermont Historical Society, Barre, VT
WAHP	William Averell Harriman Papers
WCML	Working-Class Movement Library, Salford, UK
WHJP	Walter Henry Judd Papers
WKP	William Knowland Papers
WPRL-WSU	Walter P. Reuther Library, Wayne State University, Detroit, MI

INTRODUCTION

1. "Our Weekly Letter," no. 17, 2 June 1950, Working-Class Movement Library, Salford, UK; and "Peace versus Peace," *The Economist,* 27 May 1950, 1153–1154.

2. The field of Cold War history has changed dramatically in the past two decades. It has developed into an area of study not only in the fields of diplomatic history and political science as it used to be, but social and cultural history, as well as anthropology, cultural studies, literature and film, design and art, and rhetoric and communications studies. In the first place, I have benefited from reading earlier scholarship in the field, such as the work of Walter LaFeber, John Lewis Gaddis, and Melvyn Leffler, who addressed the subject through elucidating the roles of states and policymakers—the traditional strength of diplomatic history. Even though my book raises fundamental questions about their approaches, it is their work that laid its foundation. See, for example, Walter LaFeber, *America, Russia, and the Cold War, 1945–2006,* 10th ed. (Boston: McGraw-Hill, 2008); John Lewis Gaddis, *We Now Know: Rethinking Cold War History* (New York: Oxford University Press, 1997); and Melvyn Leffler, *Preponderance of Power: National Security, the Truman Administration, and the Cold War* (Stanford, CA: Stanford University Press, 1992).

In addition, I have learned a great deal from recent scholars' work, which has expanded the objects and themes of the field, like Odd Arne Westad taking a global approach and exploring the nature of the Cold War from the angle of the Third World's decolonization processes; and Fredrik Logevall, Campbell Craig, and Thomas J. Christensen more deeply concentrating on the impact of domestic politics, examining how party politics and elections contributed to the making of the Cold War. My book is an effort to combine these two seemingly contradictory approaches—one going toward internationalization and transnationalization and, the other, in the direction of exploring domestic mechanisms—into one synthesis. See, for instance, Odd Arne Westad, *The Global Cold War: Third World Interventions and the Making of Our Times* (New York: Cambridge University Press, 2005); Fredrik Logevall, "A Critique of Containment," *Diplomatic History*, 28:4 (September 2004): 473–499; Campbell Craig and Fredrik Logevall, *America's Cold War: The Politics of Insecurity* (Cambridge, MA: Belknap Press of Harvard University Press, 2009); and Thomas J. Christensen, *Useful Adversaries: Grand Strategy, Domestic Mobilization, and Sino-American Conflict, 1947–1958* (Princeton, NJ: Princeton University Press, 1996).

Furthermore, a recent increase in studies on the Cold War by cultural, social, and labor historians, as well as by scholars in other disciplines, such as political science, anthropology, and cultural studies, has deepened my understandings of the Cold War by forcing me to reconsider the meanings and functions of the conflict. An enormous amount of literature exists, but I particularly benefited from reading Heonik Kwon, *The Other Cold War* (New York: Columbia University Press, 2010); Ted Hopf, *Reconstructing the Cold War: The Early Years, 1945–1958* (New York: Oxford University Press, 2012); Mary Kaldor, *The Imaginary War: Understanding the East-West Conflict* (Cambridge, MA: Blackwell, 1990); Jodi Kim, *Ends of Empire: Asian American Critique and the Cold War* (Minneapolis: University of Minnesota Press, 2010); and Martin J. Medhurst, *Cold War Rhetoric Strategy, Metaphor, and Ideology* (East Lansing: Michigan State University Press, 1997); as well as Robbie Lieberman and Clarence Lang, eds., *Anticommunism and the African American Freedom Movement: Other Side of Story* (New York: Palgrave Macmillan, 2009); Colleen Doody, *Detroit's Cold War: The Origins of Postwar Conservatism* (Urbana: University of Illinois Press, 2012); Shelton Stromquist, ed., *Labor's Cold War: Local Politics in a Global Context* (Urbana: University of Illinois Press, 2008); and Christina Klein, *Cold War Orientalism: Asia in the Middlebrow Imagination, 1945–1961* (Berkeley: University of California Press, 2003).

Last but not least, I am most indebted to recent scholarship, such as the work of Jeremi Suri, Mark Philip Bradley, John Fousek, as well as Patrick Major and Rana Mitter, whose work has attempted to forge bridges between two previously distant areas of literature—political and diplomatic aspects, on the one hand, and social and cultural dimensions, on the other—exploring the crossroads of politics and culture, as well as state and society. My book is an effort to explore this area further. See, for instance, Jeremi Suri, *Power and Protest: Global Revolution and the Rise of Detente* (Cambridge, MA: Harvard University Press, 2003); Mark Bradley, *Imagining Vietnam and America: The Making of Postcolonial Vietnam, 1919–1950* (Chapel Hill: University of North Carolina Press, 2000); John Fousek, *To Lead the Free World: American Nationalism and the Cultural Roots of the Cold War* (Chapel Hill: University of North Carolina Press, 2000); and Patrick Major and Rana Mitter, eds., *Across the Blocs: Cold War Cultural and Social History* (Portland, OR: Frank Cass, 2004). By the same token, I greatly benefited from reading constructivist arguments in the field of political science; see, for instance, Peter J. Katzenstein, ed., *The Culture of National Security: Norms and Identity in World Politics* (New York: Columbia University Press, 1996); Peter J. Katzenstein, *Cultural Norms and National Security: Police and Military in Postwar Japan* (Ithaca, NY: Cornell University Press, 1996); Jutta Weldes et al., *Cultures of Insecurity: States, Communities, and the Production of Danger* (Minneapolis: University of Minnesota Press, 1999); and Ted Hopf, *Social Construction of International Politics: Identities & Foreign Policies, Moscow, 1955 and 1999* (Ithaca, NY: Cornell University Press, 2002).

For more detailed historiographical discussions and overviews of the field of Cold War history, see, for example, Patrick Major and Rana Mitter, "East Is East and West Is West? Towards a Comparative Socio-Cultural History of the Cold War," in Major and Mitter, eds., *Across the Blocs*, 1–18; Odd Arne Westad, ed., *Reviewing the Cold War: Approaches, Interpretations, and Theory* (London: F. Cass, 2000); Richard H. Immerman and Petra Goedde, eds., *The Oxford Handbook of the Cold War* (New York: Oxford University Press, 2013); and Joel Isaac and Duncan Bell, eds., *Uncertain Empire: American History and the Idea of the Cold War* (New York: Oxford University Press, 2012); as well as Melvyn P. Leffler and Odd Arne Westad, eds., *The Cambridge History of the Cold War*, 3 vols. (Cambridge: Cambridge University Press, 2010).

3. The Korean War has been a topic of discussion for more than six decades. I particularly benefited from reading Bruce Cumings, *The Origins of the Korean War*, vols. *1–2* (Princeton, NJ: Princeton University Press, 1981–1990); William Stueck, *The Korean War: An International History* (Princeton, NJ: Princeton University Press, 1995); Allan R. Millett, *The War for Korea*, vols. *1–2* (Lawrence: University Press of Kansas, 2005–2010); and Sheila Miyoshi Jager, *Brothers at War: The Unending Conflict in Korea* (New York: W. W. Norton, 2013); as well as Korean scholars' recent work, such as Kim Dong-choon, *Chonjaeng kwa sahoe: Uri ege Hanguk chonjaeng un muot ionna?* [War and Society: What Was the Korean War for Us?] (Paju, South Korea: Tolbegae, 2006), and Park Myung-lim, *Hanguk 1950: Chonjaeng kwa pyonghwa* [Korea 1950: War and Peace] (Seoul: Nanam chulpan, 2002), both of which are available in Japanese translation. For more detailed discussion of Korean War historiography, see Allan R. Millett, "The Korean War: A 50-Year Critical Historiography," *Journal of Strategic Studies* 24: 1 (March 2001): 188–224.

4. George H. Nash, ed., *Freedom Betrayed: Herbert Hoover's Secret History of the Second World War and Its Aftermath* (Stanford, CA: Hoover Institution Press, 2011); David S. Foglesong, *America's Secret War against Bolshevism: U.S. Intervention in the Russian Civil War, 1917–1920* (Chapel Hill: University of North Carolina Press, 1995).

5. Alexis de Tocqueville, *Democracy in America,* vol. 1 (New York: Library of America, 2004), 476.

6. An important exception to this general trend is Jadwiga E. Pieper Mooney and Fabio Lanza, *De-Centering Cold War History: Local and Global Change* (New York: Routledge, 2012), which attempts to explore ordinary people's participation in the making of the Cold War world.

7. Gaddis, *We Now Know,* 287; and Stuart J. Kaufman, *Modern Hatreds: The Symbolic Politics of Ethnic War* (Ithaca, NY: Cornell University Press, 2001), 221.

8. There has been a surge in studies of Latin America's and Africa's experiences in the Cold War in recent years, and these studies seem to be in agreement with my argument. Hal Brands, for instance, points out that Latin America's Cold War took on peak intensity after the Cuban revolution in 1959, developing particularly between the 1960s and 1980s, and shows that it was a series of overlapping conflicts, rather than a single conflict. To explore such a variety of conflicts, Gilbert M. Joseph emphasizes the need to investigate the "*grassroots* dynamics and meanings of the Latin America Cold War," instead of seeing it merely as part of the expansion of the U.S.-USSR confrontation. In line with this, Greg Grandin urges that we view Latin America's Cold War experiences within a larger framework, namely, the "century of revolution" (and counterrevolution) in the region. By the same token, Jeffrey James Byrne points out that Africa's Cold War experience evolved after the Suez Crisis in 1956, and particularly in the 1960s and 1970s, within the contexts of decolonization, development, and the local needs of shaping nation-states. See Hal Brands, *Latin America's Cold War* (Cambridge, MA: Harvard University Press, 2010), 3–7; Gilbert M. Joseph and Daniela Spenser, eds., *In from the Cold: Latin America's New Encounter with the Cold War* (Durham, NC: Duke University Press, 2008), 16–19; Greg Grandin and Gilbert M. Joseph, *A Century of Revolution: Insurgent and Counterinsurgent Violence during Latin America's Long Cold War* (Durham, NC: Duke University Press, 2010), 1–32; Jeffrey James Byrne, "Africa's Cold War," in Robert J. McMahon, ed., *The Cold War in the Third World* (New York: Oxford University Press, 2013), 101–118.

9. Matthew Connelly, "Taking off the Cold War Lens: Visions of North-South Conflict during the Algerian War for Independence," *American Historical Review* 105: 3 (2000): 767–769; Kwon, *The Other Cold War,* 8–9.

10. Lizabeth Cohen, *A Consumers' Republic: The Politics of Mass Consumption in Postwar America* (New York: Knopf, 2003), 8.

11. Immanuel Wallerstein, "What Cold War in Asia? An Interpretative Essay," in Zheng Yangwen, Hong Liu, and Michael Szonyi, eds., *The Cold War in Asia: The Battle for Hearts and Minds* (Boston: Brill, 2010), 17.

12. Kuan-Hsing Chen, *Asia as Method: Toward Deimperialization* (Durham, NC: Duke University Press, 2010), ix–xi.

13. Jodi Kim, *Ends of Empire: Asian American Critique and the Cold War* (Minneapolis: University of Minnesota Press, 2010), 9–27.

14. Mooney and Lanza, *De-Centering Cold War History*, 3–7.

15. This idea derives from my reading of Tony Judt's analysis of "culture wars" in Eastern and Western Europe in 1947–1953. See Tony Judt, *Postwar: A History of Europe Since 1945* (New York: Penguin Press, 2005), 197–225.

1. NAMING THE UNNAMABLE

1. "Oral History Transcript for '1946: The Great Hawaii Sugar Strike,'" Center for Labor Education & Research (CLEAR), University of Hawaii at West Oahu (UHWO), Kapolei, HI, 21–22.

2. Ibid., 2; Robert N. Anderson et al., *Filipinos in Rural Hawaii* (Honolulu: University of Hawaii Press, 1984), 49; E. J. Eagen, "Reports of E. J. Eagen on Hawaiian Islands" (1940), CLEAR-UHWO, 17.

3. "Draft for '1946: The Great Hawaii Sugar Strike,'" CLEAR-UHWO, 4.

4. "Oral History Transcript for '1946,'" 21–22.

5. "Wage Not Issue," *Honolulu Star-Bulletin,* 29 October 1950.

6. ILWU Local 142 pamphlet, "1946 Sugar Strike and the ILWU" (May 1996), CLEAR-UHWO, 1; "Oral History Transcript for '1946,'" 3–6, 11; Gerald Horne, *Fighting in Paradise: Labor Unions, Racism, and Communists in the Making of Modern Hawai'i* (Honolulu: University of Hawaii Press, 2011), 3; Ruth Akamine, "Class, Ethnicity, and the Transformation of Hawaii's Sugar Workers, 1920–1946," in *Politics of Immigrant Workers: Labor Activism in the World Economy since 1830* (New York: Holmes & Meier, 1993), 189.

7. "Wage Not Issue," *Honolulu Star-Bulletin,* 29 October 1950; "Draft for '1946,'" 16; ILWU Local 142, "1946 Sugar Strike and the ILWU," 1.

8. Akamine, "Class, Ethnicity, and the Transformation of Hawaii's Sugar Workers," 186; Moon-Kie Jung, *Reworking Race: The Making of Hawaii's Interracial Labor Movement* (New York: Columbia University Press, 2006), 3, 8, 154–155.

9. A large amount of scholarship exists, but I particularly benefited from John Dittmer, *Local People: The Struggle for Civil Rights in Mississippi* (Urbana: University of Illinois Press, 1995); Pete Daniel, *Lost Revolutions: The South in the 1950s* (Chapel Hill: University of North Carolina Press, 2000); Patricia Sullivan, *Days of Hope: Race and Democracy in the New Deal Era* (Chapel Hill: University of North Carolina Press, 1996); and Thomas J. Sugrue, *Sweet Land of Liberty: The Forgotten Struggle for Civil Rights in the North* (New York: Random House, 2008).

10. "The Strange Case of 'Coke,'" *Southern Patriot* 11: 1 (January 1953), Box 288-A, Periodical Collection, Southern Labor Archives (SLA), Georgia State University (GSU), Atlanta, GA.

11. "Oral History of William P. Randall & William C. Randall" (P1989-03), SLA-GSU, 26; William B. Twitty, "GI Programs in the South: An Alabama Survey," *New South* (April 1946), Box 118, Periodical Collection, SLA-GSU, 2.

12. "Oral History of William P. Randall & William C. Randall." 6.

13. Editorial, "The Anti-Lynching Movement," *Atlanta Daily World,* 26 September 1946.

14. Jennifer E. Brooks, *Defining the Peace: World War II Veterans, Race, and the Remaking of Southern Political Tradition* (Chapel Hill: University of North Carolina Press, 2011), 13–36; Sullivan, *Days of Hope,* 197; "Oral History of W. W. Law" (P199015), SLA-GSU, 128–130; "United Veterans in March on City Hall," *Atlanta Daily World,* 5 March 1946.

15. "Oral History of W. W. Law," 132; "Oral History of William P. Randall & William C. Randall," 7–8.

16. "Antilynching Crusade," *Washington Post,* 21 September 1946.

17. "Store Strike Here Threatens General City AFL Walkout," *Oakland Tribune,* 2 December 1946; Fred Glass, "We Called It a Work Holiday: The Oakland General Strike of 1946," *Labor's Heritage* (Fall 1996): 8–9, 20.

18. Philip J. Wolman, "The Oakland General Strike of 1946," *Southern California Quarterly* 57:2 (Summer 1975): 147–178; Robert O. Self, *American Babylon: Race and the Struggle for Postwar Oakland* (Princeton, NJ: Princeton University Press, 2003), 35–46; Chris Rhomberg, *No There There: Race, Class, and Political Community in Oakland* (Berkeley: University of California Press, 2004), 96–119; George Lipsitz, *Rainbow at Midnight: Labor and Culture in the 1940s* (Urbana: University of Illinois Press, 1994), 148–152. Other cities that experienced general or city-wide strikes were: Stamford and Hartford, CT, Lancaster, PA, Rochester, NY, Camden NJ, and Houston, TX; see Fritz Steele, "A Brief History of the Oakland General Strike of 1946" (May 1995), LARC-SFSU, 4–5, 10.

19. "Betty de Losada Oral History," LARC-SFSU, 15; Dorothy Sue Cobble, *The Other Women's Movement: Workplace Justice and Social Rights in Modern America* (Princeton, NJ: Princeton University Press, 2004), 14–17; Nelson Lichtenstein, *State of the Union: A Century of American Labor* (Princeton, NJ: Princeton University Press, 2002), 88–97.

20. Cobble, *The Other Women's Movement,* 13–14.

21. Lichtenstein, *State of the Union,* 92.

22. Carmen Chaves, "Coming of Age during the War: Reminiscences of an Albuquerque Hispana," *New Mexico Historical Review* 70:4 (October 1995): 396–397.

23. Nancy Gabin, *Feminism in the Labor Movement: Women and the United Auto Workers, 1935–1975* (Ithaca, NY: Cornell University Press, 1990), 125.

24. Ibid., 126.

25. "Remembering Oakland's Big Strike," *Labor Pulse* 2:1 (Winter 1976–77): 24; Kate Rothrock, "Taking It to the Streets: The Oakland General Strike of 1946,"

Oakland Museum of California (Fall 1996); and Cobble, *The Other Women's Movement*, 21.

26. The prices of these goods in 1946 come from the following sources: "Dreams of 1946," *Life*, 25 November 1946, 60; Scott Derks, ed., *Working Americans, vol. 1: The Working Class* (Lakeville, CT: Grey House, 2000–2010), 309, 333; *vol. 2: The Middle Class*, 298; *vol. 3: The Upper Class*, 287; *vol. 7: Social Movements*, 310.

27. "Dreams of 1946," 60.

28. Derks, *Working Americans, vol. 2*, 298–299; James T. Patterson, *Grand Expectations: The United States, 1945–1974* (New York: Oxford University Press, 1996), 44.

29. Derks, *Working Americans, vol. 2*, 298–299.

30. Steele, "A Brief History of the Oakland General Strike of 1946," 4–5; and "Remembering Oakland's Big Strike." 24.

31. "Newsgram," *U.S. News and World Report* (hereafter, *USNWR*), 1 November 1946, 7.

32. Jack Metzgar, "The 1945–1946 Strike Wave," and Nicola Pizzolato, "Strikes in the United States since World War II," in Aaron Brenner, Benjamin Day, and Immanuel Ness, eds., *The Encyclopedia of Strikes in American History* (Armonk, NY: M. E. Sharpe, 2009), 222–226; George Lipsitz, *Rainbow at Midnight: Labor and Culture in the 1940s* (Urbana: University of Illinois Press, 1994); Melvyn Dubofsky and Foster Rhea Dulles, *Labor in America: A History*, 8th ed. (Wheeling, IL: Harlan Davidson, 2010). For the wartime strikes, see, for example, James T. Sparrow, *Warfare State: World War II Americans and the Age of Big Government* (New York: Oxford University Press, 2011), 194.

33. "Letters to the Editor," *Life*, 1 January 1947.

34. "The Mayor's Appeal to the Citizens of Oakland," *San Francisco Chronicle*, 4 December 1946.

35. Elizabeth A. Fones-Wolf, *Selling Free Enterprise: The Business Assault on Labor and Liberalism, 1945–60* (Urbana: University of Illinois Press, 1995), 15.

36. For detailed examples, see, for example, "Labor Management Relations in the Southern Textile Industry," Folder 27, Box 108; and Akosua Barthwell, "Trade Unionism in North Carolina: The Strike against Reynolds Tobacco, 1947" (1978), Folder 13, Box 120, both in Papers of Michael H. Ross, SLA-GSU; George Johnston's recollection in "Operation Dixie: Union Organizing for the CIO in the American South" (1987), in Folder 2, Box 2579, Stetson Kennedy Papers (SKP), SLA-GSU, 4–5, 15.

37. "Jim Crow Bars Young Veteran as a Welder," *Atlanta Daily World*, 29 March 1946.

38. George Johnston, "Operation Dixie: Union Organizing for the CIO in the American South in 1946," George Johnston Papers (GJP), Columbus State University (CSU), Columbus, GA, 34.

39. Lichtenstein, *State of the Union*, 88.

40. Gabin, *Feminism in the Labor Movement*, 119.

41. "Betty de Losada Oral History," 23–24.

42. Jason Morgan Ward, "A War for States' Rights: The White Supremacist Vision of Double Victory," in Kevin Michael Kruse and Stephen G. N. Tuck, eds., *Fog of War: The Second World War and the Civil Rights Movement* (New York: Oxford University Press, 2012), 126–127; idem, *Defending White Democracy: The Making of a Segregationist Movement and the Remaking of Racial Politics, 1936–1965* (Chapel Hill: University of North Carolina Press, 2011), 38–40.

43. Stetson Kennedy, *Southern Exposure* (Garden City, NY: Doubleday, 1946), 115–116.

44. Michael Newton, *The Ku Klux Klan in Mississippi: A History* (Jefferson, NC: McFarland, 2010), 103–104; Dittmer, *Local People*, 2.

45. "Civil Rights; Klan Parades; Negroes Scared Away from Polls," *Labor Herald*, 16 March 1946; Editorial, "Another Reason for Civil Rights," *Atlanta Daily World*, 21 March 1946.

46. Doody, *Detroit's Cold War*, 48.

47. "Police Escort Negro Children Away from White High School," *Atlanta Daily News*, 8 February 1949.

48. Brooks, *Defining the Peace*, 38.

49. C. R. Hemenway, "The Menace of the Union Shop," *Honolulu Star-Bulletin*, 30 September 1946; Albert W. Palmer, "Hawaii's Supreme Problem," *Honolulu Star-Bulletin*, 24 August 1946.

50. Editorial, "It Is Happening Here," *Honolulu Advertiser*, 19 October 1946.

51. Wendy L. Wall, *Inventing the "American Way": The Politics of Consensus from the New Deal to the Civil Rights Movement* (New York: Oxford University Press, 2008), 201–240.

52. Ibid., 17.

53. Ibid., 5, 169, 279; Julian E. Zelizer, "Confronting the Roadblock: Congress, Civil Rights and World War II," in Kruse and Tuck, *Fog of War*, 32.

54. Doody, *Detroit's Cold War*, 4, 121.

55. M. J. Heale, *McCarthy's Americans: Red Scare Politics in State and Nation, 1935–1965* (Athens: University of Georgia Press, 1998), 286–287, 296–299; see also Richard Hofstadter, *Anti-Intellectualism in American Life* (New York: Knopf, 1963), 30–42.

56. Editorial, *Honolulu Star-Bulletin*, 17 November 1946.

57. "Daily Summary of Opinion Developments" (hereafter, "DSOD"), 31 October 1946, Box 3, Daily Summary of International Topics and Foreign Policy, 1946–1948 (hereafter, Daily Summary), Office of Public Opinion Studies (OPOS), RG59, National Archives and Records Administration (NARA), College Park, MD; "Key Issues in 1946 Election: Price Control at Top of List," *USNWR*, 25 October 1946.

58. For instance, see "The Infiltration Corps: Communists and Their Friends Hold Some Key Posts," *Life,* 24 March 1947, 34–45.

59. *Newsweek,* 18 November 1946, 36–37; "The Republican Era," *Life,* 18 November 1946.

60. "DSOD," 27 and 29 January 1947, Box 3, Daily Summary, OPOS, RG59, NARA.

61. "DSOD," 17, 27, and 29 January 1947.

62. James T. Selcraig, *The Red Scare in the Midwest, 1945–1955: A State and Local Study* (Ann Arbor: UMI Research Press, 1982).

63. "Aid to Greece," Gallup Poll, vol. 1, 4 April 1947, 636; Athan Theoharis, *Seeds of Repression: Harry S. Truman and the Origins of McCarthyism* (Chicago: Quadrangle, 1971), 197.

64. SCAP originally referred to the title held by MacArthur. However, it has since been used to refer to the offices of the occupation, including both civilians and military personnel, and I follow this custom. Also, I use SCAP and GHQ interchangeably.

65. Howard B. Schonberger, *Aftermath of War: Americans and the Remaking of Japan, 1945–1952* (Kent, OH: Kent State University Press, 1989), 115; Andrew Gordon, *The Wages of Affluence: Labor and Management in Postwar Japan* (Cambridge, MA: Harvard University Press, 1998), 8; see also Joe Moore, *Japanese Workers and the Struggle for Power, 1945–1947* (Madison: University of Wisconsin Press, 1983).

66. See, for instance, letter, Roy Howard to Douglas MacArthur, January 31, 1946, Folder 2, Box 3, Bonner F. Fellers Paper (BFFP), RG44a, MacArthur Memorial Archives (MMA), Norfolk, VA; letter, Norman Thomas to Bonner F. Fellers, 7 May 1946, Folder 1, Box 5, BFFP, RG44a, MMA; see also *Life,* 2 December 1946, and *Newsweek,* 23 January 1947; Schonberger, *Aftermath of War,* 134–160.

67. Oguma Eiji, *"Minshu" to "Aikoku": Sengo Nihon no nashonarisumu to kokyosei* ["Democracy" and "Patriotism": Nationalism and Publicness in Postwar Japan] (Tokyo: Shinyosha, 2002), 175–186.

68. For a more detailed discussion on the discourse of subjectivity in postwar Japan, see J. Victor Koschmann, *Revolution and Subjectivity in Postwar Japan* (Chicago: University of Chicago Press, 1996).

69. Oguma, *"Minshu" to "Aikoku,"* 25–26, 100, 176, and 794–800.

70. "Japan and Korea, No. 8," 18 June 1946, Box 39, Public Opinion on Foreign Countries and Regions, Japan and Korea, 1945–54, OPOS, RG 59, NARA.

71. Ibid.; "Japan and Korea, No. 17," 11 March 1947, Box 39, OPOS, RG59, NARA.

72. William J. Sebald, *Nihon senryo gaiko no kaiso* [Memoir of Japanese Occupation Diplomacy] (Tokyo: Asahi shinbun, 1966), 40.

73. Correspondence, Charles A. Willoughby to G2 Staff, 9 February 1947, Folder 3, Box 18, Charles A. Willoughby Papers (CAWP), RG 23, MML.

74. Charles A. Willoughby, *Shirarezaru Nihon senryo: Wirobi kaikoroku* [Occupation of Japan Unknown: Memoir of Willoughby] (Tokyo: Bancho shobo, 1973), 136–137.

75. See "Leftist Classification of Civilian Employees," "Leftist Influence in Headquarters," and "Leftist Infiltration into SCAP," Box 18, CAWP, RG23, MML.

76. Correspondence, Willoughby to his staff, 20 February 1947, CAWP, Folder 3, Box 18, CAWP, RG23, MML.

77. Roger Baldwin, "The Reminiscences of Roger Baldwin, Occupation of Japan," 14–16, 27, Center for Oral History (COH), Columbia University (CU), New York; letter, Bonner F. Fellers to Roy Howard, February 20, 1946, BFFP, RG44a, MMA.

78. See, for instance, Sebald, *Nihon senryo gaiko no kaiso,* 94; Michael Schaller, *Douglas MacArthur: The Far Eastern General* (New York: Oxford University Press, 1989); and Sodei Rinjiro, *MacArthur no nisennichi* [MacArthur's Two Thousand Days] (Tokyo: Chuo koronsha, 1976).

79. These letters can be seen in large quantities in the "Personal Correspondence, July–December 1946," Box 12, Douglas MacArthur Papers (DMP), RG10, MMA.

80. Letter, Joseph Savage to Douglas MacArthur, December 16, 1946; letter, Nellie Gordon Curtis to MacArthur, 14 December 1946, Box 12, DMP, RG10, MMA.

81. Letter, Woodall Green to Bonner F. Fellers, April 26, 1947, BFFP, Folder 12, Box 2, RG44a, MMA. In this letter, MacArthur's aide asked Fellers to keep MacArthur posted on the current of public opinions in the United States.

82. Theodore Cohen, *Remaking Japan* (New York: Free Press, 1987), 309–311.

83. T. A. Bisson, diary entry of 20 January 1947 in *Nihon senryo kaisoki* [An Occupation Memoir] (Tokyo: Sanseido, 1983), 170.

84. Michael Schaller, *The American Occupation of Japan: The Origins of the Cold War in Asia* (New York: Oxford University Press, 1985), 131.

85. "Memorandum for Information," 23 September 1946, Box 18, RG23, CAWP, MMA.

86. Joseph Gordon, "The Reminiscences of Joseph Gordon, Occupation of Japan," 84, COH-CU; Beate Gordon, "The Reminiscences of Beate Gordon, Occupation of Japan," 166, COH-CU.

87. Cohen, *Remaking Japan,* 310.

88. Gordon, "The Reminiscences of Joseph Gordon," 208.

89. See SCAP members' memoirs, such as Bisson, *Nihon senryo kaiso ki.*

90. Schaller, *The American Occupation of Japan*; John W. Dower, *Embracing Defeat: Japan in the Wake of World War II* (New York: W. W. Norton, 1999); and Amamiya Shoichi, *Senryo to kaikaku* [The Occupation and Reform] (Tokyo: Iwanami shoten, 2008). Recent scholarship has begun focusing more on local agency. See, for instance, Hans Martin Kramer, "Just Who Reversed the Course?

The Red Purge in Higher Education during the Occupation of Japan," *Social Science Japan Journal* 8:1 (November 2004): 1–18.

91. Amamiya, *Senryo to kaikaku*; Rekishigaku kenkyukai, ed., *Senryo seisaku no tenkan to kowa* [The Shift of Occupation Policy and the Peace Treaty] (Tokyo: Aoki shoten, 1990), 4–41.

92. Schaller, *The American Occupation of Japan,* 104; and George F. Kennan, *Memoir 1925–1950* (New York: Pantheon, 1967), 368–396.

93. Schaller, *The American Occupation of Japan;* and Schonberger, *Aftermath of War*; John W. Dower, *Empire and Aftermath: Yoshida Shigeru and the Japanese Experience, 1878–1954* (Cambridge, MA: Harvard University Press, 1979).

94. Cohen, *Remaking Japan,* 125.

95. Schonberger, *Aftermath of War,* 134–160, 161–197.

96. Dower, *Embracing Defeat,* 225–273.

97. Koseki Shoichi, "Senryo seisaku no tenkan to chudo seiken" [The Change of Occupation Policy and the 'Middle-of-the-Road' Administration], in Rekishigaku kenkyukai, *Senryo seisaku no tenkan to kowa,* 25–26.

98. Nakamura Masanori, "Senryo toha nandatta noka" [What Was the Occupation?], in Rekishigaku kenkyukai, *Senryo seisaku no tenkan to kowa,* 238.

99. Ai Kume, "The Reminiscences of Ai Kume, Occupation of Japan, 1975," 23, COH-CU.

100. See Bisson's diary entries between May and August 1946 in *Nihon senryo kaisoki* 86–114.

101. Cyrus Peake, "The Reminiscences of Cyrus Peake, Occupation of Japan," 37, COH-CU.

102. Rekishigaku kenkyukai, *Senryo seisaku no tenkan to kowa,* 8, 128; Oguma, *"Minshu" to "Aikoku,"* 485–488.

103. Bisson, diary entry of 9 June 1946, *Nihon senryo kaisoki,* 94–95; Dower, *Empire and Aftermath,* 295; and Yoshida Shigeru, *Kaiso junen* [Ten Years of Recollections] (Tokyo: Shinchosha, 1957); see also Sebald, *Nihon senryo gaiko no kaiso,* 82.

104. See a series of articles, "Gyaku kousu" [Reverse Course], *Yomiuri shinbun,* 2 November–2 December 1951.

105. "Shanghaishi jingchaju zhengzhichu guanyu Shanghai gongyun xueyun qingkuang huibian ziliao [Shanghai Police Department Political Section's Collection of Documents Regarding the Situations of Shanghai Labor and Student Movements]" (hereafter, "The Situations of Shanghai Labor and Student Movements"), Q131–6–530, Shanghai Municipal Archives (SMA), Shanghai, PRC. The full text of the forum, including questions and answers between students and guests, was transcribed by three stenographers.

106. Hong Zhang, *America Perceived: The Making of Chinese Images of the United States, 1945–1953* (Westport, CT: Greenwood Press, 2002), 125–127.

107. Chiang Kai-shek, diary entry of 28 May 1946, Box 46, Chiang Kai-shek Diaries (hereafter, CKSD), Hoover Institution Library and Archives (HILA), Stanford University (SU), Stanford, CA.

108. "Beiping shi jingcha ju guanyu . . . cha xuesheng wei fanfuRi qunzhong youxing . . . deng xunling [Beijing Police Department Regarding Directives on . . . the Examination of Students Attending Mass Demonstrations of Opposing (U.S.) Support of Japan]" (hereafter, "Examination of Students"), J183–2–29849, Beijing Municipal Archives (BMA), Beijing, PRC, 13.

109. Zhang, *America Perceived*, 127–28.

110. For an overview of student movements, see, for instance, Jeffrey Wasserstrom, *Student Protests in Twentieth-Century China: The View from Shanghai* (Stanford, CA: Stanford University Press, 1991). For students' attitudes, see ibid., 241.

111. *Da Gong Bao* (Shanghai), 5 and 25 July 1946.

112. *Da Gong Bao* (Shanghai), 11 May 1948.

113. *Fei Bao,* 19 March 1947; *Fei Bao,* 15 September 1947.

114. *Da Gong Bao* (Shanghai), 5 June 1948; *Da Gong Bao* (Tianjin), 19 June 1948.

115. *Zhongyang Ribao,* 11 April 1948.

116. Chen Shutong, meeting transcript of 26 May 1948, "The Situations of Shanghai Labor and Student Movements," Q131-6-530, SMA.

117. "1947 niandu Shanghai xueyun ziliao [Materials on Shanghai Student Movements in 1947]" (hereafter, "Student Movements in 1947"), Q131–6–464, SMA; Zuo Shuangwen and Chen Wei, "1948 nian 'fan MeifuRi' yundong jiqi yu guomin zhengfu de huodong [The Movements of Opposing U.S. Support of Japan in 1948 and Its Interactions with the Nationalist Government]," *Guangdong shehui kexue* 6 (2006): 101–106.

118. Zhang, *America Perceived,* 140.

119. Ibid.

120. For detailed discussion of China's war experiences, see Rana Mitter, *Forgotten Ally: China's World War II, 1937–1945* (Boston: Houghton Mifflin Harcourt, 2013).

121. Wu Zhendong, meeting transcript of 3 June 1948, "The Situations of Shanghai Labor and Student Movements."

122. Details on the forum on 26 May 1948 can be found in "The Situations of Shanghai Labor and Student Movements."

123. Such remarks can be seen in the forums on 26 May and 3 June 1948; see "The Situations of Shanghai Labor and Student Movements."

124. *Da Gong Bao,* 11 June 1947; see also Tillman Durdin, "U.S. Help to Japan Is Alarming China," *New York Times,* 2 November 1946.

125. Amako Satoshi, *Chuka jinmin kyowa koku shi* [A History of the People's Republic of China] (Tokyo: Iwanami shoten, 2005). For the best overview of the

Chinese Civil War, see Odd Arne Westad, *Decisive Encounters: The Chinese Civil War, 1946–1950* (Stanford, CA: Stanford University Press, 2003).

126. Kubo Toru, *Chugoku kin gendai shi, vol. 4: Shakai shugi eno chosen* . [Modern Chinese History, vol. 4: A Challenge for Socialism] (Tokyo: Iwanami shoten, 2011), 14.

127. Westad, *Decisive Encounters,* 8.

128. In exploring this topic, I am most indebted to Westad, *Decisive Encounters.* I was also inspired by earlier generations of works, which tend to emphasize grassroots agency, such as Maurice Meisner, *Mao's China and After: A History of the People's Republic* (New York: Free Press, 1999); Mark Selden, *The Yenan Way in Revolutionary China* (Cambridge, MA: Harvard University Press, 1971); and Chalmers Johnson, *Peasant Nationalism and Communist Power: The Emergence of Revolutionary China* (Stanford, CA: Stanford University Press, 1962). In addition, I learned more on the roles played by the CCP in the Chinese Revolution: Steven Levine, *Anvil of Victory: The Communist Revolution in Manchuria, 1945–1948* (New York: Columbia University Press, 1987); James Gao, *The Communist Takeover of Hangzhou: The Transformation of City and Cadre, 1949–1954* (Honolulu: University of Hawaii Press, 2004); Odoric Wou, *Mobilizing the Masses: Building Revolution in Henan* (Stanford, CA: Stanford University Press, 1994); and Frederick C. Teiwes, *Politics and Purges in China: Rectification and the Decline of Party Norms, 1950–1965* (Armonk, NY: M.E. Sharpe, 1979).

129. A notable exception to this general description was the siege of Changchun in the summer of 1948, which resulted in at least 160,000 civilian deaths. See Frank Dikötter, *The Tragedy of Liberation: A History of the Chinese Revolution, 1945–57* (New York: Bloomsbury Press, 2013), 3–8.

130. Westad, *Decisive Encounters,* 13.

131. "Shanghaishi jingchaju . . . guanyu shijingju ling ge fenju chudong zhuyi Zhonggong dixiadang zai gongren xuesheng dengdi huodong xunling [Shanghai Police Department's Instruction to Branch Offices to Pay Attention to the Underground Chinese Communist Party in Labor and Student Activities]" (hereafter, "The Underground CCP"), Q144–4–1, SMA.

132. "Shanghai gaodeng tezhong xingshi fating panjue [A Judgment at the Shanghai High Special Criminal Court]," 29 May 1948, Q189–1–60, SMA.

133. "Shanghaishi jingchaju guanyu qudi fanMei xiju gequ xunling [Shanghai Police Department's Instruction to Crack Down on Anti-American Dramas and Songs]," February–April 1947, Q131–4–187, SMA.

134. "Shanghaishi shehuiju guanyu chajin jinbu shukan, vol. 2 [Shanghai Social Department Concerning Cracking Down on Progressive Books and Journals, vol. 2]," Q6–12–167, SMA, 14–31.

135. "Jiang wei jingbei silingbu daibu Shanghai shangxueyuen xuesheng youguan cailiao, 1947–1949 [Materials Related to Chiang Kai-shek's False Security Police

Headquarters Arresting Shanghai Business College Students, 1947–1949],"
Q246–1–240, SMA.

136. "The Underground CCP."

137. "'Huai zhengfu' bixu gaizu ['Broken Government' Needs to Reorganize],"
Wencui 40 (23 July 1946), D2–0–798–2, SMA; "Lun Meidi fuRi de yinmou
[Discussing the Plot of American Imperialists Helping Japan]," D2–0–753–1, SMA.

138. "Shanghaishi jingchaju guanyu qudi fanMei xiju gequ xunling."

139. "Student Movements in 1947."

140. Lou Bangyan, "Lun 'Gongran fandui zhengfu' [About 'Publicly Opposing
Government']," *Guancha* 4:22 (31 July 1948): 4–6.

141. Kubo, *Chugoku kin gendai shi,* 9.

142. "'Huai zhengfu' bixu gaizu."

143. "Beiping xuesheng beibu beishi ji [Report on Beijing Students Who Were
Arrested and Released]," *Guancha* 3:7 (3 October 1947), D2–0–2182–19, SMA;
"Ji Beiping xuesheng fanfuRi tuji da youxing [Report on Beiping's Mass Demonstra-
tions of Opposing Supporting Japan]," *Guancha* 4:17 (11 April 1948), D2–0–2193–13,
SMA.

144. Chu Anping, *Keguan* 4 (1 December 1945); Chu Anping, "Zhongguo de
zhengju [Chinese Political Situation]," *Guancha* 2:2 (8 March 1947): 3–8.

145. *Laobaixing Ribao,* 18 January 1947, 7 February 1947, and 19 and 23 March 1947.

146. *Fei Bao,* 24 October 1947.

147. *Fei Bao,* 25 October 1947.

148. *Fei Bao,* 2 October 1947 and 10 November 1948.

149. Kubo, *Chugoku kin gendai shi,* 3–4; Chiang Kai-shek, diary entry of 27 June
1948, Box 46, CKSD, HILA-SU.

150. Zhang, *America Perceived,* 77–111; Ronald Spector, *In the Ruins of Empire:
The Japanese Surrender and the Battle for Postwar Asia* (New York: Random House,
2007), 264–268.

151. "Student Movements in 1947."

152. "Lun 'fanMei' yu 'Zhong-Mei chuantong youyi' [Discuss 'Anti-America'
and 'Sino-American Traditional Friendship']," *Xin Wenhua* 3:6 (5 February 1947),
D2–0–427–1, SMA.

153. Such associations can be seen in various "reactionary" scribblings and
rumors. See "The Underground CCP"; "Student Movements in 1947."

154. Frederick C. Teiwes, "Establishment and Consolidation of the New
Regime," in John K. Fairbank, Roderick MacFarquhar, and Denis Twitchett, eds.,
The Cambridge History of China, vol. 14 (New York: Cambridge University Press,
1987), 70–77; Kenneth Lieberthal, *Governing China: From Revolution through
Reform* (New York: W. W. Norton, 1995), 53.

155. Teiwes, "Establishment and Consolidation of the New Regime," 77;
Lieberthal, *Governing China,* 85.

156. Amako, *Chuka jinmin kyowa koku shi,* 16–18, 30; Kubo, *Chugoku kin gendai shi,* 44, 68.

157. Kenneth G. Lieberthal, *Revolution and Tradition in Tientsin, 1942–1952* (Stanford, CA: Stanford University Press, 1980), 40–52; Ezra F. Vogel, *Canton under Communism: Programs and Politics in a Provincial Capital, 1949–1968* (Cambridge, MA: Harvard University Press, 1969), 95–97; and Teiwes, "Establishing and Consolidating of the New Regime," 89.

158. Zhang, *America Perceived,* 99, 107, and 124.

159. "The Red Shadow Lengthens over China," *Life,* 29 November 1948, 31.

160. For details on the life of Henry Luce, see Robert E. Herzstein, *Henry R. Luce, Time, and the American Crusade in Asia* (New York: Cambridge University Press, 2005).

161. Henry R. Luce, "The American Century," *Life,* 17 February 1941, 61–65.

162. "China," *Life,* 15 March 1948, 36.

163. "DSOD," 7 August 1947.

164. "DSOD," 7 August 1947 and 30 December 1948.

165. "DSOD," 16 February 1946. For more detailed accounts of American reactions to the Chinese Revolution, see Nancy Bernkopf Tucker, *Patterns in the Dust: Chinese-American Relations and the Recognition Controversy, 1949–1950* (New York: Columbia University Press, 1983).

166. "DSOD," 15 February 1949.

167. Craig and Logevall, *America's Cold War,* 102–105, 135.

168. Such catchy titles include: "Red Shadow Lengthens over China," "Dunkirk in the Pacific," "The Fall of Mukden," "Last Look at Peipin [Beijing]," and "Red Advance Brings Shanghai Panic." All from *Life* magazine between 1948 and 1949.

169. For more detailed discussion on the "loss" of China, see a series of articles by Warren I. Cohen, Chen Jian, John W. Garver, Michael Sheng, and Odd Arne Westad in *Diplomatic History* 21:1 (Winter 1997): 71–115; see also Thomas J. Christensen, "A 'Lost Chance' for What? Rethinking the Origins of the U.S.-PRC Confrontation," *Journal of American-East Asian Relations* 4 (Fall 1995): 249–278.

170. "DSOD," 6 September 1949.

171. Harold Isaacs, *Scratches on Our Minds: American Images of China and India* (New York: John Day, 1958), 193. See also T. Christopher Jespersen, *American Images of China, 1931–1949* (Stanford, CA: Stanford University Press, 1996).

172. "DSOD," 17 December 1948.

173. "DSOD," 9 December 1948.

174. "DSOD," 9 and 17 December 1948.

175. "DSOD," 16 December 1948.

176. "DSOD," 30 December 1948.

177. "DSOD," 10 December 1948.

178. "DSOD," 3 February 1949.

179. James T. Patterson, *Grand Expectations: The United States, 1945–1974* (New York: Oxford University Press, 1996), 172.

180. Dean Acheson, Press Club Speech and his reply to questions, 12 January 1950, John S. Service Papers (hereafter, JSSP), Folder 2, Carton 2, BANC MSS 87/21, Bancroft Library (BL), University of California, Berkeley (hereafter, BLUC), Berkeley, CA.

181. Henry A. Wallace, *The Century of the Common Man* (New York: Reynal and Hitchcock, 1943).

182. Henry A. Wallace, "American Fiasco in China," *New Republic*, 5 July 1948, 11.

183. Craig and Logevall, *America's Cold War*, 76–77; Robert David Johnson, *Congress and the Cold War* (New York: Cambridge University Press, 2006), xvi–xvii; Jonathan Bell, *The Liberal State on Trial: The Cold War and American Politics in the Truman Years* (New York: Columbia University Press, 2004), 121–159; and Zachary Karabell, *The Last Campaign: How Harry Truman Won the 1948 Election* (New York: Knopf, 2000).

184. Craig and Logevall, *America's Cold War*, 135.

185. Memorandum, September 3, 1949, Papers of the Progressive Party (PPP), Folder 2, Box 1, Special Collections & University Archives (SCUA), University of Iowa (UI), Iowa City, IA; Letter, C. B. Baldwin to Herman Wright, June 29, 1950, PPP, Folder 2, Box 1, SCUA-UI.

186. Doody, *Detroit's Cold War*, 37.

187. "Oral History Transcript for '1946: The Great Hawaii Sugar Strike,'" 33.

188. "DSOD," January 17 and 20, 1947.

189. Philip Jenkins, *Cold War at Home: The Red Scare in Pennsylvania, 1945–1960* (Chapel Hill: University of North Carolina Press, 1999), 9.

190. Editorial, "McCarthy and the Past," *Life*, 10 April 1950, 32.

191. Memorandum, Millard Tydings to Harry S. Truman, 5 June 1950, Student Research File: "McCarthyism," Box 1, Harry S. Truman Library (HSTL), Independence, MO.

192. Entry of 29 April 1950, in Eben A. Ayers, *Truman in the White House: The Diary of Eben A. Ayers*, ed. Robert Ferrell (Columbia: University of Missouri Press, 1991), 348–349.

193. Federal Civil Defense Administration, *Bert the Turtle Says Duck and Cover* (Washington, DC: GPO, 1951), Olin & Kroch Library, Cornell University (hereafter, OKL-CU), Ithaca, NY.

194. JoAnne Brown, "'A Is for Atom, B is Bomb': Civil Defense in American Public Education, 1948–1963," *Journal of American History* 75:1 (June 1988): 68–90.

195. Mickey Spillane, *The Mike Hammer Collection* (New York: New American Library, 2001).

196. Logevall, "A Critique of Containment," 497.

2. LOCAL TRANSLATION

1. Kim Song-chil, *Yoksa ap eso: han sahakcha ui 6–25 ilgi* [In the Face of History: A Historian's Diary of 6.25] (Seoul: Changjak kwa Pipyongsa, 1993), 55.

2. Ibid., 56–60.

3. Ibid., 61–62.

4. Ibid., 66–68.

5. Ibid., 68.

6. Ibid., 68–69.

7. Ibid., 69.

8. Kim Dong-choon, *Chosen senso no shakaishi: Hinan, senryo, gyakusatsu* [A Social History of the Korean War: Evacuation, Occupation, Massacre] (Tokyo: Heibonsha, 2008), 109. This is a Japanese translation of his book, *Chonjaeng kwa sahoe: Uri ege Hanguk chonjaeng un muot ionna?* [War and Society: What Was the Korean War for Us?] (Paju, South Korea: Tol Pegae, 2006).

9. Kim, *Chosen senso no shakaishi*, 110.

10. Ibid., 42, 65.

11. "War in Asia: the People," *Time*, 10 July 1950, 9.

12. Memorandum, from William J. Hassett to Charles Ross, 29 June 1950, Harry S. Truman Papers (hereafter, HSTP), OF: 471-B, Korean Emergency, Harry S. Truman Library (hereafter, HSTL), Independence, MO; Paul G. Pierpaoli, *Truman and Korea: The Political Culture of the Early Cold War* (Columbia: University of Missouri Press, 1999), 36.

13. Letter, J. L. Showalter to HST, 25 July 1950, HSTP.

14. Letter, Jimmy Balter to HST, 27 June 1950, HSTP.

15. Letter, Jean Cottrell Fleischman to HST, 26 June 1950, HSTP.

16. "Push-Button Warfare," *USNWR*, 21 July 1950, 12. A similar cartoon appeared in "Where Next?" *Ithaca Journal*, 8 July 1950.

17. Drew Pearson, "President Needs All Help in Crisis," 24 July 1950, *Washington Post*. In this period, *USNWR* forecast the possibility of World War III in the issues of August 11 and 18.

18. Steven Casey, *Selling the Korean War: Propaganda, Politics, and Public Opinion in the United States, 1950–1953* (New York: Oxford University Press, 2008), 43.

19. "World War III," 19 August 1950, *The Gallup Poll* 2, 929; "Atom Bombs," 2 August 1950, ibid., 929, OKL-CU. A similar result can be seen in the State Department's study, "Monthly Survey of American Opinion on International Affairs," no. 112 (August 1950), Box 12, Schuyler Foster Papers (hereafter, SFP), OPOS, RG59, NARA.

20. "How Prepared Are We If Russia Should Attack?" *Look*, 20 June 1950; John Lear, "Hiroshima, U.S.A.: Can Anything Be Done About It?" *Collier's*, 5 August 1950, 11–15, 68–69; "Week's Mail," *Collier's*, 23 September 1950.

21. "This Little Pig Went to Market," *Newsweek,* 7 August 1950, 64.

22. "Hoarders at Work," *Newsweek,* 7 August 1950, 64.

23. "The March of the News," *USNWR,* 25 August 1950, 2.

24. "Impact of War: A Rush to Buy—But Most Things Are Plentiful," *USNWR,* 14 July 1950, 11.

25. "Sugar for All," *Newsweek,* 21 August 1950, 70.

26. The American side of the story has been carefully examined from various angles. In particular, I am indebted to the works that explore the crossroads politics and society at the time of the Korean War. See, for example, Casey, *Selling the Korean War;* Thomas J. Christensen, *Useful Adversaries: Grand Strategy, Domestic Mobilization, and Sino-American Conflict, 1947–1958* (Princeton, NJ: Princeton University Press, 1996); Rosemary Foot, *The Wrong War: American Policy and the Dimensions of the Korean Conflict, 1950–1953* (Ithaca, NY: Cornell University Press, 1985); and Paul G. Pierpaoli, *Truman and Korea: The Political Culture of the Early Cold War* (Columbia: University of Missouri Press, 1999).

27. Eben Ayers Diary, 25 June 1950, in Robert Ferrell, ed., *Truman in the White House: The Diary of Eben A. Ayers* (Columbia: University of Missouri, 1991), 353. Washington's swift and decisive decision to dispatch U.S. forces to Korea and the Taiwan Strait is well known. See Stueck, *The Korean War,* and Glenn Paige, *The Korean Decision: June 24–30, 1950* (New York: Free Press, 1968).

28. Telegram, John Foster Dulles and John Allison to Dean Acheson and Dean Rusk, 25 June 1950, Box 71, Subject File, George M. Elsey Papers (GMEP), HSTL; "Acheson, Dean 1950," Box 47, Seeley Mudd Manuscript Library (SMML), Princeton University (PU), Princeton, NJ.

29. "President Truman's Conversation with George M. Elsey," 26 June 1950, Box 71, Subject File, GMEP, HSTL.

30. "Statement by the President," 27 June 1950, Box 71, Subject File, GMEP, HSTL.

31. "Shenyang ge jieceng dui Chaoxian zhanzheng de fanying [Reactions of Various Sections in Shenyang toward the Korean War]," 13 July 1950, *Neibu Cankao* [Internal Reference], Chinese University of Hong Kong [CUHK], Hong Kong.

32. "Guo neiwai dui Chaoxian zhanzheng he Chaoxian tanpan fanying [Responses at Home and Abroad toward the Korean War and the Korean Armistice]," 14 July 1950, No. 116–00085–01, Foreign Ministry Archives (FMA), Beijing, PRC.

33. "Chongqing gongshang, wenhuajie dui shiju de fanying [Responses in Business and Literacy Circles in Chongqing toward the Current Political Situation]," 24 July 1950, *Neibu Cankao,* CUHK.

34. "Zhonggong Shanghaishi jiaoqu gongzuo weiyuanhui guanyu Shanghaishi Hualongqu heping qianming yundong de gongzuo jianbao [CCP Rural Working Committees on Peace Signature Campaigns at Hualong District in Shanghai]," 16 July 1950, A71–2–56–9, SMA.

35. See various entries from local committees in early July 1950 in *Neibu Cankao*, CUHK, such as "Dulumen shengming fabiao hou Shanghai shichang qingkuang [The Situation of the Shanghai Market following the Announcement of Truman Statement], 1 July 1950, *Neibu Cankao*, CUHK.

36. "Jingshi gongshang jie dui muqian shiju fanying [The Reactions toward Current Affairs among Business Circles in Tianjin]," 5 July 1950, *Neibu Cankao*, CUHK.

37. "Rehe, Jinzhou dengdi ganbu qunzhong dui Chaoxian zhanshi de fanying [Reactions of Cadres and People in Rehe (Jehol), Jinzhou and Other Places toward the Korean War]," 22 July 1950, *Neibu Cankao*, CUHK.

38. Chiang Kai-shek, diary entry of 1 July 1950, Box 48, Chiang Kai-shek Diaries (hereafter, CKSD), HILA-SU.

39. Chiang Kai-shek, "Hanzhan yu shijie jushi [The Korean War and the World Situation], 3 July 1950, *Fan Gong kang-E zhong de Jiang zongtong* [Generalissimo Chiang in the Movement to Oppose Communism and Resist Russia], Dangshi-guan [Nationalist Party Archives] (NPA), Taipei, Taiwan, 42; "Zhongyang zhixing weiyuanhui tonggao [Announcement of the Central Committee of the Nationalist Party], 30 June 1950, 6–41–87: Central Reform Committee Archive, Chinese Nationalist Party Records (CNPR), 18, HILA-SU.

40. "Edi you yi qinlue xingdong [Another Invasion of Russian Imperialism], Editorial, *Zhongyang Ribao*, 26 June 1950; and "Weihe hanjian biwang qinlue bi bai [Why the Traitor Loses and the Invasion Fails]," *Gaizao*, no. 5 (1 November 1950), 101–104, NPA.

41. Memorandum, Chiang Kai-shek to Douglas MacArthur, 3 July 1950, File 3A, Box 6, RG6: Records of General Headquarters, Far East Command, MMA.

42. Guo Sifen, "Haichao [Sea Tide]," in Ge Xianning, ed., *Fan Gong kang E shixuan* [A Collection of Poems on the Oppose Communism and Resist Russia Movement] (Taipei: Zhonghua wenwu, 1952), 41–42, National Taiwan University Library (NTUL), Taipei, Taiwan.

43. Chiang Kai-shek, diary entry of 27 July 1950, Box 48, CKSD, HILA-SU.

44. Telegram, Sofia, Bulgaria, to Foreign Office, 4 July 1950, in "Bulgarian Reactions to Situation in Korea," FO371/87567, The National Archives (TNA), Kew, UK.

45. Ibid.

46. Telegram, Bucharest, Rumania, to Foreign Office, 15 July 1950, in "Rumors of Rumanian War Preparation," FO371/88073, TNA.

47. Memorandum, "Conversation between the Minister of State and the Norwe-gian Ambassador," 29 June 1950, in FO371/86538: "Norwegian Attitude towards Events in Korea," TNA.

48. Memorandum, The Hague, Netherlands, to Foreign Office, 17 July 1950, in "Netherlands Reaction to Events in Korea and to World Political Moves Relating to This Crisis," FO371/89330, TNA; "Conversation between the Minister of State

(UK) and the Norwegian Ambassador," 29 June 1950, in "Norwegian Attitude towards Events in Korea," FO371/86538, TNA.

49. Memorandum, "Greece's Attitude to Korea and Decision to Send a Battalion There," 22 July 1950, in FO371/87710: "Korea Situation: Greek Government," TNA.

50. Memorandum, Stockholm, Sweden, to Foreign Office, July 19, 1950, in "Norwegian Attitude towards Events in Korea."

51. "London Press Service: Diplomatic Summary," 22 August 1950, in "China: Political Situation," DO133/22, TNA; memorandum, Allen W. Dulles to John F. Dulles, "Memo from Conrad Adenauer," 8 September 1950, John Foster Dulles Papers, Box 47, SMML-PU. I benefited from reading Otake Hideo, *Saigunbi to nashonarizumu* [Rearmament and Nationalism] (Tokyo: Chuo koronsha, 1988) for a discussion of West Germany's rearmament.

52. Memorandum, The Hague, Netherlands, to Foreign Office, 17 July 1950, in "Netherlands Reaction to Events in Korea and to World Political Moves Relating to This Crisis."

53. "Chosen no doran to Oushu [The War in Korea and Europe]," 29 July 1950, *Asahi Shinbun.*

54. Letter, Chiba Kiyoshi to Ashida Hitoshi, Correspondence File, No. 266, Ashida Hitoshi Papers (hereafter, AHP), Modern Japanese Political History Materials Room (MJPHMR), NDL; *Asahi Shinbun,* 5 July 1950.

55. Oguma Eiji, *"Minshu" to "Aikoku": Sengo Nihon no nashonarisumu to kokyosei* ["Democracy" and "Patriotism": Nationalism and Publicness in Postwar Japan] (Tokyo: Shinyosha, 2002), 342.

56. Masuda Hajimu, "Fear of World War III: Social Politics of Japan's Rearmament and Peace Movements, 1950–53," *Journal of Contemporary History* 47: 3 (Summer 2012), 551–571.

57. Yokota Kisaburo, "Dai san ji sekai taisen no kiki to Nihon no anzen hosho [The Crisis of World War III and the National Security of Japan]," *Yomiuri Shinbun,* 30 July 1950.

58. Baba Tsunego, "Five Years since the End of the War," *Yomiuri Shinbun,* 13 August 1950.

59. Shimizu Ikutaro, "Waga jinsei no danpen [Scraps of My Life]," in *Shimizu Ikutaro chosaku shu* [The Collection of Shimizu Ikkutaro], vol. 14 (Tokyo: Kodansha, 1993), 337.

60. Ibid., 338.

61. *Mainichi Shinbun,* 1 July 1950; " 'Russia Will Go to War,' Says Bertrand Russell," *Times of India,* 2 July 1950.

62. Contents of communications among Stalin, Mao, and Kim have been well examined and published in various formats. Most notably, see CWIHP's *Bulletins,* Working Papers, and CWIHP digital archives. Also, Shen Zhihua has translated numerous Russian documents into Chinese and published them in Taiwan; Shen

Zhihua, *Chaoxian zhanzheng: Eguo danganguan de jiemi wenjian* [The Korean War: Declassified Documents from Russian Archives], 3 vols. (Taipei: Zhongyang yanjiuyuan jindaishi yanjiusuo, 2003).

63. Kim, *Chosen senso no shakaishi*, 35.

64. For instance, see Kathryn Weathersby, "'Should We Fear This?' Stalin and the Danger of War with America," CWIHP Working Paper, No. 39 (July 2002), 19; and Vojtech Mastny, *The Cold War and Soviet Insecurity: The Stalin Years* (New York: Oxford University Press, 1996). Some scholars have depicted more aggressive images of Stalin; see, for instance, Vladislav Zubok and Constantine Pleshekov, *Inside the Kremlin's Cold War: From Stalin to Khrushchev* (Cambridge, MA: Harvard University Press, 1996); and John Lewis Gaddis, *We Now Know: Rethinking Cold War History* (New York: Oxford University Press, 1997).

65. Truman was, in fact, quite reluctant even to accept the bombing of Dandong in August 1950 for fear of provoking war with China.

66. "News Quota Survey: Public Attitudes to Korean War, July 1950," SxMOA1/2/9/1/B, The Keep (TK), University of Sussex (US), Brighton, UK.

67. "Swiss Broadcasting Corporation," *Weekly Analysis of Foreign Broadcasts*, No. 450 (8 July 1950), 7, National Archives of India (NAI), Delhi, India.

68. Political cartoon, *Toronto Star,* 20 July 1950. In contrast to the *Toronto Star*'s relatively calm attitude, the *Globe and Mail,* for instance, took a much more aggressive stance, often expressing frustration and disappointment about Ottawa's decisions regarding the Korean affairs. See, for instance, editorials of the *Globe and Mail* on 27 June and 1 July 1950.

69. "No Occasion for Hoarding," editorial, *Toronto Star,* 25 July 1950.

70. "War in Korea," editorial, *Times of India,* 26 June 1950.

71. Letters to the editor, *Times of India,* 3 July 1950.

72. Letters to the editor, *Times of India,* 10 July 1950.

73. Letters to the editor, A. Datta, "India and Korea," *Amrita Bazar Patrika,* 15 July 1950, Microfilm 2816, Nehru Memorial Museum and Library (NMML), Delhi, India.

74. "Hands Off Korea," *Amrita Bazar Patrika,* 4 August 1950, Microfilm 2817, NMML.

75. "Right Policy Adopted on Korea," *Amrita Bazar Patrika,* 4 August 1950, NMML.

76. "India's Korean Policy," 3 August 1950, in *Selected Works of Jawaharlal Nehru,* vol. 15 (New Delhi, India: Orient Longman, 1972), 345–346, NMML.

77. "Communist Party Chiefs Expected to Discuss Policy on Korea War," 12 July 1950, in "Developments in Political Parties in India; Communist Activities in India," DO133/133, TNA.

78. "Indonesian Government Statement on Korea," 27 June 1950, in FO371/83725: "Indonesian Attitude to the War in Korea," TNA; telegram, Jakarta

to Foreign Office, UK, 30 June 1950, in "Indonesian Attitude to the War in Korea," FO371/83725, TNA.

79. Telegram, "Public Reactions to Korean Events," George Thompson, Malaya, to Colonial Office, UK, in "Reactions in Federation of Malaya and Singapore to Events in Korea," CO537/5965, TNA.

80. "Indonesian Wary about Korea," *Observer*, 15 July 1950, in "Various Reactions to Events in Korea," FO371/84529, TNA.

81. Telegram, Alexandria, Egypt, to Foreign Office, 1 July 1950, in "Egyptian Attitude towards Korea. Refusal to Support UN Security Council Resolution on Korea," FO371/80396, TNA.

82. Excerpt from the Cairo Radio, 1 July 1950, in "Egyptian Attitude towards Korea."

83. Ibid.

84. Ibid.

85. Telegram, Alexandria, Egypt, to Foreign Office, 4 July 1950, in ibid.

86. Memorandum, Baghdad, Iraq, to Foreign Office, 3 July 1950, in "Arab States' Views on the Situation in Korea," FO371/81920, TNA; telegram, Damascus, Syria, to Foreign Office, 13 July 1950, in "Syrian Reaction to UN Security Council Resolution on Korea," FO371/82793, TNA.

87. "Korea and Kashmir," letters to the editor, *Amrita Bazar Patrika*, 2 July 1950, Microfilm 2816, NMML.

88. For the details of the Cheju (Jeju) Incident and the Yeosu-Suncheon Uprising, see, for instance, Kim Dong-choon's *Chosen senso no shakaishi*; Bruce Cumings's *The Origins of the Korean War* Vol. 2 (Princeton, NJ: Princeton University Press, 1990); Allan Millett's *The War for Korea, 1945–1950: A House Burning* (Lawrence: University Press of Kansas, 2005); and Mun Gyonsu's *Saishuto yon san jiken* [The Cheju Island 4.3 Incident] (Tokyo: Heibonsha, 2008). Much more detailed discussions can be found in investigative reports conducted by a local newspaper in the island, which were reprinted entirely in Japan; see *Saishuto yonsan jiken* [The Cheju Island 4.3 Incident] 6 vols. (Tokyo: Shinkansha, 1994). On revolutionary movements in the North, see, for example, Charles K. Armstrong, *The North Korean Revolution, 1945–1950* (Ithaca, NY: Cornell University Press, 2003); and Suzy Kim, *Everyday Life in the North Korean Revolution, 1945–1950* (Ithaca, NY: Cornell University Press, 2013).

89. Memorandum, "Annual Political Report for Korea, 1949," Seoul, South Korea, to Foreign Office, 30 January 1950, FO371/84053, TNA.

90. Ibid.

91. Memorandum, William D. Mathews to John Foster Dulles, 21 June 1950, Box 49, JFDP, SMML-PU.

92. Ibid.

93. Kim, *Chosen senso no shakaishi*, 136.

94. Gregg Brazinsky, *Nation Building in South Korea: Koreans, Americans, and the Making of a Democracy* (Chapel Hill: University of North Carolina Press, 2007), 25.

95. Memorandum, "Annual Report for Korea, 1949," Seoul, South Korea, to Foreign Office, 30 January 1950, FO371/84053, TNA.

96. Brazinsky, *Nation Building in South Korea*, 26.

97. Memorandum, Seoul, South Korea, to Foreign Office, 30 January 1950, "Annual Political Report for Korea, 1949," FO371/84053, TNA.

98. Kim, *Chosen senso no shakaishi*, 138.

99. Ibid., 135–136.

100. Kim, *Chosen senso no shakaishi*, 115–117.

101. Park, *Senso to heiwa*, 123.

102. Kim, *Chosen senso no shakaishi*, 41–44.

3. COLD WAR FANTASY

1. Letter, Lorraine Henderson to Harry S. Truman (HST), 14 August 1950, Box 1310, OF 471B, HSTP, HSTL.

2. Joel Brinkley, "Bush and Yeltsin Declare Formal End to Cold War; Agree to Exchange Visits; U.S. Looking for New Course As Superpower Conflict Ends," *New York Times*, 1 February 1992, quoted in John Kenneth White, *Still Seeing Red: How the Cold War Shapes the New American Politics* (Boulder, CO: Westview Press, 1997), 4.

3. For example, William Stueck, *The Korean War: An International History* (Princeton, NJ: Princeton University Press, 1995); Thomas J. Christensen, *Useful Adversaries* (Princeton, NJ: Princeton University Press, 1996); Allan R. Millett, *The War for Korea, Vol. I–II* (Lawrence: University Press of Kansas, 2005–2010); and Rosemary Foot, *The Wrong War: American Policy and the Dimensions of the Korean Conflict, 1950–1953* (Ithaca, NY: Cornell University Press, 1985). For more detailed discussion, see note 7.

4. For important recent studies that have explored the Cold War's impacts on ordinary people's lives at local and grassroots levels, see, for example, Jeffrey A. Engel, *Local Consequences of the Global Cold War* (Washington, DC: Woodrow Wilson Center Press, 2007); Philip Jenkins, *Cold War at Home: The Red Scare in Pennsylvania, 1945–1960* (Chapel Hill: University of North Carolina Press, 1999); Stephen J. Whitfield, *The Culture of the Cold War* (Baltimore: Johns Hopkins University Press, 1991); and JoAnne Brown, "'A Is for Atom, B Is for Bomb': Civil Defense in American Public Education, 1948–1963," *Journal of American History* 75:1 (June 1988), 68–90.

5. George F. Kennan, 13 February 1954, Reel 2, Track 2: 4, Princeton Seminars, HSTL; *Foreign Relations of the United States (FRUS), 1950: Vol. 7* (10 July 1950), 46.

6. Averell Harriman, 14 February 1954, Reel 6, Track 1: 7, Princeton Seminars, HSTL.

7. A number of scholars have examined this topic, with particular emphases on elite policymakers' calculations and their personal traits. See, for instance, Barton Bernstein, "The Policy of Risk: Crossing the 38th Parallel and Marching to the Yalu," *Foreign Service Journal* 54:3 (March 1977), 16–22 and 29; Walter LaFeber, "Crossing the 38th: The Cold War in Microcosm," in Lynn H. Miller and Ronald Pruessen, eds., *Reflections on the Cold War: A Quarter Century of American Foreign Policy* (Philadelphia, PA: Temple University Press, 1974), 71–90; William Stueck, "The March to the Yalu: The Perspective from Washington," in Bruce Cumings, ed., *Child of Conflict: the Korean-American Relationship, 1943–1953* (Seattle: University of Washington Press, 1983), 195–237; James I. Matray, "Truman's Plan for Victory: National Self-Determination and the Thirty-Eighth Parallel Decision in Korea," *Journal of American History* 66:2 (September 1979), 314–333; Millett, *The War for Korea, 1950–1951,* vol. 2, 240; and Arnold Offner, *Another Such Victory: President Truman and the Cold War, 1945–1953* (Stanford, CA: Stanford University Press, 2002). I particularly benefited from reading the works that have explored the roles of domestic politics in relation to the decision to cross the 38th parallel: see, for example, Foot, *The Wrong War;* and Burton Kaufman, *The Korean War: Challenges in Crisis, Credibility, and Command,* 2nd ed. (New York: McGraw-Hill, 1997).

8. Federal Civil Defense Administration, *Bert the Turtle Says Duck and Cover* (Washington, DC: GPO, 1951); Brown, "'A Is for Atom, B Is Bomb.'"

9. "No Red Crabmeat," *Newsweek,* 28 August 1950, 66.

10. "Red Propaganda Discovered Hidden in Children's Card Collections," *Los Angeles Times,* 14 December 1950, in Folder 1, Box 1, "McCarthy Era Newspaper Clippings (hereafter, MENC)," M0186, Special Collections & University Archives (SCUA), SU.

11. "Rincon Annex Mural Debate," *San Francisco Examiner,* 2 May 1953; "Scudder Opens His Trial of Rincon Murals," *San Francisco Chronicle,* May 2, 1953, both in Folder 6, Box 2, MENC, SCUA-SU.

12. The point I'm making here is not to say that such "common sense" assuming the existence of Soviet espionage in America was *entirely* illusory and mistaken. As a matter of fact, declassified documents from Russian archives revealed in the 1990s that as many as 300 Americans may have worked with the Soviet intelligence agencies in the 1930s and 1940s. See John Earl Haynes and Harvey Klehr, *Venona: Decoding Soviet Espionage in America* (New Haven, CT: Yale University Press, 1999); Allen Weinstein and Alexander Vassiliev, *The Haunted Wood: Soviet Espionage in America—The Stalin Era* (New York: Random House, 1999); and Ellen Schrecker, "McCarthyism and the Red Scare," in Jean-Christophe Agnew and Roy Rosenzweig, *A Companion to Post-1945 America* (Malden, MA: Blackwell, 2006), 371–384.

My point here is, rather, why such "common sense" captured the minds of a large portion of the population and how it functioned in society and politics. For more detailed discussion on the reconsideration of McCarthyism, see Chapter 7: Social Warfare.

13. Glenn Paige, *The Korean Decision: June 24–30, 1950* (New York: Free Press, 1968).

14. "Nobody Loves a Hoarder," *Life*, 21 August 1950, 26–27.

15. "Shakedown for Decency," *Saturday Evening Post*, 19 August 1950, 10; "The Little Pig Went to Market," *Time*, 7 August 1950, 64.

16. Letter, Mary Whitman to HST, 17 July 1950, OF 471B, HSTP, HSTL.

17. Letter, A. L. Doenges to HST, 16 August 1950, Miscellaneous, OF 471B, HSTP, HSTL.

18. John Fousek, *To Lead the Free World: American Nationalism and the Cultural Roots of the Cold War* (Chapel Hill: University of North Carolina Press, 2000), 168; "Defense Cost," 23 August 1950, *The Gallup Poll* vol. 2, 934.

19. Congressional Record 82nd, 1st Session, 1950, 96, 11519–20, quoted in Paul G. Pierpaoli, *Truman and Korea: The Political Culture of the Early Cold War* (Columbia: University of Missouri Press, 1999), 35.

20. Letter, Bonner Fellers to Robert A. Taft, 19 July 1950, "1950, Korea," Box 670, Robert A. Taft Papers (RATP), Library of Congress (LC), Washington DC; "Memo of Conversation," 1 July 1950, JFDP, "Acheson, Dean 1950," Box 47, SMML-PU.

21. Paul Nitze, transcript of the BBC interview, Folder 3: "Korean War," Box 130, Paul H. Nitze Papers (PHNP), LC. In the summer of 1949, General Douglas MacArthur explained the defense line from the Aleutian Islands to Japan and Okinawa, and to Taiwan, Philippines, and Singapore. Dean Acheson delineated the same policy in a National Press Club speech on 12 January 1950.

22. "Discussions with Mr. Acheson and Officials in Washington, Saturday and Sunday, July 29th and 30th, 1950," MG26 N1 vol. 35, "Korea: Canadian Policy, 1950–51," Lester Pearson Papers (LPP), LAC.

23. Memorandum, "Conversation among Dean Acheson, John Foster Dulles, and Frank Pace," 1 July 1950, Dean Acheson File, JFDP, SMML-PU.

24. "Note of the NSC Meeting," 29 June 1950, GMEP, Subject File, Box 71, HSTL.

25. "Memorandum of Conversation, by the Ambassador at Large (Jessup)," 26 June 1950, *FRUS, 1950: Vol. 7*, 179.

26. "Editorial Note," *FRUS, 1950: Vol. 7*, 239.

27. George F. Kennan, 13 February 1954, Reel 2, Track 2:4, Princeton Seminars, HSTL; "Teleconference with MacArthur," 26 June 1950, GMEP, Subject File, Box 71, HSTL; and *FRUS, 1950: Vol. 7*, 46.

28. "Memorandum, Allison to Rusk, 13 July 1950, *FRUS, 1950: Vol. 7*, 373.

29. Letter, Clark Clifford to HST, 29 June 1950, Box 42, "Letters to and from HST," Clark M. Clifford Papers (CMCP), HSTL; memorandum, Allison to Rusk, 1 July 1950, *FRUS, 1950:* Vol. 7, 272.

30. Letter, William Mathews to John Foster Dulles, 22 July 1950, Box 49, "Letter and Memos to Dulles," JFDP; letter, John Foster Dulles to William Mathews, Box 48, "Korea, 1950," JFDP.

31. "Draft Memorandum Prepared in the Department of Defense," 31 July 1950, *FRUS, 1950: Vol. 7,* 506–507.

32. "Draft Memorandum Prepared by the Policy Planning Staff," 22 July 1950, *FRUS, 1950: Vol. 7,* 453; George F. Kennan, 14 February 1954, Reel 6, Track 1: 8, Princeton Seminars, HSTL.

33. "Memorandum Prepared in the Central Information Agency," 18 August 1950, *FRUS, 1950: Vol. 7,* 600–602.

34. "Memorandum from JCS to Secretary of Defense," 7 September 1950, Personal File, Subject File "1940–1953: NSC-Meeting File," Box 180, HSTP, HSTL.

35. "Preliminary Conversation for September Foreign Ministers' Meeting," 30 August 1950, Korean War Files, No. 17, "Tripartite Meeting of Foreign Ministers, September 1950," Box 7, HSTP, HSTL.

36. Ibid.

37. Memo, "The Implications of the Situation in Korea for British Foreign Policy," Summer 1950, CO537/5392, TNA.

38. Memoranda of conversation, "Notes re. NSC Meeting," 7 September 1950, Dean Acheson Papers (DAP), HSTL.

39. "Memorandum, Max Bishop to Jessup, 24 August 1950, *FRUS, 1950: Vol. 7,* 641.

40. "United States Courses of Action with Respect to Korea (NSC-81/2)," Personal File, Subject File, "1940–1953: NSC-Meeting File," Box 180, HSTP, HSTL.

41. "Daily Opinion Summary" (hereafter, DOS), 25 July 1950, Box 5, SFP, OPOS, RG59, NARA.

42. "Special Report American Opinion," 26 July 1950, Box 39, SFP, OPOS, RG59, NARA.

43. "DOS," 25 July 1950.

44. Ibid.

45. Editorial, "United Korea," *Ithaca Journal,* 8 August 1950.

46. "DOS," 22 August 1950.

47. "DOS," 20–25 August 1950.

48. "Monthly Survey of American Opinion on International Affairs," August 1950, Box 12, SFP, OPOS, RG59, NARA.

49. "Korea to Be Issue in November Vote," 7 August 1950, *New York Times.*

50. James T. Patterson, *Mr. Republican: A Biography of Robert A. Taft* (Boston: Houghton Mifflin, 1972).

51. Robert A. Taft, "The Korean Crisis: Caused by Wavering Foreign Policy of Administration," 28 June 1950, Speeches, Box 1446, RATP, LC.

52. "DOS," 24 July 1950; Foot, *The Wrong War,* 69.

53. Robert A. Taft, "Transcribed Edition of Capitol Report No. 63," 19 July 1950, Legislative File; Korea, 1950, Box 670, RATP, LC.

54. Letter, Robert R. McCormick to Robert A. Taft, 23 May 1950; and Taft to McCormick, 29 May 1950, General Correspondence, "1950, B-W," Box 33, PATP, LC.

55. Letter, Robert A. Taft to Bernard W. LeVander, 11 August 1950, Box 924: "Subject File: War, Korean, 1950," RATP, LC.

56. See correspondence to and from Robert A. Taft in ibid.; see also Subject File, Box 915: "Communism 1950" and Box 33: "General Correspondence 1950," as well as Political File, Box 251: "1950 Campaign-Ohio Counties," RATP, LC. On recognition of China, see Taft's letter to Carl Ryan, 25 November 1949, in Box 901: "Communism 1949," as well as his letter to Lewis Hoskins, 17 January 1950, Box 917: "Foreign Policy 1950," RATP, LC.

57. "Statement of Principles, Policies and Objectives of Republican Members of Congress," Political File "Campaign Miscellany," Box 307, RATP, LC.

58. "Liberty Against Socialism: The Issue in 1950," Political File "Campaign Miscellany," Box 307, RATP, LC.

59. John Lewis Gaddis has reminded us about this point in his earlier work published in 1972, but U.S. diplomatic historians have tended not to look at the roles of domestic and party politics in the shaping of foreign policy. Fortunately, there has been a revival in recent scholarship that focuses on this aspect. See, for instance, John Lewis Gaddis, *The United States and the Origins of the Cold War* (New York: Columbia University Press, 1972), x; Melvin Small, *Democracy and Diplomacy: The Impact of Domestic Politics on U.S. Foreign Policy, 1789–1994* (Baltimore: Johns Hopkins University Press, 1996); Fredrik Logevall, "A Critique of Containment," *Diplomatic History,* 28: 4 (2004), 473–499; Thomas Alan Schwartz, " 'Henry, . . . Winning an Election Is Terribly Important': Partisan Politics in the History of U.S. Foreign Relations," *Diplomatic History,* 33: 2 (2009), 173–190; and Andrew L. Johns, *Vietnam's Second Front: Domestic Politics, the Republican Party, and the War* (Lexington: University Press of Kentucky, 2010).

60. "Korea to Be Issue in November Vote," 7 August 1950, *New York Times.*

61. Letter, Oscar Bigler to Richard Nixon, 24 July 1950, William Knowland Papers (WKP), Carton 90: "1950 Campaign," BL-UCB.

62. "Foreign Policy Set as G.O.P. Vote Issue," 8 August 1950, *New York Times.*

63. Republican National Committee, ed., "Background to Korea," Subject File "Politics, 1950," Box 91, GMEP, HSTL.

64. Memo, "Script for the One Minute Spot on Radio," 28 October 1950, Carton 2, "1950 Campaign," WKP, BL-UCB.

65. Jenkins, *Cold War at Home,* 9.

66. Letter, Joseph McCarthy to HST, 12 July 1950, Box 872, OF 252K, HSTP, HSTL.

67. Notes, 21 July 1950, in Carton 1, JSSP, BL-UCB.

68. "Communists in Government," 7 July 1950, *Gallup Poll,* vol. 2, 924.

69. "DOS," 19 July 1950, GMEP, Subject File "Internal Security: Sen. McCarthy's Charges," Box 70, HSTL. (DOS was widely circulated at that time; on this entry, I got a copy at HSTL)

70. Dean Acheson's Press and Radio Conference, 28 September 1950, President's Secretary's File, "Secretary of State Press Conference," Box 54, HSTP, HSTL.

71. "DOS," 25 September 1950.

72. Letter, Joseph C. O'Mahoney to HST, 27 June 1950, Student File: Korean War, Box 1, HSTL.

73. Letter, Carter Clarke to Robert Fellers, 12 September 1950, BFFP, MMA.

74. See, for example, "Washington Wire," *New Republic* (25 September 1950).

75. Democratic National Committee, ed., "Questions and Answers on Foreign Policy," 3, Subject File "Politics, 1950," Box 91, GMEP, HSTL.

76. "President Address at Alexandria, VA, on Foreign Policy," 22 February 1950, and "Daily Summary of Opinion Developments," both in Subject File "Truman Administration: Speech File," Box 39, GMEP, HSTL.

77. "President Address to the American Society of Newspaper Editors," 19 April 1950, Subject File "Truman Administration: Speech File."

78. "Questions about the Battle in Korea," 2, Subject File "Politics, 1950," Box 91, GMEP, HSTL. (emphasis added)

79. "Record of Actions by the National Security Council at Its Sixty-Fourth Meeting, August 10, 1950," 10 August 1950, Personal File, Subject File, "National Security Council: Actions, 1947–1953," Box 167, HSTP, HSTL.

80. "Conversation with Congressman Clinton D. McKinnon," Subject File, "Politics, 1950: Elections," Box 92, GMEP, HSTL.

81. Memorandum, Ken Hechler to Charles Murphy, "Campaign Materials on Foreign Policy-Defense," 2 September 1950, Subject File "Politics, 1950: Elections," Box 92, GMEP, HSTL. (emphasis added)

82. Park Myung-lim, *Senso to heiwa: Chosen hanto 1950* [War and Peace: The Korean Peninsula, 1950] (Tokyo: Shakai hyoronsha, 2009) , 311–313.

83. Ibid., 314, 319–330.

84. Wada Haruki, *Chosen senso zenshi* [A Complete History of the Korean War] (Tokyo: Iwanami shoten, 2002), 191.

85. "Special Report American Opinion," 30 October 1950, SFP, Box 39, SFP, OPOS, RG59, NARA.

86. Letter, George W. Constable to HST, 12 October 1950, Official File, 471-B, Korean Emergency, HSTP, HSTL.

87. "DOS," 19 September 1950.

88. "DOS," 26 September 1950.

89. Ibid.

90. Ibid.

91. "Keep Going," *Newsweek,* 2 October 1950; "Victory Looms—So Does 38th Parallel," *Newsweek,* 2 October 1950; *U.S. News and World Report,* 25 August and 1 September 1950; and the *New Republic,* 25 September and 9 October 1950, all made similar arguments. A liberal magazine, *The Nation,* was one of the few magazines that opposed it directly. See "Deadly Parallel," 14 October 1950; "Unanswered Question," 28 October 1950; and "Threat Out of China," 11 November 1950.

92. Foot, *The Wrong War,* 69. In addition to Taft, General Dwight Eisenhower, who was already seen as another possible Republican candidate for president in 1952, similarly questioned the stopping of U.S. forces at the parallel. Eisenhower, then president of Columbia University, said that U.S. forces "[might] have to cross the 38th parallel to wage a successful war." See "Eisenhower Backs Invasion If Needed," *New York Times,* 21 July 1950.

93. "DOS," 22 September 1950.

94. Ibid.

95. Ibid.

96. "Monthly Survey of American Opinion on International Affairs," August 1950, Box 12, SFP, OPOS, RG59, NARA.

97. "DOS," 19 September 1950.

98. "DOS," 20 September 1950.

99. "Korea," 13 October 1950, *The Gallup Poll,* vol. 2, 929.

100. Elisabeth Noelle-Neumann, *The Spiral of Silence; Public Opinion—Our Skin,* 2nd ed. (Chicago: University of Chicago Press, 1993).

101. Memorandum, George F. Kennan to Dean Acheson, 21 August 1950, Student File "Korean War," Box 1, HSTL.

102. George F. Kennan, February 14, 1954, Reel 6, Track 1: 8, Princeton Seminars, HSTL.

103. "Interview with Escott Reid, Glendon College, Monday, June 9, 1969," MG31 E46 Vol. 29 "Korea," Escott Reid Papers (ERP), LAC.

104. Memorandum, Reid to Pearson, 28 September 1950, MG31 E46 vol. 29, "Korea," ERP, LAC.

105. Dean Acheson, *Present at the Creation: My Years in the State Department* (New York: W. W. Norton, 1969), 446.

106. George F. Kennan, *Memoir 1925–1950* (New York: Pantheon Books, 1967), 495.

107. Telegram, Washington DC to Foreign Office, 26 August 1950, PREM8/1156: "Suggested Visit of Prime Minister to Washington for Meeting with President Truman for Discussions with USA on International Situation, Korea and Defense," TNA.

108. Telegram, Foreign Secretary (Ernest Bevin) to High Commissioner for the UK, Delhi, India, for Pandit Nehru, September 4, 1950, in "China: Political Situation," DO133/22, TNA.

109. Memorandum, Bevin to the Cabinet, "New York Meetings: Developments in Far Eastern Policy," 6 October 1950, CAB21/2102: "The War in Korea: The Implications of, on Our Foreign Policy in Other Parts of the World: Co-operation with USA," TNA; telegram, "Yingguo waijiao dachen Beiwen zhi Zhou Enlai zongli de dian [A Telegram from British Foreign Secretary Bevin to Premier Zhou Enlai]," 10 October 1950, 110–00024–22, FMA.

110. Quoted in Foot, *The Wrong War*, 79; Allen S. Whiting, *China Crosses the Yalu: The Decision to Enter the Korean War* (New York: Macmillan, 1960), 93.

111. Telegram, High Commissioner, Delhi, to Foreign Secretary in New York, September 27, 1950, "China: Political Situation, Sept. 4–30, 1950," DO133/23, TNA.

112. Ibid.

113. Several officials continued to oppose the idea of crossing the 38th parallel, including George F. Kennan, O. Edmund Clubb, and James Webb. See, for instance, Foot, *The Wrong War*, 80.

114. Telegram, Foreign Office, UK, to Washington, 29 September 1950, "Various Reactions to Events in Korea," FO371/84529, TNA.

115. Telegram, Peking to Foreign Office, UK, 26 October 1950, "China: Political Situation, Sept. 29–Oct. 24, 1950," DO133/24, TNA.

116. *FRUS, 1950: Vol. 7*, 868–869; see also, for instance, Chen Jian, *China's Road to the Korean War: The Making of the Sino-American Confrontation* (New York: Columbia University Press, 1994), 169–170; Stueck, *The Korean War*, 230–231; and Steven Casey, *Selling the Korean War: Propaganda, Politics, and Public Opinion in the United States, 1950–1953* (New York: Oxford University Press, 2008), 99–100.

117. "Interview with Escott Reid, Glendon College, Monday, June 9, 1969," MG31 E46 Vol. 29, "Korea," ERP, LAC.

118. President's Press and Radio Conference, 31 August 1950, 21 and 28 September 1950; as well as Secretary of State's Press and Radio Conference, 30 August 1950; President's Secretary's Files, "Press Conference File," Box 53 and Box 54, HSTP; Eben Ayers Diary, 1 and 28 September 1950, Box 21, Eben Ayers Papers (EAP), HSTL.

119. Letter, James E. Webb to John W. Snyder, Box 450, James E. Webb Papers (JEWP), HSTL.

120. See, for example, correspondence in "Korean War File, Department of State," Box 6, HSTP, HSTL.

121. Letter, James E. Webb to John W. Snyder, Box 450, JEWP.

122. Averell Harriman, February 14, 1954; Reel 6, Track 1: 7, Princeton Seminars, HSTL.

123. Dean Acheson, February 14, 1954; Reel 6, Track 1: 8, Princeton Seminars, HSTL.

124. For the studies that emphasized the Truman administration's roles in "selling" aggressive programs, see, for instance, Casey, *Selling the Korean War*; Pierpaoli, *Truman and Korea*; Christensen, *Useful Adversaries*; and Frank Kofsky, *Harry S. Truman and the War Scare of 1948: A Successful Campaign to Deceive the Nation* (New York: St. Martin's Press, 1993).

125. Christensen, *Useful Adversaries*, 123. (emphasis added)

126. "Notes on Cabinet Meetings II, 1946–1953," 29 September 1950, Matthew J. Connelly Papers (MJCP), HSTL.

127. Ibid.; Foot, *The Wrong War*, 70; Offner, *Another Such Victory*, 389.

128. Dean Acheson, 13 February 1954, Reel 3, Track 2: 1, Princeton Seminars, HSTL; Dean Acheson, *Present at the Creation*, 452–463. Truman had already approved the U.S. forces' crossing of the 38th parallel on September 27th, but still requested that MacArthur submit a military plan for north of the parallel in advance. See *FRUS, 1950: Vol. 7* (27 September 1950).

129. *FRUS, 1950: Vol. 7* (29 June 1950), 826.

130. Ernest May, ed., *American Cold War Strategy: Interpreting NSC 68* (Boston: Bedford, 1993), vii; Walter LaFeber, *America, Russia, and the Cold War, 1945–2006*, 10th ed. (New York: McGraw-Hill, 2008), 103–105; idem, "Crossing the 38th: The Cold War in Microcosm," 81.

131. "Minutes of the 68th Meeting of the National Security Council held on Friday, September 29, 1950 in the Conference Room of the White House," 29 September 1950, Personal File, Subject File, National Security Council-Meeting File, Box 180, HSTP, HSTL.

132. Offner, *Another Such Victory*, 391.

133. "Makkasa zensen wo shisatsu; 'Kim-kun no demukae ha?' yumoa tappuri [MacArthur Inspects the Frontline; 'Where Is Mr. Kim?' With Humor]," *Mainichi Shinbun*, 21 October 1950; Richard H. Rovere and Arthur Schlesinger, Jr., *General MacArthur and President Truman: The Struggle for Control of American Foreign Policy* (New Brunswick, NJ: Transaction, 1992), 136; William Manchester, *American Caesar: Douglas MacArthur, 1880–1964* (Boston: Little, Brown, 1978), 599; William B. Breuer, *Shadow Warriors: The Covert War in Korea* (New York: John Wiley and Sons, 1996), 106; and David Halberstam, *The Coldest Winter: America and the Korean War* (New York: Hyperion, 2007), 11.

134. "Toward V-K Day," and "U.N.'s War in Korea Enters Its Last Phase, MacArthur's Forces Now in Position to Wipe Out Last Communist Units," 15 October 1950, *New York Times*.

135. Telegram, Peking to Foreign Office, UK, 26 October 1950, "China: Political Situation, Sept. 29–Oct. 24, 1950," DO133/24, TNA.

136. Chen, *China's Road to the Korean War*, 205–209, 288; Millet, *The War for Korea*, vol.2, 297, 542.

4. POLITICS OF IMPRESSION

1. "Yijian shu [Letter of Opinion]," 8 November 1950, in "Shi qingguan ju . . . deng danwei de tongzhi guanyu shenqing Kang-Mei Yuan-Chao de zhiyuan shu" [Volunteer Letters for Resisting America and Aiding Korea Written by Cadres of the Beijing Municipal Administration for Cleaning] (hereafter, "Volunteer Letters for Kang-Mei Yuan-Chao"), 001-009-00145, 34–37, BMA.

2. A recent study that explores individual voices is Jeremy Brown, "From Resisting Communists to Resisting America: Civil War and Korean War in Southwest China, 1950–51," in Jeremy Brown and Paul G. Pickowicz, eds., *Dilemmas of Victory: The Early Years of the People's Republic of China* (Cambridge, MA: Harvard University Press, 2008), 105–129.

3. China's entry into the Korean War has been a topic for discussion for more than half a century. I am most indebted to Chen Jian's work, such as *China's Road to the Korean War: The Making of the Sino-American Confrontation* (New York: Columbia University Press, 1994); *Mao's China and the Cold War* (Chapel Hill: University of North Carolina Press, 2001), 49–84; and "China's Changing Aims during the Korean War, 1950–1951," *Journal of American-East Asian Relations* 1 (Spring 1992), 8–41. I also benefited from reading Shu Guang Zhang, *Mao's Military Romanticism: China and the Korean War, 1950–1953* (Lawrence: University Press of Kansas, 1995); Niu Jun, "The Birth of the People's Republic of China and the Road to the Korean War," in Melvyn P. Leffler and Odd Arne Westad, eds., *The Cambridge History of the Cold War, Vol. 1* (Cambridge: Cambridge University Press, 2010), 221–243; and Simei Qing, *From Allies to Enemies: Visions of Modernity, Identity, and U.S.-China Diplomacy, 1945–1960* (Cambridge, MA: Harvard University Press, 2007), 151–168; as well as Shen Zhihua, *Mao Zedong, Sidalin yu Chaoxian zhanzheng* [Mao Zedong, Stalin, and the Korean War] (Guangzhou: Guangdong renmin chubanshe, 2007); Yang Kuisong, *Mao Zedong yu Mosike de en en yuan yuan* [Mao Zedong's Indebtedness and Bitterness toward Moscow] (Nanchang: Jiangxi renmin chuban-she, 1999); and Shu Ken'ei [Zhu Jianrong], *Mo Takuto no Chosen senso: Chugoku ga Oryokuko wo wataru made* [Mao Zedong's Korean War: China's Crossing of the Yalu River] (Tokyo: Iwanami, 2004). On the role of Moscow, I learned most from Kathryn Weathersby, "Soviet Aims in Korea and the Origins of the Korean War, 1945–50: New Evidence From the Russian Archives," CWIHP Working Paper No. 8 (November 1993) and " 'Should We Fear This?' Stalin and the Danger of War with America," CWIHP Working Paper, No. 39 (July 2002); and Alexandre Y. Mansou-rov, "Stalin, Mao, Kim, and China's Decision to Enter the Korean War, September

16–October 15, 1950," *CWIHP Bulletin* 6/7 (1995), 94–119, as well as V. M. Zubok and Konstantin Pleshakov, *Inside the Kremlin's Cold War: From Stalin to Khrushchev* (Cambridge, MA: Harvard University Press, 1996); Vojtech Mastny, *The Cold War and Soviet Insecurity: The Stalin Years* (New York: Oxford University Press, 1996); and A. V. Torkunov, *Chosen senso no nazo to shinjitsu* [The Myth and Truth of the Korean War] (Tokyo: Soshisha, 2001), a Japanese translation of Anatoly V. Torkunov, *Zagadochnaya voyna: Koreyskiy konflikt 1950–1953* [Mysterious War: War for Korea, 1950–1953] (Moscow: Rosspen, 2000).

4. Niu Jun, *Reisenki Chugoku gaiko no seisaku kettei* [Policy-Making of Chinese Diplomacy in the Cold War Period] (Tokyo: Chikura Shobo, 2007); Niu Jun, "Yueguo San-ba xian: zhengzhi junshi kaolv yu Kang-Mei Yuan-Chao zhanzheng mubiao de queding [Cross the 38th Parallel: Political-Military Considerations and the Fixation of the Aim of the Resist-America-and-Aid-Korea War]," *Zhonggong dangshi yanjiu* [CCP Historical Studies] no. 1 (2002), 17–29; Shen Zhihua, "Chaoxian zhanzheng yanjiu zongshu: Xin cailiao he xin kanfa [Summary of Korean War Studies: New Materials and New Perspectives]," *Zhonggong dangshi yanjiu* [CCP Historical Studies] no.6 (1996) 86–90. For Beijing's support for North Korea's effort and its preparation for establishing the Frontier Defense Army, see, for instance, Charles Kraus, "Zhou Enlai and China's Response to the Korean War," North Korea International Documentation Project, e-Dossier, No. 9 (June 2012); and Chen Jian, *China's Road to the Korean War*, 126–154.

5. *Renmin Ribao,* 19 and 23 July 1950.

6. *Renmin Ribao,* 23 and 25 July 1950.

7. *Renmin Ribao,* 29 July 1950.

8. *Guangming Ribao,* 6 August 1950.

9. *Jiefang Ribao,* 1 August 1950.

10. *Jiefang Ribao,* 30 August 1950.

11. For a detailed discussion of the characteristics of local newspapers in China, see Godwin Chu and Francis Hsu, eds., *Moving Mountain: Cultural Change in China* (Honolulu: University Press of Hawaii, 1979), 78; Alan Liu, *Mass Politics in the People's Republic: State and Society in Contemporary China* (Boulder, CO: Westview Press, 1996).

12. *Changjiang Ribao,* 4 July 1950.

13. *Changjiang Ribao,* 20 and 23 July 1950.

14. *Changchun Xinbao,* 28 July 1950.

15. *Changjiang Ribao,* 4 and 11 August 1950.

16. "Guanyu Wuchang Wenhua zhongxue Meiji jiaoshi jijian xuesheng an [On the Case of an American Teacher's Homosexual Activities at the Wenhua High School in Wuchang]," 15 July 1950, No. 118–00346–08, FMA.

17. "Guanyu Jiangxi Nankangxian renmin fayuan guanyu Meiguo qiaomin zong quan yaoren an panjue [On the Case of the People's Court in Jiangxi Nank-

ang Prefecture Regarding an American Letting His Dog Bite a Chinese Student on the Thigh]," 5 August 1950, No. 118–00346–07, FMA.

18. *Changjiang Ribao*, 7 September 1950.

19. "Guanyu Wuchang Wenhua zhongxue meiji jiaoshi jijian xuesheng an."

20. "Guanyu Jiangxi Nankangxian renmin fayuan guanyu Meiguo qiaomin zong quan yaoren an panjue."

21. "Guanyu fanMei buyao qianshe zongjiao de zhishi [Directive That Being Anti-American Need Not Involve Religion]," 30 July 1950, No. 118–00227–04, FMA.

22. Chen, *China's Road to the Korean War*, 158–164.

23. Park Myung-lim, *Senso to heiwa: Chosen hanto 1950* [War and Peace: The Korean Peninsula 1950] (Tokyo: Shakai hyoronsha, 2009), 241.

24. Chiang Kai-shek, 30 September 1950, Box 48, CKSD, HILA-SU.

25. Yang, *Mao Zedong yu Mosike de en en yuan yuan*, 288.

26. *Renmin Ribao*, 23 September 1950.

27. "Zhongnan qu qingnian qunzhong de sixiang qingkuang [The Thought Situations among a Mass of Youth in Zhongnan Area]," *Neibu Cankao*, 31 October 1950, CUHK.

28. "Diwu quwei, qu fulian chouweihui deng danwei guanyu Kang-Mei Yuan-Chao gongzuo de huibao, zhoubao, jianbao [Reports, Weekly Reports, and Summaries of the Fifth District Committee and Women's League of the District etc. Concerning the Work of the Resist America and Aid Korea Campaign]" (hereafter, "The Work of the Kang-Mei Yuan-Chao Campaign"), 20 October 1950, No. 040–002–00123, BMA.

29. "Beijing-shi diliu quwei gezhibu youguan Kang-Mei Yuan-Chao de quncong fanying ji xuanchuan zhihuizhan gongzuo jihua [Reports from Various Branch Offices of the Sixth District in Beijing Concerning the Common People's Reactions in the Resist America and Aid Korea Movement and Work Plans for Propaganda]" (hereafter, "The Common People's Reactions in the Kang-Mei Yuan-Chao Movement"), November 1950, No. 038–001–00023, BMA.

30. Ibid.

31. "Zhongnan qu qingnian qunzhong de sixiang qingkuang."

32. Ibid.

33. "1951 nian bannian lai jinxing Kang-Mei Yuan-Chao aiguo zhuyi jiaoyu de qingkuang baogao [Situation Report Concerning the Ongoing Patriotism Education of Resist America and Aid Korea in the First Half of 1951]" (hereafter, "The Ongoing Patriotism Education"), 21 September 1951, C21–1–108, SMA; "Wuxi, Suzhou dengdi liuchuan de yaoyan ji bufen ganbu qunzhong dui shiju de fanying [The Spread of Rumors in Wuxi and Suzhou and Other Places and Reactions among Some Cadres and the Common People toward the Current Political Situation]," *Neibu Cankao*, 11 November 1950, CUHK.

34. Ibid.; also, "The Common People's Reactions in the Kang-Mei Yuan-Chao Movement."

35. "The Work of the Kang-Mei Yuan-Chao Campaign"; "Kang-Mei Yuan-Chao yundong zhong zhongxuesheng de sixiang zhuangkuang [The Situation of Thought among High School Students in the Resist America and Aid Korea Movement]" (hereafter, "High School Students in the Kang-Mei Yuan-Chao Movement"), 21 September 1950, No. 100–001–00034, BMA.

36. "The Common People's Reactions in the Kang-Mei Yuan-Chao Movement."; "The Ongoing Patriotism Education."

37. "Meijun zai Renchuan denglu hou, Wuxi gongshangjie sixiang hunluan huangjin baozhang [The Inflation in Gold Prices and Confusion among Business Circles in Wuxi Following the Landing of U.S. Forces at Inchon]," *Neibu Cankao,* 13 October 1950, CUHK.

38. "Hunan, Zhejiang, Sunan, Shandong dengdi yaoyan huiji" [The Collection of Rumors in Hunan, Zhejiang, Sunan, Shandong, and Other Places]," *Neibu Cankao,* 25 October 1950, CUHK.

39. Ibid.

40. "Zhonggong Shanghai shi jiaoqu gongzuo weiyuanhui xuanchuanbu guanyu jiaoqu Kang-Mei Yuan-Chao xuanchuan jiaoyu gongzuo qingkuang de baogao [Report Concerning Operations of Propaganda and Education for Resist America and Aid Korea on the Outskirts of Shanghai]," A71–2–889–10, 5 January 1951, SMA; "High School Students in the Kang-Mei Yuan-Chao Movement"; and "The Common People's Reactions in the Kang-Mei Yuan-Chao Movement."

41. Ibid.

42. See news articles that appeared in, for instance, *Chiangjiang Ribao* (25 July 1950, 8 October, 5 and 24 November); *Jilin Ribao* (26 and 28 October, 1 and 5 November); *Henan Ribao* (14 and 23 November); *Shanxi Ribao* (6 August, 8 September, 21 October, and 4 December); *Guangxi Ribao* (10 and 17 December); and *Renmin Ribao* (17 October).

43. Jiang Yonghui, *San shi ba jun zai Chaoxian* [The Thirty-Eighth Army in Korea] (Shenyang: Liaoning renmin chubanshe, 2009), 14. Jiang Yonghui was an adjutant commander in the CPV during the Korean War.

44. "Zhejiang liu fenqu feite huodong jianqu changjue [Activities of Bandits and Spies Became Rampant in the Sixth District of Zhejiang]," *Neibu Cankao,* 13 October 1950, CUHK.

45. "Hubei tufei tewu eba huodong qingkuang [Situations of Activities of Local Bandits, Spies, and Local Despots in Hubei]," *Neibu Cankao,* 14 October 1950, CUHK.

46. "Xiangxi Wugang, Chengbu deng xian feite huadong zhuangkuang [Situations of Activities of Bandits and Spies in Xiangxi, Wugang, Chengbu, and Other Counties]," *Neibu Cankao,* 19 October 1950, CUHK.

47. Shu [Zhu], *Mo Takuto no Chosen senso*, 382–383.

48. Maurice J. Meisner, *Mao's China and After: A History of the People's Republic*, 3rd ed. (New York: Free Press, 1999), 71.

49. Hu Sheng et al., *Zhongguo gongchandang de qishinian* [A Seventy-Year History of the Chinese Communist Party] (Beijing: Zhonggong dangshi chuban-she, 1991), 328.

50. *Guangxi Ribao*, 10 December 1950.

51. *Guangxi Ribao*, 17 December 1950.

52. Zhou Enlai, *Zhou Enlai junshi wenxuan* [Collected Works of Zhou Enlai on Military Affairs] (Beijing: Renmin chubanshe, 1997), 60–61.

53. "Kongjun yuanfei dalu kongtou baimi [Air Force Flew Far to the Mainland to Drop White Rice]," *Minsheng Ribao*, 27 September 1950; *Neibu Cankao*, 9 November 1950, CUHK.

54. "Zijiu jiuguo zuihao shiji [The Best Opportunity to Help Ourselves and Save the Country]," 13 November 1950, in Ho Thin-shin ed., *Fan-Gong Kang-E zhong de Jiang zongtong* [Generalissimo Chiang in the Anti-Communist and Resist Russia Movement] (Taipei: Xin Zhongguo wenhua chubanshe, 1950), 66, 101–104.

55. "Pingrang jiefang hou Fuzhou, Qingdao gejie yiban sixiang qingkuang [The General Thought Situation in Various Circles in Fuzhou and Qingdao after the Liberation of Pyongyang]," *Neibu Cankao*, 23 December 1950, CUHK.

56. *Shanxi Ribao*, 8 December 1950.

57. "Meidi qinChao hou, Chasheng gedi dizhu jinxing fangong [After the U.S. Intervention in Korea, Landlords in Various Places in Cha Province Carry on Counterattack]," *Neibu Cankao*, 30 November 1950, CUHK.

58. Amako Satoshi, *Chuka jinmin kyowakoku shi* [A History of the People's Republic of China] (Tokyo: Iwanami shoten, 1999), 21.

59. "Jiangsu Zhenjiangshi gejie dui tudifa . . . de fanying [Reactions toward the Land Reform Law in the Various Circles of the City of Zhenjiang in Jiangsu]," *Neibu Cankao*, 18 July 1950, CUHK.

60. "Dui 'budong funong tudi caichan' kouhao de yiwen [Questions about Slogans of "Not Taking Lands and Properties from Rich Peasants']," *Neibu Cankao*, 8 June 1950, CUHK.

61. "Hebei, Pingyuan gejieceng dui budong funong zhengce de fanying [Reactions Among Various Levels of Society in Pingyuan, Hebei, toward the Policy of Preserving Rich Peasants]," *Neibu Cankao*, 10 July 1950, CUHK.

62. "Xinan muqian gongzuo zhongxin renwu: Deng Xiaoping zhengwei zaixinan xinwen huiyi shangde baogao zhaiyao [The Central Tasks Among Immediate Operations in the Southwest: The Summary of Deng Xiaoping's Report on the Southwest Newspaper Conference]," *Neibu Cankao*, 23 May 1950, CUHK.

63. "Yichang . . . dizhu qianfang baiji dikang pohuai [Landlords in Yichang Are Making Every Possible Effort to Resist and Destroy]," *Neibu Cankao*, 16 May 1950,

CUHK; "Tudifa gongbuhou Sunan dizhu pohuai shengchan funong fengci daji nongmin [Sunan's Landlords Sabotage Production and Rich Peasants Mock (Poor) Peasants After the Proclamation of the Land Act]," *Neibu Cankao*, 19 July 1950, CUHK.

64. Meisner, *Mao's China and After*, 92–96.

65. Teiwes, "Establishing and Consolidating of the New Regime," 84; see also Ezra Vogel, *Canton under Communism: Programs and Politics in a Provincial Capital, 1949–1968* (New York: Joanna Cotler Books, 1971), 91–106.

66. Teiwes, "Establishing and Consolidating of the New Regime," 85.

67. "Linli dui guanfei chuli bu qiadang jishi tufei chengji zaocheng qunzhong kongju [Dealings of Bandits Not Appropriate in Linli, Local Bandits Seizing the Opportunity without Delay and Spreading Rumors, and the Masses Terrified]," *Neibu Cankao*, 15 May 1950, CUHK.

68. "Xiangxi, Wugang, Chengbu deng xian feite huodong qingkuang [The Situations of Activities of Bandits and Spies in Xiangxi, Wugang, Chengbu, and Other Counties]," *Neibu Cankao*, 19 October 1950, CUHK.

69. "Hunan Yongshun dengdi tufei huodong qingkuang [The Situation of Activities of Local Bandits in Yongshun, Hunan and Other Places]," *Neibu Cankao*, 22 June 1950, CUHK; Jiang, *San shi ba jun zai Chaoxian*, 14.

70. "Zhonggong Shanghaishi jiaoqu gongzuo weiyuanhui guanyu Shanghaishi Hualongqu heping qianming yundong de gongzuo jianbao [CCP Rural Working Committees on Peace Signature Campaigns at Hualong District in Shanghai]," 4 November 1950, A71–2–56, SMA.

71. Ibid.

72. Wang Bo, *Mao Zedong de jiannan juece: Zhongguo renmin zhiyuanjun chubing Chaoxian de juece guocheng* [Mao Zedong's Difficult Decision: A Process of Decision Making over the Dispatch of the Chinese People's Volunteers to Korea], 2nd ed. (Beijing: Zhongguo shehui kexue chubanshe, 2006), 129.

73. "Mei-ji qinfan wo dongbei lingkong hou Zhenjiang qunzhong fanying [The Masses' Reactions in Zhenjiang Following American Combat Planes' Violation of Our Northeastern Territorial Sky]," *Neibu Cankao*, 12 September 1950, CUHK.

74. "Opinions Regarding the Progress of the War," a memo from the Beijing Municipal Committee to the Central Committee, 8 October 1950, in Beijing shi dang'an guan yanjiushi, ed., "Beijing shi yu Kang-Mei Yuan-Chao [City of Beijing and 'Resist America and Aid Korea' Movement]," *Lengzhan guojishi yanjiu* [Cold War International History Studies] no. 2 (Spring 2006), 396; "The Common People's Reactions in the Resist America and Assist Korea Movements"; "Zhongnan qu qingnian qunzhong de sixiang qingkuang [The Thought Situations of the Youth in the Zhongnan Region]," *Neibu Cankao*, 31 October 1950, CUHK; "Jing, Jin, Hu, Han bufen qunzhong dui muqian shiju de fanying [Reactions to the Current

Political Situations in a Portion of the Masses in Beijing, Tianjin, Shanghai, and Wuhan]," *Neibu Cankao*, 3 November 1950, CUHK, CUHK.

75. A similar observation can be seen in, for instance, Hou Songtao, "Kang-Mei Yuan-Chao yundong zhong de shehui dongyuan [The Social Mobilization in the Resist America and Aid Korea Movement]," PhD dissertation, Zhonggong zhongyao dangxiao, 2006, 29.

76. "The Common People's Reactions in the Kang-Mei Yuan-Chao Movement."

77. Beijingshi dang'anguan yanjiushi, "Report on 'Resist America and Aid Korea' Campaign," 397–398.

78. *Jilin Ribao*, 10 November 1950.

79. "The Common People's Reactions in the Kang-Mei Yuan-Chao Movement."

80. Ibid.

81. "Nanjing ge jieceng dui shiju he tugai de fanying ji gongshangjie de sixiang dongtai [Reactions on Various Levels of Society in Nanjing toward Current Affairs and Land Reform, as well as the General Trends of Thinking in Business Circles]," *Neibu Cankao*, 30 August 1950, CUHK.

82. "Zhonggong Shanghai shi Changshu quwei xuanchuanbu guanyu ge jieceng qunzhong yundong sixiang dongtai baogao [Report Written by the Propaganda Division of the Changshu District in the CCP Shanghai Committee Concerning Thought Trends among Various Sectors of the Common People]," 9 November 1950, No. A22–2–20–94, SMA.

83. "Shanghai, Tianjin deng di yaoyan yishu [A Number of Rumors in Shanghai and Tianjin and Other Places]," *Neibu Cankao*, 7 November 1950, CUHK.

84. "The Common People's Reactions in the Kang-Mei Yuan-Chao Movement."

85. Du Ping, *Zai zhiyuanjun zongbu* [At the Headquarters in the Chinese People's Volunteers] (Beijing: Jiefangjun chubanshe, 1989), 24.

86. Zhang, *Mao's Military Romanticism*, 77; UK4B-31–11, Telegram, CRO to High Commissioner in Delhi, 3 October 1950, in "China: Political Situation," DO133/24, TNA. This turned out to be a false report. The forces that crossed the 38th parallel on 1 October were South Korean, while U.S. forces crossed the parallel on 8 October.

87. Shen, *Mao Zedong, Sidalin yu Chaoxian zhanzheng*, 184; Chen, *China's Road to the Korean War*, 173.

88. Mao Zedong, *Jianguo yilai Mao Zedong wengao* [Mao Zedong's Manuscripts Since the Founding of the PRC] (hereafter, *Mao Zedong's Manuscripts*), vol. 1 (Beijing: Zhongyang wenxian chubanshe, 1987), 538.

89. Ibid., 539–541; Chen, *China's Road to the Korean War*, 175.

90. Mao, *Mao Zedong's Manuscripts*, vol. 1., 540; Chen, *China's Road to the Korean War*, 176.

91. There was considerable controversy in the mid-1990s about the credibility of the document, but, by now, historians seem to agree that Mao wrote the

document but did not send it to Moscow. See, for example, Chen, *Mao's China and the Cold War*, 56; Yang, *Mao Zedong yu Mosike de en en yuan yuan*, 290–297; and Shen, *Mao Zedong, Sidalin yu Chaoxian zhanzheng*, 179–192.

92. Lei Yingfu, "Kang-Mei Yuan-Chao zhanzheng jige zhongda juece de huiyi [Reminiscence of Major Decisions during the War of Resisting America and Aiding Korea]," *Dangde wenxian*, no. 1 (1994), 27; Yang, *Mao Zedong yu Mosike de en en yuan yuan*, 293.

93. "Ciphered Telegram from Roshchin in Beijing to Filippov [Stalin], October 3, 1950, conveying October 2, 1950 Message from Mao to Stalin," in CWIHP Digital Archives: The Korean War; also, Shen Zhihua, *Chaoxian zhanzheng: Eguo danganguan de jiemi wenjian* [The Korean War: Declassified Documents of Russian Archives] vol. 2 (Taipei: Zhongyang yanjiuyuan jindaishi yanjiusuo, 2003), 576–577; Yang, *Mao Zedong yu Mosike de en en yuan yuan*, 293–294; Xu Yan, *Mao Zedong yu Kang-Mei Yuan-Chao zhanzheng: Zhengque er huihuang de yunchou weiwo* [Mao Zedong and the War to "Resist America and Aid Korea": Correct and Glorious Operation Planning] (Beijing: Jiefangjun chubanshe, 2003), 86–87.

94. Niu Jun, "The Birth of the People's Republic of China and the Road to the Korean War," in Leffler and Westad, *The Cambridge History of the Cold War*, vol. 1, 240–242.

95. Shen, *Chaoxian zhanzheng*, vol. 2, 583–584; and "New Evidence on Cold War Crises: Russian Documents on the Korean War, 1950–1953," *Cold War International History Project Bulletin*, no. 14/15 (Winter 2003–Spring 2004), 376.

96. Shen, *Chaoxian zhanzheng* vol. 2, 582; and "New Evidence on Cold War Crises," 376–377.

97. Nie Rongzhen, *Nie Rongzhen yuanshuai huiyilu* [General Nie Rongzhen's Memoirs] (Beijing: Jiefangjun chubanshe, 2005), 585–586; Chen, *China's Road to the Korean War*, 281; Zhang, *Mao's Military Romanticism*, 80–81.

98. Scholars have scrutinized the contents of this meeting based on participants' memoirs. See, for example, Chen, *China's Road to the Korean War*, 182; Zhang, *Mao's Military Romanticism*, 80; Shen, *Mao Zedong, Sidalin yu Chaoxian zhan-zheng*, 185; Yang, *Mao Zedong yu Mosike de en en yuan yuan*, 293; Zhang Xi, "Peng Dehuai shouming shuaishi Kang-Mei Yuan-Chao de qianqian houhou [Before and After Peng Dehuai's Appointment to Command the War to 'Resist America and Aid Korea']," *Zhonggong dangshi ziliao* 31 (October 1989), 132; Zhang Min and Zhang Xiujuan, *Zhou Enlai yu Kang-Mei Yuan-Chao zhanzheng* [Zhou Enlai and the War to "Resist America and Aid Korea"] (Shanghai: Shanghai renmin chuban-she, 2000), 123. For primary sources, see, for instance, Shi Zhe, *Zai lishi juren shenbian: Shi Zhe huiyi lu* [Alongside the Great Men in History: Memoirs of Shi Zhe] (Beijing: Zhongyang wenxian chubanshe, 1991), 494; Nie, *Nie Rongzhen yuanshuai huiyilu* , 585–587; Peng Dehuai, *Peng Dehuai junshi wenxuan* [The Collected Works of Peng Dehuai] (Beijing: Zhongyang wenxian chubanshe, 1988), 320–321;

99. Li De and Shu Yun, eds., *Lin Biao riji* [Lin Biao's Journal], vol. 2 (Carle Place, NY: Mingjing chubanshe, 2009), 678; Zhang, *Mao's Military Romanticism,* 80; Shu (Zhu), *Mo Takuto no Chosen senso,* 201; Zhang and Zhang, *Zhou Enlai yu Kang-Mei Yuan-Chao zhanzheng,* 122–123; and Yang Fengan and Wang Tiancheng, *Beiwei Sanshiba du xian: Peng Dehuai yu Chaoxian zhanzheng* [The 38th Parallel: Peng Dehuai and the Korean War] (Beijing: Jiefangjun chubanshe, 2000), 93–95.

100. Zhang, "Peng Dehuai shouming shuaishi Kang-Mei Yuan-Chao de qianqian houhou," 136; Nie, *Nie Rongzhen yuanshuai huiyilu,* 587; Wang Yan, *Peng Dehuai nianpu* [A Chronological Record of Peng Dehuai] (Beijing: Renmin chubanshe, 1998), 402–403; Chen, *China's Road to the Korean War,* 183–184; Shu [Zhu], *Mo Takuto no Chosen senso,* 268–269.

101. Peng Dehuai, *Peng Dehuai junshi wenxuan,* 322; Zhang, "Peng Dehuai shouming shuaishi Kang-Mei Yuan-Chao de qianqian houhou," 53; Chen, *China's Road to the Korean War,* 183–184.

102. Nie, *Nie Rongzhen yuanshuai huiyilu,* 587.

103. Chen, *China's Road to the Korean War,* 197–200; Zhang, *Mao's Military Romanticism,* 83. Shu [Zhu] deals with this topic in detail: see his *Mo Takuto no Chosen senso,* 327–344.

104. Shen, *Mao Zedong, Sidalin yu Chaoxian zhanzheng,* 196–197; Yang, *Mao Zedong yu Mosike de en en yuan yuan,* 298–299.

105. Zhang, *Mao's Military Romanticism,* 83.

106. Chen, *China's Road to the Korean War,* 201–202.

107. Mao, document of October 13, 1950, *Mao Zedong's Manuscripts,* vol. 1, 556; Zhonggong zhongyang wenxian yanjiushi ed., *Mao Zedong wenji, Di liu juan* [The Collected Works of Mao Zedong, Vol. 6] (Beijing: Renmin chubanshe, 1999), 103–104; Chen, *China's Road to the Korean War,* 202; and Zhang, *Mao's Military Romanticism,* 184.

108. Gaddis, *We Now Know,* 80–81.

109. Shen, *Chaoxian zhanzheng,* vol. 2, 581–582; *CWIHP Bulletin,* no. 14/15 (Winter 2003–Spring 2004), 370, 375–376.

110. *CWIHP Bulletin,* no. 14/15 (Winter 2003–Spring 2004), 370.

111. Kathryn Weathersby, " 'Should We Fear This?': Stalin and the Danger of War with America," CWIHP Working Paper Series, No. 39 (July 2002), 19–20.

112. Wu Ruilin, *Kang-Mei Yuan-Chao zhong de di 42 jun* [The Forty-Two Army in the "Resist America and Aid Korea"] (Beijing: Jincheng chubansha, 1995), 80–81.

113. Chen Jian, "China's Changing Aims during the Korean War, 1950–1951," *Journal of American-East Asian Relations* 1 (Spring 1992), 26–28; Chen Jian, *Mao's China and the Cold War* (Chapel Hill, NC: University of North Carolina Press, 2001), 92–93; Zhang, *Mao's Military Romanticism,* 123; Hong Xuezhi, *Kang-Mei Yuan-Chao zhanzheng huiyi* [Memoirs of the War to "Resist America and Aid Korea"] (Beijing: Jiefangjun wenyi chubansha, 1990), 98–99.

114. Zhou Enlai, Letter to Mao Zedong, 9 December 1950, in Kraus, "Zhou Enlai and China's Response to the Korean War," 23.2014

115. "Pingrang jiefang hou Fuzhou, Qingdao gejie yiban sixiang qingkuang."

116. Editorial, *Asahi Shinbun*, 20 November 1950.

117. Shen, "Chaoxian zhanzheng yanjiu zongshu," 86–90; Niu, *Reisenki Chugoku gaiko no seisaku kettei*; idem, "Yueguo San-ba xian," 17–29.

118. With regard to Beijing's decision to cross the 38th parallel, scholars have presented several factors. First, Beijing was concerned that stopping at the 38th parallel would give U.S. forces time to recover. Second, Korean leader Kim Il-Sung visited Beijing on 3 December, pleading with Chinese authorities to advance Chinese armies southward across the parallel. Third, Beijing had obtained an American intelligence report, suggesting that the United States would withdraw fully. See, for instance, Zhang, *Mao's Military Romanticism*, 121–123; and Stueck, *The Korean War*, 143–144. Finally, scholars have presented pressures from Moscow as a driving force as well. See, for instance, "CC Politburo Decision with Approved Message to Vyshinsky in New York," 7 December 1950, in the CWIHP Virtual Archive "The Korean War"; and "Telegram from Gromyko to Roshchin Transmitting Message from Filippov to Zhou Enlai," 7 December 1950, in the CWIHP Virtual Archive "The Korean War."

119. Chen, *China's Road to the Korean War*, 215.

120. Mao, document of 13 December 1950, *Mao Zedong's Manuscripts*, vol. 1, 722.

121. Zhang, *Mao's Military Romanticism*, 126.

122. Mao, document of 21 December 1950, *Mao Zedong's Manuscripts*, vol. 1, 731–732.

123. Du Ping, *Zai zhiyuanjun zongbu* [At the Headquarters of the Chinese People's Volunteers] (Beijing: Jiefangjun chubanshe, 1989), 153.

124. Wang, *Peng Dehuai nianpu*, 460; Zhang, *Mao's Military Romanticism*, 128.

125. Zhang, *Mao's Military Romanticism*, 129; Wang, *Peng Dehuai nianpu*, 460; and Xu, *Mao Zedong yu Kang-Mei Yuan-Chao zhanzheng*, 171–172.

126. Chen, "China's Changing Aims during the Korean War, 1950–1951," 26–29, 40–41; idem, *Mao's China and the Cold War*, 61, 92–96.

5. THE TRUTH-MAKING CAMPAIGN

1. Transcript, Minutes of Regular Meeting, 9 October 1950, Folder 2, "School Defense Protest," Box 1813, Los Angeles Unified School District Board of Education Records (LAUSDBER), Library Special Collections (LSC), University of California Los Angeles (UCLA), Los Angeles, CA.

2. Letter, Nan Blair to the Los Angeles City School Board of Education, 6 February 1951, Folder 2, Box 1813, LSC-UCLA.

3. Letter, Jack J. Moore to the President of the Board of Education, 22 February 1951, Folder 2, Box 1813, LSC-UCLA.

4. Ibid.

5. Transcript, Minutes of Regular Meeting, 9 October 1950.

6. See, for instance, Steven Casey, *Selling the Korean War: Propaganda, Politics, and Public Opinion in the United States, 1950–1953* (New York: Oxford University Press, 2008); Kenneth Osgood, *Total Cold War: Eisenhower's Secret Propaganda Battle at Home and Abroad* (Lawrence: University of Kansas, 2006); Walter Hixson, *Parting the Curtain: Propaganda, Culture, and the Cold War, 1945–1961* (New York: St. Martin's Press, 1997); and Tony Shaw, *Hollywood's Cold War* (Amherst: University of Massachusetts Press, 2007).

7. Harry S. Truman, Long Hand Note File, 9 December 1950, Box 281, President's Secretary File, HSTL.

8. "Minutes of the Meeting of the President with Congressional Leaders, 11 a.m., Friday, in the White House," 1 December 1950, Folder "Attlee Meeting—December 1950," Box 149, Foreign Affairs File, Subject File, President's Secretary's Files, HSTP, HSTL.

9. For instance, see "World War III, Phase I: Soviet Ahead," *USNWR*, 24 November 1950.

10. Letter, Carter Clarke to Bonner Fellers, 18 December 1950, Folder 9, Box 1, BFFP, MMA. The underline appears in the original.

11. Correspondence, Douglas MacArthur to the Joint Chiefs of Staff, 30 December 1950, Folder 11, Box 1, DMP, MMA.

12. Press release, President Harry S. Truman's Speech, 15 December 1950, Folder "Korea," Box 1304, OF471, HSTP, HSTL; Dean Acheson, likewise, expressed a similar logic several times at the NSC meeting and the Cabinet meeting on 28 November, as well as the president's meeting with congressional leaders on 13 December. See *FRUS, 1950: Vol. 7: Korea*, 1242–1249; "Minutes of Cabinet Meeting, 4:20 p.m., Tuesday, at the White House," Folder "Attlee Meeting—December 1950," Box 149, Foreign Affairs File, Subject File, President's Secretary's Files, HSTP, HSTL; and "Minutes of the Meeting of the President with Congressional Leaders, 10:00 a.m., Wednesday, at the White House," 13 December 1950, Folder "Attlee Meeting—December 1950," Box 149, Foreign Affairs File, Subject File, President's Secretary's Files, HSTP, HSTL.

13. Letter, John Brogen to William Knowland, 12 October 1950, Box 272, WKP, BL-UCB.

14. Letter, Walter Judd to McKinley, 17 August 1950, Box 38, Walter Henry Judd Papers (WHJP), HILA-SU; see also Marguerite Higgins, *War in Korea: The Report of a Woman Combat Correspondent* (Garden City, NY: Doubleday, 1951), 215.

15. "Poll Favors Dog Tags for Bomb Attacks," *Los Angeles Times*, 25 September 1950.

16. Letter, Harold Bisbee to Harry S. Truman, 16 December 1950, Box 1307, OF471B, HSTL.

17. Letter, L. W. Neustadter to William Knowland, Box 242, WKP, BL-UCB.

18. Eugene Donald Millikin's comments in "Meeting of the President with Congressional Leaders in the Cabinet Room," 13 December 1950, Folder 3, Student File No. 44, HSTL.

19. "Meeting with the President with Congressional Leaders," 13 December 1950, Folder 3, SF 44, HSTL.

20. Ibid.

21. Letter, F. W. Stover to A. R. Guernsey, Box 1, Series I, Fred Stover Papers (FSP), SCUA-UI.

22. Norman Thomas, "Why No One Can Be Neutral," 4, in Box 11, Raymond Feely Papers (RFP), HILA-SU.

23. Memorandum, David Bruce to Acheson, "Review of Political Development During the Months of September, October, and November, 1950," 13 December 1950, *FRUS. 1950: Vol. 3: Western Europe,* 1440.

24. Stueck, *The Korean War,* 130–138.

25. For details of the Truman-Attlee conference, see *FRUS, 1950: Vol. 3, Western Europe,* 1706–1787.

26. Ibid., 1714–1715, 1725–1726.

27. Ibid., 1762–1763.

28. Ibid., 1711–1712.

29. John Dower, *War Without Mercy: Race and Power in the Pacific War* (New York: Pantheon, 1986), 142–146, 302–303.

30. Roscoe Drummond, "The State of Europe; Danger from Within," December 1950, File 2, SF No. 44. HSTL.

31. Letter, Charles R. Kennedy to HST, 4 December 1950, Box 1305, OF471-B, HSTP, HSTL.

32. Letter, Esther R. to HST, 6 December 1950, File 2, SF No. 44, HSTL.

33. Letter, A. Cumings to William Knowland, Box 272, WKP, BL-UCB.

34. Editorial, *Pittsburgh Press,* 10 December 1950.

35. See, for instance, David Lawrence, "What Do We Mean by 'Preventive War'?" *USNWR,* 8 September 1950, and "War Now? Or When? Or Never?" *Time,* 18 September 1950.

36. "Why Korea?" Twentieth Century–Fox (1950), Motion Picture Collection, HSTL.

37. Letter, Don P. West to John R. Steelman, n.d., 471-B; letter, Charles Niles to John R. Steelman, 13 January 1951, OF471B. HSTL.

38. Letter, P. J. Wood to John R. Steelman, 22 January 1951, OF471B. HSTL.

39. Walter Hixson, *Parting the Curtain: Propaganda, Culture, and the Cold War, 1945–1961* (New York: St. Martin's Press, 1997), 14–15; Kenneth Osgood, *Total Cold War: Eisenhower's Secret Propaganda Battle at Home and Abroad* (Lawrence: University of Kansas, 2006), 43; Marc J. Selverstone, *Constructing the Monolith: The*

United States, Great Britain, and International Communism, 1945–1950 (Cambridge, MA: Harvard University Press, 2009), 177.

40. Guy Oakes, *The Imaginary War: Civil Defense and American Cold War Culture* (New York: Oxford University Press, 1994), 34–38.

41. "Invitation to the first public exhibition of the Federal Civil Defense Administration's Rescue Street," Folder "Civil Defense Campaign," Box 6, Spencer R. Quick Files, Staff Member and Office Files, HSTP, HSTL.

42. "Statement by the President on the First Anniversary of Civil Defense," 12 January 1952, Folder "Feb. 1951–1953," Box 1671, OF1591, HSTP, HSTL.

43. "Federal Civil Defense Administration Press Information," No. 120, June 21, 1951, in memorandum from John T. Gibson to Irving Perlmeter, 23 June 1951, Folder "Miscellaneous, 1945–50," Box 1743, OF 2965, HSTP, HSTL.

44. "Civil Defense 1951," *Your Government: Bulletin of the Bureau of Government Research,* Lawrence, Kansas, vol. 6 (15 February 1951), Folder 4, Box 52, AFSF, UA-UCLA.

45. Letter from Alexander Stoddard to George Marshall (8 March 1951), in Folder 4: "National Security Training Classes," Box 1812, LAUSDBER, LSC-UCLA.

46. Laura McEnaney, *Civil Defense Begins at Home: Militarization Meets Everyday Life in the Fifties* (Princeton, NJ: Princeton University Press, 2000), 88.

47. Letter, J. D. Riggins to Dr. Stafford Warren, Dean of School of Medicine, UCLA, 7 August 1950, LSC-UCLA; letter, Frank Dale to HST, 17 January 1951, Folder "1945–Jan. 1951," Box 1671, OF1591, HSTP, HSTL.

48. Letter, Richard J. Kennedy to Gen. Harry H. Vaughan, 8 August 1950, Folder "1945–Jan. 1951," Box 1671, OF1591, HSTP, HSTL.

49. Letter, Richard J. Kennedy to Gen. Harry H. Vaughan, 6 September 1950, Folder "1945–Jan. 1951," Box 1671, OF1591, HSTP, HSTL.

50. Guy Oakes, *The Imaginary War: Civil Defense and American Cold War Culture* (New York: Oxford University Press, 1994), 158, 165–166.

51. "Delays in Civilian Defense," *Los Angeles Times,* 2 October 1950, Folder 4, Box 52 AFSW, UA-UCLA.

52. Memorandum, MacArthur to Joint Chiefs of Staff, 3 December 1950, File 11 Box 1, RG6, DMP, MMA.

53. Note of the President's Meeting with Congressional Leaders, 13 December 1950, Folder 3, SF 44, HSTL.

54. Ibid.; see also "Research Data of the Chinese Communist Potential for Intervention in the Korean War," in Folder 1, Box 14, RG 23, Charles A. Willoughby Papers (CAWP), MMA.

55. Shi Zhe, *Zai lishi juren shenbian: Shi Zhe huiyi lu* [Alongside the Great Men in History: Memoirs of Shi Zhe] (Beijing: Zhongyang wenxian chubanshe, 1991), 492–493; William J. Sebald, *With MacArthur in Japan: A Personal History of the*

Occupation (New York: W. W. Norton, 1965), 173; Chen Jian, *China's Road to the Korean War: The Making of the Sino-American Confrontation* (New York: Columbia University Press, 1994), 169.

56. "Research Data of the Chinese Communist Potential for Intervention in the Korean War," CAWP, MMA; see also Willoughby's Memorandum, "Brief of 'Trends of High Level Washington Estimates on Chinese Communist Intervention in Korea,'" Willoughby to MacArthur, 23 February 1951, Folder 11, Box 1, DMP, MMA.

57. Stueck, *The Korean War,* 91–96.

58. Sebald, *With MacArthur in Japan,* 173; Chen, *China's Road to the Korean War,* 169–171.

59. Willoughby, "Brief of 'Trends of High Level Washington Estimates on Chinese Communist Intervention in Korea.'"

60. David Halberstam, *The Coldest Winter: America and the Korean War* (New York: Hyperion, 2007), 370–380. Halberstam bitterly criticizes Willoughby for accommodating himself to MacArthur's wishes.

61. Bruce Cumings, *The Origins of the Korean War: The Roaring of the Cataract* (Princeton, NJ: Princeton University Press, 1990), 97. MacArthur, in fact, enjoyed talking about "Oriental psychology," which, he believed, was fundamentally different from the Western one. For example, he talked about this at length with Averell Harriman in early August 1950, telling him that Orientals would not hate to die; MacArthur explained, "They die quietly, folding their arms as a dove folding his wings, relaxing and dying." See Averell Harriman, "Trip to Korea," Box 305, William Averell Harriman Papers (WAHP), LC.

62. Chiang Kai-shek, Folder 11, Box 48, HILA-SU. Like MacArthur, White House Press Secretary Charles G. Ross told Eben Ayers on 7 November 1950 that he could not determine whether the appearance of Chinese Communist troops in North Korea represented "a full-scale attack or merely an effort on the part of the Chinese to protect utilities along the border." See Eben Ayers, *Truman in the White House: The Diary of Eben A. Ayers* (Columbia: University of Missouri Press, 1991), 380.

63. Dower, *War Without Mercy,* 99–104.

64. Ibid., 102, 105–106.

65. Harold Isaacs, *Scratches on Our Minds* (New York: J. Day, 1958), 237.

66. Ibid., 97–99.

67. Ibid., 238.

68. See Thomas Borstelmann, *The Cold War and the Color Line* (Cambridge, MA: Harvard University Press, 2001), 48–53; Michael H. Hunt, *Ideology and US Foreign Policy* (New Haven, CT: Yale University Press, 1987), 162–163.

69. Isaacs, *Scratches on Our Minds,* 226–227.

70. "Aggressive China Becomes a Menace," *Life,* 20 November 1950.

71. Iriye Akira, *Bei-Chu kankei no imeji* [Images in American-Sino Relations] (Tokyo: Heibonsha, 2002), 223–224.

72. Letter, American China Policy Association to editors of various magazines, Box 11, RFP, HILA-SU.

73. For details of the Sino-Soviet relations, see, for example, Odd Arne Westad, *Brothers in Arms: The Rise and Fall of the Sino-Soviet Alliance, 1945–1963* (Stanford, CA: Stanford University Press, 1998); Chen Jian, "The Sino-Soviet Alliance and China's Entry into the Korean War," CWIHP Working Paper No. 1 (1992).

74. T. Christopher Jespersen, *American Images of China, 1931–1949* (Stanford, CA: Stanford University Press, 1996), 188.

75. Letter, Raymond Allen to HST, 29 November 1950, Box 1306, OF 471B, HSTL.

76. "Editorial Note on Conversations between Dean Rusk and John Foster Dulles," 18 May 1951, *FRUS, 1950: Vol. 7: Korea and China, Part 2*, 1671–1672.

77. Letter, Henry A. Wallace to Jimmy Jemail, 16 December 1950, Box 38, Series III, Henry A. Wallace Papers (HAWP), SCUA-UI; Henry A. Wallace, Speech on 21 January 1951, Box 77, Series X, HAWP, SCUA-UI.

78. "Harvest Time for the 'Agrarian Reformer,'" *Saturday Evening Post*, 16 December 1950.

79. Letter, LaVere Roelfs to W. Averell Harriman, 21 November 1950, Box 309, WAHP, LC.

80. "Weihe hanjian biwang qinlue bibai [Why Traitors Will Lose and the Invasion Will Fail]," *Gaizao* [Reform], no. 5 (1 November 1950), 101–104; "Ru dazhan baofa jike chongfan dalu [If World War Explodes, We Can Return to the Mainland]," editorial, *Zhongyang Ribao*, 10 December 1950; and "Jianli dalu fanyong zhengquan fangan cao'an [A Draft for the Proposal to Establish a Political Regime to Counterattack the Mainland]," No. 014–00001–2999A, Xingzheng yuan [Office of Administration], Academia Historica [Guoshiguan] (AH), Taipei, Taiwan.

81. Minutes, Central Reform Meeting on November 1950, No. 6–41–202, CNPR, HILA-SU.

82. *Zhongyang Ribao*, 26 November 1950.

83. See, for instance, Jeremy Brown and Paul Pickowicz, *Dilemmas of Victory: The Early Years of The People's Republic of China* (Cambridge, MA: Harvard University Press, 2007), and Bai Xi, *Kaiguo dazhenfan* [Great Repression at the Time of Establishing the Country] (Beijing: Zhonggong dangshi chubanshe, 2006).

84. See, for instance, Maurice Meisner, *Mao's China and After* 3rd ed. (New York: Free Press, 1999), and Elizabeth Perry, "Reclaiming the Chinese Revolution," *Journal of Asian Studies* 67 (2008), 1147–1164.

85. For studies of close contacts among Moscow, Beijing, and Pyongyang, see, for instance, Kathryn Weathersby, "'Should We Fear This?' Stalin and the Danger of War with America," CWIHP Working Paper No. 39, July 2002; Vladislav Zubok and Constantine Pleshekov, *Inside the Kremlin's Cold War: From Stalin to Khrushchev*

(Cambridge, MA: Harvard University Press, 1996); and Sergei Goncharov, John Lewis, and Xue Litai, *Uncertain Partners: Stalin, Mao, and the Korean War* (Stanford, CA: Stanford University Press, 1993).

86. For the studies of Chinese context and aspect, see, for instance, Brown and Pickowicz, *Dilemmas of Victory*; Chen, *China's Road to the Korean War*; Shu Kenei, *Mo Takuto no Chosen senso* [Mao Zedong's Korean War] (Tokyo: Iwanami shoten, 1991); Niu Jun, *Reisen-ki Chugoku gaiko no seisaku kettei* [China's Foreign Policy Decision Making during the Cold War] (Tokyo: Chikura Shobo, 2007); and Yang Kuisong, *Mao Zedong yu Mosike de en en yuan yuan* [Mao Zedong's Indebtedness and Bitterness toward Moscow] (Nanchang: Jiangxi renmin chubanshe, 1999).

87. Letter, Carter Clarke to Bonner Fellers, 30 April 1951, Folder 9, Box 1, RG 44a, BFFP, MML.

88. "If There Ever Was a Time for the Free World to Rally!" *Kansas City Star*, 16 December 1950.

89. John King Fairbank, *The United States and China* (Cambridge, MA: Harvard University Press, 1948), xiii; John King Fairbank et al., *Next Step in Asia* (Cambridge, MA: Harvard University Press, 1949), 18.

90. Fairbank, *The United States and China*, 3–4. (emphasis in original)

91. Akira Iriye, "Culture and International History," in Michael Hogan and Thomas Peterson, eds., *Explaining the History of American Foreign Relations*, 2nd ed. (New York: Cambridge University Press, 2004), 245.

92. "American Communists," 21 August 1950, *The Gallup Poll*, vol. 2, 933, OKL-CU.

93. Ibid., 934.

94. *Counterattack* (August 1950), Tamiment Library, New York University, New York.

95. Letter, M. Keatle to HST, 11 September 1950, Box 1717, OF2750B, HSTP, HSTP, HSTL.

96. Griffin Fariello, ed., "Becky Jenkins," in *Red Scare: Memories of the American Inquisition: An Oral History* (New York: Avon Books, 1995), 71.

97. Cartoon, "Look Out for Infiltration at Home," *Ithaca Journal*, 14 August 1950; see also Jenkins, *Cold War at Home*, 1.

98. "People Fear Being Called 'Liberal,'" *Palo Alto Times*, 9 March 1951, Box 1, MENC, SCUA-SU.

99. David E. Lilienthal, *Lilienthal's Journal, Vol. II: The Atomic Energy Years 1945–1950* (New York: Harper & Row, 1964), 434; Patterson, *Grand Expectations*, 139; Alonzo L. Hamby, *Beyond the New Deal: Harry S. Truman and American Liberalism* (New York: Columbia University Press, 1973), 83.

100. Letter, Fred Behne to the Headquarter Office, 30 July 1950, Box 5, File 22, PPP, SCUA-UI. Such letters are numerous in the Progressive Party's correspondence in the summer and fall of 1950.

101. Letter, Joe Riblake to the Headquarters Office, 14 September 1950, Box 5, File 22, PPP, SCUA-UI.

102. Letter, Mike and Marilyn Gorski to the Headquarters Office, 14 September 1950, Box 5, File 22, PPP, SCUA-UI.

103. Ellen Schrecker, "McCarthyism: Political Repression and the Fear of Communism," *Social Research* 71:3 (2004), 1071.

104. Letter, anonymous to Henry A. Wallace, 9 August 1950, HAWP, SCUA-UI.

105. Letter, Felix H. Bistram to HST, 31 August 1950. HSTP, HSTL.

6. BETWEEN MOBILIZATION AND PARTICIPATION

1. Telegram, Commonwealth Relations Office (hereafter, CRO), UK, to High Commissioners, "Tightening-Up of Chinese Censorship," 24 November 1950, in "China: Political Situation," DO133/25, TNA.

2. Telegram, CRO to High Commissioners, 15 November 1950, in "China: Political Situation."

3. Telegram, CRO to High Commissioners, "Tightening-Up of Chinese Censorship." The publication of the *North China Daily News* was formally suspended in March 1951. The name of the newspaper came from a British perspective; Shanghai is in the "north" as opposed to Guangdong and Hong Kong in the "south," where the British had their territory. In Guangdong as well, all radio stations and radio transmitting equipment were required to be registered with the police in early December 1950. See letter, Trade Commissioner (Montgomery) to Board of Trade, UK, 16 December 1950, in "Reports, Comments and Information from Many Sources Showing the Extension of Power of the Ruling Chinese Communists over the Political, Social and Economic Life of the Whole of China" (hereafter, "Extension of Power of the Chinese Communists"), FO371/92192, TNA.

4. Ibid.

5. "Dianyingye tongye gonghui zai Kang-Mei Yuan-Chao yundong zhong de huodong qingkuang [Beijing Cinema Guild Concerning the Situation of Activities in the Resist America and Aid Korea Movement]," No. 022–012–00841, BMA.

6. "Shanghai shi wenhuaju guanyu Shanghai yingyuan zidong tingying Meidiguo yingpian de shenqing [The Shanghai Literacy Bureau Concerning Shanghai Theaters' Application for Voluntarily Stopping Screening of American Imperialist's Films]," 4 November 1950, B172–1–33–1, SMA; "Shanghai shi wenhuaju dui Meidiguo dianying de pipan baogao [The Shanghai Literacy Bureau's Report on American Imperialists' Films]," November 1950, B172–1–33–30, SMA; see also a British observation by telegram: CRO to High Commissioners, "Tightening-Up of Chinese Censorship."

7. *Renmin Ribao*, 25 November 1950.

8. *Renmin Ribao,* 7 December 1950.

9. *Renmin Ribao,* 8 December 1950.

10. For discussion of earlier preliminary practices of Beijing's political mobilization in the summer of 1950, see, for example, Chen Jian, *China's Road to the Korean War: The Making of the Sino-American Confrontation* (New York: Columbia University Press, 1994), 139–140.

11. "Zhonggong Shanghai shiwei xuanchuanbu jiaoqu gongzuo weiyuanhui shiyi yuefen xuanjiao gongzuo qingkuang [Summary of Propaganda and Educational Working in November Written by the Suburban Working Committee of the Propaganda Division of the CCP Shanghai Committee]," 18 December 1950, A22–2–6–210, SMA.

12. For the important accounts that stressed the top-down roles played by the CCP, with emphases more on coercive and brutal aspects, see, for instance, Frank Dikötter, *The Tragedy of Liberation: A History of the Chinese Revolution, 1945–57* (New York: Bloomsbury Press, 2013); James Gao, *The Communist Takeover of Hangzhou: The Transformation of City and Cadre, 1949–1954* (Honolulu: University of Hawaii Press, 2004); Odoric Wou, *Mobilizing the Masses: Building Revolution in Henan* (Stanford, CA: Stanford University Press, 1994); and Steven Levine, *Anvil of Victory: The Communist Revolution in Manchuria, 1945–1948* (New York: Columbia University Press, 1987). Also, see Jung Chang and Jon Halliday, *Mao: The Unknown Story* (New York: Knopf, 2005). For scholarly response to this book, see Gregor Benton and Chun Lin, *Was Mao Really a Monster?: The Academic Response to Chang and Halliday's Mao, the Unknown Story* (New York: Routledge, 2010).

13. James T. Sparrow, *Warfare State: World War II Americans and the Age of Big Government* (New York: Oxford University Press, 2011), 81–82.

14. "Beijingshi diliu quwei ge zhibu youguan Kang-Mei Yuan-Chao de quncong fanying ji xuanchuan zhihuizhan gongzuo jihua [Reports from Various Branch Offices of the Sixth District in Beijing Concerning the Common People's Reactions in the Resist America and Aid Korea Movement and Work Plans for Propaganda]" (hereafter, "The Common People's Reactions in the Kang-Mei Yuan-Chao Movement"), 2 November 1950, No. 038–001–00023, BMA.

15. "Kang-Mei Yuan-Chao baojia weiguo shengzhong Chasheng gejie sixiang dongtai [Developments in Thoughts in Various Circles in Chahar Province Amid the Voices of 'Resist America and Aid Korea, Protect Our Homes and Defend Our Country,'" 20 December 1950, *Neibu Cankao,* CUHK.

16. "Tianjin gejie dui muqian shiju de fanying [Responses in Various Circles in Tianjin Regarding the Current Political Situation]," 18 November 1950, *Neibu Cankao,* CUHK.

17. "Jin-shi dianye gonghui deng bufeng zhigong dui muqian shiju de fanying [Reflections on the Political Situation among Workers in Electronic Industry Labor Unions in Tianjin]," 24 November 1950, *Neibu Cankao,* CUHK.

18. "Shanghai, Tianjin deng di yaoyan yishu [A Number of Rumors in Shanghai and Tianjin and Other Places]," 7 November 1950, *Neibu Cankao,* CUHK.

19. "Changsha gejieceng dui muqian shiju de fanying ji liuchuan de yixie yaoyan [Widespread Rumors and Reactions Concerning the Current Political Situation among Various Sectors in Changsha]," 22 November 1950, *Neibu Cankao,* CUHK.

20. "Kang-Mei Yuan-Chao gaochao zhong Zhejiang mouxie qunzhong de sixiang qingkuang he yaoyan [Thought Situation and Rumors among the Common People of Zhejiang in a High Tide of the Resist America and Aid Korea Movement]," 14 November 1950, *Neibu Cankao,* CUHK.

21. "Nanjing gejieceng dui muqian shiju de fanying [Responses toward the Current Political Situation among Various Sectors in Nanjing]," 23 November 1950, *Neibu Cankao,* CUHK.

22. "Xi'an gejieceng dui muqian shiju de fanying he gaidi youguan shiju de yixie yaoyan [Reactions and Rumors among Various Sectors in Xi'an Concerning the Current Political Situation]," 16 November 1950, *Neibu Cankao,* CUHK.

23. "Jiangxi liuchuan de yaoyan he ge jieceng sixiang qingkuang [Widespread Rumors in Jiangxi and the Thought Situation among Various Sectors]," 9 November 1950, *Naibu Cankao,* CUHK.

24. "Changsha ge jieceng dui muqian shiju de fanying ji liuchuan de yixie yaoyan [Widespread Rumors and Reactions Concerning the Current Political Situation among Various Sectors in Changsha]," 22 November 1950, *Neibu Cankao,* CUHK.

25. "Wuxi, Suzhou dengdi liuchuan de yaoyan ji bufen ganbu qunzhong dui shiju de fanying [Rumors Widespread in Wuxi, Suzhou, and Other Places and Reactions among Some Cadres and the Common People Concerning the Current Political Situation]," 11 November 1950, *Neibu Cankao,* CUHK; "Chuanxi dizhu pohuai huodong qingkuang [The Situation of Landlords' Destructive Activities in Chuanxi]," 7 December 1950, *Neibu Cankao,* CUHK.

26. "Wuxi, Suzhou dengdi liuchuan de yaoyan ji bufen ganbu qunzhong dui shiju de fanying."

27. "Changsha gejieceng dui muqian shiju de fanying ji liuchuan de yixie yaoyan."

28. See, for instance, Thomas Borstelmann, *The Cold War and the Color Line* (Cambridge, MA: Harvard University Press, 2001), 48–53; Michael H. Hunt, *Ideology and U.S. Foreign Policy* (New Haven, CT: Yale University Press, 1987), 162–163; Bruce Cumings, *The Origins of the Korean War: The Roaring of the Cataract, 1947–1950* (Princeton, NJ: Princeton University Press, 1990), 97; Harold Isaacs, *Scratches on Our Minds* (New York: J. Day, 1958); and T. Christopher Jespersen, *American Images of China, 1931–1949* (Stanford, CA: Stanford University Press, 1996).

29. "The Common People's Reactions in the Kang-Mei Yuan-Chao Movement," 2 November 1950, No. 038–001–00023, BMA.

30. "Shenyang, Lüda zuijin qunzhong sixiang dongtai ji dite huodong qing-kuang [Recent Developments in Thoughts among the Common People in Shenyang and Lüda and the Situation of Enemy Agent Activities]," 30 November 1950, *Neibu Cankao*, CUHK.

31. "The Common People's Reactions in the Kang-Mei Yuan-Chao Movement."

32. "Liaodong, Liaoxi, Rehe, Heilongjiang deng sheng gejieceng dui shiju de fanying [Reactions toward the Current Political Situation among Various Sectors in Liaodong, Liaoxi, Rehe, and Heilongjiang Province]," *Neibu Cankao*, 18 December 1950, CUHK; "Songjiangsheng muqian ganbu, qunzhong sixiang dongtai [Recent Developments in Thoughts among Cadres and the Common People in Songjiang Province]," *Neibu Cankao*, 30 November 1950, CUHK; and "Rehe, Jinzhou deng di ganbu qunzhong dui Chaoxian zhanshi de fanying [Reactions toward the Korean War among Cadres and the Common People in Rehe and Jinzhou and Other Places]," *Neibu Cankao*, 22 July 1950, CUHK.

33. Footnote in Liu Shaoqi, *Jianguo yi lai Liu Shaoqi wengao* [Liu Shaoqi's Manuscripts Since the Founding of the PRC] (hereafter, *Liu Shaoqi's Manuscripts*) (Beijing: Zhongyang wenxian chubanshe, 2005), 593.

34. Telegram, Liu Shaoqi to Regional, Local, and Municipal Committees, 7 December 1950, *Liu Shaoqi's Manuscripts*, 593.

35. "Report on the 'Resist America and Aid Korea' Campaign," a memo from the Beijing Municipal Committee to the Central Committee, 5 November 1950, in Beijing shi dang'an guan yanjiushi, ed., "Beijing shi yu Kang-Mei Yuan-Chao [City of Beijing and 'Resist America and Aid Korea' Movement]," *Lengzhan guojishi yanjiu* [Cold War International History Studies] (hereafter, *LGY*) no. 2 (Spring 2006), 397–398; "The Second Report on the 'Resist America and Aid Korea' Campaign," a memo from the Beijing Municipal Committee to Chairman Mao, 12 November 1950, Ibid., 402–403; and "Report on the Situation Regarding Young Students, Workers, and Military Staff in Schools," a memo from the Beijing Municipal Committee to the Central Committee, 19 December 1950, Ibid., 404–405.

36. Beijing shi dang'an guan yanjiushi, "Report on the Situation Regarding Young Students, Workers, and Military Staff Schools," 405.

37. H. Y. Hsu, "Notes by H. Y. Hsu," 4 January 1951, in "Extension of the Power of Ruling Chinese Communists over the Political, Social, and Economic Life of the Whole of China," FO371/92193, TNA.

38. Letter, "Student Life in China Today," anonymous to the UK Foreign Office, 15 December 1950, in "Extension of Power of the Chinese Communists," FO371/92192, TNA.

39. "Shanghai dazhong xuexiao xuesheng choumei guannian shangwei wanquan shuli [Anti-American Perceptions Are Not Yet Well Established among College and High School Students in Shanghai]," 28 November 1950, *Neibu Cankao*, CUHK.

40. "Zhongguo jiaoyu gonghui Shanghai shi weiyuanhui guanyu Fang Ming tongzhi zuo de 'Wei baowei zuguo he qingnian ertong xingfu de jianglai er fendou' de baogao [The Shanghai Committee of the Chinese Educational Guild Concerning a Report on Fang Ming's 'Struggles for the Happy Future of the Youth and Children as Well as for the Defense of Our Mother Country']," 9 December 1950, No. C1–2–121–29, SMA.

41. Letter, "Student Life in China Today."

42. Ibid.

43. Yang Tiwei, letter to the Beijing Municipal Committee, 2 November 1950, in "Beijing Daxue deng xiao daxuesheng shenqing Kang-Mei Yuan-Chao de zhiyuanshu [Volunteer Applications for Resist America and Aid Korea (War) Written by College Students at Peking University and Other Schools]" (hereafter, "Volunteer Applications by College Students"), No. 001–009–00146, BMA.

44. Zhou Enlai, 25 November 1950, in *Zhou Enlai nianpu* [A Chronological Record of Zhou Enlai], vol. 1 (Beijing: Zhongyang wenxian chubanshe, 1997), 111.

45. *Renmin Ribao*, 29 November 1950.

46. "Volunteer Letters for Kang-Mei Yuan-Chao," November 1950, No. 001–009–00145, BMA.

47. Letters, November 1950, in "Volunteer Applications by College Students," No. 001–009–00146, BMA.

48. "Tuanshiwei deng guanyu dongyuan jqingnian canjia junxiao gongzuo de baogao ji xiaoxue Kang-Mei Yuan-Chao de huodong zonghe baogao [The Youth League Committee Concerning the Work of Mobilization of the Youth to Attend Military Schools, as Well as Its Comprehensive Report on the Resist America and Aid Korea Movement in Elementary Schools]," 29 October 1950, No. 001–009–00143, BMA.

49. "Kang-Mei Yuan-Chao shijian [Issues Related to the Resist America and Aid Korea Movement]," 22 November 1950, No. 087–042–00064, BMA.

50. "Volunteer Letters for Kang-Mei Yuan-Chao."

51. "The Work of the Kang-Mei Yuan-Chao Campaigns," December 1950, No. 040–002–00123, BMA.

52. *Changjiang Ribao*, 10 November 1950.

53. *Changjiang Ribao*, 4 December 1950; *Xi'an Qunzhong*, December 3, 1950.

54. This point has been emphasized in Patrick Major and Rana Mitter, "East is East and West is West? Towards a Comparative Socio-Cultural History of the Cold War" in Patrick Major and Rana Mitter ed., *Across the Blocs: Cold War Cultural and Social History* (Portland, WA: Frank Cass, 2004), 1–18.

55. "Zhonggong Shanghaishi Dachang quwei xuanchuanbu guanyu qingzhu pingrang jiefang de qingkuang baogao [The Propaganda Division of the Dachang District Committee of CCP Shanghai Committee Concerning a Report on the Celebration of Pyongyang's Liberation]," 15 December 1950, A71–2–883–25, SMA.

56. Ibid.

57. "Hunan Yuanjiang, Xiangxiang deng di nongmin relie yaoqiu canjun [Peasants of Yuanjiang and Xiangxiang in Hunan Province Enthusiastically Demand to Join the Army]," 29 December 1950, *Neibu Cankao,* CUHK.

58. "High School Students in the Kang-Mei Yuan-Chao Movement," 26 December 1950, No. 100–001–00034, BMA.

59. Sherman Cochran, "Capitalists Choosing Communist China: The Liu Family of Shanghai, 1948–56," in Brown and Pickowicz, *Dilemmas of Victory,* 378–379.

60. "Beijing shi tanfan Kang-Mei Yuan-Chao gongzuo jihua zongjie [Planning and Summing-up of Beijing Street Vendors' Activities of Resist America and Aid Korea]," No. 022–010–00314, pp. 23–25, BMA.

61. "Diwu quwei guanyu wuqu Kang-Mei Yuan-Chao yundong de chubu jihua, zongjie, baogao [The Fifth District Committee's Planning, Summary, and Report Concerning the Resist America and Aid Korea Movement in the Fifth District of Beijing]," 040–002–00119, BMA.

62. Ibid.

63. "Shanxi Kang-Mei Yuan-Chao yundong zhankai yilai ge jieceng sixiang dongtai [The General Trends of Thoughts on the Various Levels of Society following the Development of the Resist America and Aid Korea Movement in Shanxi]," *Neibu Cankao,* 8 December 1950, CUHK.

64. "Beijing shi yu Kang-Mei Yuan-Chao; Report on 'Resist America and Aid Korea' Campaign," a memo from Beijing Municipal Committee to the Central Committee, 5 November 1950, *LGY* no.2 (Spring 2006), 398; "The Second Report on 'Resist America and Aid Korea' Campaign," a memo from the Beijing Municipal Committee to Chairman Mao and the Central Committee, 12 November 1950, Ibid., 403.

65. "Zhonggong Shanghai shi Penglai quwei xuanchuanbu guanyu yiban sixiang qingkuang ji shishi xuanjiao gongzuo baogao [Report Written by the Propaganda Division of the Penglai District Committee in Shanghai Concerning the General Thought Situation as Well as Propaganda Working on Current Issues]," 13 November 1950, No. A22–2–20–25, SMA.

66. Ibid.

67. Ibid.; also, "Shanghai dazhong xuexiao xuesheng choumei guannian shangwei wanquan shuli [Anti-American Perceptions Are Not Yet Well Established among College and High School Students in Shanghai]," 28 November 1950, *Neibu Cankao,* CUHK.

68. "Shenyang, Lüda zuijin qunzhong sixiang dongtai ji dite huodong qingkuang."

69. "Chuangxi dizhu pohuai huodong qingkuang."

70. Ibid.

71. "Guomindang tewu zai Guiyang sanbo yaoyan [Guomingdang Agents Are Spreading Rumors in Guiyang]," 27 November 1950, *Neibu Cankao*, CUHK.

72. Ibid; see also "Chuangxi dizhu pohuai huodong zhuangkuang [The Situation of Landlords' Destructive Activities in Chuangxi]," 7 December 1950, *Neibu Cankao*, CUHK.

73. "Shenyang, Lüda zuijin qunzhong sixiang dongtai ji dite huodong qingkuang."

74. "Wuxi nongcun ganbu wufa jipo yaoyan hen kumen [Cadres in Villages of Wuxi Unable to Refute Rumors, Feeling Very Depressed]," 5 December 1950, *Neibu Cankao*, CUHK.

75. See, for instance, British diplomat's observation in a memorandum, A. A. E. Franklin to Foreign Office, 24 February 1951, in "Extension of Power of the Ruling Chinese Communists over the Political, Social, and Economic Life of the Whole of China," FO371/92194, TNA.

76. Memorandum, A. A. E. Franklin to J. S. H. Shattock, 11 January 1951, "Extension of Power of the Chinese Communists," FO371/92192, TNA.

77. Shen Zhihua, comments, "China, the Third World, and the Cold War," international conference, Hangzhou, China, 5–7 November 2010. According to Shen Zhihua, circulation was limited to high-ranking officials at the top of each communist organization. In the 1950s, only 2,400 copies were circulated nationwide.

78. "Shenyang, Lüda zuijin qunzhong sixiang huodong ji dite huodong qingkuang."

79. "The Work of the Kang-Mei Yuan-Chao Campaigns," No. 040–002–00123, BMA.

80. Ibid.

81. "Shanghai dazhong xuexiao xuesheng choumei guannian shangwei wanquan shuli."

82. "High School Students in the Kang-Mei Yuan-Chao Movement," November 1950, No. 100–001–00034, BMA.

7. SOCIAL WARFARE

1. Park Myung-lim, *Senso to heiwa: Chosen hanto 1950* [War and Peace: the Korean Peninsula 1950] (Tokyo: Shakai hyoronsha, 2009), 257–262; Bruce Cumings, *The Origins of the Korean War: Vol. 2: The Roaring of the Cataract, 1947–1950* (Princeton, NJ: Princeton University Press, 1990), 706. For a different view, see Robert L. Bateman, *No Gun Ri: A Military History of the Korean War Incident* (Mechanicsburg, PA: Stackpole Books, 2002);

2. Park, *Senso to heiwa*, 200.

3. Kim Dong-choon, *Chosen senso no shakaishi: hinan, senryo, gyakusatsu* [A Social History of the Korean War: Evacuation, Occupation, Massacre] (Tokyo: Heibonsha, 2008), 263–266.

4. Park, *Senso to heiwa,* 201.

5. Ibid., 202.

6. Similar accounts can be found in Bruce Cumings, *The Korean War: A History* (New York: Modern Library, 2010), 165–203. Also, Korean novelist Hwang Seok-yeong wrote a best-selling narrative, based on interviews he conducted, on the topic of mutual killings that occurred in Sincheon in October 1950, *Sonnimu* [The Visitors], trans. Chon Gyonmo (Tokyo: Iwanami shoten, 2004).

7. Letter, Tom Braine to Helen MacMartin, 18 July 1950, Box 3, File 12, PPP, SCUA-UI.

8. Letter, Helen MacMartin to Tom Braine, 20 July 1950, Box 3, File 12, PPP, SCUA-UI.

9. Letter, Helen MacMartin to Jessie, 6 August 1950, Box 2, File 12, PPP, SCUA-UI.

10. Local newspapers, local branches of the American Legion, and local churches often took on leadership roles in promoting local versions of "anti-communist" campaigns. In Winston-Salem, North Carolina, for instance, local newspapers conducted an "American-version" of a petition drive to counter "communist" signature-collecting campaigns. See letter, *Winston-Salem Journal* to HST, 27 September 1950, Box 1327, OF471B, HSTP, HSTL. For the roles of the Church and American Legion, see letter, Chas Beaulieu to Michael Essin, 29 October 1950, and "Legion Lashes Red-Inspired 'Peace' Effort," 27 July 1950, *Cumberland Advocate,* Wisconsin, both in File 22, Box 5, PPP, SCUA-UI.

11. Letter, Helen MacMartin to "Dear Friends," 19 July 1950, File 8, Box 2; letter, Chas Beaulieu to Michael Essin, September 13, 1950, File 22, Box 5; and letter, Carl Ramsey to Helen MacMartin, September 20, 1950, File 12, Box 3, all in PPP, SCUA-UI.

12. Letter, Helen MacMartin to Max and Grace Granich, 11 August 1950, File 12, Box 3, PPP, SCUA-UI.

13. Letter, Margaret MacMartin to Helen MacMartin, n.d., Folder 4: "Employment: Personal, circa 1951," Carton 2, Helen MacMartin Papers (HMP), Special Collections, University of Vermont, Burlington, VT.

14. Letter, Helen MacMartin to Carl Ramsey, February 7, 1951, File 13, Box 3, PPP, SCUA-UI.

15. McCarthyism has been a topic for research for more than half a century, making up an enormous quantity of literature. I am most indebted to Ellen Schrecker, *Many Are the Crimes: McCarthyism in America* (Princeton, NJ: Princeton University Press, 1999); M. J. Heale, *McCarthy's Americans: Red Scare Politics in State and Nation, 1935–1965* (Athens: University of Georgia Press, 1998); and Landon R. Y. Storrs, *The Second Red Scare and the Unmaking of the New Deal Left* (Princeton, NJ: Princeton University Press, 2013). Also, I learned about the popular aspect and local-level repression in Richard Fried, *The Russians Are Coming! The*

Russians Are Coming!: Pageantry and Patriotism in Cold-War America (New York: Oxford University Press, 1998); and Philip Jenkins, *Cold War at Home: The Red Scare in Pennsylvania, 1945–1960* (Chapel Hill: University of North Carolina Press, 1999). For more detailed discussion on the historiography of McCarthyism, see, for instance, Ellen Schrecker, "McCarthyism and the Red Scare," in Jean-Christophe Agnew and Roy Rosenzweig, eds., *A Companion to Post-1945 America* (Malden, MA: Blackwell, 2006), 371–384.

16. For the changing nature and functions of the concept of "war time," I am indebted to the analysis of Mary L. Dudziak, *War Time: An Idea, Its History, Its Consequences* (Oxford: Oxford University Press, 2012).

17. Jenkins, *Cold War at Home*, 9.

18. Letter, Mary Margaret Freese to HST, 9 August 1950, Box 881, OF263, HSTP, HSTL.

19. Letter, Mary Ann Matugeg to HST, 25 August 1950, Box 881, OF263, HSTP, HSTL.

20. Letter, Ralph W. Slone to E. L. Bartlett, 5 December 1950, Box 1307, OF471B, HSTP, HSTL.

21. "Helen MacMartin Biological Sketch," Helen MacMartin Progressive Party Papers (HMPPP), Vermont Historical Society, Barre, VT.

22. "The Reminiscences of Joseph Gordon," COH-CU.

23. See, for instance, Mary L. Dudziak, *Cold War Civil Rights: Race and the Image of American Democracy* (Princeton, NJ: Princeton University Press, 2000); Elaine Tyler May, "Postscript to the 1999 Edition," *Homeward Bound: American Families in the Cold War Era*, rev. and updated ed. (New York: Basic Books, 1999), 205–208.

24. Manning Marable, "Series Editor's Foreword," in Robbie Lieberman and Clarence Lang, *Anticommunism and the African American Freedom Movement: Other Side of Story* (New York: Palgrave Macmillan, 2009), xi.

25. Martha Biondi, *To Stand and Fight: The Struggle for Civil Rights in Postwar New York City* (Cambridge, MA: Harvard University Press, 2003), 190.

26. Pete Daniel, *Lost Revolutions: The South in the 1950s* (Chapel Hill: University of North Carolina Press, 2000), 38.

27. Letter, Herman Wright to Carter Wesley, PPP, SCUA-UI.

28. Jeff Woods, *Black Struggle, Red Scare: Segregation and Anti-Communism in the South* (Baton Rouge: Louisiana State University, 2004), 5.

29. Harold Fleming, A0363, Southern Oral History Program Online, University of North Carolina at Chapel Hill; also, Brooks, *Defining the Peace*, 55–56.

30. Thomas J. Sugrue, "Crabgrass-Roots Politics: Race, Rights, and the Reaction against Liberalism in the Urban North, 1940–1964," *Journal of American History* 82:2 (1995), 555.

31. Ibid., 556.

32. Ibid., 555.

33. Don Parson, "The Decline of Public Housing and the Politics of the Red Scare: The Significance of the Los Angeles Public Housing War," *Journal of Urban History* 33:3 (2007), 407.

34. Ibid.

35. See, for instance, Sugrue, "Crabgrass-Roots Politics," 551–578; Don Parson, "The Decline of Public Housing and the Politics of the Red Scare: The Significance of the Los Angeles Public Housing War," *Journal of Urban History* 33:3 (2007), 400–417; and Eric Fure-Slocum, "Housing, Race, and the Cold War in a Labor City," in Shelton Stromquist, ed., *Labor's Cold War: Local Politics in a Global Context* (Urbana: University of Illinois Press, 2008), 163–203.

36. Letter, Alabama State Association of Nurse Anesthetists to Pat McCarran, 17 March 1950; letter, Reno Business and Professional Women's Club to Pat McCarran, 19 June 1950, both in Box 51, Pat McCarran Papers (PMP), Nevada Historical Society (NHS), Reno, NV.

37. "Presidential Inaugural Address by Elmer L. Henderson M.D., President, American Medical Association," 27 June 1950, Box 51, PMP, NHS.

38. Seth Wigderson, "The Wages of Anticommunism: U.S. Labor and the Korean War," in Stromquist, *Labor's Cold War*, 231. On changing popular attitudes toward labor, see, for instance, "Strike in Public Service Industries," 17 April 1946; "Strikes and Lockouts," 29 April 1946; "Labor Strike," 29 May 1946; "Labor Strikes," 14 June 1946; "Strikes and Lockouts," 22 November 1946; "Factory Workers' Wage," 13 January 1947; and "Most Important Problem," 31 January 1947, in *The Gallup Poll: Public Opinion, 1935–1971: Vol. 1, 1935–1948* (New York: Random House, 1972), 570, 573, 580, 583, 608, 618, and 623. All these Gallup polls show that the majority of respondents had generally negative opinions toward labor.

39. T. Michael Holmes, *The Specter of Communism in Hawaii* (Honolulu: University of Hawaii Press, 1994), 43, 50.

40. Ibid., 172.

41. "We Owe It to Our Fighting Men," *Kansas City Star,* 13 September 1950.

42. Robert Newman, "The Lingering Poison of McCarranism," address delivered at the Carolinas Speech Communication Association Meeting, Clemson, South Carolina, 28 September 1984, in Scrap Clipping File, PMP, NHS.

43. Carl J. Bon Tempo, *Americans at the Gate: The United States and Refugees during the Cold War* (Princeton, NJ: Princeton University Press, 2008), 26–27.

44. Pat McCarran, "Speech, 1950," Box 50, PMP, NHS.

45. See, for instance, David K. Johnson, *The Lavender Scare: The Cold War Persecution of Gays and Lesbians in the Federal Government* (Chicago: University of Chicago Press, 2004); John D'Emilio, "The Homosexual Menace: The Politics of Sexuality in Cold War America," in his *Making Trouble: Essays on Gay History, Politics, and the University* (New York: Routledge, 1992), 234, 256.

46. D'Emilio, *Making Trouble,* 229.

47. "Sex Perverts in Washington," *Militant Truth* (July–August 1950), Box 269, Periodical Collection, SLA-GSU.

48. D'Emilio, *Making Trouble,* 229.

49. "Betty de Losada Oral History," 23, LARC-SFSU.

50. Congress of American Woman, "The Position of the American Woman Today" (1946), in Nancy MacLean, *The American Women's Movement: A Brief History with Documents* (Boston: Bedford/St. Martin's Press, 2009), 6; Kate Weigand, *Red Feminism: American Communism and the Making of Women's Liberation* (Baltimore: Johns Hopkins University Press, 2001), 47–48.

51. D'Emilio, *Making Trouble,* 236; Molly Ladd-Taylor and Lauri Umansky, *"Bad" Mothers: The Politics of Blame in Twentieth-Century America* (New York: New York University Press, 1998), 12–14.

52. Stephanie Coontz, *The Way We Never Were: American Families and the Nostalgia Trap* (New York: Basic Books, 1992), 30–31.

53. United States Congress House Un-American Activities Committee, *Report on the Congress of American Women* (Washington, DC: GPO, 1950), 1.

54. Storrs, *The Second Red Scare,* 3, 89.

55. May, *Homeward Bound, xviii-xxv, 205–208.*

56. Michelle M. Nickerson, *Mothers of Conservatism: Women and the Postwar Right* (Princeton, NJ: Princeton University Press, 2012); Brennan, *Wives, Mothers, and the Red Scare.*

57. Edith M. Stern, "Women Are Household Slaves," *American Mercury* (January 1949), 76; MacLean, *The American Women's Movement,* 50.

58. Nickerson, *Mothers of Conservatism,* 32.

59. Brennan, *Wives, Mothers, and the Red Scare,* 151.

60. Nickerson, *Mothers of Conservatism,* 72; Richard M. Fried, *Nightmare in Red: The McCarthy Era in Perspective* (New York: Oxford University Press, 1990), 100–101.

61. Letter, Richard Brown to HST, 10 July 1951, Box 1330, OF471-B, HSTP, HSTL.

62. Robert Justin Goldstein, *Political Repression in Modern America from 1870 to the Present* (Boston: G.K. Hall, 1978), 325.

63. Letters, John L. Linn to William Knowland, 24 October 1950, and H. A. Jarvis to William Knowland, 1 October 1950, both in Cartoon 90, "Political Files, 1950 Campaigns," WKP, BL-UCB.

64. Walter Judd, "Does China Mean World War III?" speech delivered before the Economic Club of New York, 13 March 1951, Box 40, Folder 1, WHJP, HILA-SU.

65. United States Congress House Un-American Activities Committee, *100 Things You Should Know about Communism,* rev. ed. (Washington, DC: GPO, 1950), 70.

66. "Keep Race Separate," *Militant Truth* (January–February 1947), Box 269, Periodical Collection, SLA-GSU.

67. Sherman A. Patterson, "Red Treachery Exposed," *Militant Truth* (January–February 1950), Box 269, Periodical Collection, SLA-GSU.

68. "Sex Perverts in Washington."

69. Rev. C. E. Ward, "Fathers, Mothers, and Their Children," *Militant Truth* (July–August 1950), Box 269, Periodical Collection, SLA-GSU.

70. Ibid.

71. Ralph S. Brown, *Loyalty and Security: Employment Tests in the United States* (New Haven, CT: Yale University Press, 1958), 492; Storrs, *The Second Red Scare.*

72. Eleanor Bontecou, *The Federal Loyalty-Security Program* (Ithaca, NY: Cornell University Press, 1953), 138–139; Robert Justin Goldstein, *Political Repression in Modern America from 1870 to the Present* (Boston: G.K. Hall, 1978), 303–304; and Ellen Schrecker, "McCarthyism: Political Repression and the Fear of Communism," *Social Research* 71:3 (2004), 1067.

73. "Loyalty Board Fires Service," *Rockford Morning Star,* 14 December 1951, in Oversized Box 1, JSSP, BL-UCB.

74. Brown, *Loyalty and Security,* 261.

75. William S. Hyde, "Personal History: Dr. Esther Caukin Brunauer," 9 February 1948, Federal Bureau of Investigation, Department of Justice, Box 242, Security Investigation File (SIF), RG478, NARA.

76. Stephen Brunauer, "In the Matter of the Suspension of Stephen Brunauer as an Employee of the Department of the Navy," n.d., Box 242, SIF, RG478, NARA.

77. "Statement of Mrs. Elizabeth C. Lindsay," in Patrick M. Rice, "Result of Investigation: Dr. Esther Caukin Brunauer," 19 June 1950, Box 242, SIF, RG478, NARA.

78. Elizabeth A. Collins, "Red-Baiting Public Woman: Gender, Loyalty, and Red Scare Politics," Ph.D. dissertation, University of Illinois at Chicago, 2008, 194.

79. "In the Matter of the Suspension of Stephen Brunauer as an Employee of the Department of the Navy," n.d., and "Statement of Esther C. Brunauer," 10 May 1951, both in Box 242, SIF, RG478, NARA.

80. "Statement of Esther C. Brunauer," 27 March 1950, Box 242, SIF, RG478, NARA.

81. While a large number of accusations have been considered "false" charges, the release of previously secret Russian and American documents in the mid-1990s has revealed that as many as 300 Americans may have worked with Russian intelligence agencies, mostly in the 1930s and early 1940s. See John Earl Haynes and Harvey Klehr, *Venona: Decoding Soviet Espionage in America* (New Haven, CT: Yale University Press, 1999); and Allen Weinstein and Alexander Vassiliev, *The Haunted Wood: Soviet Espionage in America—The Stalin Era* (New York: Random House, 1999).

8. "EXPOSE ENEMIES WITHIN OUR GATES!"

1. "1,200 London Buses off Roads Today," *Daily Mail,* 14 September 1950; "Rush-Hour Chaos," *Evening Standard,* 15 September 1950; "11,000 Busmen Out in London," *Daily Mail,* 15 September 1950; "Stalin's Stooges," *Sunday Graphic,* 17 September 1950; "Last Bus Strikers Vote to Go Back," *Daily Herald,* 18 September 1950; and "All Bus Service Running Today," *Time,* 18 September 1950; "Busmen Drew Up Terms: 15,700 on Strike," *Manchester Guardian,* 16 September 1950.

2. "Now Name the Traitor," *Daily Graphic,* 16 September 1950.

3. "Opinion," *Daily Express,* 16 September 1950.

4. For Isaacs's speech, see, for instance, *Daily Mail, Daily Herald,* and *Daily Express,* on 16 September 1950.

5. "Industrial Unrest," George Isaacs speech, 15 September 1950, in "London Transport Bus Dispute, September 1950" (MSS.126/TG/1165/28), Records of Transport and General Workers' Union, Modern Records Centre (MRC), University of Warwick (UW), Coventry, UK.

6. Editorial, *Daily Express,* 16 September 1950.

7. "Now Name the Traitor," *Daily Graphic,* 16 September 1950.

8. "Moscow's Mission," *Daily Mail,* 16 September 1950.

9. "Deakin Calls for Ban on Reds," *Star,* 17 September 1950; "Red Agitators May Be Outlawed," *Daily Mail,* 17 September 1950.

10. Dave Murphy, "London Gas Strikers Sentenced to Imprisonment," 20 November 1950, and "Gas Workers' Appeal," 22 November 1950, both in "Gas Workers' Strike, 1950" (MSS.233/3/3/11), MRC-UW; see also news articles, such as "Troops for Gasworkers?" *Daily Express,* 26 September 1950; "Gas Strikers Wavering," *Daily Mail,* 29 September 1950; "Gas: Navy Is Going," *Daily Express,* 3 October 1950; "The Navy's Here," *Daily Express,* 4 October 1950; "Gasman Going Back," *Daily Mail,* 6 October 1950; and " 'Repeal Order 1305' Call," *Daily Mail,* 9 October 1950.

11. Arthur Marwick, *British Society Since 1945,* 2nd ed. (New York: Penguin, 1990), 99.

12. "Public Opinion Summary, February 1951," No. 25, Conservative Central Office, Papers of the Conservative Party Papers (CPP), Duke Humfrey's Library (DHL), Oxford University (OU), Oxford, UK.

13. "Communism—And You," *Popular Pictorial* (February/March 1951), 2, National Library of Australia (NLA), Canberra, Australia.

14. "Dockers Say, 'We're Not Agitators,' " *Daily Mail,* 16 September 1950.

15. "Official Note of Meeting of London Passenger Officers, Held at Transport House Smith Square, Westminster, Monday, September 11th, 1950," 3, 18, in "London Transport Bus Dispute, September 1950" (MSS.126/TG/1165/28), MRC-UW.

16. "Why Did Strike Collapse?" *Daily Express,* 18 September 1950.

17. "Opinion Regarding Strike," 15 January 1947, SxMOA1/2/75/10/E, TK-US.

18. Ibid.

19. "All Bus Service Running Today," *Time,* 18 September 1950; "Reds Call Off Their Strike Plan," *Daily Mail,* 18 September 1950.

20. "Public Opinion Summary, February 1951," No. 25, Conservative Central Office, CPP, DHL-OU; David Childs, *Britain since 1945,* 5th ed. (New York: Routledge, 2000), 25.

21. See the Conservative Party's "Public Opinion Summary," in particular, issues published in late 1950 and 1951, Conservative Central Office, CPP, DHL-OU.

22. Frances Berner's Diary, 14 September 1950, Mass Observation Archives (MOA), TK-US.

23. Ibid.

24. "Opinion Regarding Strike," 16 January 1947, SxMOA1/2/75/10/E, TK-US.

25. Ibid.

26. "Desire Caught by Tail," *Daily Mail,* 11 October 1950.

27. Robert H., "Directive: January/February 1951," SxMOA1/3/131/1, MOA, TK-US.

28. E. Atkinson, "Directive: January/February 1951."

29. Esther Home, "Directive: January/February 1951."

30. "Public Opinion Summary, June 1951," No. 29, Conservative Central Office, CPP, DHL-OU.

31. "Public Opinion Summary, April 1951," No. 27, Conservative Central Office.

32. "It's Loneliness That Sends Most Women to Work," *Daily Mail,* 30 September 1950.

33. "You Can Fight Communism without a Tin Hat," *Popular Pictorial* (February/March 1951), 4, NLA.

34. "Public Opinion Summary, February 1951," No. 25, Conservative Central Office.

35. "Public Opinion Summary, April 1951," No. 27, Conservative Central Office.

36. "Don't Be Afraid to Have Fun," *Daily Mail,* 1 January 1951.

37. Ibid., 375; Alfred H. Havighurst, *Britain in Transition,* 4th ed. (Chicago: University of Chicago Press, 1985), 446.

38. Robert Taylor, "The Rise and Disintegration of the Working Class," in Paul Addison and Harriet Jones, eds., *A Companion to Contemporary Britain, 1939–2000* (Malden, MA: Blackwell, 2005), 376.

39. Sodei Rinjiro, ed., *Yoshida Shigeru—Makkasa ofuku shokanshu 1945–1951* [The Collection of Correspondence between Yoshida Shigeru and MacArthur 1945–1951] (Tokyo: Hosei Daigaku Shuppankyoku, 2000), 205–206.

40. Asahi Shinbunsha Reddo Paji Shogenroku Kanko Iinkai, ed., *1950-nen 7-gatsu 28-nichi: Asahi Shinbunsha no reddo paji shogenroku* [July 28, 1950: The Collection of Testimonies about the Red Purge at the Asahi Newspaper] (Tokyo: Banseisha, 1981), 28–29; Hirata Tetsuo, *Reddo paji no shiteki kyumei* [Historical Inquiry into the Red Purge] (Tokyo: Shin Nihon Shuppansha, 2002), 214.

41. We still do not know the exact number of dismissals because small businesses and companies were, from the beginning, excluded from statistics. The number given is based on statistics published in "Shakai undo tsushin [Newsletters for Social Movements]," 1 November 1950, Collections of Journals, Ohara Shakai Mondai Kenkyujo [Ohara Institute for Social Studies] (OISS), Hosei University (HU), Tokyo, Japan; see also, for instance, Miyake Akimasa, *Reddo paji to wa nani ka* [What Was the Red Purge?] (Tokyo: Otsuki Shoten, 1994), 7–10.

42. Hans Martin Kramer, "Just Who Reversed the Course? The Red Purge in Higher Education during the Occupation of Japan," *Social Science Japan Journal* 8:1 (November 2004), 1–18.

43. "Redo paji kanshi [Brief History of Red Purge]," Collections of Documents Related to the Red Purge, No. 17–4, OISS-HU.

44. Letter, Burati to Sullivan, 6 September 1950, File 12, Box 1, VBP, WPRL-WSU.

45. Robert Amis, interview in Takemae Eiji, *Shogen Nihon senryoshi: GHQ Rodoka no gunzo* [Oral Testimonies of the Occupation of Japan: The Figures in the Labor Division in the GHQ] (Tokyo: Iwanami, 1983), 324–325.

46. See, for instance, Takemae, *Shogen Nihon senryoshi;* and Miyake, *Reddo paji to wa nani ka .*

47. Letter, Burati to Sullivan, 22 August 1950, File 12, Box 1, VBP, WPRL-WSU.

48. Sasaki Ryosuke, interview in Kawanishi Hirosuke, *Kikigaki: Densan no gunzo* [A Record of Lively People in Densan] (Tokyo: Heigensha, 1992), 56.

49. "Shakei undo tsushin [Newsletters for Social Movements]," 25 October 1950, Collections of Journals, OISS-HU; see also Miyake, *Reddo paji to wa nani ka,* 87–88.

50. "Mr. Kaite's Comments on the 'Red Expulsion,'" 23 September 1950, File 11, Box 5, Valery Burati Papers (VBP), Walter P. Reuther Library (WPRL), Wayne State University (WSU), Detroit, MI.

51. "The Announcement of the President," 23 October 1950, File 12, Box 5, VBP, WPRL-WSU.

52. Letter, Valery Burati to Philip B. Sullivan, 10 May 1951, File 13, Box 1, VBP, WPRL-WSU.

53. "Mr. Amis Gives Warning to the Management," 26 October 1950, File 13, Box 5, VBP, WPRL-WSU.

54. "Memo for Mr. Amis," 24 January 1951, File 15, Box 5, VBP, WPRL-WSU.

55. Memorandum, "To Mr. Amis," n.d., File 15 Box 5, VBP; and "Memo for Mr. Amis," 8 February 1951, File 15 Box 5, VBP; WPRL-WSU.

56. "Memo for Mr. Amis," 24 January 1951, File 15, Box 5, VBP, WPRL-WSU.

57. "Exclusion of Communistic Destructive Elements in Enterprise," n. d., File 13, Box 5, VBP; and "Nikkan rodo tsushin" [Daily Labor Bulletin], 18 October 1950, File 13, Box 5, VBP, WPRL-WSU.

58. "Niigata Tekkosho File," No. 20–11, Collection of Documents Related to the Red Purge, OISS-HU.

59. Letter, Val Burati to Greechhalgh International Federation of Textile Workers' Association, UK, 23 May 1951, File 13, Box 1, VBP, WPRL-WSU.

60. Kawanishi, *Kikigaki*, 169, 239–240, 263, 303, and 373.

61. Similar remarks can be found in various statements of Densan [All-Japan Electricity Union] and Kawasaki Seitetsu [Kawasaki Steel Company] in this period.

62. Sasaki Ryosaku, interview in Kawanishi, *Kikigaki*, 77.

63. Documentation of similar experiences can be found in various court records, such as in charge sheets, which are kept in the Collection of Red Purge Documents in the OISS. A group of discharged persons at *Yomiuri, Mainichi,* and *Asashi Shinbun,* for instance, sued their companies, and their statements described these struggles; for these companies, see Files No. 20–5. See also various testimonies in *1950-nen 7-gatsu 28-nichi [July 28, 1950].*

64. See, for example, court documents in the Collection of Red Purge Documents in the OISS; see also *1950 nen 7 gatsu 28 nichi* [July 28, 1950], 66 and 132.

65. *Shiryo sengo gakusei undo* [Source Book for Postwar Student Movements], vol. 2 (1950–1951) and vol. 3 (1952–1955) (Tokyo: Sanichi Shobo, 1969).

66. *Waseda daigaku shinbun,* 1 October 1950 NRR-NDL.

67. *Todai gakusei shinbun,* 5 October 1950, NRR-NDL; *Todai toso nyusu,* 11 October 1950 and 24 October 1950, Student Movement File, OISS-HU.

68. "Sodai de kuzen no gakusei fushoji [Unprecedented Student Scandal at Waseda]," *Mainichi Shinbun,* 18 October 1950; *Asahi Shinbun,* 18 October 1950. For more detailed discussion of student and peace movements in postwar Japan, see, for example, Masuda Hajimu, "Fear of World War III: Social Politics of Japan's Rearmament and Peace Movements, 1950–53," *Journal of Contemporary History* 47: 3 (Summer 2012), 551–571.

69. *Waseda daigaku shinbun,* 1 December 1950.

70. "Sodai de kuzen no gakusei fushoji."

71. *Asahi Shinbun,* 18 October 1950.

72. *Waseda daigaku shinbun,* 21 October 1950, NRR-NDL.

73. *Asahi shinbun,* 9 December 1950; *Mainichi shinbun,* 19 December 1950.

74. Togawa Yukio, *Waseda gakusei shinbun,* 7 October 1952. NRR-NDL.

75. For the perspective of the conservatives, such as Yoshida Shigeru, see, for instance, John W. Dower, *Empire and Aftermath: Yoshida Shigeru and the Japanese Experience, 1878–1954* (Cambridge, MA: Harvard University Press, 1979).

76. See also Ronald Dore's earlier field work, such as *Land Reform in Japan* (New York: Oxford University Press, 1959) and *City Life in Japan: A Study of a Tokyo Ward* (Berkeley: University of California Press, 1958).

77. Letter, anonymous Kyoto resident to Ashida Hitoshi, Correspondence File, No. 284–3, AHP, MJPHMR-NDL.

78. Ibid.

79. Letter, Hidaka Hiroshi to Ashida Hitoshi, Correspondence File, No. 272, AHP, MJPHMR-NDL.

80. Ibid.

81. Takekura Kin'ichiro, *Kirarera batten: Shiryo reddo paji* [Got Fired: Documents on the Red Purge] (Fukuoka: Densan Kyushu Futo Kaiko Hantai Domei, 1980); see also various memoirs and local history books, such as Tokyo Hachi-ni-roku kai, ed., *1950-nen 8-gatsu 26-nichi: Densan reddo paji 30-shunen kinen bunshu* [August 26, 1950: The Thirty-Year Anniversary Collection of the Densan Red Purge] (Tokyo: Tokyo Hachinirokukai, 1983); *1950-nen 7-gatsu 28-nichi*; Amagasaki reddo paji mondai kondankai, ed., *Kaiso Amagasaki no reddo paji* [Recollections: Red Purge in Amagasaki] (Osaka: Kobunsha, 2002); and Fukushima-ken minshushi kenkyukai, ed., *Hatsudensho no reddo paji: Densan Inawashiro bunkai* [The Red Purge in Power Plant: Densan's Inawashiro Branch] (Tokyo: Koyoshuppansha, 2001).

9. PEOPLE'S WAR AT HOME

1. "Public 'Confession' and Execution," *Manchester Guardian,* 14 November 1951; "China: Mass Slaughter," *Time,* 30 April 1951; "China: Justice on the Radio," *Time,* 7 May 1951; "China: Kill Mice!" *Time,* 21 May 1951; and a report of the Shanghai Military Control Commission, *Xinwen Ribao,* 25 July 1951. Also, see memorandum, Tientsin [Tianjin] to Foreign Office, UK, 13 July 1951, in "Reports, Comments, and Information from Many Sources Showing the Extension of Power of the Ruling Chinese Communists over the Political, Social, and Economic Life of the Whole of China . . ." FO371/92204, TNA. See, also, Yang Kuisong, "Reconsidering the Campaign to Suppress Counterrevolutionaries," *China Quarterly,* no. 193 (March 2008), 111; and Julia Strauss, "Morality, Coercion, and State Building by Campaign in the Early PRC: Regime Consolidation and After, 1949–1956," in Julia Strauss ed., *The History of the PRC, 1949–1976: The China Quarterly Special Issues New Series No. 7* (New York: Cambridge University Press, 2007), 52–53.

2. "Shanghaishi junshi guanzhi weiyuanhui panchu fangeming anfan de juedingshu [Shanghai Military Control Commission's Written Verdicts on the Cases of Counterrevolutionaries]," 12 May 1951, B1–2–1050–45, SMA.

3. Ibid., 18 April 1951, B1–2–1050–62, SMA.

4. Ibid., 28 May 1951, B1–2–1063–12, SMA.

5. Norimura Kaneko, *Zanryu shoujo no mita chousen sensou no koro* [The Time of the Korean War through the Eyes of a War-Displaced Japanese Girl] (Tokyo: Shakai shisosha, 1992), 96–98.

6. Ibid., 98–102.

7. Ibid., 102–105.

8. Luo Ruiqing, "Weida de zhenya fangeming yundong [The Great Campaign to Suppress Counterrevolutionaries]," *Renmin ribao*, 1 October 1951.

9. See telegrams, memorandums, and reports sent from Beijing, Shanghai, Tianjin, Wuhan, Nanjing, and other places to the Foreign Office, U.K. between March and July 1951. These documents can be found in a series of files, called "Extension of Power of the Chinese Communists," from FO371/92192 to FO371/92206, TNA.

10. Telegram, Beijing to Foreign Office, 6 April 1951, in "Extension of Power of the Chinese Communists," FO371/92196, TNA.

11. These numbers were based on Deputy Public Security Minister Xu Zirong's report in 1954, which was recounted in Yang, "Reconsidering the Campaign to Suppress Counterrevolutionaries," 120–121. Frank Dikötter estimates the scale of terror much larger, with an estimate of total death at "close to 2 million people." See Frank Dikötter, *The Tragedy of Liberation: A History of the Chinese Revolution, 1945–57* (New York: Bloomsbury Press, 2013), x, 99–100. In fact, a British diplomat who was in Shanghai at that time reported that, in his opinion, actual figures of the death toll would far exceed those acknowledged officially. See a telegram from Shanghai to Foreign Office, 8 June 1951, in "Extension of Power of the Chinese Communists," FO371/92198, TNA.

12. Yang, "Reconsidering the Campaign to Suppress Counterrevolutionaries," 102–121; idem, "Xin Zhongguo zhenfan yundong shimo [The Story of the Suppression of Counterrevolutionaries in New China]" and "Shanghai zhenfan yundong de lishi kaocha [Historical Examination of the Campaign to Suppress Counterrevolutionaries in Shanghai]," in Yang Kuisong, *Zhonghua renmin gongheguo jianguo shi yanjiu* [A Study of the History of the Establishment of the People's Republic of China], vol. 1 (Nanchang: Jiangxi renmin chubanshe, 2009), 168–217 and 218–259; Strauss, "Morality, Coercion, and State Building by Campaign in the Early PRC," 37–58; Julia Strauss, "Paternalist Terror: The Campaign to Suppress Counterrevolutionaries and Regime Consolidation in the People's Republic of China, 1950–1953," *Comparative Studies in Society and History*, 44:1 (January 2002), 80–105; Frederic Wakeman Jr., " 'Cleanup': The New Order in Shanghai," in Jeremy Brown and Paul Pickowicz, eds., *Dilemmas of Victory: The Early Years of the People's Republic of China* (Cambridge, MA: Harvard University Press, 2007), 21–58; Konno Jun, *Chugoku shakai to taishu doin: Mo takuto jidai no seiji kenryoku to minshu* [Chinese Society and Mass Mobilization: Political Power and People in the Era of Mao Zedong] (Tokyo: Ochanomizu shobou, 2008); and Izutani Yoko, *Chugoku kenkoku shoki no seiji to keizai: Taishu undo to shakai shugi taisei* [Politics and Economy in the Early Period of the People's Republic of China: Mass Movements and Socialist Regime] (Tokyo: Ochanomizu shobou, 2007).

13. Yang, "Reconsidering the Campaign to Suppress Counterrevolutionaries," 104–105, 107–108.

14. Ibid., 106.

15. Ibid., 117–119.

16. "Gong'anbu guanyu qunzhong dui chuli waiji fan geming fenzi de fanying [Memorandum from the Ministry of Public Security Concerning Popular Responses Toward Dealing with Foreign Counterrevolutionaries]," June 25, 1951, No. 118–00306–15, FMA. For the official policy of the Foreign Affairs Ministry, see, for instance, "Zhongyang guanyu waiguo fangeming de chuli wenti dao gedi de zhishi dian [Directive from the Central Government to Various Regions Concerning the Issue of Dealing with Foreign Counterrevolutionaries]," 2 August 1951, No. 118–00306–01, FMA. In this telegram, Beijing declared that, in general, foreigners who were considered counterrevolutionaries would be deported from the country, and basically would not be executed.

17. "Zhongnanqu guanyu zhenya fangeming de zhishi de dianbao [Telegram of the Mid-South Regional Bureau Concerning the Directive of Suppression of Counterrevolutionaries]," 30 November 1950, No. 118–00306–16, FMA.

18. Yang, "Reconsidering the Campaign to Suppress Counterrevolutionaries," 106.

19. Ibid., 107.

20. "Beijing shi tanshang Kang-Mei Yuan-Chao jingsai yundong youguan wenjian [Documents Related to Beijing Street Vendors' Movements to Resist America and Aid Korea]," No. 022–012–00497, pp. 25, 142, 185–187, and 194, BMA.

21. Ibid., 194.

22. Ibid., 196.

23. "Dong'an shichang Kang-Mei Yuan-Chao aiguo yundong [Kang-Mei Yuan-Chao Patriotic Movements in the Dong'an Market]," 14 May 1951, in "Beijing shi tanfan Kang-Mei Yuan-Chao gongzuo jihua zongjie [Planning and Summing-Up of Beijing Street Vendors' Work of Resisting American and Aiding Korea]" (hereafter, "Beijing Street Vendors' Work of Kang-Mei Yuan-Chao"), 42–43, No. 022–010–00314, BMA.

24. Ibid., 15 May 1951, 96, No. 022–010–00314, BMA.

25. Ibid., 132–134, No. 022–012–00497, BMA.

26. Izutani Yoko, *Chugoku kenkoku shoki no seiji to keizai: Taishu undo to shakai shugi taisei* [Politics and Economy in the Early Period of the People's Republic of China: Mass Movements and the Socialist Regime] (Tokyo: Ochanomizu shobou, 2007), 224–225.

27. Ibid., 225.

28. Arif Dirlik, "The Ideological Foundations of the New Life Movements: A Study of Counterrevolution," *Journal of Asian Studies,* 34: 4 (August 1974), 954–958.

29. "A New Pattern of Life," *Manchester Guardian,* 20 November 1950.

30. "Beijing qunzhong dui zhenya fangeming de fanying [Popular Reactions in Beijing Toward the Suppression of Counterrevolutionaries]," 9 April 1951, *Neibu Cankao,* CUHK; "Lanzhou zhenya fangeming fenzi hou de shehui fanying [Social

Reactions after the Suppression of Counterrevolutionaries in Lanzhou]," 9 April 1951, *Neibu Cankao,* CUHK; and Strauss, "Morality, Coercion, and State Building by Campaign in the Early PRC," 51.

31. Konno, *Chugoku shakai to taishu doin,* 119–120.

32. "1951 nian shangbannian yilai jinxing Kang-Mei Yuan-Chao aiguo zhuyi jiaoyu de qingkuang baogao [A Report on Situations Concerning the Ongoing Patriotism Education to Resist America and Aid Korea in the First Half of 1951]," 21 September 1951, C21–1–108–13, SMA.

33. "Jiaoqu funü Kang-Mei Yuan-Chao aiguo yundong 4 yue zongjie [The Summary of Women's Activities of the Resist America and Aid Korea Patriotic Movements on the Outskirts of Beijing in April]," April 1951, No. 084–003–00008, BMA; and "China: Mass Slaughter," *Time,* 30 April 1951.

34. "Qingnian tuan Shanghai shiwei guanyu zai Kang-Mei Yuan-Chao, zhenya fangeming yu tudi gaige yundong zhong dui shehui qingnian gongzuo de zongjie [The Youth Group in the Shanghai City Committee's Final Report Concerning The Activities Toward the Youth During The Movements of Resisting-America and Assisting Korea, Suppression of Counterrevolutionaries, and Land Reform]," 17 October 1951, No. C21–1–143, SMA.

35. Jingshi fangeming fenzi luxu tanbai dengji jiaochu wuqi [Counterrevolutionaries in Beijing Are Confessing, Registering, and Surrendering Their Weapons One After Another, But There Are Some Special Agents and Bandits Who Still Refuse to Realise Their Errors and Continues Their Activities]," 13 April 1951, *Neibu Cankao,* CUHK.

36. "Shanghai Shijiao quwei guanyu zhenya fangeming de qingkuang tongjibiao; fangeming fenzi zisha dengji biao [Statistical Tables Concerning the Situation of Suppression of Counterrevolutionaries on the Outskirts of Shanghai; Tables Registering the Suicides of Counterrevolutionaries]," 25 July 1951, No. 71–2–94, SMA.

37. Ibid.

38. Memorandum, Beijing to Foreign Office "A Final Report on China," October 1951, in "Extension of Power of the Chinese Communists," FO371/92206; telegram, Beijing to Foreign Office, 19 January 1951, ibid., FO371/92192; telegrams, Beijing to Foreign Office, 3 and 6 March 1951, ibid., FO371/92194; as well as telegram, Foreign Office to Embassies, 11 May 1951, "China: Political Situation," DO133/27; and Telegram, Beijing to Foreign Office, 7 April 1952, ibid, DO133/28, all at TNA. Also, see Strauss, "Morality, Coercion, and State Building by Campaign in the Early PRC," 46–48.

39. Telegram, Beijing to Foreign Office, 3 March 1951, "Extension of Power of the Chinese Communists," FO371/92194, TNA.

40. Fukumoto Katsukiyo, *Chugoku kakumei o kake nuketa autorotachi: dohi to ryubo no sekai* [Outlaws in the Chinese Revolution: The World of Local Rebels and Rogues] (Tokyo: Chuo koronsha, 1998).

41. Konno, *Chugoku shakai to taishu doin*, 102.

42. "*'Gongchang sanfan yundong tongbao'* 1951 nian di 2 hao ['*Bulletin of Sanfan movements in Factories'* Vol. 2, 1951]," 12 February 1952, in "*'Gongchang sanfan yundong tongbao'* ji gongchang sanfan zonghe qingkuang ['*Bulletins of Sanfan movements in Factories'* and the comprehensive situation of the Sanfan movements in Factories]," cited in Konno, *Chugoku shakai to taishu doin*, 127.

43. Luo Ruiqing, "Weida de zhenya fangeming yundong [The great campaign to suppress counterrevolutionaries]," *Renmin Ribao,* 1 October 1951; Konno, *Chugoku shakai to taishu doin*, 92–93.

44. Yang, "Xin Zhongguo zhenfan yundong shimo," 203–204.

45. Ibid., 204.

46. "The Credit in the Balance-Sheet," *Manchester Guardian,* 17 November 1950.

47. Ibid.

48. "Beijing Street Vendors' Workings of Kang-Mei Yuan-Chao," 23–25, No. 022–010–00314, BMA.

49. Yang, "Reconsidering the Campaign to Suppress Counterrevolutionaries," 105.

10. DECOLONIZATION AS RECOLONIZATION

1. Qiu Guozhen, *Jindai Taiwan canshi dang'an* [Records of Tragic History in Modern Taiwan] (Taipei: Avanguard, 2007), 205. For descriptions of similar executions, see, for example, Chen Yingtai, *Huiyi: Jianzheng baise kongbu* [Recollections: Testifying the White Terror] (Taipei: Tangshan chubanshe, 2005), 109.

2. Lin Shuyang, *Cong 2.28 dao 50 niandai baise kongbu* [From 2.28 to the White Terror in the 1950s] (Taipei: Shibao wenhua chubanshe, 1992), 132; Lan Bozhou, *Baise kongbu* [The White Terror] (Taipei: Yangzhi wenhua shiye, 1993), 43; and Li Wanbei, "Baise kongbu shounan zhe jiashu Ko-Tsai A-lee nüshi shengming gushi tanjiu [An Inquiry into a Life Story of Mrs. Ko-Tsai A-lee, Who Was a Family Member of a Victim in the White Terror]," master's thesis, National Kaohsiung Normal University, 22.

3. Hui Xunhui, "Taiwan wuling niandai guozu xiangxiang zhong 'gongfei / feidie' de jian'gou [The Construction of 'Communist Bandits/Spies' in the the Imagination of the Nationalists in Taiwan in the 1950s]," master's thesis, Tunghai University, 2000, 74.

4. Li, "Baise kongbu shounan zhe jiashu Ko-Tsai A-lee," 21.

5. Editorial, "Lun sujian gongzuo [Discussing a purge of traitors]," *Minsheng ribao,* 29 September 1950; see also, for instance, Lin, *Cong 2.28 dao 50 niandai baise kongbu,* 132; and Lan, *Baise kongbu,* 43.

6. Chen Cuilian, "Taiwan jieyan shiqi de tewu tongzhi yu baise kongbu fenwei [The Reign of Spying during Martial Law in Taiwan and the Atmosphere of the White Terror]," in Zhang Yanxian and Chen Meirong, eds., *Jieyan shiqi baise*

kongbu yu zhuanxing zhengyi lunwenji [The Collection of Articles on Transitional Justice and the White Terror during the Martial Law Rule] (Taipei: Wu Sanlian Taiwan shiliao jijinhui chubanshe, 2009), 65–66.

7. Lan, *Baise kongbu*, 21, 48.

8. Su Ching-hsuan, "Guojia jianzhi yu baise kongbu: Wushi niandai chuqi Taiwan zhengzhi anjian xingcheng zhi yuanyin [State-Building and the White Terror: The Causes of Political Persecution in the Early 1950s in Taiwan]," master's thesis, National Taiwan University, 2008, 14–15.

9. Lin, *Cong 2.28 dao 50 niandai baise kongbu*, 133.

10. Ibid., 133; Lan, *Baise kongbu*, 43–44.

11. Lin, *Cong 2.28 dao 50 niandai baise kongbu*, 133.

12. Watan Tanaga (Lin Zhaoming), Kikuchi Kazutaka trans., "1950 nendai Taiwan hakusyoku tero junan no kaioku [Recollections of Sufferings in Taiwan's White Terror in the 1950s]," *Kindai Chugoku kenkyu iho* [Bulletin for Modern Chinese Studies] no. 21 (1999), 49, 81.

13. See, e.g., Lan, *Baise kongbu*.

14. Ibid., 66; Su, "Guojia jianzhi yu baise kongbu," 45.

15. Lin Yixu, interview in Lü Fangshang, ed., *Jieyan shiqi Taibei diqu zhengzhi anjian xiangguan renshi koushu lishi: Baise kongbu shijian chafang* [Oral Histories Concerning Political Cases in Taipei Area in the Period of the Martial Law: Inquiries into the White Terror] (Taipei: Taibeishi wenxian weiyuanhui, 1999), 18.

16. Lin Enkui, interview in Lan Bozhou, ed., *Gaoxiong xian 228 ji wuling niandai baise kongbu minzhong shi* [A History of People in Gaoxiong County Concerning the 2.28 Incident and the White Terror in the 1950s] (Gaoxiong: Gaoxiong xian zhengfu, 1997), 306–312.

17. Qiu, *Jindai Taiwan canshi dang'an*, 173.

18. Chin Shou'ei (Chen Shaoying), *Gairai seiken asseika no sei to shi: 1950 nendai Taiwan hakushoku tero, ichi junansha no shuki* [Life and Death Under the Tyrannic Rule of the Foreign Regime: A Sufferer's Personal Account of Taiwan's White Terror in the 1950s] (Tokyo: Shuei shoo, 2003).

19. Qiu, *Jindai Taiwan canshi dang'an*, 266–268.

20. Ibid., 199–200.

21. Lan, *Baise kongbu*, 116; Su, "Guojia jianzhi yu baise kongbu," 9–11; and Wakabayashi Masahiro, *Taiwan* (Tokyo: Chikuma shobo, 2001), 101.

22. Wang Huan, *Liehuo de qingchun: Wuling niandai baise kongbu zhengyan* [Blazing Youth: Testimonies of the White Terror in the 1950s] (Taipei: Renjian chubanshe, 1999), 124–125; Lin Shuzhi, *Baise kongbu X dang'an* [X Files of the White Terror] (Taipei: Qianwei chubanshe, 1997), 24.

23. Chen Mingzhong, interview in *Gaoxiong xian 2.28 ji wuling niandai baise kongbu minzhong shi*, 328–330; Wang, *Liehuo de qingchun*, 49–54; Qiu, *Jindai Taiwan canshi dang'an*, 166–167.

24. Moguang Xinye [Suemitsu Kin'ya], *Taiwan gekidou no sengoshi: 228 jiken to sono zengo* [Taiwan's Turbulent Postwar History: Before and After the 2.28 Incident] (Taipei: Zhiliang, 2006), 54–56.

25. Ibid., 56–58.

26. Ibid., 70–74.

27. Ibid., 66.

28. Ibid., 81–83.

29. Ibid., 80.

30. Ibid., 89–138; Qiu, *Jindai Taiwan canshi dang'an*, 77–78.

31. Suemitsu, *Taiwan gekidō no sengoshi*, 138–149; Qiu, *Jindai Taiwan canshi dang'an*, 79–80.

32. Lin, *Cong 2.28 dao wuling niandai baise kongbu*, 141.

33. Xu Jinfa, "Zuoqing zhishi qingnian de suqing [The Elimination of Left-Leaning Young Intellectuals]," in *Jieyan shiqi baise kongbu yu zhuanxing zhengyi lunwenji*, 98.

34. Wang, *Liehuo de qingchun*, 5.

35. Lu Zhaolin, interview in *Jieyan shiqi Taibei diqu zhengzhi anjian xiangguan renshi koushu lishi*, 620–622.

36. Huang Guanghai, interview in *Jieyan shiqi Taibei diqu zhengzhi anjian xiangguan renshi koushu lishi*, 652.

37. Xu, "Zuoqing zhishi qingnian de suqing," 135.

38. Qiu, *Jindai Taiwan canshi dang'an*, 180–181 and 258–259.

39. Ibid., 266–267; Watan Tanaga (Lin Zhaoming), Kikuchi Kazutaka trans., "1950 nendai Taiwan hakushoku tero junan no kaioku," 57–61.

40. Huang Yukun, interview in *Jieyan shiqi Taibei diqu zhengzhi anjian xiangguan renshi koushu lishi*, 237–240; Xu, "Zuoqing zhishi qingnian de suqing," 128–130.

41. Suemitsu, *Taiwan gekidou no sengoshi*, 194–204.

42. "Kouhao [Slogans]," *Minsheng Ribao*, 7 August 1950.

43. "Dongyuan fangong, jianshe Jiayi, difang zizhi bi chenggong [Mobilize Anti-Communism, Build Jiayi; Local Governing Must Succeed]," 5 August 1950, *Minsheng Ribao*.

44. "Guili [Discipline]," *Minsheng Ribao*, 7 August 1950.

45. Ibid., 7 August 1950.

46. Hui, "Taiwan wuling niandai guozu xiangxiang zhong 'gongfei / feidie' de jian'gou," 45–46.

47. Ibid.

48. Ibid.

49. "Zhanshi shenghuo yundong [The Wartime Life Movement]," *Mingsheng Ribao*, 7 August 1950.

50. Wakabayashi, *Taiwan*.

51. Chiang Kai-shek, diary entry of 23 August 1950, Box 48, CKSD, HILA-SU.

52. Chiang Kai-shek, "Fan-Gong Kang-E de gongzuo gaoling he nuli fangmian [Main Tasks and Areas that Need Efforts for the [Campaign] of the 'Oppose Communism and Resist Russia']," 3 April 1951, No. 132–142, NPA.

53. Qiu, *Jindai Taiwan canshi dang'an*, 132; Hui, "Taiwan wuling niandai guozu xiangxiang zhong 'gongfei / feidie' de jian'gou," 138–139, 171–172.

54. Qiu, *Jindai Taiwan canshi dang'an*, 132.

55. Zhou Kunru, interview in *Jieyan shiqi Taibei diqu zhengzhi anjian xiangguan renshi koushu lishi*, 593; and Chen, "Taiwan jieyan shiqi de tewu tongzhi yu baise kongbu fenwei," 66.

56. Tan Yimin ed., Ziyou Zhongguo minzhong Fan-Gong yundong [People's Anti-communist Movements for Free China] (Taipei: Gaizao chubanshe, 1953), 21–24.

57. Wang, *Liehuo de qingchun*, 53–54.

58. Ibid., 68 and 80–81.

59. Wakabayashi, *Taiwan*, 101; Tamura Shizue, *Hijo joshi no hito bito: Taiwan to Nihon no uta* [The People of Hijo-joshi: Songs of Taiwan and Japan] (Tokyo: Shobunsha, 1992), 162–163; Lin, *Cong 2.28 dao 50 niandai baise kongbu*, 137; and Lan, *Baise kongbu*, 48.

60. Qiu, *Jindai Taiwan canshi dang'an*, 16–37; Suemitsu, *Taiwan gekidou no sengoshi*, 22–28.

61. Memorandum, Manila to Foreign Office, UK, "Trial of Twenty-Six Members of the Communist Party of the Philippines on May 12th," 28 May 1951, in "Internal Affairs in the Philippines; Outlawing of the Communist Party," FO371/92932, TNA.

62. Ibid.

63. Special Committee on Un-Filipino Activities, *Report on I. The Illegality of the Communist Party of the Philippines. II. The Functions of the Special Committee on Un-Filipino Activities* [hereafter, *The Illegality of the Communist Party*] (Manila, 1951), 13, Institute of Southeast Asian Studies (ISEAS), Singapore.

64. Ibid., 14.

65. "Report on the Illegality of the Communist Party of the Philippines," 15 May 1951 by the Special Committee on Un-Filipino Activities, in Internal Affairs in FO371/92933: "Internal Affairs in the Philippines; Outlawing the Communist Party," TNA.

66. Ibid.

67. "Report on the Functions of the Special Committee on Un-Filipino Activities," 15 May 1951, the Special Committee on Un-Filipino Activities, in FO371/92933: "Internal Affairs in the Philippines; Outlawing of the Communist Party," TNA.

68. For the studies on American colonial rule and its colonization efforts in the Philippines, I benefited from reading Paul A. Kramer, *The Blood of Government: Race, Empire, the United States, and the Philippines* (Chapel Hill: University of

North Carolina Press, 2006); Julian Go and Anne L. Foster, *The American Colonial State in the Philippines: Global Perspectives* (Durham, NC: Duke University Press, 2003); Alfred W. McCoy, *Policing America's Empire: The United States, the Philippines, and the Rise of the Surveillance State* (Madison: University of Wisconsin Press, 2009); Alfred W. McCoy and Francisco A. Scarano, *The Colonial Crucible Empire in the Making of the Modern American State* (Madison: University of Wisconsin Press, 2009); and Warwick Anderson, *Colonial Pathologies: American Tropical Medicine, Race, and Hygiene in the Philippines* (Durham, NC: Duke University Press, 2006).

69. Albert Lau, *Southeast Asia and the Cold War* (Oxon, UK: Routledge, 2012), 3.

70. Ibid., 3.

71. Report, L. H. Foulds, "Philippines: The Hukbalahap," 27 May 1950, FO371/84303: "Communism in the Philippines, 1950," TNA.

72. Ibid.

73. Benedict J. Kerkvliet, *The Huk Rebellion: A Study of Peasant Revolt in the Philippines* (Berkeley: University of California Press, 2002); Suzuki Sizuo, *Firipin no rekishi* [A History of the Philippines] (Tokyo: Chuo koronsha, 2008).

74. Report, L. H. Foulds, "Philippines: The Hukbalahap," 27 May 1950, in "Communism in the Philippines, 1950," FO371/84303, TNA.

75. Report, Russell H. Fifield, associate professor of political science, University of Michigan, to Myron M. Cowen, ambassador at U.S. Embassy, Manila, 10 August 1950, in "Communism in the Philippines, 1950," FO371/84303, TNA.

76. Ibid.

77. Ibid.

78. Kerkvliet, *The Huk Rebellion*, 210.

79. Telegraph, Foulds to Bevin, "HukBalahap Attack in Central Luzon," 29 August 1950, FO493/4: "Correspondence Respecting the Philippines: Part 4"; and Foulds, "Philippines: Annual Review for 1950," 12 February 1951, 3–4, FO371/92930, TNA.

80. Vina A. Lanzona, *Amazons of the Huk Rebellion: Gender, Sex, and Revolution in the Philippines* (Madison: University of Wisconsin Press, 2009), 7–14.

81. Ibid., 96, 265.

82. "The Current Situation in the Philippines," 30 March 1949, Central Intelligence Agency, 4, NARA.

83. *The Illegality of the Communist Party*, 124–125.

84. Ibid.

85. Committee on Un-Filipino Activities, *General Report on Communism and the Communist Party* [hereafter, *Communism and the Communist Party*] (Manila: Committee on Un-Filipino Activities, 1949), 50–52, NLA.

86. Ibid.

87. Lanzona, *Amazons of the Huk Rebellion*, 96.

88. "Report on the Functions of the Special Committee on Un-Filipino Activities," published by the Special Committee on Un-Filipino Activities, 15 May 1951, in "Internal Affairs in the Philippines; Outlawing of the Communist Party," FO371/92933, TNA.

89. Kerkvliet, *The Huk Rebellion*, 254–256.

90. Special Committee on Un-Filipino Activities, *Communism in the Philippines* (Manila: Committee on Un-Filipino Activities, 1952), 20, NLA; memorandum, Manila to Foreign Office, "Trial of Twenty-Six Members of the Communist Party of the Philippines on May 12th," 28 May 1951, "Internal Affairs in the Philippines; Outlawing of the Communist Party," FO371/92932, TNA.

91. Ibid.

92. William O. Douglas, "The Black Silence of Fear," *New York Times,* 13 January 1952.

EPILOGUE

1. "My Ideas and Hopes for Post War Conditions," British Legion Essay Competition 1944, "Post War Hopes 1944," SxMOA1/2/40/1/A, MOA, TK-US.

2. Ibid.

3. Barbara W. Tuchman, *The Guns of August: The Outbreak of World War I* (New York: Presidio Press, 2004), 523–524.

4. See, for example, Sekhara Bandyopadhyaya, *Decolonization in South Asia: Meanings of Freedom in Post-Independence West Bengal, 1947–52* (New York: Routledge, 2009)

5. For the study of policymakers' use (and misuse) of historical lessons, see Ernest May, *"Lessons" of the Past: The Use and Misuse of History in American Foreign Policy* (New York: Oxford University Press, 1973).

Archives Consulted

AUSTRALIA

National Library of Australia, Canberra

CANADA

Library and Archives Canada, Ottawa

CHINA

Beijing Municipal Archives, Beijing
Cold War History Research Center, East China Normal University, Shanghai
Foreign Ministry Archives, Beijing
Jilin University Library Archives, Changchun
National Library of China (Zhongguo guojia tushuguan), Beijing
Northeast Normal University Library, Changchun
Peking University Library, Beijing
Shanghai Municipal Archives, Shanghai
Tianjin Municipal Archives, Tianjin

HONG KONG

Chinese University of Hong Kong Library, Hong Kong

INDIA

National Archives, Delhi
Nehru Memorial Museum and Library, Delhi
West Bengal State Archives, Kolkata

JAPAN

Diplomatic Archives (Gaiko shiryo kan), Tokyo
National Diet Library, Tokyo
Ohara Institute for Social Research (Ohara shaken), Hosei University, Tokyo
Osaka Municipal Library, Osaka
Osaka Prefectural Central Library, Higashi–Osaka
Tokyo Metropolitan Library, Tokyo
University of Tokyo Library, Tokyo

SINGAPORE

Institute of Southeast Asian Studies, Singapore
National University of Singapore Central Library, Singapore

TAIWAN

Academia Historica (Guoshiguan), Taipei
National Taiwan Library, Taipei
National Taiwan University Library, Taipei
Nationalist Party Archives (Dangshiguan), Taipei

UNITED KINGDOM

British Library Newspaper Reading Room, Colindale
Duke Humfrey's Library, University of Oxford, Oxford
The Keep, University of Sussex, Brighton
Llyfrgell Genedlaethol Cymru / National Library of Wales, Aberystwyth
Modern Records Centre, University of Warwick
The National Archives, Kew
Working Class Movement Library, Salford

UNITED STATES

Auburn Avenue Research Library on African American Culture and History, Atlanta, GA
Bancroft Library, University of California at Berkeley, Berkeley, CA
Center for Labor Education and Research, University of Hawaii–West Oahu, Kapolei, HI
Center for Oral History, Columbia University, New York City, NY
Center for the Studies of the Korean War, Independence, MO
Hamilton Library, University of Hawaii at Manoa, Honolulu, HI
Harry S. Truman Library, Independence, MO
Hoover Institution Library and Archives, Stanford University, Stanford, CA
Labor Archives and Research Center, San Francisco State University, CA
Libraries Special Collections, University of Southern California, Los Angeles, CA
Library of Congress, Washington, DC
Library Special Collections, University of California at Los Angeles, Los Angeles, CA
MacArthur Memorial Archives, Norfolk, VA
National Archives and Records Administration, College Park, MD
Nevada History Society, Reno, NV
New-York Historical Society, New York, NY
Oakland Historical Room, Oakland Public Library, Oakland, CA
Oakland Museum of California, Oakland, CA
Olin and Kroch Libraries, Cornell University, Ithaca, NY
Seeley G. Mudd Manuscript Library, Princeton University, Princeton, NJ
Southern Labor Archives, Georgia State University, Atlanta, GA
Special Collections, Columbus State University, Columbus, GA
Special Collections, University of Vermont, Burlington, VT
Special Collections and University Archives, Stanford University, Stanford, CA
Special Collections and University Archives, University of Iowa, Iowa City, IA
Tamiment Library, New York University, New York City, NY
University Archives, University of California at Los Angeles, Los Angeles, CA
Vermont Historical Society, Barre, VT
Walter P. Reuther Library, Wayne State University, Detroit, MI

Acknowledgments

Looking back on the years spent on this book, I feel anew that I have been extremely fortunate to work with exceptional scholars and friends at Cornell University and the National University of Singapore (NUS). Fredrik Logevall has consistently encouraged me in completing my project even when it sounded too ambitious. He has read all drafts, chapter by chapter, and given me straightforward and practical advice, as well as constructive criticism, with high standards in terms of accuracy and style in writing, providing me with a model of a mentor and scholar. Chen Jian, in a different way, has provided a model of an international scholar who is active and enthusiastic in research and lecturing in both China and the United States. He has rigorously read my written work since it took the form of term papers and provided numerous comments on almost every page, often alerting me to various aspects I had overlooked. J. Victor Koschmann has always given me valuable comments from the viewpoint of an intellectual historian, with insights that would never have occurred to me otherwise, and assisted me in viewing and discussing my project in a theoretical and conceptual manner. I am also grateful to Walter LaFeber, Peter J. Katzenstein, and Katsuya Hirano, who read earlier chapters and helped me to elaborate on ideas and develop arguments.

Beyond Cornell, Marilyn B. Young, Mark Philip Bradley, Laura E. Hein, and David S. Foglesong have shown great enthusiasm for this project when it was still scattered parts of dissertation chapters, reading portions of earlier manuscripts, and never failing to encourage me to pursue the project. Also, I deeply thank William Stueck, who agreed to read the entire manuscript and provided critical comments, with a keen eye on the accuracy of details. Also, I thank three colleagues at NUS who have read the entire manuscript and given friendly but constructively critical feedback: Bruce Lockhart, Lee Seung-Joon, and John P. DiMoia. Finally, Jay S. Winston, with a careful eye and concern over style, has patiently read all my chapters, helped me to sharpen their arguments, and forced me to clarify otherwise ambiguous points.

In the past nine years, all chapters—and, in some cases, each section of those chapters—have been presented at nearly two dozen academic conferences and international workshops in France, Britain, China, Singapore, and the United States, including the annual meetings of the Society for Historians of American Foreign Relations (SHAFR) in 2008, 2009, 2010, 2011, and 2012; the Association for Asian Studies in 2008, 2011, and 2013; and the American Historical Association in 2013. Many people have attended my presentations or read my conference papers, given both positive and critical feedback, and encouraged me in pursuing this project. I am deeply grateful to Michael Allen, Balogh H. Balogh, Gregg Brazinsky, Alexander Bukh, Julia C. Bullock, Adam Cathcart, Bo Chen, Mario Del Pero, Richard Filipink, the late Ilya Gaiduk, Hope M. Harrison, Gail Hershatter, Christian A. Hess, Walter Hixson, Denise Y. Ho, Linda Hoaglund, Minoru Iwasaki, Andrew Johns, Nick Kapur, Hiroshi Kitamura, Mark Kramer, Melvyn Leffler, Christopher R. Leighton, Li Danhui, Xiaobing Li, Tehyun Ma, Andrew Mertha, Jennifer M. Miller, Viren Murthy, Kenneth Osgood, Christian Ostermann, Park Tae Gyun, James Person, Sergey Radchenko, Andrew Rotter, Wesley Sasaki-Uemura, Thomas A. Schwartz, Franziska Seraphim, Shen Zhihua, Naoko Shibusawa, Setsu Shigematsu, Jason Scott Smith, James T. Sparrow, Patricia Steinhoff, Julia C. Strauss, Lu Sun, Yuko Torikata, Kathryn Weathersby, Odd Arne Westad, Yafeng Xia, Jiro Yamaguchi, Daqing Yang, Yang Kuisong, Salim Yaqub, and Yang Zhang, for their comments, critiques, and, in many cases, enthusiasm for my project. In particular, I thank Chen Jian, Steven I. Levine, and James Z. Gao, as well as Bill Miscamble and Arnold Offner, who candidly and straightforwardly gave me invaluable critical feedback.

Furthermore, I thank Pierre Journoud, Zhao Ma, Chen Jian, Katsuya Hirano, and S. R. Joey Long, as well as Amy King and Jon Howlett, for inviting me to their thought-provoking conferences and workshops in Paris, Shanghai, Hangzhou, Ithaca, Singapore, and Bristol, respectively. These scholars' feedback at numerous venues forced me think and rethink, contributing to an improvement in the manuscript in ways I could not have achieved otherwise. In a similar way, I benefited from feedback at smaller gatherings and colloquiums. I am indebted to participants including Edward Baptist, Brett de Bary, Sherman Cochran, Duane Corpis, Matthew Evangelista, Durba Ghosh, T. J. Hinrichs, Mary Beth Norton, Jon Parmenter, Judith Reppy, Aaron Sachs, Naoki Sakai, and Claudia Verhoeven, as well as Claudine Ang, Deokhyo Choi, Mari Crabtree, Brian Cuddy, Sean Fear, Noriaki Hoshino, Christopher Jones, Peter Lavelle, Sujin Lee, Daegan Miller, Jorge Rivera Marin, Shohei Sato, Mike Schmidli, Rebecca Tally, Christopher Tang, Irene Vrinte, Yuanchong Wang, We Jung Yi, and Taomo Zhou, for their comments on various parts of earlier drafts. Above all, I am deeply grateful to the members of a dissertation writing group at Cornell: Chris Ahn, Samson Lim, Honghong Tinn, Chunyen Wang, and Akiko Ishii.

Although I spend most of my time in my carrel or office during the academic year, I have spent almost all of my summer and winter breaks on research trips to fifty-eight archives and libraries in Japan, China, Taiwan, Hong Kong, Singapore, India, Britain, Canada, and the United States. In the course of dozens of research trips, I have become indebted to numerous archivists, librarians, and scholars. In China, in particular, I received research assistance from Shen Zhihua, Li Danhui, and Zhou Na at East China Normal University; Yu Qun and Zhang Yang at Northeast Normal University; and Xiao Jin at the Chinese University of Hong Kong. In particular, I thank Shen Zhihua, who wrote reference letters and gave me valuable practical advice on archival research in China. Also, I thank Gao Yanjie, Yin Ling, Ji Fengliang, and Chehui Peh, who helped me to check Pinyin spelling and to obtain permissions for images from Chinese archives and newspapers.

In other places as well, my research could not have been completed without the meticulous support and, in some cases, almost intuition of archivists. I am especially thankful to David Clark and Samuel Rushay at the Harry S. Truman Library, James W. Zobel at the MacArthur Memorial Archives, Paul Edwards and Gregory Edwards at the Center of the Study for the Korean War, William Puette at the University of Hawaii West-Oahu's CLEAR Archives, Peter J. Roberts at Georgia State University's Southern Labor Archives, David Owings at the Columbus State University Library, Catherine Powell at San Francisco State University's Labor Archives and Research Center, William W. Lefevre at Wayne State University's Walter P. Reuther Library, Kathryn Hodson at the University of Iowa's Special Collections, Prudence Doherty at the University of Vermont's Special Collections, Liz Wood at Warwick University's Modern Records Centre, and Jeremy McIlwaine at Oxford University's Bodleian Library. Without their support, I would not have been able to write this book. These research trips provided me with not only fruitful outcomes in terms of research but also a great deal of enjoyment visiting new places, meeting new people, and eating new food, which satisfied my taste for the joy of traveling and backpacking.

Such extensive and worldwide research in the past decade would have been inconceivable without plentiful—indeed, more than two dozen—research and travel grants, as well as generous fellowships from the Peace Studies Program, East Asia Program, American Studies Program, Mario Einaudi Center for International Studies, Department of History, and Graduate School at Cornell, as well as the Faculty of Arts and Social Sciences at NUS: Sage Fellowships, Robert Smith Fellowships, the Peace Studies Graduate Fellowship, Bluestone Fellowship, Boldt Fellowship, and Graduate School Research Fellowship at Cornell; and the Start-up Grant, Staff Research Support Scheme, and Book Grant Scheme at NUS. In addition, these institutions awarded me numerous conference grants. In addition, SHAFR provided a one-year Dissertation Completion Fellowship and Samuel Bemis Research Grant in 2010–2011, giving me a crucial, privileged period during which most of my chapters, which were still scattered pieces of writing, could be brought together in an organically unified narrative.

The Department of History at NUS provided a friendly, supportive, and intellectual community and allowed me a nonteaching semester at a critical moment before completing my book. I sincerely thank Yong Mun Cheong, Ian Gordon, Bruce Lockhart, Malcolm Murfett, Brian Farrell, Lee Seung-Joon, and John P. DiMoia for their cordial support and friendship. I am also grateful to my friends, professors, language teachers, and colleagues—Rob Stothart, Steve Thulin, and Mary Baumann, as well as Harriet Bloom-Wilson and Richard Wilson at Northwest College; Michael Adas, David S. Foglesong, Norman Markowitz, Donald Roden, and Richard Simmons at Rutgers University; Stewart Markel, Ingrid M. Arnesen, Frances Yufen Lee Mehta, and Qiuyun Teng at Cornell; Tim Amos and Ryoko Nakano at NUS; and my former colleagues at *Mainichi Shinbun*, who inspired me in many ways and helped me to grow intellectually over the years. I also thank Kathleen McDermott, my editor at Harvard University Press, who expressed great enthusiasm for my project when it was still scattered pieces and kept encouraging me, patiently waiting for completion of this book. Debra Soled provided wonderful copyediting, scrupulously reading every sentence and raising innumerable questions to help me clarify otherwise obscure points.

Finally, I owe the greatest thanks to my parents, Masuda Hiroshi and Masuda Emiko, who have cultivated my curiosity about writing, history, and traveling since I was young by buying me countless fiction and nonfiction books, and taking me to temples, shrines, and museums and on short trips during summer breaks. More than anything else, I am grateful that they have never forced me to follow a particular way of life and have patiently and warmly encouraged my journey all along.

Most of all, I want to thank my wife, Akiko Ishii, and our beautiful child, Kousei. Since we first met at a graduate seminar and together took on the role of discussants of a thick history book on Stalinism, I have been continually amazed by her intellectual ability to discuss history in a conceptual and abstract manner—introducing me to aspects that I had totally neglected. Since then, whenever I come up with new findings and arguments, I always test them with her; when she is excited, I further develop them, and, if not, I reconsider them. In this way, in all processes of conducting research, forming ideas, testing arguments, and writing and rewriting my book, Akiko has been always the first and most candid—often most critical—listener and reader of my work. Indeed, this book could not have been completed without her constant encouragement, enduring camaraderie, and unfailing trust and love. Kousei, who arrived in this world just one month before the delivery of the manuscript to the publisher, of course complicated my writing schedule at the last moment, yet provided enormous delight and joy. Although thousands of days will pass before he can possibly read this book, I hope that he will, someday. This book, thus, is dedicated to my parents and my family.

Index